The Organization of Islamic Cooperation and Human Rights

PENNSYLVANIA STUDIES IN HUMAN RIGHTS

Bert B. Lockwood, Series Editor

A complete list of books in the series
is available from the publisher.

The Organization of Islamic Cooperation and Human Rights

Edited by
Marie Juul Petersen and Turan Kayaoglu

PENN

UNIVERSITY OF PENNSYLVANIA PRESS

PHILADELPHIA

Published by
University of Pennsylvania Press
Philadelphia, Pennsylvania 19104-4112
www.upenn.edu/pennpress

Printed in the United States of America on acid-free paper

10 9 8 7 6 5 4 3 2 1

Library of Congress Cataloging-in-Publication Data

Names: Petersen, Marie Juul, editor. | Kayaoglu, Turan, editor.
Title: The Organization of Islamic Cooperation and human rights / edited
by Marie Juul Petersen, Turan Kayaoglu.
Other titles: Pennsylvania studies in human rights.
Description: 1st editon. | Philadelphia : University of Pennsylvania Press, [2019] |
Series: Pennsylvania studies in human rights | Includes bibliographical references
and index.
Identifiers: LCCN 2018047537 | ISBN 9780812251197 (hardcover)
Subjects: LCSH: Organisation of Islamic Cooperation. | Human rights. |
Human rights—International cooperation. | Human rights—Islamic countries.
Classification: LCC KZ5286 .O74 2019 | DDC 341.4/8091767—dc23
LC record available at https://lccn.loc.gov/2018047537

CONTENTS

The Organization of Islamic Cooperation and Human Rights

Introduction

Marie Juul Petersen and Turan Kayaoglu

"The United Nations of the Muslim world" is how the Organization of Islamic Cooperation (OIC) often refers to itself. The OIC is an intergovernmental organization, established in 1969 with the purpose of strengthening solidarity among Muslims. Headquartered in Jeddah, Saudi Arabia, the OIC today consists of fifty-seven states from the Middle East, Asia, Africa, and Latin America. The OIC's longevity and geographic reach, combined with its self-proclaimed role as the UN of the Muslim world, raise certain expectations as to its role in global human rights politics. However, to date these hopes have been unfulfilled. This volume sets out to demonstrate, by way of various methods of analysis, the potential and the shortcomings of the OIC and the obstacles (sometimes set by OIC members themselves) on the paths this group has navigated.

Historically, the OIC has had a complicated and conflict-ridden relationship with the international human rights regime and with the concept of universal human rights. Palestinian self-determination—a political problem with a strong human rights dimension—was an important catalyst for the founding of the OIC in 1969. Nonetheless, the OIC did not develop a comprehensive human rights approach in its first decades. In fact, human rights issues were rarely, if at all, mentioned at the organization's summits or the annual conferences of foreign ministers. Instead, the OIC tended to focus on protecting Islamic holy sites and increasing economic cooperation among member states.

As other international and regional organizations expanded and strengthened the international human rights system in the 1990s, the OIC began to pay greater attention to human rights, although not always in a way that aligned with Western states' conceptions of human rights. In particular, two initiatives came to shape the organization's human rights agenda and its (reactionary) human rights image in the eyes of the West throughout the 1990s.

First, in 1990, the OIC introduced the Cairo Declaration on Human Rights in Islam, which presented a set of religiously defined human rights. The OIC often argued that the declaration was complementary, not a substitute or alternative, to the Universal Declaration on Human Rights (UDHR) and true to Islamic principles. At the same time human rights activists and Western states widely denounced the declaration. These detractors argued that subjugating human rights to religious limitations, as promoted in the Cairo Declaration, conflicted with essential principles of the UDHR, including the core principles of equality and nondiscrimination, thus undermining it.

Second, in 1999, the OIC introduced the first of a series of UN resolutions to the Human Rights Commission, asking governments to combat "defamation of religions" by limiting freedom of expression and criminalizing defamatory statements. According to the OIC, this was a much-needed step in the fight against rising Islamophobia in the West. Specifically, the OIC claimed that the defamation of Islam often led to anti-Muslim discrimination. Western states considered the resolutions contrary to freedom of expression and saw such efforts as an attempt to universalize anti-blasphemy laws. Coupled with harsh human rights violations in many OIC member states and the OIC's unwillingness to address these violations either through its own protocols or as a participant in international human rights proceedings, the OIC gained a reputation as a spoiler organization in the international human rights system.

The mid-2000s saw the OIC engaging with international human rights in a slightly more constructive manner. Internally, as part of a larger reform of the OIC, its Ten Year Program of Action (TYPOA) was published in 2005, introducing an explicit focus on universal human rights and highlighting the importance of incorporating human rights concerns into all programs and activities. Notably, the plan also stressed "the responsibility of the international community, including all governments, to ensure respect for all religions and combat their defamation." The new approach was most clearly manifested in the 2011 establishment of an OIC human rights mechanism, the Independent Permanent Human Rights Commission (IPHRC). The IPHRC was charged with supporting member states in their implementation of international human rights obligations.

A number of other initiatives also had the potential to positively influence the OIC's human rights agenda, including the establishment of the OIC Humanitarian Affairs Department, known as ICHAD (2007); mechanisms for cooperation with humanitarian nongovernmental organizations (NGOs) (2012); the Peace, Security and Mediation Unit (2013); and the Women's Development Organization (2013). Externally, the OIC also showed signs of a more constructive approach at the UN. In 2011, the organization cosponsored a UN resolution that linked religious discrimination with combating hate speech.[1] At least on the surface, this resolution signaled a move away from the anti-defamation agenda and, more generally, a willingness to engage positively with mainstream human rights conceptions rather than promoting a parallel system of religiously defined human rights.

Simultaneously, however, the OIC has continued to voice its criticism of certain human rights. Either as an organization or through the voices of its members, the OIC has opposed efforts concerning the rights of LGBTI people as well as certain women's rights, such as reproductive rights. Together with Russia, the OIC has cosponsored a set of resolutions on "traditional values," emphasizing the importance of conservative religious values in the interpretation of human rights. Furthermore, the OIC's internal organizational developments also invite serious questions regarding its commitment to their stated 2005 agenda. The OIC's main vehicle for human rights advancement, the IPHRC, was born with a severely restricted mandate and a minimal budget. Other instruments with the potential to impact the OIC's human rights agenda—such as the Peace, Security and Mediation Unit and the Women's Development Organization—took years to establish. The OIC's weak embrace of the organs that could further its human rights agenda reflects a lack of support by member states, testifying to the fact that state sovereignty and noninterference are still the defining features of the OIC.

These developments reveal the OIC to be an increasingly important actor in the field of international human rights but show that its human rights involvement is inconsistent, contradictory, and at times counterproductive to the promotion, protection, and further development of human rights. This makes it necessary to better understand the OIC, its actions, its motivations, and its organizational framework. In recent years, a number of scholars have begun to study the organization's engagement with human rights issues, including analyses of the Cairo Declaration and the Covenant of the Rights of the Child in Islam (Mayer 2012; Farrar 2014), the defamation of religion agenda and Resolution 16/18 (Rehman and Berry 2012; Petersen and Kayaoglu

2013; Bettiza and Dionigi 2014; Kayaoglu 2014; Langer 2014; Limon et al. 2014; Skorini and Petersen 2017), the IPHRC (Petersen 2012; Kayaoglu 2013), civil society cooperation (Ameli 2011), humanitarianism (Svoboda et al. 2015), counterterrorism (Samuel 2013), the OIC's status in international law (Cismas 2014), and the OIC and LGBTI rights (Chase 2012). Expanding on much of this work and presenting new analyses, this book aims to provide a comprehensive examination of the OIC's human rights approach with a focus on both the factors shaping this approach and the OIC's influence on wider human rights developments.

Human Rights, Intergovernmental Organizations, and Global Islam

Presenting a nuanced and detailed case study of the OIC, the book not only provides essential empirical and theoretical insights on the OIC and human rights, it also contributes to the broader scholarly discussions centered around contemporary challenges to human rights, intergovernmental organizations, and global Islam.

Earlier literature on human rights was premised on an (implicit) assumption that human rights diffusion is a linear process resulting in institutionalization and "closure." As such, this literature has difficulties accounting for challenges to human rights. Contemporary research—emerging from international relations, anthropology, and sociology—has shown that human rights are not definitively accepted when internalized in hard law and institutions (Redhead and Turnbull 2011:186) but remain contested even after their internalization. As such, human rights are better conceived as open-ended processes in which "co-optation, drift, accretion and reversal of a norm—including disputes over whether it is a norm at all—are constant possibilities" (Krook and True 2012:104) and the risk of decay and erosion is ever-present (Panke and Petersohn 2012). Recent research has explored processes of norm reconceptualization (Krook and True 2012), localization and vernacularization (Merry 2006; Acharya 2011; Zwingel 2012), and contestation (Wiener 2012). Questioning conceptions of human rights as fixed and static norms, this literature instead directs attention to the various ways in which human rights are constantly challenged, appropriated, co-opted, and rejected. As such, human rights discourses and practices are best conceptualized as "politics" in the sense of power struggles to fix meaning, decision-making, and resource allocation, or as attempts to constitute the social in certain ways (Laclau and Mouffe 1985).

Through an examination of the OIC's engagement with human rights discourses and practices, this volume explores the ways in which human rights are not only challenged and rejected, but also—and perhaps increasingly so—co-opted and reconceptualized. The volume comprises new perspectives, extensive research, and differing insights, providing empirical information on a key—but often overlooked—actor in contemporary human rights politics.

Thus the volume presents new perspectives on the recent expansion of the international human rights regime. Challenges to human rights, we argue, no longer come primarily from outside the human rights system but also from within the expanded system, offered up in the same human rights language as the regime itself was constructed—that of those who are criticized. This dynamic also means that traditional dichotomies between universalism and relativism fall short of explaining contemporary challenges to human rights. While the OIC does still deploy a relativist critique of human rights at times, in other instances the organization's critique is formulated in terms of an alternative universalism, making the conflict over human rights as much a conflict between competing universalisms (Halliday 1995) as it is between universalism and relativism. Furthermore, this volume's analyses of the OIC's direct attention to the crucial fact that differences in values and worldviews are not the only source of conflict over human rights, and that competing policy priorities, power relations, and historical experiences all play an equally important role in understanding contemporary challenges to human rights.

In this politics of human rights, international organizations are often seen as key sites for the construction and diffusion of global norms, ideas, and practices (Barnett and Finnemore 2004). Much international relations literature on human rights has foregrounded the role of international organizations in the creation, diffusion, and internalization of these international norms (Finnemore and Sikkink 1998; Finnemore and Sikkink 2001). Research to date has included analysis of how and when international organizations frame human rights issues, set the agenda of state negotiations, and alter the positions of states (Checkel 1999; Risse et al. 1999; Ratner 2000). However, as Bettiza and Dionigi (2014) argue, much scholarship is marked by considerable Western-centrism, apparent in the overwhelming focus on "good" global norms, promoted by Western-based actors, in non-Western contexts (2). This Western-centrism is also evident in a tendency to assume a one-way process of norm diffusion from the West to the rest of the world.

A focus on the OIC brings a new perspective, shedding light on the ways in which non-Western actors engage with human rights, not only as norm-takers but also as norm-makers, seeking to promote and internationalize their own beliefs, values, and principles (Bettiza and Dionigi 2014:2). At the same time, an analysis of the OIC's engagement with human rights issues can contribute to modifying expectations concerning the power and influence of international organizations. Although international organizations can be placed on a continuum of supranationalism and intergovernmentalism, human rights scholars tend to study supranational organizations and how these organizations use their autonomy from and power over member states to advance human rights agendas. This tendency creates the image of international organizations as valuable for human rights. The OIC is a good example of an intergovernmental organization that has very little autonomy from and power over member states. Its human rights agenda and occasionally unhelpful role in human rights politics and governance challenge the expected positive role of international organizations in human rights literature.

As several chapters in this volume demonstrate, the OIC is an important actor in the UN, capable of effectively framing human rights issues on its own terms, but the OIC has (and seeks) little influence at the level of its own member states. There are few examples of the organization having altered the human rights positions of OIC member states or influenced their negotiations on human rights issues. In fact, the OIC rarely engages in discussions on human rights issues in member states, thus reflecting the importance that the OIC member states place on the principle of noninterference and pointing to the disproportionate power of (certain) states in shaping the organization's human rights approach.[2]

Finally, an analysis of the OIC's engagement with human rights issues can contribute to understanding the inherent heterogeneity of international organizations in general and the OIC in particular. Consisting of fifty-seven member states, each with its own political, economic, cultural, and religious characteristics, the OIC is constantly struggling to maintain organizational unity. From this perspective, the OIC's ambiguous, ambivalent, and sometimes outright contradictory human rights discourses and practices are not only expressions of opportunistic realpolitik but are just as much strategies for organizational survival, designed to contain internal disagreements and conflicts.

In this, religious discourses and practices play an important role for the OIC, making it a key actor in contemporary struggles to define global Islam.

In literature on global Islam, the role of the OIC as a pan-Islamic organization is severely under-researched (notable exceptions are Haynes 2001; Akbarzadeh and Connor 2005; Kayaoglu 2015). Instead, analyses of global Islam have tended to focus on "political Islam." This analytical perspective has led to studies of organizations and movements working for the establishment of a political order based on Islam and Sharia whether through the nonviolent capture of state power, as is the case with the Muslim Brotherhood, or through violent means, as is the case with the Islamic State and Al-Qaeda (Mandaville 2014). Recent years have witnessed an increasing interest in other manifestations of global Islam, highlighting the emergence of a "civil Islam" that focuses on values and morality, whether through charity, education, or other forms of social action in civil society (Hefner 2000; Krause 2012).

Neither expressing a straightforward political Islam, nor a civil Islam (but in part and at times relying on both), the OIC presents an alternative Islamic response to the challenges of globalization and modernity, invoking religion as a relevant factor in global value politics (Cismas 2014). As an Islamic organization, the OIC claims to speak on behalf of not only its member states but, controversially, on behalf of Islam and the *umma*, the worldwide Muslim community (Kayaoglu 2015). However, as the contributions to this volume demonstrate, this is a difficult role. Since member states differ widely in terms of their interpretations of Islam and its place in the public sphere, the Islam that the OIC represents must necessarily be an eclectic, flexible, and "thin" Islam, capable of accommodating a wide variety of positions but also inherently ambiguous and at times contradictory. Within the OIC, where are the conflicts over the meaning and role of Islam? What conceptions of Islam are prioritized over others? When is Islam invoked as a relevant factor? Exploring such questions, the chapters in this volume not only shed light on the identity of the OIC as a "religionist organization" (Cismas 2014) but also contribute to a broader study of the contemporary politics of Islam.

Foundations, Interventions, and Intersections: Structure and Themes of the Book

Gathering perspectives from some of the world's leading scholars on the OIC, this volume explores the nexus between the OIC and the international human rights regime, assessing and clarifying the OIC's vision, role, and influence in the field of international human rights. Exploring the OIC's human rights activities at many levels—in the UN, in the organization's own institutions, and at member state level—the volume's twelve chapters assess many aspects of the OIC's approach to human rights, identifying priority areas of involvement and underlying conceptions of human rights, analyzing the factors that shape these OIC actions and understandings, and discussing the consequences they may have for the broader human rights field. While the twelve chapters in this volume take diverse disciplinary approaches, emphasize various analytical levels (state-centric, organizational, or transnational) and focus on different aspects of the relationship between the OIC and human rights, they all seek to explore and answer three main questions.

First, contributors to this volume ask what the OIC's approach is to human rights and human rights-related issues. In answering this question, the chapters present in-depth, empirical descriptions of the OIC's human rights discourses and practices, analyzing the organization's human rights agendas, exploring their historical development, comparing divergent conceptions of human rights within the OIC, and discussing areas of conflict and congruence between the OIC's human rights discourses and practices and those of the international human rights regime. In so doing, the volume points to an emerging human rights perspective in the OIC—that being one which approaches human rights from a place that is ideologically conservative, rather than Islamist; is oriented toward state security, rather than human security; and exhibits a strong preference for human rights diplomacy, rather than human rights advocacy. At the same time, however, the writers of this volume demonstrate that this perspective is far from consolidated in the organization but ambiguous and unstable, pointing to inherent contradictions in the OIC's organizational identity as well as deep-seated disagreements among member states, between headquarters and certain member states, and between organizational entities.

Second, the authors ask why the OIC favors this particular approach to human rights, exploring various explanatory factors and models. Directing attention to the organizational politics and internal dynamics of the OIC, each author explores issues of power and authority in order to analyze the roles that member states, organizational entities, and individuals play in shaping the OIC's human rights agenda. The intergovernmental nature of the OIC; the organization's endemic lack of financial, human, and political resources; the dominance of conservative members, in particular Saudi Arabia, Iran, and Pakistan; the marginalization of civil society actors in OIC activities; and the lack of human rights expertise among OIC leaders have all shaped the OIC's human rights approach. However, the OIC's approach is not determined solely by internal dynamics. Rather, the OIC's human rights approach is also subject to influence by external actors as well as political, social, economic, and cultural structures, thereby creating conditions of possibility and constraint for particular human rights interpretations. For example, the lack of both a strong OIC and a broader Muslim voice in the UN Security Council has contributed to the OIC's strategy of using the Human Rights Council instead, effectively resulting in a highly politicized and securitized perspective toward human rights.

Third, each chapter addresses the wider consequences of the OIC's human rights approach. Placing the OIC in the larger context of global politics, the authors present informed suggestions as to what the organization's human rights engagement means for the development of an international human rights regime. Has the OIC succeeded in influencing the human rights agenda? If so, in what ways? If not, why not? Will the organization's human rights discourses and practices contribute to strengthening or weakening human rights? Will they broaden or limit the scope of human rights? Will they substantially change the meaning of human rights? In Chapter 4, Ann Mayer argues that the OIC's human rights policies at the UN involve injecting incongruous religious factors that undermine human rights because these factors ultimately serve to discredit the freedoms espoused by Western democracies. Other contributors are slightly more positive: Petersen, for example, argues that the OIC's increased cooperation with humanitarian organizations may present an opportunity for greater human rights engagement in relation to economic, social, and cultural rights.

The book is divided into three sections. Part I, Foundations, establishes the theoretical and organizational foundations of the book. In Chapter 1, "Setting the Scene," Anthony Tirado Chase presents a theoretical and conceptual framework for analyzing and understanding the OIC and human rights. Will the OIC's engagement with human rights advance human rights in the Muslim world or are these efforts a problematic strategy to co-opt or even subvert human rights? And, more broadly, what does the OIC's engagement with human rights say about the ways in which human rights norms are independently affected by international organizations, either positively or negatively? Answering these questions, Chase argues that an international organization such as the OIC, dominated by conservative, authoritarian states, is unlikely to create political opportunity structures to advance human rights. Indeed, the OIC's record shows that, if it has had any independent impact on human rights at all, the effect has been to create regional and international opposition to the expansion of human rights.

Opposing Chase's skepticism in Chapter 2, "Human Rights Agenda of the OIC: Between Pessimism and Optimism," Mashood A. Baderin offers a cautiously optimistic account of the OIC's contribution and future potential as a human rights actor. Baderin argues that OIC activities and challenges should be perceived as attempts to contribute to the "inclusive universalism in the international human rights system." Thus, the OIC complements the UN human rights system by offering a regional human rights system rather than undermining it by offering its human rights system as an alternative. In the process, the OIC has been challenged to "harmonize . . . Islamic values with international human rights standards." Baderin presents a three-pronged critique of the OIC's human rights agenda in the context of an "is-ought" analysis with regard to the conceptualization, standard-setting, and implementation of human rights. Juxtaposing pessimistic and optimistic perspectives on OIC activities, he strongly asserts why we should be optimistic about the OIC's activities and their potential as a human rights actor.

Moving from the theoretical and conceptual aspects of the OIC's human rights involvement to the organizational ones, Turan Kayaoglu's "The OIC's Human Rights Regime" (Chapter 3) provides an introductory overview of the OIC institutions relevant to understanding the organization's human rights involvement. Kayaoglu examines the OIC mechanisms, documents, organs, and actors that produce and implement the organization's human rights agenda, whether directly—such as the Cairo Declaration on Human Rights in Islam, the OIC's UN offices in New York and Geneva, and the Independent Permanent Human Rights Commission—or more indirectly, such as the Department on Muslim Minorities and Communities, the Islamophobia Observatory, and the Humanitarian Affairs Department.

Part II, Interventions: Rights and Values, addresses the OIC's involvement in issues directly framed as human rights issues, focusing on those human rights that have been particularly challenged by the OIC and exploring the ways in which the OIC approaches and conceptualizes these rights in UN debates and within its own institutions. The section's five chapters present analyses of the OIC's approach to rights such as freedom of expression, freedom of religion, women's rights, and children's rights. In Chapter 4, "The OIC's Human Rights Policies in the UN: A Problem of Coherence," Ann Elizabeth Mayer asks whether the OIC can articulate a coherent philosophy on how Islamic concerns relate to human rights. Mayer argues that the OIC appears incapable—or unwilling—to distinguish between secular principles of international law and religious precepts of Islamic doctrine and that its attempt to subjugate the former to the latter would impose Islamic censorship worldwide.

In Chapter 5, "OIC and Freedom of Expression: Justifying Religious Censorship Norms with Human Rights Language," Heini í Skorini zooms in on one of the OIC's most controversial human rights policies, the so-called defamation of religions resolutions presented by the OIC to the UN Human Rights Council each year from 1999 until 2010. Tracing the historical trajectory of these resolutions, the chapter explores the conflict between the OIC and Western states over the right to free speech and protection of religious sentiments, analyzing the shifting strategies and terminologies of the OIC.

In "Competing Perceptions: Traditional Values and Human Rights," Chapter 6, Moataz El Fegiery explores another UN debate in which the OIC has played a key role, namely the debate on the role of traditional values in the promotion of human rights. Focusing on the 2009 resolution "Promoting Human Rights and Fundamental Freedoms Through a Better Understanding of Traditional Values of Humankind," presented to the Human Rights Council by Russia and vehemently supported by the OIC, El Fegiery examines how the concept of traditional values is defined and promoted as a way to limit or block certain human rights, in particular LGBTI rights and certain women's rights.

Ioana Cismas further explores the position of the OIC on women's rights in Chapter 7, "The Position of the OIC on Abortion: Not Too Bad, Ugly, or Just Confusing?" Cismas analyzes relevant provisions related to the topic of abortion in OIC human rights instruments and documents, and contrasts these with the organization's statements in UN forums and the practices of selected member states. While the organization's position on aspects related to sexuality is commonly described as strongly conservative, Cismas demonstrates that its stance on abortion is far more complex and at times contradictory and incoherent. In an effort to deconstruct this disharmony, the study explores religious, legal, political, and sociohistorical factors and argues for the need to build legitimacy from within the OIC in order to advance a progressive OIC sexuality agenda.

The last chapter in this section, Mahmood Monshipouri and Turan Kayaoglu's "The OIC and Children's Rights," focuses on (in the eyes of the OIC) a less controversial set of rights, namely children's rights. In fact, the OIC's 2005 Covenant on the Rights of the Child in Islam is the organization's only potentially binding human rights document. Monshipouri and Kayaoglu present the OIC's position and activities on children's rights, comparing the Covenant with UN standards on children's rights and discussing the ways in which the OIC seeks to align children's rights with respect to Islamic traditions. They argue that even when the OIC has prioritized the development of a covenant on the rights of children, the organization has been ineffective in implementing these standards, reflecting among other things the ambiguous nature of the covenant.

Part III, Intersections: Conflicts and Cooperation, focuses on areas of the OIC's work that are not explicitly framed in terms of human rights but which are nonetheless highly relevant to understanding the organization's position and influence in the field of human rights. Exploring the OIC's involvement in the areas of conflict resolution, humanitarian and development aid, refugee law, and civil society cooperation, this section analyzes the role that human rights play (or do not play) in this involvement, pointing to similarities with and differences from the ways in which the OIC engages in more explicit human rights issues. Chapter 9, Hirah Azhar's "The OIC and Conflict Resolution: Norms and Practical Challenges" analyzes the role of human rights in the OIC's conflict resolution efforts. For many regional and international organizations, the protection of human rights forms the very cornerstone of their conflict resolution discourse and involvement. Analyzing the OIC's engagement in conflict resolution, including the Peace, Security and Mediation Unit and the Network of Religious and Traditional Peacemakers, Azhar argues that the OIC has largely ignored the issue of human rights in its conflict resolution efforts, reflecting the interests of certain influential member states.

Evren Tok and Martin Lestra's chapter, "Fragmented Aid? The Institutionalization of the OIC's Foreign Aid Framework," looks at the OIC's involvement in humanitarian and development aid. Reflecting the organization's wish to institutionalize "Islamic solidarity," the OIC has engaged in this issue since its early days, manifested in the establishment of, for example, the Islamic Development Bank, the Islamic Solidary Fund, and—more recently—the Humanitarian Affairs Department. Tok and Lestra posit that, theoretically, foreign aid presents an area in which the OIC could act as a credible, effective, and cohesive alternative to established frameworks. In practice, however, what started as a promising political enterprise led to a puzzling outcome, characterized by fragmentation and ineffectiveness.

Chapter 11, Zeynep Mencütek's "Governance of Refugees in the OIC," explores another area in which the OIC has the potential to become an important actor on the international scene. As both the main source of and as host to refugees and internally displaced persons, the OIC might well be expected to develop a policy to address the causes as well as consequences of internally or externally displaced populations. However, as Mencütek demonstrates, the organization has been slow in developing such a framework and lacks an integrated approach, often limiting its activities to humanitarian aid during refugee crises.

In Chapter 12, "The OIC and Civil Society Cooperation: Prospects for Strengthened Human Rights Involvement?" Marie Juul Petersen explores the OIC's relations with civil society. Parallel to its increased attention to human rights, the OIC has claimed a willingness to strengthen its cooperation with civil society, including, among other things, the introduction of "consultative status" to certain NGOs. How, if at all, does this strengthened cooperation with civil society influence the OIC's human rights involvement? Building on an empirical analysis of the OIC's relations with civil society, Petersen contends that the inherent potential of civil society organizations is impeded by the fact that the OIC prioritizes cooperation with apolitical, service-oriented organizations, the majority of them conservative Islamic NGOs engaged in the provision of humanitarian aid rather than human rights advocacy organizations.

The perspectives of the authors gathered here vary widely and present an interdisciplinary mosaic intended to provoke discourse on their role in the global community. Since the OIC's inception in 1969, its place in the world of international diplomacy has evolved, changed, and been strengthened over time. The analysis of its role—past, present, and future—is both timely and worthwhile. The value lies not only in the analysis but in the critical engagement with an international organization with an abundance of potential to effect change in critical times.

Notes

1. The title of the resolution is "Combating Intolerance, Negative Stereotyping and Stigmatization of, and Discrimination, Incitement to Violence and Violence Against, Persons Based on Religion or Belief," also known as Resolution 16/18.

2. This does not mean that the OIC's human rights engagement will not at some point lead to changes at the member-state level. As noted by Chase in his contribution to this volume, even hypocritical human rights rhetoric can have an entrapment effect, and the OIC's mouthing of platitudes about human rights at the UN level may inadvertently constrain the

organization from acting in ways that are too obviously contradictory to its platitudes in relation to member states.

Works Cited

Acharya, Amitav. 2011. "Norm Subsidiarity and Regional Orders: Sovereignty, Regionalism and Rule-Making in the Third World." *International Studies Quarterly* 55 (1): 95–123.

Akbarzadeh, Shahram, and Kylie Connor. 2005. "The Organization of the Islamic Conference: Sharing an Illusion." *Middle East Policy* 12 (2): 79–92.

Ameli, Saied Reza. 2011. "The Organization of Islamic Conference: Accountability and Civil Society." In *Building Global Democracy? Civil Society and Accountable Global Governance*, ed. Jan Aart Scholte, 146–62. Cambridge: Cambridge University Press.

Barnett, Michael, and Martha Finnemore. 2004. *Rules for the World: International Organizations in Global Politics*. Ithaca, NY: Cornell University Press.

Bettiza, Gregorio, and Filippo Dionigi. 2014. "How Do Religious Norms Diffuse? Institutional Translation and International Change in a Post-Secular World Society." *European Journal of International Relations* 21 (3): 621–46.

Chase, Anthony T. 2012. *Human Rights, Revolution, and Reform in the Muslim World*. Boulder, CO: Lynne Rienner.

Checkel, Jeffrey T. 1999. "Norms, Institutions, and National Identity in Contemporary Europe." *International Studies Quarterly* 43 (1): 83–114.

Cismas, Ioana. 2014. *Religious Actors and International Law*. Oxford: Oxford University Press.

Farrar, Salim. 2014. "The Organization of Islamic Cooperation: Forever on the Periphery of Public International Law?" *Chinese Journal of International Law* 13 (4): 787–817.

Finnemore, Martha, and Kathryn Sikkink. 1998. "International Norm Dynamics and Political Change." *International Organization* 52 (4): 887–917.

———. 2001. "Taking Stock: The Constructivist Research Program in International Relations and Comparative Politics." *Annual Review of Political Science* 4 (1): 391–416.

Halliday, Fred. 1995. "Relativism and Universalism in Human Rights: The Case of the Islamic Middle East." *Political Studies* 43 (1): 152–67.

Haynes, Jeff. 2001. "Transnational Religious Actors and International Politics." *Third World Quarterly* 22 (2): 143–58.

Hefner, Robert W. 2000. *Civil Islam: Muslims and Democratization in Indonesia*. Princeton, NJ: Princeton University Press.

Kayaoglu, Turan. 2013. "A Rights Agenda for the Muslim World? The Organization of Islamic Cooperation's Evolving Human Rights Framework." Brookings Doha Center Analysis Papers. Doha: Brookings Institution.

———. 2014. "Giving an Inch Only to Lose a Mile: Muslim States, Liberalism, and Human Rights in the United Nations." *Human Rights Quarterly* 36 (1): 61–89.

———. 2015. *The Organization of Islamic Cooperation: Politics, Problems, and Potential*. London: Routledge.

Krause, Wanda. 2012. *Civil Society and Women Activists in the Middle East: Islamic and Secular Organizations in Egypt*. London: I.B. Tauris.

Krook, Mona Lena, and Jacqui True. 2012. "Rethinking the Life Cycles of International Norms: The United Nations and the Global Promotion of Gender Equality." *European Journal of International Relations* 18 (1): 103–27.

Laclau, Ernesto, and Chantal Mouffe. 1985. *Hegemony and Social Strategy: Towards a Radical Democratic Politics*. London: Verso.

Langer, Lorenz. 2014. *Religious Offence and Human Rights: The Implications of Defamation of Religions*. Cambridge: Cambridge University Press.

Limon, Marc, Nazila Ghanea, and Hilary Power. 2014. *Combatting Global Religious Intolerance: The Implementation of Human Rights Council Resolution 16/18*. Geneva: Universal Rights Group.

Mandaville, Peter. 2014. *Islam and Politics*. London: Routledge.

Mayer, Ann Elizabeth. 2012. *Islam and Human Rights*. 5th ed. Boulder, CO: Westview.

Merry, Sally Engle. 2006. "Transnational Human Rights and Local Activism: Mapping the Middle." *American Anthropologist* 108 (1): 38–51.

Panke, Diana, and Ulrich Petersohn. 2012. "Why International Norms Disappear Sometimes." *European Journal of International Relations* 18 (4): 719–42.

Petersen, Marie Juul. 2012. "Islamic or Universal Human Rights? The OIC's Independent Permanent Human Rights Commission." Danish Institute for International Studies Working Papers. Copenhagen: DIIS.

Petersen, Marie Juul, and Turan Kayaoglu. 2013. "Will Istanbul Process Relieve the Tension Between the Muslim World and the West?" *Washington Review of Turkish and Euroasian Affairs*, September 30.

Ratner, Steven R. 2000. "Democracy and Accountability: The Criss-crossing Paths of Two Emerging Norms." In *Democratic Governance and International Law*, ed. Gregory H. Fox and Brad R. Roth, 449–90. Cambridge: Cambridge University Press.

Redhead, Robin, and Nick Turnbull. 2011. "Towards a Study of Human Rights Practitioners." *Human Rights Review* 12 (2): 173–89.

Rehman, Javaid, and Stephanie E. Berry. 2012. "Is 'Defamation of Religions' Passé? The United Nations, Organisation of Islamic Cooperation, and Islamic State Practices: Lessons from Pakistan." *George Washington International Law Review* 44 (3): 431–72.

Risse, Thomas, Stephen C. Ropp, and Kathryn Sikkink, eds. 1999. *The Power of Human Rights: International Norms and Domestic Change*. Cambridge: Cambridge University Press.

Samuel, Katja. 2013. *The OIC, the UN and Counter-Terrorism Law-Making: Conflicting or Cooperative Legal Orders?* Oxford: Hart.

Skorini, Heini, and Marie Juul Petersen. 2017. "Hate Speech and Holy Prophets: Tracing the OIC's Strategies to Protect Religion." In *Religion, the State and Human Rights*, ed. Anne Stensvold, 44–61. London: Routledge.

Svoboda, Eva, Steven A. Zyck, Daud Osman, and Abdirashid Hashi. 2015. "Islamic Humanitarianism? The Evolving Role of the Organisation for Islamic Cooperation in Somalia and Beyond." Humanitarian Policy Group. https://www.odi.org/sites/odi.org.uk/files/odi-assets/publications-opinion-files/9457.pdf.

Wiener, Antje. 2012. *A Theory of Contestation*. Heidelberg: Springer.

Zwingel, Susanne. 2012. "How Do Norms Travel? Theorizing International Women's Rights in Transnational Perspective." *International Studies Quarterly* 56 (1): 115–29.

PART I

FOUNDATIONS

CHAPTER 1

Setting the Scene

Anthony Tirado Chase

The OIC and Human Rights: Promise and Problems

Any introduction to the Organization of Islamic Cooperation (OIC) and human rights must start by noting the great hopes that have been invested in the OIC as a vessel to advance human rights. These hopes have been inspired by how—after years of being perceived by virtually all observers as, at best, a marginal actor in both regional and global politics—in recent years the OIC has increasingly raised its profile. It has done so, in part, by virtue of adopting rights language in its own declarations and, hence, affirming human rights as a legitimate global regime of which the OIC (and the Muslim world) are an integral part (Kayaoglu 2015b). For such a conservative, state-centric actor to have done this formally contradicted the notion that human rights were foreign to the Muslim world. More importantly, it suggested that the OIC's human rights engagements might be a means to bring even the most conservative Muslim states into the fold of states that see human rights as an extension of their own values and interests. These hopes, however, have been simultaneously raised and frustrated. This is largely because their rhetorical embrace of human rights has meant very little in terms of substantive policy by the OIC and its member states. Indeed, it could be argued that the theoretical adoption of human rights language has been a tool used by the OIC to subvert human rights in practice.

This ambiguity in the OIC's current policies on human rights is mirrored by ambiguity in the OIC's historical relations with the international human rights regime. On the one hand, the OIC has had a consistent history of resisting human rights, both collectively in international forums and within its leading member states such as Iran and Saudi Arabia. On the other hand, all of its member states have signed on to human rights treaties and many of its states have significantly engaged in building the human rights regime, including the drafting of its basic legal instruments, well beyond the pro forma signing of a few treaties (Waltz 2004). This ambiguous history may help explain why the OIC's current policies on human rights are both promising and problematic.

In a promising sense, the OIC's position on human rights has seemingly evolved in affirmative ways in recent years. Specifically, the OIC has moved from opposing human rights as such to proactive engagement, including the use of human rights language to defend its positions in international forums and, more importantly, the establishment of the Independent Permanent Human Rights Commission (IPHRC) in 2011 (Cismas 2011). This presents the tantalizing potential of giving the international human rights regime purchase within an important bloc of states that—despite their differing human rights positions and records—have at times presented themselves as collectively opposed to important expansions of human rights norms (Kayaoglu 2013).

This enticing promise, however, also raises a number of problematic questions, both practical and theoretical (Petersen 2012). A first set of questions regards whether the OIC's future engagement can or will substantively advance human rights in the Muslim world or whether it is even meant to do so: Perhaps it is more a strategy to co-opt or block human rights than expand them? A second set of questions raised by the OIC's human rights engagement is especially relevant to human rights and international relations scholarship: What does the OIC's engagement with human rights say about the ways in which human rights norms do or do not spread around the globe and how, in those continual processes, may they be redefined for better or for worse?

This chapter argues in regard to the first set of questions that, as tantalizing as the promise of the OIC's engagement with human rights may be, this engagement has more potential to be irrelevant or even somewhat problematic than helpful in advancing human rights. There are three reasons for this. One, the future of human rights within the vastly diverse member states of the OIC depends on domestic, transnational, and international factors distant from the OIC's human rights initiatives. The OIC is simply not in a position to have a determinative impact on advancing human rights given its minimal on-the-ground presence within its member states. If the OIC is to have any substantial impact, it will most likely be at the international level working as a bloc at the UN in opposition to rights' expansions, not in terms of implementing rights at the domestic level within its own states.

Two, there is strong reason to doubt that the OIC initiatives are even meant to advance human rights at the domestic level. It is certainly the case that the OIC's leading states increasingly see human rights—and, more specifically, how human rights norms and law have increasingly informed the demands of social movements attempting to change the status quo power structures within such states—as a threat both internally and regionally. They are, thus, being proactive rather than passive in addressing this threat; Saudi Arabia (the OIC's leading funder) has been particularly proactive in the wake of the Arab Uprisings (2010–2012) in attacking movements for greater democracy and popular empowerment within the Arab world—and has had considerable success in that counterrevolutionary process (Hashemi 2017). That states are using the OIC as a tool in this strategy is a far more realistic explanation for why and how it is that the OIC is engaging with human rights—that is, the OIC can help state efforts to co-opt and contain human rights. It may even be that OIC initiatives will result in changes to how human rights are defined in favor of state-centric interests. That the OIC's human rights concerns seem to center on the interests and identities of elites that dominate OIC states rather than those states' disempowered groups indicates that its initiatives remain contrary to a consistent idea in human rights instruments: that they should aim to bring more groups into states' political communities, not reinforce existing power hierarchies in authoritarian governments with only narrow bases of support, as is the case with many leading OIC states.

Three, no matter what the OIC's on-the-ground position or geopolitical intentions, structurally it is not clear that the OIC is an international organization with the ability to be an independent actor, at least in respect to advancing human rights. International organizations are unlikely to be leaders in advancing human rights unless they are constituted in significant ways by states and nonstate social movements that either push them to do so or, at least, give that international organization substantial purview to act independently. While this is sometimes the case for international organizations, there is no evidence that it is the case for the OIC, as the organization remains dominated by nondemocratic states that are threatened by the sort of popular empowerment envisioned in a human rights framework (Graham 2014). Indeed, if an international organization such as the OIC that is dominated by authoritarian states is to have any impact at all, it is more likely to be negative. Even such a negative impact, however, helps us understand how increasingly contested human rights are—a backhanded testament to their importance. Despite (or perhaps due to) that importance, the OIC is joining a battle that shows how vulnerable human rights are to being co-opted and used against, ironically, the purposes with which they are most commonly associated: protections of minorities and vulnerable populations from majoritarian state power.

These three arguments lead to one overarching conclusion: that what will move the pendulum toward greater human rights implementation are political opportunity structures created by a dialectic among various actors, not an organization such as the OIC, disposed to oppose human rights. First among these actors are social movements potentially acting both as instigators of changing norms and mobilizers of political pressures advancing human rights in domestic and international spaces (Blakeley 2013; Brysk 2013). Second among these actors are vigorously democratic states that give a context in which human rights–related social movements can flourish and have an impact in pushing states to support human rights, in some sense, in their own interest (Moravcsik, 2000; Schulz, 2002). And, third, when an international organization is in active dialogue with such states and social movements it has the potential to develop as an independent actor that can act to advance human rights (Landolt 2013). It is in *that* context that an international organization can be an independent actor interacting with states and social movements in ways that create political opportunity structures that can be seized on to advance human rights (Barnett and Finnemore 2004). The OIC as currently structured, however, does not present a significant opportunity to advance human rights protections.

In short, there is no reason to assume that the OIC's invocation of human rights will necessarily lead to the advancement of human rights. Until now, there has been little evidence that the OIC is anything but a tool of its most powerful states, a tool that has consistently been used to limit human rights' use by social movements within those states, transnationally and internationally. Hence the provisional conclusion that the OIC's engagement with human rights is unlikely to have positive impacts until the OIC is more fully constituted by democratic states and independent domestic and transnational civil society movements. The barometer for a more optimistic conclusion will be if the OIC's human rights initiatives ever turn toward empowering the disadvantaged and marginalized in their state members' societies, something that has so far been lacking (Brysk and Wehrenfennig 2010).

This is not to say, however, that the OIC's engagements with human rights are academically uninteresting. To the contrary, getting a handle on the implications of these engagements is essential to a clear-eyed take on the OIC's role at the UN (especially at the Human Rights Council) and within its member states. The way in which the OIC may be having a negative impact on human rights spread is important to take into account when thinking about the impacts of international organizations. Reflecting on the OIC in this regard yields two important insights. The first of these is that, as already indicated, it can help us understand what actually advances human rights and what is a mirage in that regard: what actors and what contexts influence the spread or failure of human rights?

A second question may be of particular interest to scholars of human rights: how have the OIC's human rights initiatives affected battles over what human rights are and will become? Studying the OIC can help us understand how human rights are constantly being contested and rolled back just as often as they are moved forward. It is important to conceptualize human rights as objects of such contestations that take place in intersections among many actors, as the case of the OIC makes clear. In that sense, the OIC can help us better grasp that the spread of human rights is not about core principles being progressively implemented through efforts by elites who dominate international organizations. To the contrary, human rights are continually being expanded, continually being blocked, and, in those processes, continually being reconceptualized at multiple levels. Those reconceptualizations can be about furthering human rights potential to empower marginalized populations. Just as easily, however, they can be about furthering a contradictory conception, one that perversely uses human rights language to advance the power of states and their elites. It would seem that the OIC's aims in invoking human rights are in line with the latter.

To justify the argument just outlined, the second section in this chapter addresses a number of background questions: What is the OIC? What is its history with human rights by reference to the Cairo Declaration on Human Rights in Islam? What does that history say about what human rights are more generally understood to be? What have been the OIC's human rights initiatives? Against that backdrop, the third section looks specifically at the OIC's Independent Permanent Human Rights Commission (IPHCR) and addresses what its establishment says about a fundamental question: Will the OIC's recent human rights initiatives advance human rights or are they even meant to advance human rights? Finally, on that basis, in the fourth section we ask: What is the role of international organizations in the spread and redefinition of human rights norms?

The OIC, Human Rights, and the OIC's Human Rights Initiatives

What Is the OIC?

The OIC currently consists of fifty-seven member states, more than double its initial twenty-five members when founded in 1969 as the Organization of the Islamic Conference. Despite agreeing on a charter in 1972 and growing into a membership that makes it the world's second-largest international organization, the OIC, in Marie Juul Petersen's terms, "has remained a peripheral, and in many ways irrelevant, figure on the international scene" (Petersen 2012). The OIC pales in comparison to the United Nations and its family of agencies as a focal point of global politics, nor does it have anything close to the profile of regional organizations like the Organization of American States, the African Union, the European Union, or even the Association of Southeast Asian States. The OIC has had no particularly cogent unifying impetus other than vague invocations of Islam that ignore both Islam's diversity and conflicts among states and movements claiming to act under Islam's mantle. Beyond that, historically the OIC's most powerful states have had geopolitical rivalries—specifically intense splits among its most powerful members, Iran, Pakistan, Saudi Arabia, and Turkey—that long kept the organization from having a focused agenda, commonality of purpose, or any substantial on-the-ground programming. This peripheral status to which Petersen refers was evidenced by its minimal programming, small budgets ($17.6 million in 2006; Johnson 2010), and lack of a permanent building. This only began to change with the 2005 Ten Year Program of Action (TYPOA).

Human Rights and the OIC: From the Cairo Declaration on Human Rights in Islam to the 2008 OIC Charter

The 2000s found attempts by the OIC to forge at least the foundation for greater common purpose and activity. This included a new charter in 2008,[1] changing the name to the Organization of Islamic Cooperation in 2011, and the funding and awarding of an ambitious design for a permanent headquarters in Jeddah. Most notably, the 2008 charter references human rights, but does so in a way that entirely passes over what had been the instrument for which the OIC had likely gained the most attention and certainly the most controversy during its first decades: its 1990 Cairo Declaration on Human Rights in Islam (whose emphasis on privileging state power over human rights is discussed in Chapter 4).

The 2008 charter makes three notable pronouncements regarding human rights that distinguish it from the Cairo Declaration. One, in its prologue it calls on the OIC to "promote human rights and fundamental freedoms, good governance, rule of law, democracy and accountability in Member States in accordance with their constitutional and legal systems."[2] Two, the charter "reaffirms," in its opening "Objectives and Principles" section, the OIC's "support for the rights of peoples as stipulated in the UN charter and international law." What is significant here is that, unlike in the Cairo Declaration, human rights are sourced from the United Nations and international law, not state interpretations of Islam. Nor are specific human rights provisions assumed to be overridden by Sharia, as in the Cairo Declaration. Three, the charter calls for the Independent Permanent Commission of Human Rights which, as noted, was formally established in 2011.

There had long been criticism by domestic and international human rights activists regarding the Cairo Declaration's shortcomings. The new OIC charter's failure to even reference the Cairo Declaration is indicative of two key points. One, an acceptance by the OIC that, as Turan Kayaoglu writes, its "shortcomings render the Cairo Declaration ineffective as a mechanism for the promotion and protection of human rights. In fact, Muslim advocacy groups, Muslim scholars of human rights, and even Ekmeleddin İhsanoğlu—

OIC secretary-general at the time of the OIC's human rights initiatives—largely ignored the Declaration in their discussions of Islam and human rights" (Kayaoglu 2013). While not formally repudiated, in short, the failure to even mention the Cairo Declaration seems to affirm the OIC's acceptance of the wide-ranging criticisms to which it had been subjected, though the OIC's position on the Cairo Declaration's salience to its current work remains ambivalent if not contradictory, it is certainly fair to note the Cairo Declaration's lack of impact on any level (Cismas 2014).

What Are Human Rights?

These criticisms of the Cairo Declaration speak to a further point of importance: what human rights are or, in this context, what they are not. Kayaoglu summarizes four bases for rejecting the Cairo Declaration that, collectively, speak to what human rights are not. Human rights are based in international law that has sought to make state obligations both increasingly specific and increasingly informed by civil society and other non-state actors, and in which regional human rights instruments supplement rather than contradict international human rights. How the Cairo Declaration contradicts international law, its deliberate ambiguity that allows states to determine what human rights they accept or reject, and its disempowerment of civil society together indicate how the Cairo Declaration—unlike other regional instruments—seeks to supplant international law.

These criticisms speak to predominant conceptions of what human rights have come to be understood to be. While human rights have continued to evolve and to be contested, there has emerged through international treaties a tentative global consensus that anchors human rights to certain core continuities. Most generally, as noted above, human rights are meant to limit the power of the state as well as to make clear the state's obligations to those under their jurisdiction, rather than reinforce the power of the state and elite groups that dominate their states. More specifically, internationally agreed on human rights standards are conceptualized as a framework to advance pluralist political communities, rather than ground political communities in norms identified with only one community. Human rights advocacy attempts to advance that pluralism through norms such as nondiscrimination, rather than legitimize discrimination based on religious (or other) norms. The rights regime has aimed to develop specific legal and political avenues to give those subject to discrimination or other rights' violations by the state tangible tools to resist such violations, rather than further empower the state. In short, human rights as defined in internationally agreed on instruments have aimed both to make states take into account their pluralism rather than deny it and to limit the power of the state to discriminate in favor of its dominant groups and against minorities and the marginalized.

Human rights have been elaborated on with increasing precision in literally hundreds of legal instruments on which states have reached consensus. Despite the development of such specifics, its nondiscrimination principle remains as concise a definition of human rights' core commitment as is possible. That commitment underpins the varied legal and political pathways through which human rights have grown into an avenue to limit and regulate the otherwise increasingly powerful modern state. Most importantly, to the degree that commitment has taken hold it means that human rights have moved away from being invoked on behalf of ethnic solidarity, per the European colonial model of insisting on the right to "protect" fellow Christians or the Cairo Declaration's focus on the rights of fellow Muslims, and into what Brysk and Wehrenfennig call "inter-ethnic solidarity."

OIC Engagements with Human Rights

In the context of this brief review of the OIC, controversies over its Cairo Declaration, and what criticisms of this declaration indicate about what human rights have become and how they remain contested, one last piece of important background is how the OIC has engaged with human rights in recent years. More specifically, with what conceptualization of human rights do these engagements connect? On the surface, the OIC's move from the Cairo Declaration to the Independent Permanent Human Rights Commission is part of a progressive embrace of human rights as embedded in the international treaties that have emerged out of global consensus around certain issues. Rather than trying to create a parallel structure in which human rights are subsumed within an Islamic framework, the OIC has adopted the language of both international law and an implied universality of human rights. Is this shift substantial in the sense that, per this chapter's concerns, it indicates that the OIC has either the incentive or the ability to advance human rights, that is, pay serious attention to the rights of various minorities—ethnic, religious, geographic, gender, or even sexual—within their state societies?

There have been three representative OIC human rights-related initiatives through which one can test this commitment. First, at the UN General Assembly and Human Rights Commission, the OIC led a high-profile agenda to criminalize "defamation of religion," beginning in 1999 and gaining momentum in the wake of the 2005–2006 Danish cartoon crisis. As a signifier of its changing discourse, the OIC did not frame this agenda as a desire to limit free expression as such. Instead, in its annual resolutions, the OIC argued for limits on free speech under the aegis of human rights, both in terms of human rights treaties' references to legitimate restrictions on hate speech and, importantly, as an extension of the right to freedom of religion by extending that into a protection of religion.[3]

As Peter Henne writes, support for the defamation of religions resolutions actually continued to diminish each year until their annual introduction was eventually abandoned in 2011. More importantly, however, Henne demonstrates that support for the annually introduced resolution was centered among states with the lowest levels of democracy and highest levels of repression of religion. This would indicate that it is naïve to take at face value OIC claims to be acting on behalf of actual freedom from religious discrimination (Henne 2013). To the contrary, Henne's analysis indicates that the underlying motive for these actions was a desire for nondemocratic regimes—such as those that have a leadership role in the OIC—to gain support from their domestic religious elites as a way to "justify their restrictive policies" (Henne 2013:512). In other words, despite rhetoric to the contrary, human rights as a way to be inclusive toward minorities was not the driver of these actions. Rather, human rights language was deployed to help elites further consolidate their domination over such minorities. In that context, the OIC attempting to use human rights to protect majoritarian religious orthodoxies from mocking or even blasphemous satire should be seen clearly for what it is: an obvious departure from the normative impulses that have led to human rights being invoked by disenfranchised groups in many parts of the world. To put a fine point on it, these OIC initiatives were about justifying the empirical fact that defamation and blasphemy laws, as a rule, have been harshly implemented by state authorities to attack religious minorities, including those within leading OIC states such as Iran, Pakistan, and Saudi Arabia.

Second among these human rights-related initiatives, the OIC has taken the lead at the UN Human Rights Council in opposing an emerging movement to conceptualize human rights as applicable to sexual orientation and gender identity. Interestingly, it has done so in language that, rhetorically, positions itself as a defender of human rights and its true essence rather than an opponent. The OIC has done this in cooperation with Russia and other conservative non-Islamic UN member states as well as the Vatican, and in a way that again raises doubts if this engagement on human rights is about commitment to an understanding of human rights as extending to the disenfranchised or if it is more about protecting the status quo. As explained by Iranian IPHRC commissioner Mostafa Alaei at a Danish Institute for Human Rights workshop in Copenhagen, from his point of view the OIC can use "human rights as a way to protect the rights of Muslims, especially Muslims in Europe, not LGBT [Lesbian, Gay, Bisexual, Trans] groups. . . . LGBT groups do not have human rights."[4] Leaving aside debates about LGBT or sexual orientation and gender identity-related rights (Chase 2016), what is problematic here is an ethno-nationalist notion of human rights more as a tool to protect the rights of one's own sectarian group rather than the rights of nondominant sectors.

The position of Muslim minorities in Europe (and elsewhere) is a valid human rights concern, and it is vital to direct pressure at European states in that regard. Making this a primary aim of the OIC's human rights initiatives, however, is more problematic and reminiscent of U.S. and European concerns—from the colonial to the contemporary eras—with protecting the rights of their overseas Christian brethren. This conceptualization is contrary to what human rights have become and what has lent them increasing normative power: an attempt to acknowledge and give a frame to the necessity of coming to terms with pluralisms of different sorts—especially ethnic pluralism—rather than remaining moored to ethnic nationalist solidarities.

As is clear, this is by no means uncontested. Everything from the OIC's hypocritical invocations of human rights to the United States' equally hypocritical use of human rights justifications for overseas occupations show how states often employ human rights language for their own purposes. Opposition to sexual orientation, gender identity, and expression (SOGIE)-related rights is indicative of how the OIC has not moved toward extending human rights to groups on its margins, but rather conceptualizes human rights as a way to justify majoritarian identity politics that depend on demonizing vulnerable minorities (Appadurai 2006). Politicizing homophobia, as Bosia and Weiss discuss, has become a way for authoritarian states to instrumentally mobilize domestic support, showing how such popular mobilizations—even in a democratic context—can be problematic if not limited by rights principles (Weiss and Bosia 2013). Not only does the OIC reflect this politicization of homophobia in some of its member states, but it is also using it to give itself reason to exist as an international organization. As noted previously, the OIC has had very little common purpose, and opposition to SOGIE-related rights conveniently gives it an "other" against which to define itself in a politically useful manner. But, again, it is in a manner that is problematic from the perspective that holds that human rights should be informed by a commitment to nondiscrimination and to moving beyond ethnic solidarity.

So, in regard to these first two initiatives, there seem to be three problems. The first is the use of human rights to justify repression of already disenfranchised religious and sexual minorities at the domestic level. The second is an attempt to move those justifications into internationally recognized human rights language, with the effect of downgrading the possibility of rights being protected and expanded. And the third is that these two initiatives regarding human rights have nothing to do with the implementation of human rights *within* OIC member states in a way that would protect those states' minorities—ethnic, gender, ideological, or sexual—from violations.

The IPHRC as a Tool to Advance Human Rights: Actions and Intentions

If these two initiatives are problematic, this leaves the aforementioned IPHRC as the only remaining test of whether or not the OIC's human rights initiatives represent a substantial commitment to human rights, or whether the move toward using international and universal language is merely superficial. In that regard, the IPHRC stands out for its failure to date to initiate any programming based on addressing internal human rights policies of OIC states. It is early yet, but there is certainly no reason beyond blind optimism to assume that the OIC will diverge from its previous policies. As Ann Mayer argues, conceptually the IPHRC is not so substantially different from the Cairo Declaration . . . old wine in new bottles as it were (Mayer 2014). Empirically, there has been no substantive human rights programming to point to an intent to use the IPHRC to advance human rights (Kayaoglu 2015a).

It is notable in this regard that, as part of its aggressive countermeasures in the wake of the Arab Uprisings, Saudi Arabia has bankrolled and otherwise supported antidemocratic forces around the Arab world. It has also moved to assert more direct control over the OIC (Kayaoglu 2015a). This began before the Arab Uprisings with the insistence that Jeddah would be the site of the OIC headquarters, overriding proposals that the OIC's diversity be highlighted by having its headquarters in a country such as Indonesia. Saudi Arabia's bureaucratic dominance was strengthened further after the Arab Uprisings when, against previous precedent that only non-Saudis would lead the OIC, it insisted the new secretary-general be the Saudi, Iyad Madani. On taking office, Madani made a point of thanking above all others Saudi King Abdullah bin Abdulaziz for his nomination, giving a clear signal of the OIC's hierarchy. This represented a geopolitical shift toward Saudi power, informed as it is by antipluralist and antihuman rights politics. As Kayaoglu notes, with Madani taking over from Ekmeleddin İhsanoğlu, this shift was also reinforced at the individual level. It had been the relatively liberal İhsanoğlu who initiated the move away from the Cairo Declaration and toward the IPHRC (Kayaoglu 2015a).

So, in short, the test regarding this first set of questions (whether the OIC's future engagement can or will substantively advance human rights in the Muslim world, or if it is even meant to do so) is straightforward: is there evidence in the OIC's three main human rights initiatives that the OIC is using human rights to empower minorities of different sorts within its various borders? At best, there is no evidence of principled engagement with human rights in ways that would allow space to confront dominant power groups in OIC member states. At worst, one could argue these initiatives are about reinforcing dominant majoritarian constructs of power internally and externalizing those problematic hierarchies into becoming regional and international legal norms.

This is most easily summarized by realities at the domestic, regional, and international levels. Domestically, the OIC has little on-the-ground human rights programming nor does it have the normative presence in its member states to give it the legitimacy to act effectively at the rhetorical level to advance human rights. The OIC is simply not in a position to be an active, effective actor in this regard. Secondly, the OIC does not have a geopolitical incentive to do so. The OIC has been, in fact, a redoubt of authoritarian states in the Middle East looking to counter democratic voices emerging from the street seeking to represent the region's pluralism (al-Qassemi 2013). The OIC's failure to have any substantial human rights programming, its association with Saudi Arabia's geopolitical agenda, and its shared interests with other authoritarian states give the empirical lie to the more human rights friendly rhetoric of the IPHRC.

The point is not that human rights cannot become tools of state power to reinforce dominant power structures. In fact they can and have been by many states and blocs—once human rights became a globally resonant language such co-optation has proven to be useful to states. That is precisely why these OIC engagements need to be taken seriously. They indicate that the OIC is not serious about human rights as they are most commonly understood, but is very serious about seeking to turn human rights more toward being instruments of state power.

International Organizations: An Independent Actor Advancing or Obstructing Human Rights?

This leads into the second set of questions I posed. Moving beyond the issues of OIC's on-the-ground position or geopolitical intentions, there is the larger theoretical issue of whether or not any international organization is able to independently influence human rights. This debate can be framed in two ways. One, if the OIC's human rights' initiatives mattered, they might be indicative of such an impact, but if these initiatives are unlikely to advance human rights then they lend support to the notion that international organizations are mere tools of their state members, not independent actors. In regard to this first frame, the evidence presented so far shows that the OIC is a case in which an international organization remains a tool of its most powerful state-members.

There is, however, also a second way to look at this debate. Could it be, on the one hand, that the OIC's adopting human rights as part of its mandate will unintentionally, even if inadvertently, advance human rights? Or, on the other hand, even if it is the case that the OIC is not advancing human rights, could it be that the OIC is still independently affecting human rights in a significant, albeit negative, manner? Looking at the OIC with these two more counterintuitive impacts in mind—either inadvertent or negative—may more insightfully engage with the puzzle that the OIC's human rights initiatives present.

Regarding the more optimistic possibility that there may inadvertently be positive impacts from the OIC's human rights initiatives, such as when OIC members sponsored a 2015 HRC resolution on the Rohingya Muslims in Burma, some international relations theorists have convincingly argued that such state rhetoric—whatever the instrumental intentions—can have an entrapment effect. In other words, mouthing platitudes about human rights or democracy inadvertently constrains these same states from acting in ways that are too obviously contradictory to their platitudes (Fleay 2011). The United States can be held up an example of this. International embarrassment over Jim Crow segregation in the context of Cold War rhetoric regarding freedom was one factor that pushed the United States toward desegregation (Ignatieff 2005). Similarly, the embarrassing contradiction between the U.S. democratization rhetoric and its support for authoritarian Latin American dictators is believed to be part of what led to a decline in U.S. support for those dictatorships (Sikkink 2004). Could something analogous be the case in regards to the OIC and human rights—that is, could the OIC's open embrace of human rights, however cynical, end up unintentionally advancing human rights by entrapping the OIC into taking actions to sustain its new rhetoric?

It is, in fact, certainly reasonable to expect that a public embrace of human rights by the OIC takes the steam out of some states' persistent objections against the theoretical validity or practical relevance of human rights. It is not just that cultural relativist arguments regarding human rights, already increasingly marginalized, become even more untenable when an OIC led by Saudi Arabia and Iran are, publicly at least, touting human rights' relevance. More important is that, flowing out of this on a practical level, there may indeed be some specific issues on which this will open space for the expansion of discourse on human rights within the Muslim world. Nonetheless, if the OIC is indeed engaging with human rights as a means to cannily contain their spread, while constructivist IR theories of entrapment (Risse 2000) may be one optimistic possibility, it must at least be considered that a strategy of engaging with human rights in order to contain their spread may also succeed. The effectiveness of this strategy in numerous states indicates that not all rhetoric leads to effective entrapment. Certainly, in regard to the OIC, there is no evidence yet of any sort of normative entrapment effect.

The overarching issue regarding this more optimistic take is whether or not the OIC presents a political opportunity structure for actors concerned with advancing human rights. If so, then it may indeed be an actor independently advancing human rights, even if it intends the opposite. Kollman and Waites speak directly to such opportunity structures in writing—regarding the inroads that SOGIE-related human rights have made in the international realm—that: "Political opportunity structure includes factors such as how institutionalized a particular policy area in the international realm is, how open these institutions are to non-state actors, and how many allies advocacy groups can find within them. Because of the successful institutionalization of the international human rights regime and the widespread acceptance of human rights rhetoric, human rights NGOs have often found the international political opportunity structure reasonably favourable" (Kollman and Waites 2009).

Kollman and Waites point correctly to fruitful intersections between social movements and international institutions regarding human rights (even controversial SOGIE-related rights) and give useful markers regarding the degree to which the OIC has facilitated those sorts of intersections.

However, they leave out a key variable: the state. Despite an increasingly complex roster of actors in global politics, states remain central. The state is particularly relevant in that its power can rebuff or advance attempts to limit political opportunity structures for social movements attempting to advance human rights. This takes place on the domestic level with attempts to repress social movements working to advance democracy and human rights; on the transnational level with attempts to frustrate such movements' abilities to forge transnational connections; and, on the international level, with attempts to block their access to international organizations (Tarrow 2005). In fact, the OIC is dominated by states that have a track record of working proactively in all three of the above-mentioned dimensions to block rather than advance voices that advocate human rights' relevance to the intersection of economic, political, and social issues.

This points to the necessity of highlighting the state as a key actor in a dialectic with social movements and international organizations. Positive advances on human rights are a particularly good example of this. Even if international organizations are neither wholly independent nor the most important actor, they can have significant impacts in the context of being empowered by democratic states and pushed by vigorous civil societies. The Inter-American Commission and Court of Human Rights, for example, ended up able to act to expand the scope of human rights' implementation, well beyond the political priorities of even its democratic member states. This dialectic played a substantial role in Latin America's regional move in the direction of democracy and greater human rights protections, a move that was simulated by powerful local and transnational social movements.

This sort of role for an international organization, however, becomes more and more unlikely the less an international organization's state members are committed to democracy and the more they are able to limit the voice of their domestic and regional civil societies and social movements. It is, therefore, unsurprising that the OIC is doing little to advance human rights given the context in which it works. Its engagements with human rights are more about blocking their use by local social movements than furthering human rights in any substantive manner. The optimistic "entrapment" argument regarding the OIC and human rights has to deal, thus, not just with the weight of evidence that shows the OIC is not working to advance human rights, but also with the underlying issue that the OIC is constituted primarily by antidemocratic states. This insulates it structurally from the sorts of states that can open passageways for civil society pressures. Such pressures could potentially give the OIC a more forceful push regarding human rights beyond what these states could or would do on their own. Indeed, how the OIC remains dominated by authoritarian states that are threatened by the sort of popular empowerment envisioned in a human rights framework indicates that, if the OIC does have an impact, it will be in a contrary, negative direction.

There are two ways in which the OIC may be an actor that is in some sense independent in ways that are having a negative impact. One, the OIC may be having some impact in normatively legitimizing conservative constructs of Islam held by states like Saudi Arabia; less conservative Muslim-majority states seem to be accepting such positions as default in international forums. This has helped make conservative readings of Islam—some of which see human rights as in conflict with Islam—mainstream among OIC states. Two, this has had its most tangible expression in the OIC vote as a bloc at the United Nations—particularly at the Human Rights Council—in ways that have had some success in blocking important human rights' expansions.

In other words, the OIC's initiatives may have an independent impact on human rights, but not in the way one might assume at first blush when presented with the IPCHR. States are not being affected in the sense that they are being pushed to implement human rights within their domestic jurisdictions. Instead, the pluralism of OIC member states—including the voices of states and, in the cases of more democratic states such as Indonesia, their peoples—is being subsumed into an organization that constricts the "Islamic world's" diversity into the tight confines of the OIC's positions on human rights. This is problematic for the internal politics of OIC state-members, reinforcing norms and structures that see human rights as a threat.

The OIC has externalized this by becoming a prominent player on the UN Human Rights Council, in regard to defamation of religions, gender identity-related rights, and other issues. This has had a significant impact on the Human Rights Council, slowing conceptual advancement of rights and blocking many state actions from the council's purview. At the same time, however, as noted above, support for the OIC defamation of religions resolutions diminished over time such that the OIC stopped introducing the resolution. The most recent vote at the Human Rights Council on sexual orientation, gender identity, and expression-related rights represented a similar setback for the OIC position. A resolution on combating violence and discrimination based on sexual orientation and gender identity was adopted on September 26, 2014, over strong lobbying by OIC states and after defeating numerous OIC-proposed amendments. It is notable that there has been an increase in Human Rights Council support since 2011 for attention to SOGIE-related rights, represented by this resolution being co-sponsored by 46 states (analogous to how the OIC gradually lost ground on defamation of religions). Perhaps even more notably, OIC states' unanimous opposition to SOGIE-related rights fractured, with several OIC states abstaining rather than opposing the resolution. So, while the OIC may be having negative effects, they are by no means uncontested, including from forces within the Muslim world (Chase 2012a).

Conclusion

This chapter has argued that the OIC's initiatives regarding human rights are both much less *and* much more than meets the eye. It is not just that they are unlikely to advance human rights within OIC state-members. The more global impact appears to be blocking or helping to block human rights' expansion or, perhaps more dangerously, advancing a conceptualization of human rights as a tool of state power. It is worth noting the theoretical assumption that underlies this argument: that human rights need to be understood not as a fixed entity, but rather as a legal-political language that can be invoked to advance any number of positions and interests (Chase 2012a).

The reason the OIC's human rights initiatives are important, thus, is not so much that they have had a large impact. Their importance comes from how human rights are changed as their conceptualization is fought over in battles in which the OIC is now fully engaged. Indeed, human rights' increasing centrality as a language of global politics has led those groups with conflicting positions and interests to attempt to control how human rights are defined and applied. It is certainly true that human rights have been most commonly articulated as resistance to illegitimate and discriminatory authority. In that spirit they have informed many struggles by marginalized populations, be that marginalization based on ideology, ethnicity, gender, or sexuality. Human rights language, however, has also been commonly appropriated by powerful actors for reasons that include justifying actions—including military invasions, in the case of the United States—that are motivated by reasons that have little to do with empowering the marginalized. Much evidence would place the OIC's initiatives firmly in that category. This makes them a disappointment for those living within OIC states which may hope for better implementation of their government's human rights commitments. It is also problematic for those tracking normative changes in terms of what human rights are and what they are becoming: Will human rights become more a tool of state power than a tool with which to contest state power?

This is part of continuing normative, political, and legal contestations over what constitutes human rights. Beyond the general binary in terms of what human rights can be used to justify—state power or contesting state power—there are any number of more specific battles in terms of how human rights' meanings continue to evolve. Are human rights simply about protecting citizens, or can they be extended to those on the margins of nation-states, including indigenous peoples or undocumented refugees? Are human rights about protecting free expression or limiting it in regard to hate speech? Are human rights about protecting the right to practice religion in ways that are contrary to dominant orthodoxies or are they about protecting those orthodoxies from what can be considered blasphemous attacks? To what degree can human rights move beyond supposed "core" protections to include those marginalized on the basis of gender identity or sexual orientation? The role human rights plays in global politics has become increasingly complicated and contradictory—both contesting and advancing state power—and is at the center of continuing battles over how human rights are reimagined and defined.

In short, human rights should be seen as a site of struggle that can be contested from many sides. It is in that context that the OIC's recent human rights initiatives become particularly interesting. The OIC shows that international organizations can be an important part of such contestations, but not necessarily in the ways and with the results that might be optimistically anticipated.

Notes

1. Charter of the Organization of Islamic Cooperation. Dakar, March 14, 2008. http://ww1.oic-oci.org/english/charter/OIC%20Charter-new-en.pdf.

2. Ibid.

3. UN Human Rights Council. *Combating Defamation of Religion*, A/7/19. http://ap.ohchr.org/documents/E/HRC/resolutions/A_HRC_RES_7_19.pdf.

4. Ambassador Mostafa Alaei represented the IPHR Commission at a seminar on OIC and Human Rights, held by the Danish Institute for Human Rights in Copenhagen on September 13, 2013. See http://www.oic-iphrc.org/en/activities/, accessed May 2, 2016. Notes from Ambassador Alaei's comments on file with the author.

Works Cited

Appadurai, Arjun. 2006. *Fear of Small Numbers: An Essay on the Geography of Anger*. Durham, NC: Duke University Press.

Barnett, Michael, and Martha Finnemore. 2004. *Rules for the World: International Organizations in Global Politics*. Ithaca, NY: Cornell University Press.

Blakeley, Ruth. 2013. "Human Rights, State Wrongs, and Social Change: The Theory and Practice of Emancipation." *Review of International Studies* 39 (3): 599–619.

Brysk, Alison. 2013. *Speaking Rights to Power: Constructing Political Will*. New York: Oxford University Press.

Brysk, Alison, and Daniel Wehrenfennig. 2010. "'My Brother's Keeper'? Inter-ethnic Solidarity and Human Rights." *Studies in Ethnicity and Nationalism* 10 (1): 1–18.

Chase, Anthony. 2012a. *Human Rights, Revolution, and Reform in the Muslim World*. Boulder, CO: Lynne Rienner.

———. 2012b. "Legitimizing Human Rights: Beyond Mythical Foundations and into Everyday Resonances." *Journal of Human Rights* 11 (4): 505–25.

———. 2016. "Human Rights Contestations: Sexual Orientation and Gender Identity." *International Journal of Human Rights* 20 (6): 703–23.

Cismas, Ioana. 2011. "Introductory Note to the Statute of the OIC Independent Permanent Human Rights Commission." *International Legal Materials* 5 (6): 1148–60.

———. 2014. *Religious Actors and International Law*. Oxford: Oxford University Press.

Fleay, Caroline. 2011. "China and the Limits of Transnational Human Rights Activism: From Tiananmen Square to the Beijing Olympics." In *Power and Transnational Activism*, ed. Thomas Olesen, 111–29. Abingdon: Routledge.

Graham, Erin. 2014. "International Organizations as Collective Agents: Fragmentation and the Limits of Principal Control at the World Health Organization." *European Journal of International Relations* 20 (2): 366–90.

Hashemi, Nader. 2017. "The ISIS Crisis and the Broken Politics of the Arab World: A Framework for Understanding Radical Islamism." In *Routledge Handbook on Human Rights and the Middle East and North Africa*, ed. Anthony Chase, 83–103. Abingdon: Routledge.

Henne, Peter. 2013. "The Domestic Politics of International Religious Defamation." *Politics and Religion* 6 (3): 512–37.

Ignatieff, Michael, ed. 2005. *American Exceptionalism and Human Rights*. Princeton: Princeton University Press.

Johnson, Toni. 2010. "The Organization of the Islamic Conference: A Council on Foreign Relations Backgrounder." Council on Foreign Relations. https://www.cfr.org/backgrounder/organization-islamic-conference.

Kayaoglu, Turan. 2013. "A Rights Agenda for the Muslim World? The Organization of Islamic Cooperation's Evolving Human Rights Framework." Brookings Doha Center Analysis Papers. Doha: The Brookings Institution.

———. 2015a. "The OIC's Independent Human Rights Commission: An Early Assessment." *Matters of Concern* series working paper. Copenhagen: Danish Institute for Human Rights. https://www.humanrights.dk/publications/oics-independent-permanent-human-rights-commission-early-assessment.

———. 2015b. *The Organization of Islamic Cooperation: Politics, Problems, and Potential.* London: Routledge.

Kollman, Kelly, and Matthew Waites. 2009. "The Global Politics of Lesbian, Gay, Bisexual, and Transgender Human Rights: An Introduction." *Contemporary Politics* 15 (1): 1–17.

Landolt, Laura K. 2013. "Externalizing Human Rights: From Commission to Council, the Universal Periodic Review and Egypt." *Human Rights Review* 14 (2): 107–29.

Mayer, Ann Elizabeth. 2014. "The OIC's Human Rights Policies in the UN: A Problem of Coherence." *Matters of Concern* series working paper. Copenhagen: Danish Institute for Human Rights. https://www.humanrights.dk/publications/oics-human-rights-policies-un-problem-coherence.

Moravcsik, Andrew. 2000. "The Origins of Human Rights Regimes: Democratic Delegation in Postwar Europe." *International Organization* 54 (2): 217–52.

Petersen, Marie Juul. 2012. *Islamic or Universal Human Rights? The OIC's Independent Permanent Human Rights Commission.* DIIS report. Copenhagen: Danish Institute for International Studies.

Qassemi, Sultan Sooud al-. 2013. "Gulf States Embrace Post-Brotherhood Egypt." *Al Monitor,* July 10, 2013. http://sultanalqassemi.com/articles/gulf-states-embrace-post-brotherhood-egypt.

Risse, Thomas. 2000. '"Let's Argue!': Communicative Action in World Politics." *International Organization* 54 (1): 1–39.

Schulz, William. 2002. *In Our Own Best Interest: How Defending Human Rights Benefits Us All.* Boston: Beacon Press.

Sikkink, Kathryn. 2004. *Mixed Signals: U.S. Human Rights Policy and Latin America.* Ithaca, NY: Cornell University Press.

Tarrow, Sidney. 2005. *The New Transnational Activism.* Cambridge: Cambridge University Press.

Waltz, Susan. 2004. "Universal Human Rights: The Contribution of Muslim States." *Human Rights Quarterly* 26 (4): 799–844.

Weiss, Meredith L., and Michael J. Bosia, eds. 2013. *Global Homophobia: States, Movements, and the Politics of Oppression.* Urbana: University of Illinois Press.

CHAPTER 2

The Human Rights Agenda of the OIC: Between Pessimism and Optimism

Mashood A. Baderin

Introduction

In contrast to the general pessimism with which the human rights agenda of the Organization of Islamic Cooperation (OIC) is often perceived in relation to the international human rights system, this chapter critically assesses the OIC's human rights agenda with a balance of optimism. It identifies not only its failings but also its prospects and proposes how the system can be enhanced to reinvent itself and contribute more positively to the effectiveness of the international human rights system. The chapter pinpoints the complexity of the politics of international human rights and highlights the complementary utility of the OIC's human rights agenda to the UN human rights agenda, with reference to the promotion and protection of human rights in the Muslim world but also its potential for contributing to desired inclusive universalism in the international human rights system. This is premised on the fact that, as "the Muslim world's only intergovernmental body—the largest such system outside of the United Nations" (İhsanoğlu 2010, inside back cover), the OIC must project itself, and be seen, as an organization that has an important role to play in the promotion and protection of human rights in the Muslim world and to contribute to the desired universalization of human rights for a more encompassing international human rights system. The chapter presents a three-pronged critique of the OIC's human rights agenda in the context of an "is-ought" analysis with regard to the conceptualization, standard-setting, and implementation of human rights.

The Problematique of "the Politics of Human Rights"

Certainly, the promotion and protection of human rights is well-established today as a global project advanced by the UN through international cooperation. The moral legitimacy of human rights is grounded in the inalienable inherent dignity of every human being. However, the legal foundation for the current international human rights system was laid in Article 1(3) of the UN charter, which specifies international cooperation in promoting respect for human rights and all fundamental freedoms as one of the main purposes of the UN. There is often a tendency to perceive the international human rights project linearly and sometimes simplistically as a fully settled and incontestable universal experience. To the contrary, it is evident that apart from its moral and legal persuasions, the international human rights project also embodies what is often referred to as "the politics of human rights." In the words of Tony Evans, the politics of human rights "place[s] human rights within the context of power, hegemony and interests" (T. Evans 2003:158). This exposes the international human rights system to different ideological, cultural, and political contestations in the form of tactful counter-hegemonic responses from different stakeholders. Evans has further observed that "the politics of human rights . . . offers a troublesome discourse, useful perhaps when discussing the pivotal role of power relations in the creation of the United Nations, the drafting of the Universal Declaration of Human Rights, but less so when attempting to construct a human rights narrative and proclaim its success" (159). The pivotal role of such power relations within the international community greatly influences how the international human rights narrative is formulated and assessed, and how its success is proclaimed.

Different voices, especially from the Global South, have challenged the international human rights system as being embedded with neocolonial, hegemonic, and complicit political nuances of the powerful developed states of the Global North (Rajagopal 2006; Hopgood 2013; Mutua 2016). Human rights are, in the words of Rajagopal (2006:770), "seen as the language of military intervention, economic reconstruction and social transformation—a totalising discourse." The OIC and its member states, being mostly Muslim-majority states from the Global South, fall into this category of contesting stakeholders, seeking to present a counterhegemonic discourse to, presumably, protect Islamic norms from the hegemonic tendencies of the politics of human rights. This is reflected, for example, in OIC Resolution No. 51/25-P of 1998 titled *On Coordination Among Member States in the Field of Human Rights*, which, on the one hand, acknowledges the importance of promoting and encouraging respect for human rights, but on the other hand refers to "the attempts [by the powerful states of the Global North] to exploit the issue of human rights to discredit the principles of Islamic Shariah and to interfere in the affairs of Islamic States." It identifies "the need for close coordination among [OIC] Member States in resisting the moves to exploit human rights for political purposes including selective targeting of individual countries for undeclared reasons" and requests the OIC secretary-general to "provide ways and means to convey the OIC stance on different issues in the field of human rights . . . with a view to furthering OIC positions on human rights at the UN." This position is reiterated in later OIC resolutions such as Resolution No. 1/38-LEG of 2011. While such counterhegemonic rhetoric from the OIC may provide a legitimate contribution to the politics of the international human rights system, it needs to be complemented by the organization's commitment to improve the practical human rights situation in its own member states.

The OIC's human rights agenda cannot be divorced from the ideological and political dissensions of its member states against perceived hegemonic politics within the international human rights system. Such dissensions should not, however, be presumed instinctively as depicting a general negative stance by the OIC against the UN's universal human rights agenda but should be subjected to two tests: whether they constructively challenge perceived Westernization of human rights to engender recognition of non-Western contributions to international human rights discourse, or whether they are mere attempts to undermine the international human rights system. In essence, the politics of human rights (including counterhegemonic claims) should not be seen as all bad; there can also be good politics of human rights. Bad politics of human rights is, on the one hand, to use the claims of universalism as a means of imposing hegemonic controls on other civilizations or, on the other hand, to use dubious counterhegemonic rhetoric to undermine the international human rights system. Conversely, challenging contentious universalist or relativist human rights assumptions to engender necessary "overlapping consensus" (Rawls 1987) and motivate effective realization of international human rights globally must be seen as good politics of human rights. A critical reflection about the OIC's human rights agenda reveals apparent fluctuations between good and bad politics of human rights over the past forty years. But rather than simplistically construing the OIC as hindering the UN's universal human rights agenda, it should be critically engaged with as a legitimate stakeholder that could bring justifiable critique into international human rights discourse to highlight its shortcomings and lead to improving its appeal and effective implementation globally. As observed by Kayaoglu (Chapter 3), the fact that the OIC has declared its desire to work with and through the UN as opposed to working against it or presenting itself as an alternative to it, provides a strong basis for such complementary engagement.

The OIC's Human Rights Agenda in Context

Empirically, the human rights agenda of the OIC has evolved normatively over the past forty-five years from what can be described as a conservative Islamic agenda to an accommodative agenda that seeks to harmonize adherence to Islamic values with international human rights standards. Obviously, the promotion and protection of human rights was not the main impetus for the formal founding of the OIC. Rather the objectives, as stated in Article II(A) of the 1972 OIC charter, were to, inter alia, "promote Islamic solidarity among member states," "support of the struggle of the people of Palestine, and help them to regain their rights and liberate their land," and "strengthen the struggle of all Muslim peoples with a view to safeguarding their dignity, independence, and natural rights."[1] The charter was basically a statement of Islamic solidarity rather than of universal human rights. It was, however, registered as an international treaty with the UN in 1974 in conformity with Article 102 of the UN charter and thus could be invoked before all UN organs pursuant to Article 102(2). In October 1975 the UN General Assembly adopted a resolution inviting the OIC to participate as an observer in the sessions and work of the assembly and its subsidiary organs (UNGA Res. 3369 (XXX) of October 10, 1975), followed by different resolutions on cooperation with the OIC.[2] Today, the OIC has permanent observer status at the UN and enjoys representation at the Human Rights Council, where it advocates the collective view of its member states on human rights issues, particularly in relation to the Muslim world.

There is some debate about whether the OIC can be considered a regional organization within the context of Article 52 of the UN charter. The view advanced in this chapter is that the OIC can certainly be considered a regional arrangement within the context of Article 52 of the UN charter. The concept of regionalism or regional arrangements in the UN charter is not limited strictly to geographical proximity but could also accommodate arrangements based on common heritage and cultural solidarity (M. Evans 2012:271). Similar to other regional arrangements, the OIC, as an organization uniting its member states on the basis of Islamic values, can play a significant role in the promotion and protection of human rights in the Muslim world and thereby contribute positively to the realization of an inclusive universalism in international human rights law.

In contrast to its 1972 charter, it is notable that the issue of human rights has become more visible on the OIC's agenda, with its "Ten Year Program of Action," adopted in 2005, listing human rights as one of its priorities and its new 2008 charter specifically acknowledging a commitment to the promotion and protection of human rights. The 2008 charter mentions not only the organization's adherence and commitment to the principles of the UN charter in its preamble but also the determination of the member states to "promote human rights and fundamental freedoms, good governance, rule of law, democracy and accountability in member states in accordance with their constitutional and legal systems." This declared human rights commitment in its 2008 charter suggests a new human rights agenda of the OIC, which is significant for the realization of an inclusive universalism in the international human rights system.

Nevertheless, there is still a view that the OIC's new human rights agenda is constrained by its parallel "Islamic" ethos, which is seen as incompatible with the UN's "secular" universal human rights agenda. This requires a critical interrogation of the evolution and current state of the OIC's human rights agenda from both a pessimistic and optimistic perspective, to identify its failings and prospects of contributing positively to the UN's universal human rights agenda within its stated determination of preserving Islamic values. Notably, there is no rule in international law or international relations that precludes an organization such as the OIC from being part of and contributing to the UN's universal human rights agenda because of its declared Islamic religious ethos.

Pessimistic Perspective

A pessimistic analysis of the OIC's human rights engagement would involve a basic empirical assessment without considering the ideological challenges or counterhegemonic argument that the OIC brings to international human rights discourse. It would typically scrutinize the OIC's human rights agenda against an idealized universalism under the international human rights system, without appreciating the hegemonic nuances and problematique of the "politics of human rights" earlier discussed. Such an approach would consider the OIC human rights regime as a hindrance to the universalist perception of human rights—one which should be discouraged or eliminated, without considering the potential of the OIC as a necessary regional arrangement for the promotion and protection of international human rights in the Muslim world. The justification commonly advanced for such an eliminative approach is that the universality of human rights is now fully established, with all states having an obligation to promote universal respect for all human rights. However, while the universality of human rights is acknowledged, the conceptual understanding of its "universal nature" remains a subject of academic and policy debate within human rights scholarship and practice. That debate is not meant to undermine the universality of human rights but rather to foster the search for an enduring, inclusive universalism in human rights through some form of overlapping consensus among the different civilizations and cultures of the world (Donnelly 2007, 2010; Goodhart 2003, 2008).

This author's sustained view on the debate about universality (Baderin 2003:23), is that the universal nature of human rights should be understood from two connotations, namely, the "universality of human rights" and the "universalism in human rights." It is important to appreciate that the two connotations are different contextually. On the one hand, the phrase "universality of human rights" signifies the universal quality or conceptual acceptance of the human rights idea as a necessary international humanist venture, which has become fully established over the past sixty-eight years after the adoption of the Universal Declaration of Human Rights (UDHR). Thus, no state today would unequivocally accept that it is a violator of human rights. All states, including the OIC member states, generally acknowledge the concept of human rights, thus establishing its universal quality. On the other hand, the phrase "universalism in human rights" implies the existence of a common universal consensus for the interpretation and application of international human rights law globally, which, unlike its *universality*, continues to be contested both academically and politically. While significant progress has been made, the full realization of "universalism in human rights" is still an aspiration and continues to be a subject of debate within the international human rights system.

Practically, the differences in the interpretation of human rights norms are not often about the substantive rights themselves. Rather they are about the scope of limitations that different states place on those rights, apparently based on ideological and political grounds but often argued under familiar legal limitation clauses such as "protection of national security," "protection of public safety," "protection of public order," or "protection of morals"—all of which are variously recognized under international human rights law as reflected, for example, in Articles 18, 19, 21, and 22 of the International Covenant on Civil and Political Rights (ICCPR). Thus, for example, while all state parties to the ICCPR recognize the rights to freedom of religion (Article 18), freedom of expression (Article 19), peaceful assembly (Article 21), and freedom of association (Article 22), there are often differences of interpretation regarding the scope of limitations under the respective provisos in those articles subjecting these rights to public order and public safety clauses. There are many practical examples of the problems that this poses to the concept of universalism in the case law of different human rights regimes. However, that is not to say that universalism in human rights cannot be achieved but rather that it should be consensually negotiated. It demands the evolution of a universal consensus in the interpretation of human rights norms, through conscientious cross-cultural engagements in an accommodative manner that would lead to the realization of an inclusive theory of universalism, to which the OIC has the potential of contributing with respect to Islamic values. Encouragingly, there has been some degree of narrowing down of interpretational differences already in that regard, with reference to Islamic relativism as exemplified by the revision of both the Arab Charter on Human Rights (ArCHR) by the Arab League and the Moroccan family code (*Mudawwanah*) by the government of Morocco in 2004 to bring each of them in closer harmony with international human rights principles consistently with Islamic values. This brings us to the optimistic contextual perspective of the OIC's human rights agenda.

Optimistic Perspective

An optimistic analysis of the OIC's human rights agenda favors an inventive approach entailing not just empirical scrutiny but also an appreciation of and critical engagement with the interpretative dissensions and counterhegemonic arguments that the OIC human rights agenda brings into international human rights discourse.

Based on the earlier submission that the OIC is a regional arrangement within the context of Article 52 of the UN charter, the assessment of its human rights agenda should not merely be a descriptive analysis of whether or not it *is* in harmony with the perceived ideals of the UN universal human rights project. Rather, it must include a prescriptive counternarrative of why and how it *ought* to, as a matter of necessity, contribute positively to the international human rights system as envisaged under Article 52(1) of the UN charter, which allows regional arrangements "provided that such arrangements or agencies and their activities are consistent with the Purposes and Principles of the United Nations" and acknowledged under Article 2(1) of the current OIC charter itself that "All Member States commit themselves to the purposes and principles of the United Nations Charter." This relates to the "is-ought" question, which has been identified as the central issue in moral philosophy—that is, "[h]ow is what *is* the case related to what *ought* to be the case—statements of fact to moral judgements?" (Hudson 1969:11).

As most of the chapters in this volume address the question of what *is* the case of the OIC's human rights agenda in relation to the UN's universal human rights project, it remains imperative to address what *ought* to be the case, that is, applying those factual assessments to the moral judgments of both human rights and Islamic values.

It is submitted that the OIC *ought* to aim at continually improving its human rights practices with regards to conceptual articulation, standard-setting, and implementation, which are the three main stages of human rights development.

Conceptual Critique

According to both the UN charter and the current OIC charter, the human rights agenda of the OIC, as a regional arrangement, must complement the UN's universal human rights project but this cannot be divorced from the declared Islamic ethos of the OIC. Clearly, the OIC makes no pretentions about its commitment to Islamic values. The organization's charter indicates that in pursuing the organization's objectives, "they shall be guided and inspired by the noble Islamic teachings and values." While the OIC charter states that member states are committed to the principles of the UN and international law, it also states that they will be guided by Islamic values, as noted in Article 1(14): "[The charter aims t]o promote and to protect human rights and fundamental freedoms including the rights of women, children, youth, elderly and people with special needs as well as the preservation of Islamic family values." But ought this commitment to Islamic values necessarily create a conceptual conflict between the UN and OIC human rights agendas, respectively?

The influence of Islamic religious teachings and values is perceived by many commentators as one of the main impediments restricting the OIC's human rights agenda in relation to perceived ideal universal human rights norms (Kayaoglu 2013:5). This has also led to the question of whether the OIC's human rights agenda is aimed at establishing an alternative Islamic human rights system or complementing the UN's universal human rights agenda (Petersen 2012). While it is true that a hardline conservative perception of Islamic teachings could negatively restrict the human rights agenda of the OIC, this ought not necessarily to be the case. Similar to the debates about universalism analyzed above, the concept of what is "Islamic" is not monolithic and the understanding of Islamic values has evolved over time. Islamic values and law, as derived from Sharia by jurists, can be understood and applied in either hardline conservative or in moderate evolutionary ways. When perceived in hardline conservative ways, understandings of Islamic values are often restricted to the traditional rulings of classical jurists as if those rulings were immutable. This often creates a reductionist approach, based on the disputed claim of the "closing of the gate of legal reasoning (*ijtihad*)" in Islamic legal theory. That claim restricts Islamic understandings to the rulings of classical jurists as recorded in the traditional treatises of the different schools of Islamic jurisprudence, which date back to the tenth century, and essentially portrays Islamic values and law as static and non-evolutionary. The idea of the "closing of the gate of legal reasoning" under Islamic legal theory has been challenged both in theory and practice within contemporary scholarship on Islamic law (Hallaq 1984). It is a conservative perception of Islamic values and law that would sustain the view that the OIC and the UN human rights agendas are totally irreconcilable and consequently promotes pessimism.

By contrast, while an evolutionary perception of Islamic values and law does see a rich source of jurisprudence in the traditional rulings of the classical jurists, it also recognizes the continual evolution of Islamic values and law through the continued process of legal reasoning by qualified contemporary Islamic jurists. This outlook perceives Islamic law and values as a system that evolves in necessary response to the dynamic nature of human life, responds effectively to the challenges of modern human rights norms, and thereby contributes positively to the enhancement of the UN's universal human rights agenda. The OIC has apparently acknowledged the importance of adopting an evolutionary approach to Islamic values and law by indicating in Article 1(11) of its current charter that its commitment to Islamic teachings and values would be "based on moderation and tolerance," which encourages optimism.

Through the adoption of a moderate and tolerant perception of Islamic teachings and values, the OIC human rights agenda can positively complement the UN universal human rights venture by reflecting what Habermas describes as "Janus-faced," with one side related to the "Islamic" and the other side related to the "universal" but both aligned for the effective realization of international human rights and protection of the inherent dignity of all human beings without discrimination in the Muslim world. This perception is similar to Habermas' presentation of law and morals as aligned rather than rival concepts (Habermas 1996; Flynn 2003). What we get from this approach, with reference again to Habermas, is a "dialogical principle of universalization," and this *ought* to be the human rights agenda that the OIC should adopt for an effective and pragmatic universalization of human rights in the Muslim world. For this conceptualization to be effective, the OIC has to adopt an evolutional interpretation of the Sharia that explores the possibilities offered by alternative, moderate, and legitimate Islamic jurisprudence in relation to human rights. This will enable it to bring constructive challenges to the conceptual understandings of human rights under the UN's human rights system in ways that would not only enhance the effectiveness of the system but also contribute positively to the realization of the required cross-cultural conceptual consensus.

The OIC has yet to effectively demonstrate such a constructive conceptual approach in its engagement with the international human rights system. Currently its human rights conceptual narrative appears to replicate the bad politics of human rights, using Islamic values to defend the poor human rights practices of its member states in the international forum. The OIC

International Islamic Fiqh Academy (IIFA), as the organization's Islamic jurisprudential organ, has an important role to play in transforming the OIC's human rights conceptual narrative. It is overdue for the IIFA to provide a comprehensive and evolutional Islamic jurisprudential resolution on the concept of human rights to establish a contemporary Islamic theoretical foundation for it among the OIC member states. While the IIFA has adopted Islamic resolutions and recommendations on some contemporary issues, such as Islamic banking and finance, organ transplant, birth control, incorporeal rights, the role of women in development of Muslim society, the rights of children and the aged, and so forth (IDB and IFA 2000), it has yet to adopt a specific substantive resolution on the concept of human rights in Islam. The IIFA adopted Resolution No. 68/6/7 in May 1992 *On International Rights in Islam*, resolving that a committee be set up to look further into the topic and submit a report to it at its eighth session. No record could be found of whether the IIFA followed up on this resolution.

One pertinent example of Islamic conceptual stimulus that the OIC could bring to international human rights discourse is in respect to the conventional conception of human rights as a vertical relationship between the individual and the state. This conception is problematic in two ways. First, it understates the importance of duties in the protection of human rights, and second, it does not facilitate a direct and holistic protection of human rights across the horizontal dimensions of human interaction. This has led to considerable debate about the horizontal effects of human rights laws generally. In contrast, the Islamic conceptualization of human rights can be perceived from four dimensions: the personal, relating to the self; the horizontal, relating to the other; the vertical, relating to state authority; and the pivotal, relating to God, which is the fulcrum or driving force for the first three dimensions. All four dimensions emanate from the Qur'an, sura 17:70, which states unequivocally that God has bestowed innate dignity on every human being: "And surely We have bestowed dignity on the progeny of Adam [i.e., human beings] and elevated them on land and sea and provided them of all good things and made them to excel above most of Our creation."[3] Through those four dimensions, the Islamic conceptualization of human rights balances between rights and duties in human rights discourse and facilitates a holistic and effective protection of human rights across all perceivable dimensions of human interaction. It is submitted that this is an important area in the conceptualization of human rights where the OIC, based on its declared Islamic religious ethos, can positively influence the

UN's universal human rights agenda and thereby bring original and innovative perspectives to the debate on the international conceptualization of human rights that will be accommodative to all.

Standard-Setting Critique

After proper conceptual appreciation, standard-setting is the second important step in human rights strategy to ensure a clear specification of human rights content. Compared to other regional human rights regimes, the OIC has only taken minimal practical steps with regards to specific standard-setting in its human rights agenda and *ought* to improve its performance in that regard.

The first substantive attempt at human rights standard-setting by the OIC was through the adoption of its Cairo Declaration on Human Rights in Islam (CDHRI) in 1990. In its preamble, the CDHRI made no reference to the UDHR or to any international human rights instrument preceding it but rather began by stating that the CDHRI "will serve as a general guidance for Member States in the field of human rights." It then stated the wish of the member states "to contribute to the efforts of mankind to assert human rights, to protect man from exploitation and persecution, and to affirm his freedom and right to a dignified life in accordance with the Islamic *shari'ah*." The member states also expressed their belief that

> fundamental rights and universal freedoms in Islam are an integral part of the Islamic religion and that no one as a matter of principle has the right to suspend them in whole or in part or violate or ignore them in as much as they are binding divine commandments, which are contained in the Revealed Books of God and were sent through the last of His Prophets to complete the preceding divine messages thereby making their observance an act of worship and their neglect or violation an abominable sin, and accordingly every person is individually responsible and the *Ummah* collectively responsible for their safeguard.

These words of the CDHRI preamble create expectations of very high substantive human rights standards from both Islamic and international human rights perspectives. Based on those preambular statements, one would reasonably expect the CDHRI to set much higher substantive standards for human rights in Islam above the standards of the UDHR or other human rights instruments before it.

In many ways, however, the substantive rights guaranteed under the CDHRI demonstrate lower human rights standards than the UDHR, both in language and scope, even when evaluated from an Islamic perspective. Thus, applying the concept of immanent or internal critique (Kellison 2014:719), it can be argued that the CDHRI's substantive human rights standard neither measures up to its own very high objectives nor, fully, to Islamic standards of human rights. The language and scope of the rights in the CDHRI are mostly vague and subjected to Sharia claw-back clauses, with Article 24 generally subjecting all the rights "to the Islamic *shari'ah*," and Article 25 stating that "Islamic *shari'ah* is the only source of reference for the explanation or clarification of any of the articles of this Declaration." There is no clarification of what this means in practice regarding whose interpretation of Islamic Sharia prevails in the case of differences of jurisprudential views on the scope of any of the articles.

Many commentators have criticized the CDHRI on these grounds, claiming that it undermines rather than complements the UDHR. Areas of concern include the limited scope of women's rights and the right to freedom of religion or belief. For example, rather than providing for the specific substantive right to freedom of religion or belief as guaranteed within Islamic teachings, the CDHRI states tersely in its Article 10 that "Islam is the religion of true unspoiled nature. It is prohibited to exercise any form or pressure on man or to exploit his poverty or ignorance in order to force him to change his religion to another religion or to atheism." Similarly, a number of specific rights, such as the right to nationality, right to peaceful assembly and association, right to social security, right to cultural life, and right to effective remedy for human rights violations, are not fully provided for. As the primary human rights instrument of the OIC, the scope and standard of the CDHRI could have gone much further to cover all conceivable rights under Islamic law to substantiate the inference in the preamble that Islam could provide a higher standard of human rights. Also, the subjection of many of the rights in the CDHRI to Sharia claw-back clauses has attracted particular criticism. Practically, subjecting the provisions of the CDHRI to the Sharia should itself not be unexpected, since it clearly states that it is a declaration on "human rights in Islam." The obstacle, however, is that there is no definition of what this means in practice, despite the fact that the term "Sharia" could have different meanings both theoretically and practically

(Baderin 2009:186–87). Adopting a hardline conservative interpretation would certainly restrict the scope of most of the rights guaranteed in the CDHRI, which could defeat the Sharia's higher objectives (*maqāsid*) of promoting human welfare. Conversely, a contextual evolutional interpretation could enhance the respective scope of the different rights guaranteed in the CDHRI.

Institutionally, the OIC's human rights stance in relation to many of the issues covered in this volume reflects a conservative approach. A pessimistic way of reacting to that situation is to consider the OIC's human rights regime as a drawback for international human rights standards that should be abolished. That would, however, not necessarily lead to the improvement of human rights in the OIC member states. An optimistic and constructive way would be to instigate the OIC to modify its human rights standards in ways that would enhance the effectiveness of human rights in its member states. The OIC needs to move beyond mere rhetoric and encourage among its member states the practical interpretation of Islamic values in a manner that enhances the realization of international human rights (Baderin 2003:228). That would entail a revision of the CDHRI to reflect higher human rights standards as promoted by both international human rights law and Islamic teachings. The greater human rights commitment reflected in the 2008 OIC charter, adopted eighteen years after the CDHRI, provides a strong basis for advocating such revision. In 2012, at the first meeting of the Islamic Permanent Human Rights Commission (IPHRC) in Jakarta, former OIC Secretary-General Ekmeleddin İhsanoğlu indicated this need for a revision and update of the CDHRI and other OIC instruments.

Such a revision is possible within the objectives of the OIC without the need to discard its adherence to Islamic values. One could look to the Arab League's 2004 revision of the ArCHR or the Moroccan government's 2004 revision of the country's family code (*Mudawwanah*) for examples, both of which reflect, despite their Islamic predispositions, higher human rights standards than their earlier versions.

It is noteworthy that in its Resolution No. 50/25-P of 1998, *Follow-Up of the Cairo Declaration on Human Rights in Islam,* the OIC identified the need to follow up the CDHRI with a set of binding Islamic covenants on human rights to expand the scope of the specific rights recognized in the CDHRI such as women and children's rights. Consequently, the OIC Covenant on the Rights of the Child in Islam (CRCI) was adopted in June 2005. However, the CRCI still has not been brought into force thirteen years after its adoption.

A source from the OIC headquarters in Jeddah confirmed that only two member states, Gambia and Mauritania, have currently ratified the covenant, a far cry from the twenty ratifications required for the covenant to enter into force. To bring it into force expediently, and in conformity with current international treaty practices, it is proposed that Article 23(1) of the covenant be amended to reduce the required number of ratifications to two so that the covenant would go into force immediately for those state parties that have ratified it.

Another step relevant to the issue of human rights standard-setting by the OIC was its adoption of the Ten Year Program of Action to Meet the Challenges Facing the Muslim Ummah in the 21st Century in December 2005. Through the Ten Year Program of Action, the leaders of the OIC apparently demonstrated an appreciation of the need to seek a necessary means of harmonization between Islamic values and international human rights norms through the flexibility of Islamic jurisprudence. Notably, Part 1 Section IV was titled "Multiplicity of Islamic Jurisprudence" which underlined "the need to strengthen dialogue among Islamic Schools"—in other words using an evolutionary approach to Islamic law through *ijtihād*. It also "condemns extremism in all its forms and manifestations as it contradicts Islamic and human values" and "emphasizes inter-civilizational dialogue" and "the teaching of Islamic education, culture, civilization, and the jurisprudence and literature of difference; calls on member states to cooperate amongst themselves in order to develop balanced educational curricula that promote values of tolerance, human rights, openness, and understanding of other religions and cultures; reject fanaticism and extremism, and establish pride in the Islamic identity."

Despite these commendable aspirations very little has been achieved in practice between 2005 and 2018. The Ten Year Program of Action reached its deadline in December 2015 without the CRCI coming into force, and neither the proposed Covenant on the Rights of Women in Islam nor any other binding charter of human rights in Islam has been adopted as of the time of this writing, as was envisaged. This calls into question the practical implementation of the standard-setting aspirations of the OIC.

Implementational Critique

The final important stage of ensuring practical realization of human rights is the implementation of the standards set in human rights instruments. To that end, the international human rights regime has established nonjudicial human rights treaty bodies conferred with the competence of monitoring state parties' implementation of the different international human rights instruments. The different regional human rights regimes have also established similar nonjudicial bodies and created judicial institutions with jurisdiction to adjudicate cases of human rights violations brought before them under the respective regional human rights instruments.

This author had, in 2003, proposed the need for an implementational mechanism under the OIC's human rights agenda (Baderin 2003:228). In 2005, the CRCI provided, in its Article 24(1), for the establishment of an Islamic Committee on the Rights of the Child made up of representatives of all state parties to the covenant; the committee was to meet every two years with the limited role of examining the progress made in the implementation of the covenant. As the covenant has not yet entered into force, the committee has not been established and no specific rules of procedure have been adopted for its operation.

In 1987 the OIC attempted to establish an International Islamic Court of Justice (IICJ) by adopting the Statute of the Islamic Court of Justice with competence to hear, inter alia, cases that OIC member states refer to it and cases "whose referral to the Court is provided for in any treaties or conventions in force" (Article 25). The IICJ statute has not entered into force as of this writing, and the court has not yet been established, although it is listed as one of the OIC charter organs in Articles 5(5) and 14 of the 2008 OIC charter, which states that "the International Islamic Court of Justice established in Kuwait in 1987 shall, upon entry into force of its Statute, be the principal judicial organ of the Organisation." To enter into force, Article 11 of the IICJ statute requires ratification of two-thirds (or thirty-eight) of the OIC member states. A source from the OIC office in Jeddah confirmed that the IICJ statute has currently been ratified by only thirteen states: Bahrain, Egypt, Gambia, Jordan, Kuwait, Libya, Mauritania, Maldives, Pakistan, Palestine, Qatar, Saudi Arabia, and Sudan. In OIC Resolution No. 49/25P, adopted at the Twenty-Fifth Session of the Conference of Foreign Ministers in 1998, the OIC expressed its wish to speed up the establishment of the IICJ, urging members to "accelerate the completion of the ratification procedure . . . so that the quorum needed for the Court to become operational may be attained," a request which was reiterated in Resolution No.3/38-LEG of June 30, 2011. This apparently demonstrates the organization's ongoing collective political will for creating the court, subject, however, to the member states' individual political will to ratify the statute to bring the court into existence.

Long gaps between adoption and ratification of international instruments are not unique to the OIC. For example, after the adoption of the ICCPR and the International Covenant on Economic, Social and Cultural Rights (ICESCR) by the UN General Assembly in 1966, it took another ten years for each of the two covenants to come into force (in 1976), subject to the individual political will of the UN member states. Also, it took another forty-two years from 1966 for the UN General Assembly to adopt an optional protocol to the ICESCR in 2008, and five years thereafter to attract the needed ten individual member state adoptions to bring it into force in 2013. That was after prolonged, optimistic lobbying and agitation by international human rights and civil society groups. Thus, the individual political will of the OIC member states to ratify the IICJ statute and other adopted instruments can (and should) be boosted through positive encouragement and efficient lobbying by relevant human rights and religious groups, as has often been done within the UN and regional human rights regimes.

Similar to other OIC instruments, Islamic law features prominently in the IICJ statute, with Article 27 of the statute providing that Islamic Sharia shall be the fundamental law of the court. However, the court can also refer to international law, international conventions, customary international law, and general principles of law or judgments of other international tribunals. The court therefore has the potential of being able to reconcile areas of differences between Islamic law and international human rights norms, thereby developing an Islamic jurisprudence in relation to different international law issues, including human rights. Michele Lombardini has identified the need and possible advantage of the IICJ as follows: "The International Islamic Court of Justice . . . further shows the will of a group of states to be governed by a special judicial system that constitutes an alternative forum for the peaceful resolution of international conflicts. The interpretation and the implementation of the norms applicable to the IICJ would probably have the effect of consolidating the block of Muslim countries spread all over the world, paving the way for a future of increased co-operation and solidarity" (2001:679).

A pertinent question would be whether the proposed IICJ has jurisdiction over human rights cases. Regarding its jurisdiction *ratione materiae*, the IICJ statute does not specifically mention human rights, but its Article 25 on jurisdiction is broad enough to accommodate human rights cases. Article 25(a) states that the court shall have jurisdiction for all matters that the concerned member states of the OIC agree to submit to it. Also, Article 25(b) provides that the court has jurisdiction to hear "all matters considered relevant to the competence of the Court in any treaty or convention in force," while Article 25(d) gives the court the competence to "examine any matter of international law." These provisions would accommodate human rights claims, first, where concerned states agree to submit such cases to the court; second, based on human rights treaties in force for concerned states; and, third, as a matter of international law. With respect to its jurisdiction *ratione personae*, the IICJ statute does not specifically provide for the right of individuals to bring human rights claims before the court. Rather, its Article 21 indicates states as the main possible parties before the court. This lack of access for individuals before the court is similar to the position under the UN International Court of Justice (ICJ), which has been challenged by different leading legal scholars (Vicuna 2001; Scheinin 2007), and would apparently limit the potential for bringing human rights cases before the court. To enhance the human rights implementational regime of the OIC, the current lack of access for individuals before the IICJ ought to be corrected.

In the years since the adoption of the IICJ statute, it has not attracted the required number of ratifications to bring the court into operation. This long delay begs the question of whether the OIC member states really have the required individual political will to give effect to the creation of the court. Some would consider this as dousing the hope of actualizing the IICJ as a possible human rights implementational mechanism under the OIC human rights agenda. However, the optimistic option would be to identify what necessary steps the OIC *ought* to take to bring the IICJ statute into force as an effective implementational mechanism for its human rights agenda.

To this end four main steps are identified and proposed. First, it *ought* to revisit and amend the IICJ statute to strengthen its provisions on human rights protection by including a specific provision recognizing the right of access for individuals to bring claims of human rights violations against OIC member states before the court. With regards to Islamic law, there is precedent in the classical *Mazālim* jurisdiction recognizing the right of individuals to bring complaints of injustice or rights violations against the authorities of state under Islamic law. It would also be more reasonable and economical to expand the jurisdiction of the IICJ to specifically cover human rights cases rather than propose the creation of another human rights court for that purpose under the OIC human rights agenda. This is exemplified by the 2004 merging of the African Court of Justice and the African Court of Human and Peoples Rights into a single regional judicial mechanism with human rights jurisdiction, named the African Court of Justice and Human Rights. Second, the OIC *ought* to amend Article 11 of the IICJ statute on the number of ratifications required to bring it into force. The amendment should reduce the number of required ratifications to two so that the statute can go into force for those member states that have already ratified it. Third, the OIC must be prepared to fund the court adequately after it takes off to ensure that it is fully able to discharge its functions effectively. And fourth, after its establishment, the court must be very innovative when drafting its rules of procedure and enlist competent experts in both international human rights law and Islamic law to ensure the adoption of an appropriate rules of procedure that will enable it to discharge its functions effectively.

With regard to having a nonjudicial human rights implementational mechanism under the OIC human rights agenda, Articles 5(6) and 15 of the 2008 OIC charter provided for the establishment of the Independent Permanent Human Rights Commission (IPHRC) that "shall promote the civil, political, social and economic rights enshrined in the organization's covenants and declarations and in universally agreed human rights instruments, in conformity with Islamic values." This makes the IPHRC a general OIC charter body responsible for promoting the implementation of all human rights under the OIC human rights agenda. The mandate of the IPHRC under Article 15 of the OIC charter is quite broad, which probably led former OIC Secretary-General Ekmeleddin İhsanoğlu to express high optimism about the proposed commission in 2010 before its establishment: "The establishment of the IPHRC will have a very positive impact on the OIC and on the commitment of its member states to uphold the principles of human rights" (quoted in Demir and Gamm 2010).

The IPHRC statute was adopted through OIC Resolution No. 2/38-LEG in June 2011. Notably, the first preambular paragraph of the resolution indicated the mindfulness to empower the OIC "with a mechanism to strengthen and protect human rights in the member states." The preamble of the IPHRC statute itself refers to the CDHRI and "relevant international instruments, charters and conventions." However, when compared to the mandate of other nonjudicial human rights mechanisms under the UN and regional human rights regimes, it obviously falls short of important functions such as receiving and reviewing mandatory periodic state reports on the human rights situation from respective member states, receiving interstate or individual complaints of human rights violations, monitoring the human rights situations in OIC member states, investigating human rights violations in the member states, and undertaking other protective functions. The only monitoring mandate of the commission under the IPHRC statute is its mandate to monitor observance of the human rights of Muslim communities and minorities in non-OIC member states.

Thus, the specific mandate of the commission under the IPHRC statute disappointingly falls short of the possible scope of the broad mandate conferred on it under Article 15 of the current OIC charter. Again, a pessimistic view would consider this as an indication of lack of political will on the part of the OIC to give the IPHRC the necessary mandate to monitor and report on human rights violations under its human rights agenda in a similar way as other nonjudicial bodies under the UN and regional human rights systems. The commission, however, demonstrated some optimism through adopting a relatively upbeat rules of procedure in September 2012, approved by the OIC Council of Ministers. The rules of procedure identified the commission as the principal human rights organ of the OIC, including that it should exercise its functions in an independent manner and in conformity with universally recognized human rights norms and standards, with the added value of Islamic principles of justice and equity. Through its rules of procedure, the commission endeavored to relatively enhance its functions by expanding the interpretation of its mandate under the OIC charter and the IPHRC statute.

However, the important functions of receiving mandatory state reports on the human rights situation from respective member states, receiving interstate or individual complaints of human rights violations, monitoring the human rights situation in OIC member states, investigating human rights violations in member states, and undertaking protective functions are still not specifically covered by the rules of procedure. The significance of these omitted functions for the effective performance of a nonjudicial human rights body cannot be overemphasized. This begs the question of whether the IPHRC can still find a way to legitimately perform these functions within its current mandate. With optimism, the IPHRC could learn from the long experience, good practices, and dynamism of the UN human rights treaty bodies and other regional human rights treaty bodies in legitimately finding ways around restrictions in their mandates to enhance their effectiveness.

Some commentators have expressed deep skepticism about the role of the IPHRC as an effective human rights mechanism under the OIC human rights agenda (cf. Blitt 2016:16–28). Other commentators have expressed optimism about the ability of the commission to find progressive ways of discharging its role effectively in accordance with international good practices. For example, Cismas notes that "nothing in the [commission's] mandate prevents the commissioners from exploiting a variety of working methods" to get around the apparent limitations in its mandate (2014:298). Article 17 of the IPHRC statute and Rules 64 and 65 of the rules of procedure, she argues, have the potential for the commission to adopt general comments and to conduct country missions to observe and report on the human rights situation in the OIC member states. She also notes that "although individual complaints were not included in the mandate of the IPHRC, nothing prevents the commissioners from making use of diplomatic channels to address various human rights violations" in member states (299).

The OIC's implementational credentials *ought* to improve significantly to enable the organization to demonstrate its complementary utility as a regional arrangement to the UN's human rights system. As the principal human rights organ of the OIC that is committed to "advance human rights and fundamental freedoms in member states . . . in conformity with the universally recognized human rights norms and standards and with added value of Islamic principles of justice and equality" (IPHRC Rules of Procedure: Rule 2), the IPHRC *ought* to adopt a progressive approach in its functions in conformity with the optimistic view. The IPHRC can certainly learn from the practices of earlier regional mechanisms such as the African Commission on Human and Peoples' Rights, which has acted optimistically over the years and succeeded substantially in "unshackling itself from the strictures of the African Charter," and expanded its mandate to justify its role as a relevant and necessary mechanism for the effective implementation of human rights under the African human rights system (Kufuor 2010:37).

Conclusion: Optimism over Pessimism

This chapter has critically explored the human rights agenda of the OIC from the perspectives of pessimism and optimism. It is obvious that the OIC has come a long way in its human rights journey since its establishment in 1972. Departing from its conservative beginnings, the organization made a significant positive shift in 2005 when it adopted its Ten Year Program of Action, followed by a revised charter in 2008. Both instruments contain aspirational declaratory commitments that could significantly transform the OIC's human rights agenda, subject to the collective political will of the organization and the individual political will of its member states to dynamically pursue the transformation of the human rights aspirations of both instruments into full reality.

Retrospectively, this author had proposed in 2003 (Baderin 2003:230) that for the OIC to enhance its human rights agenda and contribute positively to the realization of international human rights in the Muslim world, it ought to take three main steps. First, renew its human rights commitment and adopt a more comprehensive and binding Islamic human rights covenant to be ratified by all its member states. While this was reflected in its 2005 Ten Year Program of Action, that aspiration has not yet been fully transformed into reality. Second, establish a mechanism with a comprehensive mandate to monitor the implementation of human rights in all the OIC member states. It was proposed that the implementational mechanism should, inter alia, have jurisdiction to adjudicate allegations of human rights violations against any of the OIC member states; have the mandate to interpret the scope of the rights guaranteed under the CDHRI, subsequent instruments and rights guaranteed under the Sharia in general; be composed of highly qualified jurists in both Islamic law and international human rights law; and adopt an evolutionary approach in its interpretation of the law and consciously develop a progressive human rights jurisprudence within the context of both international human rights law and Islamic law that would serve as a specific departure point for human rights practice in the Muslim world. Third, the implementation mechanism should have compulsory jurisdiction for individual complaints against human rights violations in the OIC member states, and there should be cooperation between it, the UN human rights bodies, and other regional human rights bodies, with the aim of combining the best in the different civilizations and legal traditions for the realization of an inclusive universalism for human rights.

In the years since those propositions were made, the OIC has partly adopted them in aspiration only and has been very slow in transforming them into full reality. This should, however, not douse optimism about the ability of the OIC to improve its human rights regime as advanced in this chapter. Certainly, it is optimism that has sustained the whole notion of human rights over the years, "even when human rights seem to be about slow and piecemeal reform" (Moyn 2010:4). This optimism is bolstered by Tony Evans's observation that "[although] human rights of all people may not yet be protected . . . the march of international human rights regime is inexorable" (T. Evans 2003:156). It is envisaged that the OIC would not be inclined to being left behind in that inexorable human rights march forward. Thus, with regard to transforming the OIC's human rights aspirations into full reality, those earlier propositions are still substantially valid today, and, going forward, they still underpin the suggestions made in this chapter with respect to the conceptualization, standard-setting, and implementation of human rights under the OIC's human rights agenda. It is submitted that the OIC *ought* to, optimistically, take these propositions seriously and implement them in pursuance of its declared enhanced commitment to human rights in its current charter to secure a place for itself in the inexorable forward march of international human rights.

This chapter thus proposes optimism over pessimism in respect of the OIC's human rights agenda into the future. Despite the apparent shortcomings of the OIC's human rights agenda, rather than pessimistically writing it off, we would be more reasonable, in the quest for genuine inclusive universalism in human rights, to continue encouraging the organization to live up to its obligations—it being the Muslim world's only intergovernmental body and the largest of such after the UN that has committed to the promotion and protection of human rights as one of its charter objectives.

Notes

1. See https://treaties.un.org/doc/Publication/UNTS/Volume%20914/volume-914-I-13039-English.pdf.

2. See, for example, UN General Assembly Resolutions A/RES/37/4 of October 22, 1982; A/RES/57/42 of January 16, 2003; A/67/L.29 of December 4, 2012; and A/RES/67/264 of August 16, 2013.

3. Author's translation.

Works Cited

Baderin, Mashood. A. 2003. *International Human Rights and Islamic Law*. Oxford: Oxford University Press.

———. 2009. "Understanding Islamic Law in Theory and Practice." *Legal Information Management* 9 (3): 186–90.

Blitt, Robert C. 2016. "Equality and Nondiscrimination Through the Eyes of an International Religious Organization: The Organization of Islamic Cooperation (OIC) Response to Women's Rights and Sexual Orientation and Gender Identity Rights." University of Tennessee Legal Studies Research Paper Series, no. 291.

Cismas, Ioana. 2014. *Religious Actors and International Law.* Oxford: Oxford University Press.

Cruft, Rowan, S. Matthew Liao, and Massimo Renzo, eds. 2015. *Philosophical Foundations of Human Rights.* Oxford: Oxford University Press.

Demir, Gul, and Niki Gamm. 2010. "OIC Leader Circles Globe to Represent Voice of Muslim World." *Hürriyet Daily News*, July 18, 2010.

Donnelly, Jack. 2007. "The Relative Universality of Human Rights." *Human Rights Quarterly* 29 (2): 281–306.

———. 2010. "International Human Rights: Universal, Relative or Relatively Universal?" In *International Human Rights Law: Six Decades After the UDHR and Beyond*, ed. Mashood A. Baderin and Manisuli Ssenyonjo, 31–48. Farnham: Ashgate.

Evans, Malcolm D. 2012. "The Future(s) of Regional Courts on Human Rights." In *Realizing Utopia: The Future of International Law*, ed. Antonio Cassese, 261–74. Oxford: Oxford University Press.

Evans, Tony. 2003. "Universal Human Rights: 'As Much Round and Round' as Ever Onward." *International Journal of Human Rights* 7 (4): 155–68.

Flynn, Jeffrey. 2003. "Habermas on Human Rights: Law, Morality, and Intercultural Dialogue." *Social Theory and Practice* 29 (3): 431–57.

Goodhart, Michael. 2003. "Origins and Universality in the Human Rights Debates: Cultural Essentialism and the Challenge of Globalization." *Human Rights Quarterly* 25 (4): 935–64.

———. 2008. "Neither Relative nor Universal: A Response to Donnelly" *Human Rights Quarterly* 30 (1):183–93.

Habermas, Jürgen. 1996. *Between Facts and Norms.* Cambridge, MA: MIT Press.

Hallaq, Wael B. 1984. "Was the Gate of Ijtihad Closed?" *International Journal of Middle East Studies*, 16 (1): 3–41.

Hopgood, Stephen. 2013. *The Endtimes of Human Rights.* Ithaca, NY: Cornell University Press.

Hudson, W. D., ed. 1969. *The Is-Ought Question: A Collection of Papers on the Central Problem in Moral Philosophy.* Controversies in Philosophy 1. London: Macmillan.

IDB and IFA. 2000. *Resolutions and Recommendations of the Council of the Islamic Fiqh Academy, 1985–2000.* Jeddah: Islamic Research and Training Institute.

İhsanoğlu, Ekmeleddin. 2010. *The Islamic World in the New Century: The Organisation of the Islamic Conference, 1969–2009.* London: Hurst.

Kayaoglu, Turan. 2013. "A Rights Agenda for the Muslim World? The Organization of Islamic Cooperation's Evolving Human Rights Framework." Brookings Doha Center Analysis Papers. Doha: Brookings Institution.

Kellison, Rosemary B. 2014. "Tradition, Authority, and Immanent Critique in Comparative Ethics." *Journal of Religious Ethics* 42 (4): 713–41.

Kufuor, Kofi Oteng. 2010. *The African Human Rights System: Origin and Evolution.* New York: Palgrave Macmillan.

Lombardini, Michele. 2001. "The International Islamic Court of Justice: Towards an International Islamic Legal System?" *Leiden Journal of International Law* 14 (3): 665–80.

Moyn, Samuel. 2010. *The Last Utopia: Human Rights in History.* Cambridge: Belknap Press of Harvard University Press.

Mutua, Makau. 2016. *Human Rights Standards: Hegemony, Law, and Politics.* Albany: State University of New York.

Petersen, Marie Juul. 2012. *Islamic or Universal Human Rights? The OIC's Independent Permanent Human Rights Commission.* DIIS Report. Copenhagen: Danish Institute for International Studies.

Rajagopal, Balakrishnan. 2006. "Counter-Hegemonic International Law: Rethinking Human Rights and Development as a Third World Strategy." *Third World Quarterly* 27 (5): 767–83.

Rawls, John. 1987. "The Idea of an Overlapping Consensus." *Oxford Journal of Legal Studies* 7 (1): 1–25.

Scheinin, Martin. 2007. "The ICJ and the Individual." *International Community Law Review* 9 (2): 123–37.

Vicuna, Francisco Orrego. 2001. "Individuals and Non-State Entities Before International Courts and Tribunals." *Max Planck Yearbook of United Nations Law* 5 (1): 53–66.

CHAPTER 3

The OIC's Human Rights Regime

Turan Kayaoglu

Introduction

The Organization of Islamic Cooperation's (OIC's) human rights regime is an eclectic patchwork informed by the interests of leading countries, the pressures of the broader political environment, and the OIC's organizational needs. This regime displays a semblance of consistency because of excessive and vague references to Islam, Sharia, and the *umma*. This chapter explains their regime in five sections. The first section provides a broad overview of the current global human rights regime. The second section focuses on key OIC forums through which the member states decide on its human rights regime. The third section examines the activities of the Independent Permanent Human Rights Commission (IPHRC), the OIC's most important human rights instrument. The fourth section describes other agencies within the OIC that work to implement aspects of its human rights agenda, such as the Department on Muslim Minorities and Communities; the Islamophobia Observatory; the Peace, Security and Mediation Unit; and the Humanitarian Affairs Department. The fifth section examines how the OIC works through and with other organizations to advance its human rights agenda at the international level.

An Islamic Human Rights Regime?

An international human rights regime is defined as a set of standards and decision-making procedures that a group of states accept as authoritative

(Krasner 1983; Donnelly 1986:602; Donnelly 2003). The UN human rights system is an international human rights regime; a variety of regional regimes complement and support the UN human rights system. Human rights regimes typically include four types of instruments: a declaration, a charter, a commission, and a court. A declaration establishes the regime's broad principles in a non-binding framework; a charter (or covenant) elaborates these principles in a binding treaty; a commission monitors the implementation of these rights; and a court adjudicates disputes over these rights. As Table 3.1 illustrates, the evolution of regional human rights regimes has been uneven and not all regimes have all four of the above instruments (Donnelly 2013:95–103).

The strength of a regional human rights system depends on the level of authority it has over member states in terms of standard-setting, monitoring, and enforcement. In a 2013 assessment of regional human rights systems, Jack Donnelly characterized Europe as having a strong "enforcement regime," with authoritative regional norms and regional judicial enforcement. The inter-American system can be considered "promotional," where a set of regional norms exists with some monitoring and enforcement in place. He terms the African system as a "declaratory" or "promotional" system in which there are weak standards replete with exemptions and there exists little monitoring and enforcement. Donnelly argues that Asia and the Arab world, meanwhile, lack any effective human rights regimes, though he points to emergence of a weak declaratory regional system in the Arab world under Arab League's leadership and in Asia under Association of Southeast Asian Nations' (ASEAN) leadership (Donnelly 2013: 106). He omits the OIC and the Muslim world.

Once established, human rights regimes often evolve by gradually acquiring more authority over their member states. The African system has developed considerably over the past twenty years: broad guidelines have given rise to stronger norms and even a "promotional regime" in which an international body encourages or assists governments in implementing these norms. Typically, once leading states in the organization commit—even rhetorically—to human rights values, these values tend to spread and a mechanism to implement them is often established by the organization in conjunction with member states. These steps, however, often meet strong resistance from at least some member states.

The development of regional human rights regimes is subject to a range of complicating factors, including states' level of commitment to human rights, the level of democratization within member states, and the influence

Table 3.1. International and Regional Human Rights Regimes

	Declaration	*Charter*	*Commission*	*Court*
Universal (The UN System)	Universal Declaration of Human Rights (1948)	International Covenant on Civil and Political Rights (1966); International Covenant on Economic, Social, and Cultural Rights (1966)	Human Rights Committee (1977); Commission on Economic, Social, and Cultural Rights (1985)	None
European System (Council of Europe)	None	European Convention on Human Rights (1950)	European Commission of Human Rights (1954–1998)	European Court of Human Rights (1959)
Inter-American System (Organ-ization of American States)	American Declaration of the Rights and Duties of Man (1948)	American Convention on Human Rights (1969)	Inter-American Commission on Human Rights (1959)	Inter-American Court of Human Rights (1979)
African System (African Union)	None	African Charter on Human and Peoples' Rights (1981)	African Commission on Human and Peoples' Rights (1986)	African Court on Human and Peoples' Rights (1998)
Arab System (Arab League)	None	Arab Charter on Human Rights (2004; revised)	Arab Human Rights Committee (2009)	None (Arab Court of Human Rights proposed in 2014)
Asian System (Association of Southeast Asian Nations)	ASEAN Human Rights Declaration (2012)	ASEAN Charter (2007)	ASEAN Intergovernmental Commission on Human Rights (2009)	None
Islamic System (Organization of Islamic Cooperation)	Cairo Declaration of Human Rights in Islam (1990)	Covenant on the Rights of the Child in Islam (2004)	Independent Permanent Human Rights Commis-sion (2011)	None

of external actors. Regional organizations are also important actors in this process. The Council of Europe, which has gradually extended its authority over member states, is an apt illustration of the key role of other regional organizations in the human rights regime development process. The EU's membership demands and the overall democratization in Europe have been the main reasons for the Council of Europe's success in building a rigorous human rights regime. But the gradualist approach taken by institutions such as the Council of Europe, the European Commission, and the European Court of Human Rights was also extremely instrumental in creating a strong human rights regime in Europe (Forsythe 2000:133). An incremental approach allowed the European system to evolve from its initial focus on the promotion of human rights (the 1950s) to a phase that embraced the monitoring of human rights (the 1960s), and finally to the enforcement of human rights (the 1970s) (Donnelly 2013:95–96, 106–7).

In the OIC region, some of the components of an international human rights regime are in place. The Cairo Declaration, the Covenant on the Rights of the Child in Islam, and the Independent Permanent Human Rights Commission all in principle provide the OIC with an important basis from which to demand that member states improve their human rights practices. The IPHRC has the potential to strengthen the international human rights system for OIC member states. However, its ultimate success will depend on the willingness of member states to grant it standard-setting and monitoring capabilities as well as on the ability of the OIC to establish some degree of authority over member states.

The OIC and Human Rights Law-Making

The OIC has two main decision-making bodies, the Islamic Summit and the Islamic Council of Foreign Ministers, which share responsibility for defining the OIC's human rights policies. The first Islamic Summit was held in 1969; the OIC was formally established at this meeting. Composed of heads of state, the Islamic Summit remains the most important platform for representing and advancing Muslim solidarity, achieving the objectives outlined in the organization's charter and addressing the problems of member states and the *umma*, the worldwide Muslim community. The framers envisioned the summit as the core of the organization and as the locus of the "supreme authority of the Organization" (OIC charter, Article 6). Convening once every three years, the summits have become meaningfully symbolic, akin to Muslim intergovernmental pilgrimages. Moreover, the various host states tend to be states looking to publicize their Islamic credentials and visibility. To date the Islamic Summit has met thirteen times, most recently in Istanbul in 2016. Despite the OIC's claims of Islamic solidarity, the Islamic Summits have often highlighted the fractures and disagreements that exist among some members, resulting in some states boycotting the summits or only participating minimally.

Still, Islamic Summits have the authority to pass resolutions, communiqués, and declarations that establish the OIC's priorities. Most of the discussions at the Islamic Summit are not substantive policy discussions. What takes place at the Islamic Summit has often already been discussed and agreed on at the Council of Foreign Ministers (previously Islamic Conference of Foreign Ministers or ICFM), an annual meeting between foreign ministers of OIC member states. As the main forum for deliberation and decision-making in the OIC, the council wields the power over the fate of OIC resolutions, declarations, and treaties.

Since 2002, in addition to the annual meetings, the council has also met regularly in New York to coordinate member states' policies and to develop a common Islamic strategy at the UN. The coordination meetings in New York are considered to be of high importance to the OIC. This indicates the organization's emphasis on diplomacy and its desire to project the image of an able and active umma prepared to present a united front in international diplomacy, despite the divisions among member states on many key issues. These meetings attempt to build consensus on thematic issues such as UN reform, terrorism, and responses to Islamophobia. The council meetings in New York also aim to establish a common Islamic stance on issues such as Kashmir, Cyprus, Sudan, Somalia, Rohingya Muslims, and, particularly, the Israeli-Palestinian conflict.

The OIC General Secretariat, located in Jeddah, Saudi Arabia, is the OIC's administrative arm. The OIC General Secretariat remains weak, with a small staff and shoestring budget. As with other international organizations, the administrative staff is composed of officials and civil servants whose work supports the organization. While not a formal staff requirement, in practice all staff members are Muslims. While the secretariat was essentially designed to organize conferences such as the Islamic Summits and the ICFM, it has gained a modest amount of authority beyond the role of conference organizer and responsibility with the daily implementation of policies and strategies—even though deference to state sovereignty continues to be salient within the OIC.

The OIC's tripartite summit-council-secretariat structure resembles the structure of other international organizations. Unlike most other intergovernmental organizations, which pass binding resolutions on human rights, monitor state compliance, and enforce decisions, the OIC has relied largely on unbinding resolutions and declarations (Cismas 2014; Kayaoglu 2015b). In essence, three factors—a diverse membership, a weak enforcement capability, and a deference to state sovereignty—prevent the OIC from establishing a strong human rights regime.

First, the OIC has a diverse group of member states in comparison with other regional organizations, such as the Organization of American States, the European Union, and the African Union. The OIC's fifty-seven member states (including Palestine) are scattered across four continents (Africa, Asia, Europe, and South America). These members include some of the world's richest countries, such as Qatar, and some of the poorest countries, such as Yemen. OIC members include all Muslim majority states but also some states with Muslim minorities, such as Ghana, Guyana, and Suriname. Some of the members are theocracies, such as Iran and Saudi Arabia, while others are secular, such as Azerbaijan and Kazakhstan. Given this diversity, the organization has refrained from establishing strong governance structures and relies mostly on declarative resolutions; the weak enforceability of these resolutions means that states tend not to object to them.

Second, despite an emphasis on solidarity and a preference for passing resolutions with consensus, the organization lacks any monitoring or enforcement power, apart from naming and shaming member states, denying member states access to resources from the Islamic Development Bank, and the drastic measure of expulsion, as with Egypt in 1980 after the Camp David Accords (Egypt was readmitted to the organization in 1984) or the suspension of Syria's membership in 2012. Essentially, the OIC relies on member states' willingness to implement resolutions and to act on the basis of a vaguely defined sense of Islamic solidarity. The OIC resolutions potentially have soft power, moral authority grounded in the collective will of member states, but only if there is a strong consensus in support of them. For example, in 2012, Albania, Cameroon, Togo, and Bosnia (an OIC observer) were named and shamed in various OIC platforms and publications when they abstained from voting for nonmember status for Palestine at the UN; the rest of the OIC member states were in support of this because nonmember observer state status represented an upgrade relative to Palestine's prior status of observer entity. Agreement among the members also signals to the international community the Islamic stance on issues in world politics.

The third reason for the weak human rights regime in the OIC is its deference to state sovereignty. In part reflecting its postcolonial and anti-imperialist orientation, respecting state sovereignty, accepting the primacy of domestic legislation, and refraining from interfering in each other's domestic affairs undergird the OIC charter. The OIC resolutions appeal to a state's voluntary compliance, avoid asking for any supranational monitoring and enforcement, and steer clear from singling out any OIC member for criticism. Reflecting this deference to state sovereignty, the OIC has been reluctant to interact with civil society; only in the 2010s—and in a very restricted manner—has it allowed civil society actors to have a voice in the organization (see Chapter 12).

With a strong emphasis on sovereignty and a relatively weak secretariat and civil society voice, the OIC is a quintessential *inter*governmental organization that is closely controlled by its member states (Kayaoglu 2015b). The leading member states of the OIC are Saudi Arabia, Iran, Pakistan, and Turkey. They are among the main funders of the organization and are the strongest voices in the organization. With respect to the OIC's human rights agenda, Iran has arguably been the most ideologically driven: It was the main force behind the Cairo Declaration on Human Rights in Islam. Pakistan has been the coordinator of the OIC group in Geneva for many years, and its activities at the UN Human Rights Council have been influential in framing and driving the OIC's "defamation of religions" agenda. While Saudi Arabia prefers a less public approach, it has also played a major role in shaping the human rights agenda, determining what issues or agencies could get funding. Unlike Iran, Pakistan, and Saudi Arabia, Turkey is a secular state and has a comparatively better human rights record. Significantly, Turkey also falls under the jurisdiction of the European Court of Human Rights. Turkey has promoted a human rights agenda within the OIC, especially during the tenure of Ekmeleddin İhsanoğlu, a Turkish national, as head of the organization. Saudi Arabia, Iran, and Pakistan have historically used the OIC's diplomatic powers to shield themselves from criticism of their human rights records in the UN Human Rights Council.

Despite the OIC's intergovernmentalism, OIC bureaucrats and leaders exert some influence on the organization's human rights agenda. As the public face of the organization, secretaries-general, in particular, can articulate human rights positions and contribute to shaping the organization's agenda and priorities. One example is the significant difference between the human rights leadership of the past OIC secretary-general, İhsanoğlu, and his successor, Secretary-General Madani. A Turkish academic-cum-diplomat, İhsanoğlu was arguably a "moderate universalist" who wanted to align the OIC's human rights agenda with that of the international human rights system, while Madani, the former Saudi minister of information and culture, seemed to be more skeptical of human rights. Madani has publicly criticized the supposed "Western character" of human rights protections and has questioned their compatibility with Islamic values (Kayaoglu 2015a).

Similarly, the first IPHRC chairperson, Siti Ruhaini Dzuhayatin, an Indonesian academic and women's rights activist, advocated for universal human rights. The second chair, Mohammed Kawu Ibrahim, a Nigerian diplomat, emphasized Muslim societies' distinctiveness and primacy of state sovereignty when it comes to human rights (Kayaoglu 2015a). The difference between Ambassador Ufuk Gokcen, who represents the OIC at the UN in New York, and Ambassador Zamir Akram, the permanent representative of Pakistan in Geneva, who coordinates OIC activities on human rights in Geneva at the UN Human Rights Council (HRC), is also telling. While Gokcen has espoused universal human rights and has established strong connections with civil society and NGO communities in New York, Akram has been an apologist for the human rights records of OIC members and a force behind the defamation of religions agenda, a policy that has been criticized by many human rights NGOs as compromising freedom of speech by universalizing blasphemy laws.

Although its diverse membership, weak enforcement capabilities, and deference to state sovereignty only allow the OIC to rely on unbinding resolutions, the common moral discourse, Islamic symbolism, and the soft power of the collective religious identity of the OIC provide these resolutions with additional weight (Samuel 2014). The normative discourse on Sharia and Islam plays multiple roles in the OIC: It builds consensus within the OIC, it projects an image of the OIC as the spokesperson of the Muslim world, it adds moral weight to the organization's mostly toothless resolutions, and, paradoxically, it upholds state sovereignty within the organization (Kayaoglu 2013). The discourse on Islam tends to remain at a very general, abstract level, in which Islam and Sharia are treated as an ethical system or a moral code shared by OIC member states as the lowest common denominator. This allows states with a variety of state-religion interactions—including secular OIC members, such as Kazakhstan, Senegal, and Turkey—to agree to OIC resolutions and declarations. When it comes to specific issues within the OIC, however, conservative Islamic states often define what "Islamic" means, and they frequently impose a highly restrictive understanding of Islam in the OIC's discourse and resolutions. Yet, when it comes as a normative system, with the broad flexibility of Sharia and without an authoritative interpreter of Sharia, references to Sharia in resolution declarations essentially allow states to interpret these documents to suit their needs.

The Independent Permanent Human Rights Commission

In 2011, the OIC inaugurated its own Independent Permanent Human Rights Commission. It is the only agency within the OIC with a mandate to promote human rights in member states and to protect Muslim minorities worldwide.

There were several reasons behind the OIC's push for a human rights commission. First, it was part of the proposed organizational reforms under İhsanoğlu's leadership, reforms that were designed to make the OIC a more effective international organization (İhsanoğlu 2010). A further motive behind the establishment of the IPHRC was a desire to increase the OIC's credibility among both Muslims and the broader global public. The commission can also be seen as an extension of a new humanitarian agenda that emphasizes aid, disaster relief, and collaboration with civil society organizations (Petersen 2012:13). The internal dynamics of the OIC also played a critical role in the creation of the IPHRC. The traditional dominance of Saudi Arabia, Iran, and Pakistan within the organization has been countered by the growing involvement of countries such as Turkey, Malaysia, Morocco, and Indonesia, which are comparatively friendlier toward international human rights.

Of the eighteen experts elected to the IPHRC in 2011, equal numbers came from Arab, Asian, and African states, and in its current first cohort, four of the eighteen members—those from Afghanistan, Indonesia, Malaysia, and Sudan—were women (IPHRC 2016). The members were mostly diplomats, bureaucrats, and academics. While some were well-respected in the international human rights community, others were "known for their strong opposition to at least parts of the universal human rights agenda" (Petersen

2012:35). None of the eighteen representatives was a religious scholar, but most had strong ties to their states' bureaucracies, indicating the desire of OIC members to retain influence over the commission. The IPHRC members came from different backgrounds, but, in effect, most were state employees, such as diplomats, with little autonomy or independence (30).

The diverse backgrounds of the commissioners were undoubtedly an asset to making the commission more effective in human rights diplomacy, but the varied life experiences of commissioners do not necessarily make them strong human rights advocates. Human rights *diplomacy* acknowledges the primacy of sovereignty and requires international actors to work with the state, understand the concerns of state leaders, and reason with governments to improve human rights. By contrast, human rights *advocacy* aims to mobilize international and nonstate actors to apply moral pressure to induce states to address human rights violations. Many of the experts elected to the IPHRC are human rights diplomats with experience in national, regional, and international human rights organizations. An optimist would argue that this level of experience and connection is an asset for their work on the commission; pessimists, however, would stress the limited independence of the supposed "independent" experts from member states.

The commission has more of a consultative than a protective function. Its duties include conducting "studies and research" on human rights and provide technical support to the member states for capacity building and helping them meet the reporting requirements of human rights mechanisms.[1] These functions allow only a limited, supporting role for the commission; its actions are largely dependent on the OIC or the requests of member states.

A major tool in the arsenal of international human rights organizations is the ability to publish country reports and resolutions that, in effect, "name and shame," creating moral pressure to curb the violations of human rights (Risse-Kappen, Ropp, and Sikkink 1999). The downside of this strategy is that it can sometimes backfire, producing defensive responses or outright denials from member states. The OIC thus publishes thematic rather than country-specific reports and resolutions on controversial issues related to member states. This strategy is consistent with the OIC's strategy at the UN HRC. One OIC representative at the UN Commission argued that the UN and HRC resolutions "were often politically motivated and did not help in the promotion and protection of human rights" (Steiner, Alston, and Goodman 2008:979). The OIC sees the issue-specific focus of the thematic reports as depoliticizing the human rights problems identified, thereby allowing countries to address human rights issues without losing face. In other words, rather than human rights advocacy through moral pressure, the OIC envisions the commission engaging in human rights diplomacy through persuasion.

Three structural problems will likely limit the commission's effectiveness. First, the IPHRC has only a few, relatively weak mechanisms. All other human rights systems have monitoring mechanisms, such as periodic review of state reports, country visits, and complaint mechanisms for interstate problems or individual grievances. However, OIC members have carefully guarded their sovereignty and have denied their commission any significant independent authority.

Second, there has been no integration of civil society organizations into the IPHRC. While the OIC charter allows cooperation with "Islamic and other organizations" (Article 26), the OIC lacks a clear and inclusive mechanism for NGO accreditation and has traditionally excluded civil society from its official business. While the IPHRC's statute specifies that "the Commission will promote and support member state-accredited NGOs" it also enumerates additional burdensome requirements for inviting an OIC-accredited NGO to participate in IPHRC meetings (Article 15).

Third, the jurisdictional reach of the commission is both ambitious and problematic. Allowing for a potentially universal jurisdiction, the IPHRC founding statute asks the commission "to monitor observance of the human rights of Muslim communities and minorities" (Article 10). Many international human rights issues, such as combating Islamophobia and addressing the defamation of religions, have a prominent place on the OIC's human rights agenda. In these instances, the OIC presents itself as an advocate for the rights of Muslim minorities. Yet the basis for the OIC's claim to speak on behalf of Muslims in nonmember states remains unclear. This is especially vexing as the OIC's state-centric organization does not allow for the formal representation of these Muslim minorities in nonmember states. Finally, there is a notable double standard at play: While the IPHRC's founding statute calls for monitoring the human rights of Muslim minorities in nonmember states, it denies the commission a similar function regarding human rights issues in OIC member states.

The establishment of the IPHRC signaled a newfound commitment to human rights issues within the OIC. Five years after its establishment, however, the IPHRC's track record and trajectory had at best disappointed the hopes of optimists and justified the fears of the skeptics. As yet, the IPHRC has failed to develop a single major initiative to promote and protect human rights in the Muslim world. Of greater concern are that the comments of the OIC and IPHRC leaders, as well as the debates and resolutions of the commission itself, provide a bleak picture of the commission's commitment to international human rights. The universalist and progressive tendencies toward human rights that were present at the start of the commission have been replaced by parochial and reactionary attitudes (Kayaoglu 2015a).

Iran and Saudi Arabia have been notably strategic and competitive about the OIC's human rights agenda. The competition between the two countries has been evident in discussions regarding the location of the IPHRC headquarters. Both countries sought to house the IPHRC; eventually, Iran conceded. While some OIC bureaucrats and moderate Muslim states lobbied for Indonesia as a host country, Indonesia immediately backed down when the two leading OIC states entered the game, demonstrating the internal power structures of the organization.

The OIC and Human Rights Implementation

In addition to the IPHRC, several other agencies within the OIC system have mandates that intersect with issues related to human rights.

The Islamophobia Observatory

Islamophobia has been of particular concern to the OIC. As Skorini discusses in Chapter 5, anti-Islam and anti-Muslim speech, or blasphemous speech, has been on the OIC's agenda since the 1980s. Iranian leader Khomeini's fatwa calling for the killing of British-Indian novelist Salman Rushdie—a response to Rushdie's *The Satanic Verses*, a novel which some Muslims found blasphemous—further highlighted the willingness of some Muslims to call for violence when faced with blasphemous speech. While the OIC refrained from endorsing Khomeini's fatwa, it nonetheless condemned Rushdie. In the late 1990s, the OIC started to refer to anti-Islam and anti-Muslim speech as the "defamation of Islam." The OIC then began a campaign to require states to combat the "defamation of religions," encouraging states to criminalize defamatory anti-Islamic speech. Later, the OIC exerted great efforts to promote the term "Islamophobia," understood to mean a fear and hatred of Islam and Muslims. The OIC has accepted and endorsed the use of the term within the UN, giving the term "Islamophobia" additional legitimacy within international human rights discourse comparable to the term anti-Semitism (Kayaoglu 2011).

In 2007 the OIC established the Islamophobia Observatory in its headquarters in Jeddah to monitor speech and acts that defame Islam and are prejudicial toward Muslims. Since its establishment, the observatory has published monthly reports, cataloguing—albeit unsystematically—various incidents deemed Islamophobic. Without a set of criteria or a clear definition of Islamophobia however, the OIC reports include a wide range of speech and actions. While some of them can be considered as incitement of hatred and thus are banned under international human rights law, others can be categorized as blasphemous or critical speech about Islam and Muslim—thus creating confusion about the OIC's intent with the "combatting defamation of religions" agenda. The reports also focus disproportionately on speeches and events in North America, Europe, and Australia, suggesting the OIC's desire to criticize Western liberal states in retribution because these states often criticize the OIC member states for human rights violations.[2]

Islamophobia has been a useful rhetorical tool for the OIC. The existence of the term provides a shorthand in OIC efforts to name and shame Western countries, to criticize the dominant liberal approach to international human rights, and to draw a distinction between "Western" and Islamic approaches to human rights.

The Department of Muslim Communities and Minorities

Especially in the OIC's early years, the status of Muslim minorities in Bulgaria, Cambodia, China, Myanmar, and the Philippines were important issues. To address these issues, the organization established the Department of Muslim Minorities in 1978 (later renamed the Department of Muslim Communities and Minorities). The department was charged with collecting information on Muslim minorities, facilitating the OIC's relations with these minority communities, and protecting and promoting the interests of these communities.

Unlike issues related to Islamophobia, which often lead the OIC to criticize Western states, the OIC follows a different approach in addressing the problems of Muslim minorities in non-Western states: It frames its advocacy within the human rights and minority rights protections provided by the international human rights regime and shies away from directly criticizing host governments. The organization often collaborates with host states and tries to avoid the appearance of interfering in the domestic affairs of host states (İhsanoğlu 2010:127–29). OIC documents frequently refer to the organization's desire to help Muslim minorities "within the framework of respect for the sovereignty of these countries."[3] Moreover, the OIC encourages host countries to join the OIC as observer states in order to allow the OIC to work more closely with the Muslim minorities within the state. Some states with Muslim minorities such as Russia and Thailand already have observer status within the OIC. Only when the host countries refuse to work with the OIC does the OIC use its power in diplomatic corridors of the United Nations to argue that Muslim minorities should have a voice on these platforms. In addition to regular OIC agenda items, such as Palestinians and Muslims of India-controlled Kashmir, in the past the organization was instrumental in helping Bosnian Muslims gain access to international platforms (Karčić 2013) and at the time of this writing, the OIC has been vocal about the rights of Rohingya Muslims in Myanmar.

The Peace, Security and Mediation Unit

In the early 2000s, conflict resolution became a priority for the OIC, and the organization launched the Peace, Security and Mediation Unit (PSMU) in 2013. As detailed by Hirah Azhar in Chapter 9, the PSMU consists of a Wise Persons' Council (WPC) of Muslim leaders to provide guidance, and special envoys to implement initiatives on the ground. Projects undertaken by the special envoys require approval by the Council of Foreign Ministers, suggesting that even fairly weak units within the OIC are tightly controlled by the member states.

The PSMU also represents the OIC in the Network for Religious and Traditional Peacemakers. Launched in 2013, the network is a joint initiative in which the OIC has partnered with Finn Church Aid (FCA), the UN Mediation Support Unit (MSU), the UN Alliance of Civilizations (UNAOC), and Religions for Peace (RfP). In addition to embracing aspects of traditional peacemaking, such as mediation, reaching out to local leaders, and conducting fact-finding missions, the network also aims to involve traditional and religious leaders in conflict resolution and peace building. One issue that the network is likely to tackle in the future is violence motivated by religious extremism.

In Chapter 9, Azhar also shows that the PSMU, being underfunded and understaffed, relies on the supplemental OIC budget, funding for which is mostly provided by Saudi Arabia, and external expertise and practical knowledge, largely provided by the MSU. The lack of resources and the reliance on the UN suggest that the OIC sees its role in conflict resolution as complementary to the UN and regional organizations, rather than as an independent leader of peacekeeping initiatives.

The OIC and Human Rights Diplomacy

In addition to its internal practices with regard to human rights lawmaking and implementation, the OIC works with other intergovernmental organizations to articulate and advance its human rights perspective. Notwithstanding the OIC's human rights activities on the ground and within OIC member states, the organization's human rights efforts are most evident at the international level (Chase 2012; Freedman 2013).

The United Nations

Despite occasional claims by those who wish to see the OIC as a parallel Muslim UN, the OIC upholds the UN as an international authority and has chosen to forge partnerships on a range of issues, including terrorism, conflict resolution, and development, rather than present itself as an alternative. In other words, the OIC sees itself as a supplementary organization to the UN, rather than a substitute. OIC-UN ties received a big boost in 1975 when the OIC joined the UN as an observer. Since then, the OIC and the UN have built partnerships on issues ranging from economic development and interfaith dialogue to humanitarian aid and conflict resolution. Over the years, and particularly under OIC Secretary-General İhsanoğlu's tenure from 2004 to 2013, the OIC's influence within the UN system has grown. Secretary-General Ban Ki-moon was the first UN secretary-general to visit the OIC headquarters in Jeddah in 2012. That same year, in a UN-OIC coordination meeting, the UN and the OIC declared their commitment to cooperate in addressing the problems of OIC member states and working to improve the status of Muslim minorities worldwide.

The OIC has developed four primary tools to promote itself within the UN system. First, the OIC has established two missions—one in New York and one in Geneva—to coordinate its activities at the UN. These missions monitor UN activities, reach out to UN bureaucrats, and organize formal OIC-UN cooperative efforts. Second, the OIC has launched biennial coordination meetings to foster cooperation between the two organizations on a range of issues, from food security to conflict resolution and from environment to education.[4] Third, the specialized agencies and subsidiary organs of both the OIC and the UN have expanded their collaborative efforts. OIC leaders have claimed that the IPHRC, for instance, was created with an eye toward cooperation with UN human rights organs. As Mencütek elaborates in Chapter 11, the OIC and UNHCR have been cooperating since the 1980s; Azhar further elaborates on the cooperation between the OIC's PSMU and the UN's MSU. Fourth, since 1983, the OIC has held its ICFM annual coordination meetings alongside UN meetings in New York. In these meetings, OIC members work to develop a common stance on UN agenda items. They also determine who they will support for various UN positions.

The OIC has ultimately been successful in creating and sustaining a powerful UN voting bloc on certain issues, namely the Palestinian cause and the defamation of religions agenda. While the organization's membership size provides it with a strong base at the UN, the fact that the OIC is a cross-regional organization with members in four continents means that its geographical extent further amplifies its potential influence. This is because regional and bloc politics often shape the debates and voting at various UN agencies, as well as the HRC. The OIC shares a large number of states with the UN's African and Asian Groups, which allows the OIC to lobby and mobilize these UN groups for OIC causes (Freedman 2013:124). For example, the African Group and the Asian Group each have thirteen states, which are seated at the HRC. Even though some of these are not part of the OIC, OIC members establish a critical mass and sometimes chair these regional groups. OIC states can thus influence their regional neighbors to vote in line with the OIC position, especially on issues that are not of great concern to other Asian and African states. These twenty-six votes amount to a majority of the

HRC's forty-seven votes, making the OIC, in the words of human rights scholar Rosa Freedman, "the dominant group at the Council" (126).

Buoyed by its numerical advantage and regional allies in the HRC, the OIC uses group voting to shield its members from criticism while maintaining a dual focus on issues related to Israel and Palestine (Freedman 2013:128) and its decade-long attempt to combat and criminalize defamation of religions (Kayaoglu 2014a). Overall, the OIC counters Western liberal states in the council by rejecting country-specific resolutions. Two notable exceptions to this are resolutions concerning Israel, which the OIC views as thematic because of its occupation, and resolutions concerning countries that have attracted international opprobrium for their conduct toward a Muslim minority population within their borders, such as Myanmar. On the general subject of country-specific resolutions, the OIC argues that the council should work with those states that violate human rights to help them improve their human rights records, rather than naming and shaming member states that are violating human rights. The organization also advocates for conservative positions on issues such as gender rights, LGBT rights, free speech restrictions, and the noninterference in domestic affairs on the part of the HRC. To this end, the OIC often collaborates with Christian rights groups as well as the Vatican to counter progressive agendas in the council (Bob 2012:37; Chase 2012:160). As discussed by El Fegiery in Chapter 6, the OIC has been working with Russia to advance a traditional values agenda in the UN.

Although the OIC's numerical advantage and its ability to mobilize other states have given it significant leverage in some UN forums, especially in the UN General Assembly and at the HRC, the OIC has not been able to wield much influence in the Security Council (UNSC). The OIC's limited influence at the UNSC stems both from permanent members with veto powers and the American willingness to use its veto to shield Israel from official UNSC criticism. Gradually, however, the OIC has strengthened its collaboration with the UNSC. In October 2013, the UNSC unanimously adopted a "presidential statement" calling for strengthening its partnership with the OIC on issues related to international peace and security. OIC and UN leaders seem to agree that the OIC's unique faith-based identity, its ability to access groups and localities that the UN has difficulty reaching, and its expertise in the Muslim world equip the OIC with a soft power (UN Security Council 2013). Despite its limited resources, the OIC continues to work to complement the UN on issues such as mediation, conflict-resolution, and peacekeeping efforts, and addressing refugee problems (see Chapters 6 and 11 for further discussions).

The Non-Aligned Movement

The OIC and the Non-Aligned Movement (NAM) share strong ties due to the fact that many OIC members are also NAM members. Of the OIC's fifty-seven members, fifty-one are among NAM's 120 members—OIC states thus comprise about 40 percent of NAM's total members. NAM's strong anti-imperialist stance gives the OIC a natural platform from which to mobilize an international partner in order to advance its pro-Palestinian agenda and decry American intervention in the Muslim world. Beginning in the late 1990s, NAM supported the OIC's campaign highlighting the reluctance of Western states to address the rise of Islamophobia. Further, the OIC has successfully inserted Islamophobia as a form of racism worthy of attention in NAM discourse and resolutions. For its part, the OIC has consistently supported NAM's challenge to industrialized countries' stance on issues including globalization, free trade, and the dominance of Western media in the global public sphere.

The African Union

There are also strong ties between the OIC and the African Union (AU), due to overlapping member states in both groups and a degree of ideological similarity between the groups of member states in each organization. In fact, twenty-seven of the fifty-four AU member states are also OIC members. The OIC and the AU have long supported each other as allies on international issues and within international organizations. The OIC and the AU share an anticolonial and anti-imperialist perspective. The OIC supported the anti-apartheid campaign led by the Organization of African Unity (the predecessor to the AU). Further, the AU has consistently supported the OIC's position on the Palestinian cause. When African issues related to non-OIC members are raised in international organizations, the OIC often follows the lead of the AU (Khan 2001:177). In situations where a dispute arises between two OIC members that are also AU members, the OIC often defers to the AU for conflict resolution—a sign of trust and also of general deference to regional organizations on matters of conflict resolution. For example, the OIC supported the AU's peacekeeping forces in Darfur and Somalia (Freedman 2013:128).

The AU and the OIC often act in solidarity in the UN, particularly in the HRC, in order to shield their members from official criticism, condemnation, and interference. For example, in the HRC discussions about Darfur, the OIC and the AU collaborated to protect Sudan (Freedman 2013:299). When the International Criminal Court indicted Sudanese President Omar Bashir for the crimes of genocide, war crimes, and crimes against humanity, the OIC and the AU together condemned the indictment.

The League of Arab States, the Gulf Cooperation Council, and the Arab Maghreb Union

All twenty-two members of the League of Arab States (LAS), all six members of the Gulf Cooperation Council (GCC), and all five members of the Arab Maghreb Union (AMU) are also OIC members. Oftentimes, the OIC and these organizations have very similar aims in international affairs and cooperate closely with each other on regional and international issues. Occasionally, however, the OIC experiences internal friction between Arab and non-Arab members. For example, during the Iran-Iraq war, an Arab member of the OIC, Iraq, fought a non-Arab member of the OIC, Iran. In this case, the LAS acted within the OIC to advance Arab states' interests in condemning Iran.

The most influential among the three organizations is the LAS. The leadership of the OIC and the LAS meet regularly to develop a common stance on regional and global issues. Representatives from each organization regularly attend meetings of the other organization and also hold their own coordination meetings. The OIC ultimately trusts the LAS enough that it has endorsed the league's Arab Peace Initiative in response to the Israeli-Palestinian conflict, rather than developing its own initiative.

The European Union

Unlike other international organizations, such as NAM, the UN, the LAS, and ASEAN, which share some common members with the OIC, the OIC and the EU do not share any member states. But geographical proximity, past interactions, economic ties, and the presence of an estimated 20 million Muslims in the EU have pulled the EU and the OIC closer (Nielsen 2013). Additionally, Turkey has been an EU candidate country since 1999. EU leaders see the OIC as an actor in the EU's Euro-Mediterranean Partnership program, which aims to promote EU economic integration with non-EU Mediterranean states and to foster democratic reforms, human rights, and good governance in the region.

In spite of these connections, however, the OIC and the EU have developed few institutional ties. In 2013, the OIC took the initiative to institutionalize ties: It opened a permanent observer mission to the EU in Brussels. Working with the European Parliament and the European Council, the OIC mission in Brussels will, in the words of former OIC Secretary-General İhsanoğlu, "fight against Islamophobia to further strengthen ties between the Islamic world and Europe" through interfaith and intercultural dialogue (*Hürriyet* 2013). This mission, however, will likely remain a symbolic diplomatic presence rather than an effective lobbying body due to limited resources. As of the writing of this chapter, the mission lacks a website and looks all but dormant.

Additionally, the OIC has attempted to pursue a more activist agenda regarding the protection of human rights for Muslims in Europe. It has sought to raise its profile throughout Europe, by asserting its claim to speak on behalf of Muslim minorities as well as its member states (Kayaoglu 2011, 2014a) at a time when many European countries struggle with issues related to the rising Islamophobia, Islamic symbols in the public sphere, and the human rights of Muslim minorities (Kayaoglu 2014b).

Indeed, the OIC partnerships with the EU will not be easy. The rise of Islamophobia in Europe and the OIC's commitment to restrict free speech as a way to combat Islamophobia have the potential to sour the OIC-EU relationship. The EU countries were the main target of the OIC's campaign to establish an international norm requiring states to combat the defamation of religions. The EU collectively and many of its members individually have vigorously countered the OIC's anti-defamation campaign at the UN (Kayaoglu 2014a; Chapters 4 and 5, this volume). The EU would not accept the OIC's claim of being a representative—let alone the sole representative—of all Muslims, including Muslims in Europe. Finally, the rift between the EU and the OIC at the HRC on issues such as gender rights, LGBT rights, religious freedom, and blasphemy laws is likely to continue to feed the EU's perception of the OIC as a conservative and reactionary organization.

Yet some signs point to the possibility that the EU and the OIC could bridge the gap and work together to address some thorny issues. One such example is UNHCR Resolution 16/18 concerning combating religious intolerance. The EU hosted a conference for the implementation process for the resolution, yet disagreements on key issues, such as the threshold for the criminalization of the incitement of religious hatred, still remain.

Conclusion

The OIC's human rights activities—its legal instruments, organs, and collaborations with other international organizations—amount to a human rights regime. Although this regime is weak, incomplete, and eclectic, a collective Islamic identity and discourse, a deference to state sovereignty, and the OIC's internal and external activities give the regime a level of coherence and visibility and hope for the future (see Chapter 2).

The Independent Permanent Human Rights Commission is—at least in principle—the OIC's main human rights body. The IPHRC has raised expectations regarding the OIC's willingness to be a reliable partner to advance international human rights even though it lacks the monitoring and enforcement authority enjoyed by other regional human rights bodies. However, five years after its establishment, the IPHRC assumed a conservative and defensive stance on human rights, rather than a progressive and proactive one.

In addition to the IPHRC, the OIC has several other agencies whose work deals with aspects of human rights. While these agencies have a narrower focus and are thus better positioned to have targeted influence, they are underfunded and understaffed. Apart from the Department of Muslim Minorities and Communities, these agencies will require significant capacity-building before they are able to have any discernible impact.

However, the most visible human rights work done by the OIC is not in the streets of its member states but in the corridors of international organizations. The OIC's fifty-seven member states provide it with significant voting power that allows the OIC to punch above its weight in the UN and other organizations. Working within organizations such as the African Union and G-77, the OIC is able to present a formidable voting bloc to advance its human rights agendas, protect its member states, and oppose Western liberal progressive human rights agendas in the UN.

Notes

1. OIC's Independent Permanent Human Rights Commission's webpage can be found at https://www.oic-iphrc.org/en/home. The relevant documents, including IPHRC's statute can be found at https://www.oic-iphrc.org/en/oic-human-rights-RI&T.

2. OIC's Islamophobia Observatory can be found at http://www.oic-oci.org/page/?p_id=182&p_ref=61&lan=en.

3. "Resolutions on Muslim Communities and Minorities in Non-OIC Member States." Adopted by the 11th Session of the Islamic Summit Conference, Dakar, Senegal. https://www.oic-oci.org/docdown/?docID=36&refID=9.

4. "Strengthening the Partnership Synergy Between the UN and the OIC." October 3, 2013. http://undocs.org/S/2013/588.

Works Cited

Bob, Clifford. 2012. *The Global Right Wing and the Clash of World Politics*. Cambridge: Cambridge University Press.

Chase, Anthony T. 2012. *Human Rights, Revolution, and Reform in the Muslim World*. Boulder, CO: Lynne Rienner.

Cismas, Ioana. 2014. *Religious Actors and International Law*. Oxford: Oxford University Press.

Donnelly, Jack. 1986. "International Human Rights: A Regime Analysis." *International Organization* 40 (3): 599–642.

———. 2003. *Universal Human Rights in Theory and Practice*. 2nd ed. Ithaca, NY: Cornell University Press.

———. 2013. *International Human Rights*. 4th ed. Boulder, CO: Westview.

Forsythe, David P. 2000. *Human Rights in International Relations*. Cambridge: Cambridge University Press.

Freedman, Rosa. 2013. *The United Nations Human Rights Council: A Critique and Early Assessment*. London: Routledge.

Hürriyet Daily News. 2013. "OIC Launches Europe Mission in Brussels." June 26, 2013. http://www.hurriyetdailynews.com/Default.aspx?pageID=238&nid=49469.

İhsanoğlu, Ekmeleddin. 2010. *The Islamic World in the New Century: The Organization of Islamic Conference*. London: Hurst.

IPHRC. 2016. "Composition." http://www.oic-iphrc.org/en/about.

Karčić, Hamza. 2013. "In Support of a Non-member State: The Organisation of Islamic Conference and the War in Bosnia, 1992–1995." *Journal of Muslim Minority Affairs* 33 (3): 321–40.

Kayaoglu, Turan. 2011. "Islamophobia, Defamation of Religions, and International Human Rights." In *Human Rights in the Middle East: Frameworks, Goals, and Strategies*, ed. Mahmood Monshipouri, 73–89. New York: Palgrave-Macmillan.

———. 2013. "A Rights Agenda for the Muslim World? The Organization of Islamic Cooperation's Evolving Human Rights Framework." Brookings Doha Center Analysis Paper. Doha: The Brookings Institution.

———. 2014a. "Giving an Inch only to Lose a Mile: Muslim States, Liberalism, and Human Rights in the United Nations." *Human Rights Quarterly* 36 (1): 61–89.

———. 2014b. "Trying Islam: Muslims Before the European Court of Human Rights." *Journal of Muslim Minority Affairs* 34 (4): 345–64.

———. 2015a. "The OIC's Independent Permanent Human Rights Commission: An Early Assessment." *Matters of Concern* series working paper. Copenhagen: Danish Institute of Human Rights. https://www.humanrights.dk/publications/oics-independent-permanent-human-rights-commission-early-assessment.

———. 2015b. *The Organization of Islamic Cooperation: Politics, Problems, and Potential.* London: Routledge.

Khan, Saad. 2001. *Reasserting International Islam: A Focus on the Organization of the Islamic Conference and Other Islamic Institutions.* London: Oxford University Press.

Krasner, Stephan, ed. 1983. *International Regimes.* Ithaca, NY: Cornell University Press.

Nielsen, Jørgen S. 2013. "The New Muslim Europe." In *Islam in the Modern World*, ed. Jeffrey T. Kenney and Ebrahim Moosa, 335–50. London: Routledge.

Petersen, Marie Juul. 2012. *Islamic or Universal Human Rights: The OIC's Independent Permanent Human Rights Commission.* DIIS report. Copenhagen: Danish Institute for International Studies.

Risse-Kappen, Thomas, Stephen C. Ropp, and Kathryn Sikkink, eds. 1999. *The Power of Human Rights: International Norms and Domestic Change.* Cambridge: Cambridge University Press.

Samuel, Katja L. 2014. *The OIC, the UN, and Counter-Terrorism Law-Making: Conflicting or Cooperative Legal Orders?* London: Hart.

Steiner, Henry J., Philip Alston, and Ryan Goodman. 2008. *International Human Rights in Context: Law, Politics, Morals.* Oxford: Oxford University Press.

UN Security Council. 2013. "Security Council Advocates Greater Ties with Organization of Islamic Cooperation to Resolve Conflict in Middle East, Other Strife-Torn Regions." October 28. Available at http://www.un.org/News/Press/docs/2013/sc11161.doc.htm.

PART II

INTERVENTIONS: RIGHTS AND VALUES

CHAPTER 4

The OIC's Human Rights Policies in the UN: A Problem of Coherence

Ann Elizabeth Mayer

Introduction

Over the last few decades the Organization of Islamic Cooperation (OIC) has asserted confused positions in discussions of human rights in international forums. Chapters 1 and 5 in this volume provide background for the following assessment, which examines how the OIC has failed to enunciate and follow a coherent philosophy on the role that Islamic law should play in defining human rights rules affecting freedom of expression. The incoherence in the OIC's statements flows from its efforts to inject incongruous Islamic qualifications into international human rights law while seeking to convince the world that it adheres to the UN human rights system—where it aspires to play a powerful role.

As this chapter demonstrates, where the human right to freedom of expression is concerned, the OIC displays deep ambivalence, sometimes professing to adhere to the UN system of international human rights law, a secular law, and at other times speaking as if it were applying Islamic law. It also wavers between claiming that international human rights law is unacceptably Western and indicating that it merely wants to see that law fine-tuned in some areas. While advocating inserting distinctive Islamic rules that clash dramatically with the values of the UN human rights system, it claims to be trying to advance secular goals including fighting Islamophobia and deterring the hate speech prohibited in the International Covenant on Civil and Political Rights (ICCPR).

The OIC deploys human rights rhetoric in a highly politicized manner, harshly attacking the treatment of Islam and Muslims in the West while mostly disregarding the egregious violations of religious freedom occurring on the territories of OIC members. Admittedly, employing double standards is hardly peculiar to the OIC. One might, for example, cite the striking inconsistences in the way the United States treats human rights abuses in allied states versus those that occur in states with which it has sour relations. Nonetheless, the OIC's level of inconsequence stands out.

This chapter examines aspects of the OIC's human rights record at the UN, facets of the 1990 Cairo Declaration on Human Rights in Islam, and UN Human Rights Council resolutions sponsored by the OIC starting in 1999 calling for combating defamation of religions along with the contrasting resolutions that the OIC began sponsoring in 2011, the first in the series being the Human Rights Council Resolution 16/18 on "combating intolerance, negative stereotyping and stigmatization of, and discrimination, incitement to violence and violence against, persons based on religion or belief."[1] Statements by the OIC Secretaries-General Ekmeleddin İhsanoğlu, who headed the organization from 2004–2014 and acted as the OIC's point man on human rights issues, and his immediate successor, Iyad Ameen Madani, will be covered, as will some positions taken by the OIC Independent Permanent Human Rights Commission (IPHRC), which was established in 2011.

The OIC—A State-Based Organization Asserting an Unexplained Religious Mandate

A baffling aspect of the OIC's varying stances on human rights is the lack of explanation as to why they uphold Islamic doctrine at the expense of international law. It should be noted that the word "Islamic" in the OIC's name does not signal that the organization is a religious entity but refers instead to the demographic profiles of its member states; as one reads in Article 3(2) of the OIC's 2008 charter, member states are to have Muslim majorities. Neither of its two charters assigns it any religious function. The repeated references to "Member States" in its 1974 charter underline its character as a state-centered entity. Far from prioritizing Islamic law over conflicting rules of international law, the preamble affirms that the OIC was committed to "the UN Charter and fundamental Human Rights" (Moinuddin 1987:187–88). Occasional Islamic references in the 1974 charter appear, such as calls for preserving "Islamic spiritual, ethical, social and economic values" in the preamble, promoting "Islamic solidarity among member states" in Article II/A/1, and safeguarding "the Holy Places" in Article II/A/5. These merely amounted to statements of programmatic goals; they did not make the entity itself religious. The preamble to the significantly revised 2008 charter reaffirms that the OIC aims "to uphold the objectives and principles of the present Charter, the Charter of the United Nations and international law."[2]

The OIC's terminology shifts in its revised 2008 charter, where the original commitment to UN human rights is altered, with the OIC pledging "to uphold the objectives and principles of the present Charter, the Charter of the United Nations and international law as well as international humanitarian law while strictly adhering to the principle of non-interference in matters which are essentially within the domestic jurisdiction of any State."[3] In a significant omission, the original phrase "the UN Charter and fundamental Human Rights" was dropped, with the replacement, "humanitarian law," being distinct from human rights law. Highlighting noninterference in matters falling within the domestic jurisdiction of states implies a repudiation of a basic principle of international human rights law, which entitles observers to pierce the veil of state sovereignty to assess whether violations of international human rights law are occurring. The 2008 charter also calls for the OIC "to promote human rights and fundamental freedoms, good governance, rule of law, democracy and accountability in Member States in accordance with their constitutional and legal systems." In context, inserting the qualification "in accordance with their constitutional and legal systems" means that international human rights law will be overridden by the application of OIC members' domestic standards, which frequently include rules taken from Islamic law.

Although the 2008 charter, like its predecessor, gave no indication that the OIC was entitled to determine Islamic doctrine, it did state in the preamble and in Article 1(11) that the OIC would promote Islamic values, and in Article 1(12) offered a new pledge "to protect and defend the true image of Islam, to combat defamation of Islam."[4] The pledge correlated with wording in UN resolutions proposed by the OIC starting in 1999, which proposed that international law should incorporate a duty to criminalize "defamation of Islam."

Manifesting an incongruous presumption to be able to rule on religious questions, in 1989 the OIC publicly condemned Salman Rushdie's novel *The Satanic Verses* as blasphemy and classed him as an apostate from Islam.

Although not expressly endorsing the death edict that Iran's clerical leader Ayatollah Khomeini had issued shortly before, the OIC failed on this occasion—and on others as well—to criticize Iran for calling for the assassinations of Rushdie and others associated with the publication of his novel. Underlying the OIC's denunciation of Rushdie was a theory that Islamic criminal law governed expression by British citizens living in Britain. As it often did, the OIC disregarded relevant aspects of international law, acting as if Islamic rules on blasphemy determined the legality of expression in the West.

Over time, the OIC's way of characterizing its position evolved. After manifesting its conviction that Westerners should be penalized when they failed to adhere to Islamic censorship rules, it later tried to convince the international community that it was merely calling for punishing incidents of hate speech, hate speech being prohibited by Article 20(2) of the ICCPR. Of course, this entailed reading the ICCPR as supporting the OIC position that insults to Islam had to be prohibited. If one accepted the OIC's view, since international human rights law was binding on all UN members, Western democracies could be castigated for their noncompliance when they allowed Rushdie to go unpunished after insulting Islam.

In 1990, shortly after its intervention in the Rushdie Affair, in the period between the issuance of its two charters, the OIC chose to set forth the Cairo Declaration on Human Rights in Islam, purporting to embody Islamic teachings. Adopted at a meeting of OIC foreign ministers, the declaration significantly reduced the menu of civil and political rights afforded in secular UN human rights instruments and upheld the supremacy of Islamic principles over human rights. Left unexplained was on what basis the OIC could justify this move when its own foundational documents required it to adhere to the UN charter and international law. Also left unexplained was on what grounds the OIC had concluded that the principles contained in the Cairo Declaration amounted to a definitive Islamic doctrine on rights. In Islamic law, it is crucial to demonstrate how principles are derived from the Islamic sources, but the OIC offered no references to relevant works by any learned and respected Islamic jurists, nor any specification of the methodology that had been employed to mine the Islamic sources for guidance. From the information that the OIC has chosen to release, it seems that the Cairo Declaration emerged from a consensus by foreign ministers representing OIC member states. That is, in making this document on Islamic human rights, the OIC imitated the voting methods employed by the UN General Assembly in approving the 1948 Universal Declaration of Human Rights, which expressed the consensus of UN member states on human rights. Producing a UN declaration that rests on the consensus of states makes sense, but it is highly problematic for any group of nation states to claim that their consensus can determine religious doctrines on human rights or any other subject. Moreover, OIC Secretary-General İhsanoğlu, the OIC's main spokesperson on human rights, in a 2013 interview affirmed that the OIC was not a religious institution (*Al Jazeera* 2013). That is, İhsanoğlu did not pretend that the OIC possessed a status akin to that of the Vatican, which can speak both as the supreme religious authority on Catholicism and as a UN permanent observer.

Although the OIC has in superficial ways adjusted to working within the UN system of international human rights law, in practice it frequently acts more like an advocacy organization that serves the interests of a particular religion or religious community. It resembles in this regard organizations that operate outside the UN system such as the Catholic League for Religious and Civil Rights, which has the mission of fighting anti-Catholic discrimination and defamation but, unlike the OIC, does not claim to be part of the UN human rights system.

A comparison can illustrate the problematic nature of the OIC's presumption to enunciate Islamic doctrine on human rights. Consider what would happen if another state-centric entity attempted to promulgate religious rules to curb the rights afforded in international human rights law. What if the Organization of American States (OAS) claimed the right to set forth the definitive Christian teachings on human rights, promulgating a set of principles that clashed with international human rights law? Even though the majority of the people in OAS member states are Christian, any assertion by the OAS of supreme authority in matters of Christian doctrine would be rejected. Thus, if the OAS decreed, say, that the right to marry and divorce as guaranteed in international law had to be restricted by relevant Christian doctrines or that freedom of expression had to be curbed in order to protect Christian sanctities, such a presumption would be scoffed at. Observers would readily concur that the OAS lacked any basis to enunciate Christian doctrines, let alone doctrines at odds with human rights.

One needs to stress that the OIC could not rely on settled Islamic teachings in promulgating its stances on human rights. Like Christianity, Islam today is riven by deep sectarian splits and ideological cleavages. Moreover, the various domestic laws affecting human rights endorsed by OIC member states diverge widely. Thus, the OIC was far from engaged in restating an Islamic consensus on human rights.

"Islamic" Human Rights in Opposition to "Western" Human Rights

OIC members did not in practice implement the Cairo Declaration, merely treating it as a tool to be used when expedient. It was of use in the 1990s when they were collaborating with other undemocratic states including China, which asserted that the imperative to uphold "Asian values" justified deviating from international human rights law. Thus, the OIC's appeals to Islam were of a piece with the way many states were invoking supposed cultural particularisms at UN human rights forums to excuse their bad human rights records. Of course, attributing their estrangement from human rights to "cultural" differences amounts to a gross oversimplification; lurking under such "cultural" rationales analysts could identify a variety of other reasons for appeals to "Asian values" (Engle 2000). Among other things, OIC members welcomed having a separate set of "Islamic" human rights to which they could appeal in the face of Western critiques of their human rights violations.

While joining with states invoking "Asian values," the OIC seemed to want to have its own Cairo Declaration—an embodiment of cultural particularism in the human rights domain—treated as a respectable human rights instrument. As a result of OIC pressures, the Cairo Declaration became included in the UN documents issuing from the 1993 World Conference on Human Rights in Vienna (Office of the High Commissioner for Human Rights 1997:475–76). This recognition implied that the Cairo Declaration was a legitimate Islamic alternative to documents such as the ICCPR.

Indicating its continued viability, in 2014 OIC Secretary-General Madani endorsed the Cairo Declaration as "the OIC's most complete statement on human rights in Islam" (Shaikh 2014). He deprecated international human rights laws, claiming that they were based on Western values and presented "a number of issues that go beyond the normal scope of human rights and clash with Islamic teachings" (ibid.). Among other things, on the matter of limitations on freedom of expression and gender equality, Madani reaffirmed that OIC member states would uphold domestic standards using their own constitutional and legal systems (ibid.). He underlined his conviction that the OIC's Islamic human rights were to be viewed as normative, proposing that what was needed was "a yardstick that each individual member state can look at to measure the distance between the Islamic human rights model and its own laws and practices" (ibid.).

The OIC's Attempts to Inject Islamic Censorship Criteria into International Law

In a peculiar twist, after producing an alternative Islamic human rights declaration, the OIC decided to launch a campaign to insert its Islam-based limitations on freedom of expression into international law, a campaign that is reviewed in Chapter 5. The campaign reflected Article 22 of the Cairo Declaration, which imposes Sharia-based limits on freedom of expression and prohibits "information" that violates "sanctities and the dignity of prophets":

> Article 22:
>
> (a) Everyone shall have the right to express his opinion freely in such manner as would not be contrary to the principles of the Shari'ah.
>
> (c) Information is a vital necessity to society. It may not be exploited or misused in such a way as may violate sanctities and the dignity of Prophets, undermine moral and ethical values or disintegrate, corrupt or harm society or weaken its faith.[5]

Such religious restrictions on freedom of expression clash starkly with the ICCPR. The UN Human Rights Committee warned in 2011 that the ICCPR does not accommodate prohibitions of blasphemy in General Comment 34 on the ICCPR: "Blasphemy laws are incompatible with the International Covenant on Civil and Political Rights."[6]

In 1999 the OIC began sponsoring UN resolutions that called for international law to criminalize what it initially called "defamation of Islam." Terms like "blasphemy" or "sacrilege" would have seemed more apposite than "defamation" for incidents where the OIC was complaining of insults to Islamic sanctities. The term "defamation" was likely preferred because more accurate terms like "blasphemy" were too obviously tied to religious doctrines, which would have gotten in the way of OIC efforts to persuade the UN that its Islamic censorship rules belonged as part of international human rights law. International human rights law does encompass prohibitions of conduct such as group defamation and defamation that violates the right to reputation, so the term "defamation" could be linked to existing, secular UN terminology. Although the OIC treated defamation of Islam as a criminal offense, it never bothered to define the term with any precision. The OIC treated it as a rubric with an amorphous, malleable character and applied it to very dissimilar acts.

Struggling to persuade skeptical UN members that its resolutions belonged in the UN system, over the years the OIC diluted their specifically Islamic character, often using wording like defamation of "religions," even though Islam remained the preoccupation, and adding numerous references to principles in the UN human rights system. The wording in the various resolutions varies, but by picking any of the later resolutions in the series, one gets a general sense of how the OIC portrayed bans on insults to religion as serving the goals of the international human rights system. The 2007 Human Rights Council Resolution 4/9 *Combating Defamation of Religions* is offered as an example, using numerical designations of the paragraphs in the preamble language, which are unnumbered in the original.[7]

The resolution repeatedly cites mainstream human rights principles, such as invoking freedom of religion and belief (para. 8), a principle that was deliberately eliminated from the Cairo Declaration and that OIC members routinely violate without the OIC taking them to task. Religious censorship is treated as a positive measure, and the resolution asserts that defamation of all religions (not merely Islam) causes problems of racism and xenophobia (para. 7) and human rights violations (para. 9). Article 4 claims that religious defamation serves as "an aggravating factor that contributes to the denial of fundamental rights and freedoms of target groups, as well as their economic and social exclusion."

The language shifts back and forth from concerns about defamation of religions generally to specific references to attacks on Islam and discrimination against Muslims (e.g., paras. 4, 5, 6, and 10). It includes calls for respect for different religions and beliefs (Article 9) and deplores the use of the media to incite acts of violence, xenophobia, or related intolerance and discrimination toward Islam or any other religion (Article 11). In a pattern commonly found in the OIC resolutions, Resolution 4/9 posits a link between discrimination and intolerance affecting Muslims and Arabs and broader human rights problems of racism, racial discrimination, xenophobia, and related intolerance (e.g., para. 6). Islam remains, however, the main concern: a complaint is made that "religions, and Islam and Muslims in particular," are increasingly being attacked in human rights forums (para. 10). In the aftermath of the 9/11 attacks, the problems of defamation of religions and profiling of Muslim minorities are said to be increasing (Article 3), and measures that monitor Muslims and Arabs and legitimize discrimination are mentioned (see Articles 3, 5)—with the implication that these problems are concentrated in the West, where since the 9/11 attacks Muslim minorities are often stigmatized as potential terrorists.

Significantly, the 2007 resolution seeks to square the religious censorship that it envisages with Articles 19 and 20 of the ICCPR on freedom of expression. Article 7 of the resolution cites ICCPR's Article 20(2)—but only with a major modification. The original prohibits hate speech, providing "any advocacy of national, racial or religious hatred that constitutes incitement to discrimination, hostility or violence shall be prohibited by law." To that secular language the OIC resolution adds wording that calls for prohibiting "material aimed at any religion or its followers." The additional phrase vastly widens the grounds for censorship; the original ICCPR wording does not shield religions.

Article 19(3) of the ICCPR limits restrictions on freedom of expression to what is necessary for "respect of the rights or reputations of others" as well as for "protection of national security or of public order (*ordre public*), or of public health or morals." To this original ICCPR formulation the OIC resolution in Article 10 adds wording permitting curbs on freedom of expression necessary for "respect for religions and beliefs," thereby changing the ICCPR provision by adding major new constraints aimed at protecting religion and beliefs from insults.

Resolution 4/9 *Combating Defamation of Religions* embodies the OIC's thesis that religious censorship advances the cause of human rights. In reality, evidence on the ground proves that imposing the kind of Islamic censorship that the OIC favors correlates with patterns of egregious human rights violations. The link between blasphemy laws and patterns of human rights violations has been studied by, among others, the NGO Human Rights *First*, which has published an account focused mostly on OIC countries (Human Rights *First* 2012). In OIC states, accusations of religious offenses including blasphemy and apostasy are deployed by religious establishments, governmental institutions, demagogues, religious zealots, and politicians in ways that inflame religious antagonisms and have particularly harsh consequences for dissident intellectuals, members of the political opposition, critics of governmental religious policies, and vulnerable or unpopular religious communities. The harmful consequences that come from blasphemy laws have been documented in many human rights reports, including the annual U.S. International Religious Freedom Reports.[8]

How eventually the OIC came to abandon its campaign to insert bans on defamation of religions into international human rights law is detailed in Chapter 5. After facing defeats in the UN, in 2011 the OIC sought to recharacterize its position, trying to convey the impression that it was not calling for protecting religion from aspersions but was aiming to protect believers from human rights violations that flowed from insults to their religions. The OIC frequently stumbled, however, inadvertently revealing that it was still trying to make international law serve as a vehicle for criminalizing acts of blasphemy regardless of whether any significant setbacks for human rights resulted.

The Danish Cartoons and Islamophobia

As had happened with the fury over Rushdie's novel, the fury over the Danish cartoons was deliberately inflamed by certain Muslim agitators bent on stirring up outrage over alleged Western insults to Islam. In both cases the original publications were misrepresented; malign motives and anti-Islamic animus were reflexively attributed to the authors with a view to provoking indignation.

The controversy erupted after cartoon depictions of the Prophet Muhammad were published in September 2005 in *Jyllands-Posten*, an obscure Danish-language newspaper with a circulation of about 120,000. The cartoon that was later singled out as most outrageous was a drawing by Kurt Westergaard of the Prophet with a bomb poking out of his black turban. The announced objective of the newspaper in publishing the cartoons was resisting mounting pressures for self-censorship in order to avoid offending Muslims, pushing back against pressures for Danes in Denmark to abide by Islamic criminal law. The paper indicated that it wanted to break with the political correctness that did not allow treating Muslims like any other religious group (Klausen 2009:15). Of course, because there was a simultaneous wave of strong anti-immigrant sentiment in Denmark and because the newspaper was widely seen as belonging to the political right wing (traditionally critical of immigration), many interpreted the cartoons as expressing xenophobia and hostility to Muslims.

Imposing Islamic censorship seems natural in the setting of OIC member states, but in Europe it seemed incongruous. As an EU study has documented, European laws are overwhelmingly secularized, and the occasional blasphemy laws that remain on the books are rarely used (Directorate-General for Internal Policies of the Union 2015:85–107). In this context, the Danish cartoonists not surprisingly reacted against what they found an absurd situation, one where the result of the protracted process of European secularization had left Europeans free to express negative and scornful views about Jesus Christ and Christianity, Europe's dominant religion, but where they were admonished to abstain from any expression that would be blasphemous by Islamic definitions.

While most Danish Muslims protested the cartoons through peaceful demonstrations and debates in the Danish media, a small number launched a campaign to incite international protests, internationally disseminating the very cartoons that they claimed should have been suppressed (Klausen 2009:86–89). A delegation traveled to Egypt, Lebanon, and Syria with a view to inciting protests against Denmark (89). Significantly, the dossier that was distributed included pictures that were far more inflammatory than the original set of cartoons published by *Jyllands-Posten*. For example, an image from a French pig-squealing contest was included as if it had figured among the cartoons, creating the false impression that the Prophet had been depicted as a pig (Klausen 2009:91). Various Middle Eastern governments exploited the occasion, seeking to whip up popular outrage and inflame anti-Western resentments and in the process to divert attention from their own domestic problems. As demagogues worked to exacerbate tensions, aggrieved Muslims called for boycotting Danish products and some even for killing the cartoonists—thereby providing ammunition for right-wing Islamophobic demagogues in Europe who sought to portray Muslims as violent and dangerous. Threatened with assassination, Kurt Westergaard had to live under guard and was nearly killed when an armed Muslim terrorist broke into his home in 2010. Instead of trying calm matters or to promote dialogue, the OIC worked to mobilize worldwide Muslim outrage over the cartoons (Klausen 2009:39).

Secretary-General İhsanoğlu protested when the OIC's demands for punishing the cartoonists were rejected by the Danish government. Indicating the kind of harsh censorship regime that he expected Denmark to adopt and rejecting the idea that independent courts should protect human rights, he denounced a Danish court ruling upholding freedom of the press, also condemning European support for Denmark:

> We expected from the European Governments . . . to take a political and ethical stand against uncivilized transgressions in the name of freedom of expression. To our dismay, what we found in return was an official common European position in support of the stance of the Danish government who refrained for a long time to take any political or ethical responsibility on the grounds that the laws of the country guarantee the freedom of the press and that there is no government authority or responsibility over this matter as it is completely up to the court to determine if what was published was within the boundaries of law or not. (İhsanoğlu 2013)

In January 2006 the OIC espoused the cause of the Muslims condemning the Danish cartoons at the UN and asked for a binding resolution "banning contempt for religious beliefs and providing for sanctions to be imposed on contravening countries or institutions" (Abdul Ghafour and Tago 2006). As the wording indicates, this OIC campaign had the goal of prohibiting insults to religious beliefs, not protecting individual Muslims' human rights.

Pivoting to a stance that could—at least superficially—be reconciled with the philosophy of human rights, in an interview with *Jyllands-Posten* in October 2008, İhsanoğlu changed the nature of his complaint. With disregard for the internal logic of his statements, he asserted that his objections to the cartoons were not at all religiously based but concerned instead the cartoonists' violation of the ICCPR ban on hate speech in Article 20(2). He offered no evidence whatsoever to support the notion that the Danish cartoonists had violated Article 20(2) of the ICCPR by deliberately engaging in advocacy of religious hatred with an aim of inciting discrimination, hostility, or violence and ignored the fact that they were asserting a right to exercise the freedom of expression under applicable Danish law. He deliberately avoided dealing with the role that the OIC had played in inflaming religious antagonisms and did not concede that the destructive conflicts that followed had resulted from a controversy that was quite deliberately ginned up by the machinations of Muslim politicians and demagogues whose attacks on everything Danish were designed to incite outrage and provoke retaliation.

In the same 2008 interview, İhsanoğlu incongruously protested that curbing freedom of expression was not at all the OIC's objective, insisting that the OIC's sole concern was deterring hate speech—as opposed to punishing insults to Islam—and speaking as if the OIC's complaint was that the cartoonists had been intentionally sowing hatred against Muslims:

> I am quite surprised to see in the Danish press insinuations that I or the OIC are opponents of freedom of expression who are endeavoring to stifle this freedom by calling for banning of criticism of religions. Everybody is entitled to criticize anybody or anything. . . . We have no problem whatsoever with this. However, when freedom of expression is abused to ridicule and demonize with the intention to sow seeds of hatred against a group of peoples or citizens, then problems start because the rights of the victims of this incitement comes to the fore. (OIC 2008)

Having charged Denmark with violating secular human rights law in failing to punish the cartoonists and *Jyllands-Posten*, he claimed that, in contrast to Denmark, the OIC was following the mandate of international human rights law in trying to curb hate speech that engendered hostility and endangered the lives of Muslims: "What we are against is not the criticism of religion per se but rather the intended objective of this criticism which is, in this case, jeopardize [*sic*] Muslim rights, by creating an atmosphere of hostility and rancor which make [*sic*] their life unsafe and strewn with prejudices of all kinds, and this is what international law prohibits" (OIC 2008).

Hate speech had been prohibited under ICCPR Article 20(2) since 1966. If one took seriously İhsanoğlu's claims that the OIC's objective was halting hate speech, one would wonder why the OIC had undertaken its protracted campaign to win UN support for its resolutions on combating defamation of Islam and defamation of religion. These resolutions rested on Islamic criteria for defining prohibited speech and did not belong in the secular hate speech category defined by ICCPR Article 20(2). In reality, the OIC's claims that its campaign to get international law to criminalize insults to Islam and the Prophet had the same objectives as those in ICCPR Article 20(2) were not credible in context.

Elsewhere, İhsanoğlu claimed that the Danish cartoons were both religious crimes and hate speech, as in a lecture that he gave in 2006 in Moscow, where he first employed the religious category "blasphemy" then equated it to the secular category of hate speech directed at Muslims (İhsanoğlu 2006). According to the transcript of the lecture, he complained that the Danish cartoons were "blasphemous cartoons which offended the image of the Prophet of Islam, and depicted him in a way to arouse hatred to Islam and Muslims." Without adducing any proofs, İhsanoğlu accused the cartoonists of engaging in the "advocacy of national, racial or religious hatred," prohibited under the ICCPR, and asserted that their intended objective was "inciting hatred against [the] Muslim population in Denmark and elsewhere and exposing them to prejudice and threats" (ibid.).

Sometimes the OIC's pretenses of concern for punishing hate speech were dropped. In a June 2013 interview with *Al Jazeera*, İhsanoğlu reverted to language indicating that his objections to the cartoons were owing to their sacrilegious character, complaining that they insulted a prophet who was venerated by Muslims (*Al Jazeera* 2013). He seemed to be particularly outraged by the cartoon of the Prophet with a bomb in his turban, a depiction that, he asserted, offended vast numbers of Muslims by portraying the Prophet as a terrorist. İhsanoğlu was obviously relying on the rule in the OIC's Cairo Declaration in Article 22(c) prohibiting "information" that "may violate sanctities and the dignity of Prophets," not any ICCPR provision. This could not be reconciled with claims that he had made elsewhere that his objections were based on the ICCPR ban on hate speech.

In the same interview İhsanoğlu maintained that this cartoon violated the ICCPR by denigrating religious symbols. In this connection he referred to UN Human Rights Council Resolution 16/18 calling for "combating intolerance, negative stereotyping and stigmatization of, and discrimination, incitement to violence and violence against, persons based on religion or belief"—as if this thoroughly secular UN resolution strengthened his claim that publishing a cartoon insulting the Prophet was prohibited (*Al Jazeera* 2013). Although the OIC was officially a sponsor of Resolution 16/18, İhsanoğlu spoke as if oblivious to its content. The resolution did not call for criminalizing insults aimed at religions or sacred figures, condemning instead "any advocacy of religious hatred that constitutes incitement to discrimination, hostility or violence," and, as Skorini points out, calling on states to take "measures to criminalize incitement to imminent violence based on religion or belief."

The confusion created by the way that the OIC has continued to mix up religious and secular restrictions on freedom of expression was exacerbated by the OIC's practice of equating its campaign to impose Islamic censorship with fighting "Islamophobia." How the OIC defined "Islamophobia" was left vague, sometimes seeming to resemble ICCPR hate speech but on other occasions denoting sacrilege. Significantly, in an interview with *Al Jazeera* in 2013 when the interviewer asked İhsanoğlu what Islamophobia consisted of, İhsanoğlu hesitated before suggesting various offenses that it might cover. Some were offenses that were clearly religious in nature such as desecrating tombstones, defaming religion, and writing a book insulting the Prophet. (This last was probably a reference to Rushdie's *The Satanic Verses*, which would entail retroactively calling it a work of Islamophobia.) İhsanoğlu also mentioned an entirely secular offense—politicians using xenophobic rhetoric and discriminating against immigrants based on social and economic concerns (*Al Jazeera* 2013). According to İhsanoğlu, both secular and purely religious offenses could fit in the Islamophobia category.

One of the many failings in the OIC's denunciations of Westerners such as the Danish cartoonists is the casual way it ascribes criminal intent to them, irrespective of whether it can offer any supporting evidence. Establishing intent is essential before deciding whether expression falls within the ICCPR Article 20(2) category of hate speech, where the aim must be one of inciting "discrimination, hostility or violence." Such intent is blatantly displayed by prominent Islamophobes in the West. A few of the more notorious ones include Steven Emerson, Pamela Geller, Robert Spencer, and Geert Wilders, who regularly spew bigoted venom. It is remarkable that İhsanoğlu shied away from vigorously attacking these prominent hate-mongers and instead repeatedly hurled opprobrium at the Danish cartoonists, when the basis for classing the cartoons as hate speech is dubious. Among other things, the cartoonists offered entirely plausible assertions that their cartoons were designed as pushback against illegitimate demands to submit to Islamic censorship. Such pushback against religious censorship is demonstrably common in the West without having connections to ICCPR hate speech.

When one observes how individual Danish cartoonists are singled out for vehement condemnation whereas direct confrontations with assertive Islamophobes like Geller are avoided, one finds the lack of proportion in the OIC response striking. This pattern suggests that the OIC's positions are not made based on serious assessments of who is engaged in hate speech.

The OIC's repeated conflating of blasphemy and hate speech in cases where the two were easily distinguishable contrasts with other cases where experts concur that the differences between blasphemy and hate speech are less than clear. As a detailed study by the Directorate-General for Internal Policies of the Union of the EU Parliament shows, there are borderline cases where making the distinctions can be difficult (Directorate-General for Internal Policies of the Union 2015). OIC spokespersons had little motivation to master such distinctions, because the OIC was seeking to squeeze religious crimes into the same category as hate speech.

Mixed Western reactions to the January 2015 terrorist attack on the Paris offices of Charlie Hebdo show how insults to religion can be construed as Islamophobic polemics when observers ignore the context and motivations. Reflecting anticlerical ideas and militant secularism that date back to the era of the French Revolution, the iconoclastic French newspaper *Charlie Hebdo* was notorious for publishing rude insults directed at Christianity and other religions. Its sacrilegious cartoons occasionally depicted the Prophet Muhammad, which provoked Muslim extremists to launch the 2015 attack. When a PEN award was given to *Charlie Hebdo* in New York for "freedom of expression courage" some PEN members protested, claiming that the cartoons had been Islamophobic, thereby conflating polemics of Islamophobes like Pamela Geller with *Charlie Hebdo*'s mockery of all religions. Surviving members of the *Charlie Hebdo* team objected, specifically underlining the difference between their mission and Geller's (Gladstone 2015).

While appreciating this difference, one could nonetheless concede that *Charlie Hebdo*'s policies on religious cartoons were insensitive and problematic. For example, observers could fairly complain that *Charlie Hebdo* had exhibited a blameworthy indifference to a social context in France where Muslims felt beleaguered, living as a disadvantaged minority, or that the publication had used double standards, refraining from publishing material with potential anti-Semitic implications while failing to weigh whether cartoons had potential Islamophobic implications. Nonetheless, on careful examination of the patterns in *Charlie Hebdo*'s transgressive satires and savage mockery of religions, one would be drawn to conclude that they did not belong in the same category as Geller's Islamophobic broadsides, where animus toward Islam was the central motivation.

The OIC's Anti-Western Bias

The OIC's credibility on human rights is undermined by the fact that for decades it has spoken as if the problems of Muslim minorities suffering from religiously based insults and related harms were concentrated in the West. Rarely does it protest problems suffered by Muslim minorities elsewhere. The OIC has complained about the persecutions of the Rohingya Muslims of Burma, but it eschews denunciations of how China and Russia abuse and discriminate against Muslims. On a side note, the OIC does, of course, lambaste Israeli policies that harm Palestinians, but the Palestinian situation is too complex to fit inside a framework detailing "problems suffered by Muslim minorities."

When the West resists demands for Islamic censorship, the OIC criticizes the West for allegedly failing to comply with Resolution 16/18 on "combating intolerance, negative stereotyping and stigmatization of, and discrimination, incitement to violence and violence against, persons based on religion or belief." This complaint rests on the OIC's flawed assumption that hate speech encompasses insults to religion. The OIC may plausibly claim that incidents of what it would deem blasphemous expression like the Danish cartoons occur more frequently in the West than in OIC member states; what it cannot plausibly maintain is that religiously grounded hate speech prohibited under ICCPR Article 20(2) or Resolution 16/18 occurs with greater frequency in the West than on the territories of its own members.

The OIC seems to discount the ways that various Muslim groups and movements hurl gross insults at the beliefs of Muslim dissenters and Muslims belonging to rival Islamic factions, often castigating them as infidels or heretics. The viciousness of Muslims' invective directed at their coreligionists can be ascertained by perusing the actual wording, such as the attacks documented in a 2015 BBC program (*BBC News* 2015). Such intra-Muslim polemics have exacerbated socioreligious tensions and sectarian enmities with terrible consequences such as religious persecutions and terrorist bombings of mosques and religious ceremonies, with OIC member states often either reacting with indifference or conniving in the violence (as will be discussed in the following). By November 2013 campaigns to inflame Sunni hostility toward Shias had escalated to the point that the Iranian foreign minister asserted they were probably the most serious security threat not only to the Middle East but to the world at large (*BBC News* 2013). In 2014, after tracking religious restrictions and religious hostilities around the world, the Pew Research Center reported that the Middle East and North Africa was the region most afflicted by sectarian violence in 2012 (Pew Research 2014).

Of course, hate speech by Muslims directed against other Muslims is not what immediately comes to mind when "Islamophobia" is discussed, because the attacks are not on Islam per se but on despised subgroups or dissenters within Muslim societies. But any entity that is as committed to fighting violations of the principles in ICCPR Article 20(2) and in Resolution 16/18 as the OIC claims to be would be expected to treat this as a major problem. That the OIC instead chooses to berate Danish cartoonists is telling.

Real-world patterns of religious antagonisms and violence engendered by hate speech cannot be reconciled with the OIC's theory that criminalizing insults to Islam is vital for securing religious harmony and tolerance. Although the OIC regularly fulminates about how the West's failure to impose Islamic censorship leads to harming Muslims, the human rights protections that Muslims enjoy in the West actually remain comparatively strong. Muslims suffering from religiously based persecutions and terror in OIC member states where blasphemy is criminalized keep fleeing in vast numbers to Western democracies, calculating that they will be far safer. These uncomfortable realities have been glossed over by İhsanoğlu. When an *Al Jazeera* interviewer in 2013 asked İhsanoğlu why, if Western Islamophobia was endangering Muslims, so many Muslims were fleeing Muslim countries and seeking asylum in the West, he abruptly deflected the question, quickly launching into a digression on an unrelated matter (*Al Jazeera* 2013). He could not explain away the evidence that millions of Muslims who lived in OIC member states wracked by religious conflicts were risking grave dangers to seek safe havens in the West, where, according to his depiction of events, the failure to criminalize insults to Islam would make their lives hellish.

Speaking in June 2013 at a Geneva meeting on the implementation of Resolution 16/18 İhsanoğlu insisted that the OIC was attuned to the need to fight discrimination and intolerance, asserting that combating discrimination and intolerance was a vital OIC concern (OIC 2013). Instead of a logical follow-up, which would have been to address the extensive and destructive religious intolerance blighting the lives of Muslims in OIC states, İhsanoğlu chose to denounce minor incidents in the West, which he placed under the label of Islamophobia even though they would more appropriately be classed as incidents of sacrilege. Thus, he lamented the alarming increase in Western intolerance and discrimination against Muslims, specifically mentioning "the burning of [the] Quran by the Florida Pastor and release of the reprehensible trailer [meaning *Innocence of Muslims*] on YouTube" (OIC 2013).

That is, İhsanoğlu singled out two U.S. incidents that both fell in the category of sacrilege, involving insults to Islam, denouncing a disreputable celebrity-seeking Florida pastor named Terry Jones who had publicly burned a copy of the Quran, as well as an obscure Egyptian immigrant with a criminal record who had posted on the internet the *Innocence of Muslims* video, a clumsy and amateurish production that vilified the character of the Prophet Muhammed. Given the low status of the perpetrators, by themselves their acts—though reprehensible—had little potential to cause actual harm to Muslims.

In the same speech, İhsanoğlu made the choice to complain about "the Utøya massacre in Norway," where young Norwegian campers on Utøya Island were massacred by Anders Breivik, a deeply disturbed and isolated Norwegian. Breivik's slaughter of his fellow Norwegians was far from embodying a straightforward example of Islamophobic intolerance and violence. True, Breivik admired Islamophobes like Pamela Geller and vehemently objected to Muslim immigration, but his deluded fantasy that he was a paladin of the ancient order of the Knights Templar—despite being alienated from Christianity and venerating the pagan god Odin—and his obsession with fighting against cultural Marxism and the humiliating subjugation of Norwegian men by feminists make it difficult and misleading to treat his horrendous crime as a product of classic Islamophobia.

One is struck by the lack of proportion in İhsanoğlu's denunciation of these U.S. incidents of sacrilege by marginal figures and the massacre of Norwegians by a delusional Norwegian misfit in the context of an international meeting that was designed to deal with the follow-up to Resolution 16/18—a time when the lives of millions of Muslims in OIC member states were blighted by intra-Islamic conflicts and religiously based terrorist attacks.

The OIC's Independent Permanent Human Rights Commission (IPHRC) might have been expected to distinguish sacrilegious speech, which does not violate human rights, from ICCPR hate speech. In actuality, the IPHRC has turned out to be concerned with denouncing sacrilege, a religious offense. For example, it denounced the *Innocence of Muslims* video for "ridiculing Islam and Prophet Mohamed" (OIC IPHRC 2012). Nonetheless, the IPHRC did seek to make some linkage to human rights, claiming that, because believers felt injured by such ridicule, the "denigration of religions for many of their followers becomes a direct assault on their own selves" (ibid.).

As if it were reconsidering, in its initial response to the *Charlie Hebdo* murders, the IPHRC gave a tentative sign that it might be moving away from the position that the OIC had once taken in the Rushdie Affair, when it had failed to oppose Iran's call for assassinating Rushdie. On January 12, 2015, the IPHRC "condemned in the strongest terms possible the terrorist attack . . . on the offices of *Charlie Hebdo*." Instead of lambasting France for failing to punish the cartoonists for insulting the Prophet, the IPHRC stated that it "regretted the barbaric act and expressed solidarity with the bereaved families, and the French nation for this tragic loss." Offering no sympathy for the killers of the cartoonists, who claimed to be avenging insults to the Prophet, the IPHRC instead spoke as if international human rights law governed and proclaimed "its strong rejection of radicalism, intolerance and terrorism in all its forms and manifestations, wherever they exist" (OIC 2015a). Moreover, rather than demanding Islamic censorship, the IPHRC is reported as saying that "responsible use of freedom of expression in accordance with international human rights law is fundamental for building peaceful and progressive democratic societies" (ibid.).

In contrast, on January 18, 2015, in responding to the same incident Secretary-General Iyad Madani, who had succeeded İhsanoğlu in 2014, chose to denounce the wrongfulness of *Charlie Hebo*'s conduct, advising that the OIC would seek to sue the paper and asserting that "freedom of speech must not become a hate speech and must not offend others. No sane person, irrespective of doctrine, religion or faith, accepts his beliefs being ridiculed" (Withnall 2015). This mixing of the very different offenses of hate speech and ridiculing religious beliefs—as if the two belonged in the same category—suggested that, like his predecessor, Madani continued to class sacrilege as a dimension of ICCPR hate speech. Also on January 18, 2015, the IPHRC issued a second statement, one that sharply diverged from its previous call for upholding international human rights law. In this second statement the IPHRC pivoted and reverted to the OIC's practice of protesting insults to religious sanctities as criminal acts and classing them as hate speech. It pronounced itself "appalled by the recent repeated publication of sacrilegious caricature of Prophet Mohammad (PBUH) by the French magazine *Charlie Hebdo* and squarely condemns this act as an intolerant, disrespectful and manifest expression of hatred," going on to condemn "this extreme act of malicious provocation and hatred based on ill-founded presumption of the right to insult and defame the faith, values and cultures of others in the name of freedom of expression" (OIC 2015b). This alteration of its previous stance indicated that the IPHRC was reverting to the typical OIC view that states had a duty to prohibit expression that offended religion.

Self-contradictions continue to plague the OIC's recent efforts to portray itself as respectful of the ICCPR. For example, in August 2015 the IPHRC disingenuously warned against the promotion of "non-universal and divisive concepts as human rights," asserting that this would "undermine the existing unity that is essential to upholding and ensuring the implementation of present universally agreed human rights regime" (OIC IPHRC 2015). This stance, given the timing, was likely related to the OIC's opposition to the emerging support in the UN for protecting the human rights of all people regardless of sexual orientation, which the OIC has tried to delegitimize, blaming this on "selectivity" and decisions to serve "the interests of particular groups" (Mayer 2012:164–65). No one familiar with the OIC's record could fail to note, however, that in continuing to cling to the Cairo Declaration the OIC had manifested its determination to uphold Islamic particularism at the expense of the UN human rights system.

Conclusion

Despite having made numerous pronouncements since 2011 averring that it embraces ICCPR principles, in the area of freedom of expression the OIC effectively disregards international human rights law and persists in promoting Islamic censorship rules, which it seeks to extend beyond the borders of the Muslim world to criminalize expression in the West. The OIC's regular invocations of the ICCPR and Resolution 16/18 are made opportunistically, being used to give plausibility to its campaign to make international law criminalize insults to Islam.

The OIC has become entangled in incompatible claims that variously affirm principles of international human rights law that uphold freedom of expression and demand that the West should apply Islamic censorship rules that assume that Islamic law overrides international law. As it struggles to paper over the inconsistences, the OIC has strained to convince an international audience that insults to Islamic sanctities, offenses that can only be determined within the framework of Islamic doctrine, belong in the same category as the secular hate speech banned under the ICCPR. Unless and until the OIC backs away from its excessively politicized stances on human rights and manages to disentangle Cairo Declaration values—where primacy is given in all cases to upholding Islamic law at the expense of human rights—from the principles actually set forth in international human rights law, it has little chance of articulating a coherent human rights philosophy.

Notes

1. UN Human Rights Council. 2011. *Combating Intolerance, Negative Stereotyping and Stigmatization of, and Discrimination, Incitement to Violence and Violence Against, Persons*

Based on Religion or Belief, A/16/18. Available from http://www2.ohchr.org/english/bodies/hrcouncil/docs/16session/A.HRC.RES.16.18_en.pdf.

2. Charter of the Organization of Islamic Cooperation. https://www.oic-oci.org/page/?p_id=53&p_ref=27&lan=en.

3. Ibid.

4. Ibid.

5. *The Cairo Declaration on Human Rights in Islam.* http://www.oic-oci.org/english/article/human.htm.

6. "Blasphemy Laws Are Incompatible with the International Covenant on Civil and Political Rights." September 12. http://www2.ohchr.org/english/bodies/hrc/docs/gc34.pdf.

7. *Combating Defamation of Religions,* A/4/9. Available from http://ap.ohchr.org/documents/E/HRC/resolutions/A-HRC-RES-4-9.doc.

8. U.S. Department of State. 2001–2016. *International Religious Freedom.* http://www.state.gov/j/drl/rls/irf/.

Works Cited

Abdul Ghafour, P. K., and Abdul Hannan Faisal Tago. 2006. "OIC, Arab League Seek UN Resolution on Cartoons." *Arab News,* January 30. http://www.arabnews.com/node/279660.

Al Jazeera. 2013. "Ekmeleddin İhsanoğlu: Combating Islamophobia. The Secretary-General of the OIC Discusses Discrimination, Freedom of Expression and Religious Persecution in the West." June 11. http://www.youtube.com/watch?v=fv0DarFDgHY.

BBC News. 2013. "Iran FM: Sectarian strife is worst threat in world." November 11. http://www.bbc.com/news/world-middle-east-24893808.

———. 2015. "Freedom to Broadcast Hate: An Investigation into the Extreme Religious TV Channels, Both Sunni and Shia, That Are Broadcasting Sectarian Views and Stoking Hate Across the Arab World." January 4. http://www.bbc.co.uk/programmes/n3csv0c4.

Directorate General for Internal Policies of the Union. 2015. *The European Legal Framework on Hate Speech, Blasphemy and Its Interaction with Freedom of Expression.* http://www.europarl.europa.eu/RegData/etudes/STUD/2015/536460/IPOL_STU(2015)536460_EN.pdf.

Engle, Karen. 2000. "Culture and Human Rights: The Asian Values Debate in Context." *NYU Journal of International Law and Politics* 32: 291–333.

Gladstone, Rick. 2015. "Charlie Hebdo Editor Seeks to Distance Newspaper from Anti-Islam Causes." *New York Times,* May 5. http://www.nytimes.com/2015/05/06/world/europe/charlie-hebdo-editor-seeks-to-distance-newspaper-from-anti-islam-causes.html.

Human Rights *First.* 2012. *Blasphemy Laws Exposed: The Consequences of Criminalizing "Defamation Of Religions."* New York: Human Rights *First.* http://www.humanrightsfirst.org/wp-content/uploads/Blasphemy_Cases.pdf.

İhsanoğlu, Ekmeleddin. 2006. "Building Bridges: Intercultural Dialogue Identities and Migration." Lecture presented at the Organization of the Islamic Conference, Mgimo University, Moscow. https://mgimo.ru/files/118373/2006-06-08_Ihsanoglu.doc.

———. 2013. *Moderation and Modernization: Vision for the Muslim World: Selected Speeches, 2005–2013.* Jeddah: OIC.

Klausen, Jytte. 2009. *The Cartoons That Shook the World.* New Haven, CT: Yale University Press.

Mayer, Ann Elizabeth. 2012. *Islam and Human Rights: Tradition and Politics.* Boulder, CO: Westview.

Moinuddin, Hasan. 1987. *The Charter of the Islamic Conference and the Legal Framework of Economic Co-operation Among Its Member States.* Oxford: Oxford University Press.

Office of the High Commissioner for Human Rights (OHCHR). 1997. *Human Rights: A Compilation of International Instruments,* vol. 2, *Regional Instruments.* Geneva: OHCHR, 475–76.

OIC. 2008. "The Full text of the Interview of the Secretary-General with the Danish Daily Jyllands Posten, which was published on 28 October 2008." http://www.oic-oci.un.org/english/article /Jyllands%20Posten%20Interview.pdf (accessed July 17, 2005).

———. 2013. "Statement by His Excellency the Secretary-General at the 3rd Istanbul Process Meeting on the Follow-up of Implementation of HRC Resolution 16/18." June 21. https://oichumanrights.wordpress.com/tag/tolerance/.

———. 2015a. "IPHRC Condemns Terrorist Attack on *Charlie Hebdo* Magazine in France." January 12. http://www.oic-oci.org//topic/?t_id=9678&t_ref=3849&lan=en.

———. 2015b. "OIC, IPHRC Strongly Condemns the Recent Publication of Blasphemous Caricatures of Prophet Mohammad (PBUH) by the French Magazine *Charlie Hebdo.*" January 18. http://www.oic-iphrc.org/en/data/docs/Media/Press%20Statements/EV/iphrc_charlie_hebdo_2015.pdf.

OIC IPHRC. 2012. "The OIC Human Rights Commission Strongly Condemns the Release of the Anti-Muslim Film as a Deliberate Act of Incitement." http://www.oic-iphrc.org/en/data/docs/media/Press%20Statements/EV/IPHRC%20-%20Press%20Release%20-%20Anti%20Muslim%20Film%20-%20Sept%202012%20-%20EV.pdf.

———. 2015. "Message on "Islamic Human Rights and Human Dignity Day." http://www.oic-iphrc.org/en/press_details/?id=63.

Pew Research. 2014. "Religious Hostilities Reach Six-Year High." January 17. http://www.pewforum.org/2014/01/14/religious-hostilities-reach-six-year-high/.

Shaikh, Habib. 2014. "OIC Seeks Rights Debates Based on Islamic Values." *Arab News,* February 4. http://www.arabnews.com/news/520321.

Withnall, Adam. 2015. "Saudi Muslim Leader Organising 'Legal Action Against Charlie Hebdo' Over Mohamed Cartoons." *The Independent,* January 18. http://www.independent.co.uk/news/world/middle-east/saudi-muslim-leader-organising-legal-action-against-charlie-hebdo-over-mohamed-cartoons-9985984.html.

CHAPTER 5

The OIC and Freedom of Expression: Justifying Religious Censorship Norms with Human Rights Language

Heini í Skorini

Introduction

In recent years, several incidents have illustrated the tensions between free speech ideals and religious sensitivities. The most violent examples are probably the Danish cartoon affair—triggered by twelve cartoons of the prophet Mohammed in September 2005—and the *Charlie Hebdo* massacre in Paris in January 2015, which echoed the Rushdie Affair back in 1989. In all cases, blunt religious satire had deadly and bloody consequences. However, tensions between contrasting free speech ideals are as old as religion itself and have caused fierce power struggles since the birth of the UN. In fact, the drafting history of UN covenants and declarations is permeated with conflicts between divergent ideals regarding free speech, especially with regard to speech targeting religion (Farrior 1996; Mchangama 2011b; Aswad 2013). In 1999, Pakistan launched the first ever draft resolution combating "defamation of Islam" in the UN Commission on Human Rights on behalf of the OIC,[1] and the resolution—later titled "defamation of religions" after European pressure—was adopted every year until 2010. But the genealogy of the resolution can be traced back to the late 1970s, when the OIC started adopting its own resolutions committed to combat what was perceived as unacceptable vilification of the Islamic religion.[2] Much has been written about the defamation debate on free speech and religion in the UN system between 1999 and 2010 (Grinberg 2006; Khan 2007; Dobras 2009; Graham 2009; James 2009; Blitt 2010, 2011a, 2011b; Mayer 2015), but the historical background paving the way for the OIC's first resolution in 1999 has not attracted the same scholarly attention.

This chapter approaches the OIC as an innovative norm entrepreneur and a vehicle for norm diffusion in the sphere of international normative politics, which may counterbalance the overwhelming preoccupation in constructivist scholarship with how liberal norms spread in the non-Western world (Bettiza and Dionigi 2014). The OIC's agency in UN human rights forums is a case study that illustrates norm diffusion in the opposite direction—the attempt to spread nonliberal norms at the international level—and how self-proclaimed religiously motivated actors also seek to promote and internationalize their own values and beliefs. Needless to say, this does not mean that the OIC should be approached as one homogenous international actor. Contrary to the external perceptions of the OIC as a coherent entity with a clear and consistent logic, and contrary to the internal and rather idealized attempts to portray the OIC as representing the Islamic *umma* or the "concrete manifestation . . . of Islamic solidarity" (İhsanoğlu 2010:13), it provides much more conceptual clarity to understand the organization as an arena, where different nation states pursue their own national interests. Often they clash, but sometimes they are able to identify common goals and act in concert, not least regarding the tense relationship between free speech and religious sensitivities.

This chapter's main purpose is to unravel OIC attempts to redefine international free speech norms and justify religious censorship. In recent years, this endeavor has been carried out by employing a predominantly liberal and secular discourse at the UN that embraces the idea of universal human rights and liberal individualism. But conceptualizing the UN conflict on freedom of expression vis-à-vis religious sensitivities as a clash between liberal universalism and nonliberal cultural relativism may miss the point, both because OIC's human rights terminology is permeated with the pledge to promote universalism and because OIC's representatives in recent years have framed religious censorship as a way of protecting individual believers from the harm caused by defamation. Therefore, it is perhaps more relevant to ask not how the OIC challenges the concept of universality, but how it seeks to redefine the content of universal norms, reinterpret international law, and renegotiate the substantial meaning of "universality."

To study how human rights norms spread across the globe is important, but such studies must take into account how the content, the meaning, and the implications of each and every norm are contested by different political actors (Krook and True 2012). Norms are not fixed entities; they are dynamic discursive battlegrounds. On the basis of these reflections, this chapter argues that, despite the OIC's discursive transformation from religious particularism toward a secular and individualistic terminology, the OIC represents a nonliberal version of universalism, which in practice challenges the liberal human rights tradition. In order to assess the implications of the OIC's policies, one needs only see how blasphemy laws are employed in many of the OIC's leading member states. These laws empower the ruling elites and reinforce existing structures of power against deviating groups and dissenting individuals.

The chapter is divided into four main sections. The first section examines the OIC's historical position regarding freedom of expression vis-à-vis religion from the first internal resolution on the issue in 1979 up to the Rushdie Affair and the adoption of the Cairo Declaration on Human Rights in Islam in the early 1990s. The second section examines the circumstances that paved the way for the OIC's decision to launch the controversial resolution on religious defamation in the UN in 1999. This section highlights growing tensions in the UN throughout the 1990s and how powerful OIC member states have enforced strict legislation against blasphemy. The third section explores the norm struggle in the UN from 1999 onward, and the fourth and final section examines the 2011 consensus Resolution 16/18. This section concludes that Resolution 16/18 has by no means ended the diplomatic conflict on freedom of expression and religious sensitivities.

Norm Formation Within the OIC: Efforts to Prohibit Blasphemy and Defamation of Religions Prior to 1999

Historically, the OIC has been characterized by profound geopolitical conflicts, severe internal rivalries, and sectarian diversity, obstructing the OIC's influence and significance on the world stage. However, the attempt to combat and outlaw blasphemous speech internationally is an issue where OIC member states have been able to act in concert and vote as a relatively homogenous group in the UN. The OIC's decision to launch the debate on defamation of religions in the UN Commission on Human Rights in 1999 was neither a sudden move nor an abrupt decision. Quite the contrary, the OIC's preoccupation with defending Islam from defamation, vilification, blasphemy, denigration, or insult is visible in the organization's official documents from the late 1970s, and if we go further back, the drafting history of UN conventions and declarations shows that Muslim-majority states fought against liberal free speech ideals long before the establishment of the OIC in 1969 (Farrior 1996:21; Aswad 2013:1320).[3]

While anti-blasphemy laws are diminishing in Western countries, as both a legal and practical concept (Pew Research 2014), blasphemy remains a serious crime throughout the Muslim world, not least in influential OIC member states such as Egypt, Pakistan, and Saudi Arabia, which indicates a correlation between domestic policies and international activism (Freedom House 2010:21–34, 69–88, 29–55; Alfandari, Baker, and Atteya 2011; Marshall and Shea 2011:21–34, 61–100; *Economist* 2014).

The first OIC resolution explicitly addressing the necessity to protect Islam from criticism was adopted at the annual summit of OIC foreign ministers in 1979 in Morocco and was titled "Measures to Counter Propaganda Against Islam and Muslims."[4] Prompted by a supposedly blasphemous (and relatively unknown) film appearing on Japanese television in the late 1970s, the text was adopted by consensus and was the first of many similar resolutions throughout the 1980s. The resolution notes a recent "intensification of propaganda against Islam" and calls on all member states to adopt measures in order to "counter propaganda directed against Islam and Muslims inside and outside the Islamic countries." Two years later, in 1981, the OIC heads of state adopted a resolution that called for "an international information order characterized by justice, impartiality and morality, so that our nation may be able to show to the world its true qualities, and refute the systematic media campaigns aimed at isolating, misleading, slandering and defaming our nation."[5] Besides condemning hostile attacks from the non-Muslim world, the same paragraph identified the enemy within, pledging to "cleanse our societies of the manifestations of moral laxity and deviation" and "purify Islamic thought of all that may be alien or divisive." At the same summit in Mecca in 1981, OIC heads of state also adopted a resolution in order "to eliminate those ideas that are contrary to the essence of Islam."[6] The OIC's discourse was characterized by a well-delineated "us" and "them"; Islam was under siege by external and internal forces, which polluted and challenged the religious-political order. Nonetheless, the resolutions were vague and avoided mentioning specifically what forces, actors, or entities were undermining societal values in OIC member states.

Throughout the 1980s, all OIC summits between foreign ministers and heads of states presented resolutions and final communiqués reiterating the pledge to defend Islam against insult, vilification, or defamation. According to OIC diplomats from the period, this agenda was promoted and controlled by religiously conservative OIC members with distinctive theocratic jurisprudence, in particular Saudi Arabia and its allies together with Pakistan and postrevolutionary Iran, while many African OIC members were generally more preoccupied with economic development. The Southeast Asian countries followed suit without taking the lead. The secular republic of Turkey usually had a sobering effect on OIC's religious discourse, which dated back to the very establishment of the OIC in 1969, when Turkey advocated for a charter that defined the OIC in political rather than religious terms.[7] In other words, the domestic role of religion and the restrictive jurisprudence on blasphemy and apostasy in self-proclaimed Islamic states such as Iran, Pakistan, and Saudi Arabia seem to explain at least partly how these countries acted in the OIC arena. In the wake of the Danish cartoon affair triggered in 2005, Egypt has, together with Pakistan, played an important role in promoting the blasphemy agenda internationally in UN corridors.[8] However, during the 1970s and the 1980s, Egypt was not among the dominant OIC members, first and foremost due to its controversial peace agreement with Israel in 1979 and its subsequent suspension from the OIC.

Another factor determining state behavior during the 1970s and the 1980s was the rise of Islamism in civil society and the religious resurgence throughout the region (Mayer 2006), which prompted state representatives to demonstrate their religious commitment as a way of countering opposition and claiming the authority to define the true version of Islam. According to an OIC researcher and civil servant in one of the influential OIC member states, the Iranian revolution also triggered an interstate rivalry between Iran and Saudi Arabia on who was the true global guardian of Islam. Saudi Arabia's symbolic power was threatened, as many Sunni Islamists—despite sectarian differences—admired Khomeini's political achievements. The basic debate on the necessity of protecting Islam from unacceptable defamatory speech was largely shaped by these two countries and was characterized by a fierce theological rhetoric. Meanwhile, Pakistan was also undergoing a religious political revival under General Zia ul-Haq in the 1980s, when the country's notorious blasphemy laws inherited from British rule were severely tightened. These radicalizing currents in the Muslim world contributed to shaping the OIC's approach to the tense relations between freedom of expression and religious sensitivities.[9]

In the wake of the publication of *The Satanic Verses*, Khomeini's fatwa against Salman Rushdie, and the international attention surrounding the affair, OIC official discourse became more concrete and vociferous. Speaking on behalf of the OIC, the Libyan delegate in the UN General Assembly in 1989 made it clear that the publication of *The Satanic Verses* was "punishable under the Sharia" and that "no one could insult Muslims without expecting a reaction on their part."[10] When the OIC's foreign ministers gathered that same year, they strongly condemned Rushdie's novel and issued a declaration to combat "blasphemy against Islam."[11] This was the first time the word "blasphemy" had appeared in the OIC's official documents. But the declaration never went as far as Khomeini's fatwa, which sentenced Rushdie to death (Chase 1996). The final communiqué of the conference urged all states to "coordinate their efforts" in attempts to "effectively combat blasphemy against Islam and abuse of Islamic personalities," and these efforts should be "based on the Sharia." The member states further declared "that blasphemy could not be justified on the basis of freedom of thought or expression," and they "strongly condemned the blasphemous publication Satanic Verses" and declared the author—Salman Rushdie—an "apostate." Finally, OIC member states "appealed to all members of the International community to ban the book and take necessary measures to protect the religious beliefs of others."[12]

In hindsight this statement is informative in many regards. First, and despite the absence of any clear definition, it confirmed the OIC's commitment to Sharia. Second, it made clear that blasphemy, in the opinion of the OIC, was not and should not be protected by existing international standards. Third, by appealing for an outright international ban on the book, the statement indicated the OIC's ambition to internationalize domestic blasphemy prohibitions.

Two years later—and for the first time ever—the OIC heads of states voiced their demand for a new international legal instrument combating blasphemous speech at the Sixth Islamic Summit Conference in Dakar. Having affirmed that "belief in the same Islamic spiritual values is the very essence of the Organization of the Islamic Conference,"[13] the heads of state requested the OIC's secretary-general "to take the necessary measures for the drafting of an international convention to ensure respect for sanctities and values."[14] The call for an international convention was a decisive shift in the OIC's discourse and demonstrated a new level of ambition, which came to characterize OIC rhetoric for many years.

Another decisive feature in the OIC's discourse is the juxtaposition of words and deeds. When the re-publication of Salman Rushdie's novel was condemned by the OIC's foreign ministers in 1993, the same resolution also condemned the killing of Muslims in Bosnia-Herzegovina, India, Jammu and Kashmir, and Palestine, as well as the Israeli aggression against the Al-Aqsa Mosque in Jerusalem and the destruction of the historical Babri Mosque by Hindu militants.[15] Under the headline "A Unified Stand on the Belittling of Islamic Sanctities and Values," the resolution indirectly equates the publication of a book with the killing of Muslims in war-torn areas, which illustrates how serious a crime the OIC perceived the publication of a so-called blasphemous novel to be.[16] In other words, OIC member states seemed to perceive anti-Muslim or anti-Islamic speech as part of a broader campaign, and as both an indication of and a reason for discrimination and attacks against Muslims. However, it would be naïve to ignore the fact that the issue was also opportunistically utilized by political elites for strategic and political purposes. As pointed out below, the religious resurgence throughout the region combined with the gradual globalization of mass media, and the subsequent intensification of interaction across cultural and religious boundaries throughout the 1980s and 1990s was indeed fertilizing religious and cultural-identity politics. These tendencies may have motivated domestic political actors to publicly demonstrate a desire to protect and safeguard the Islamic religion against defamatory expressions.

The efforts to eliminate blasphemous speech are also reflected in the OIC's Cairo Declaration on Human Rights in Islam, which was unanimously adopted in 1990, the result of a meeting in Teheran the year before by a committee of legal experts. With regard to freedom of expression, Article 22 of the Cairo Declaration states that "everyone shall have the right to express his opinion freely in such manner as would not be contrary to the principles of the Shari'ah." Furthermore, free speech must not be "exploited or misused in such a way as may violate sanctities and the dignity of Prophets, undermine moral and ethical values or disintegrate, corrupt or harm society or weaken its faith."[17] The Cairo Declaration was a controversial document, promoting a duty-based, theological communitarianism as opposed to a rights-based, secular individualism, and has been subject to severe criticism from human rights advocates, but OIC members did not back down. At the UN World Conference on Human Rights in Vienna in 1993, the OIC circulated the Cairo Declaration as its contribution to the World Conference.[18] Such references to the Cairo Declaration indicate the normative significance ascribed to the declaration by the OIC. Indeed, on the website of the OIC's Independent Permanent Human Rights Commission, the Cairo Declaration is referred to as one of the OIC's key legal instruments.[19]

Besides the aforementioned religious resurgence throughout the Muslim world, structural factors on the international level have also shaped the OIC's growing preoccupation with freedom of expression and religion. It was during the 1980s when Western media was globalized that Muslim-majority states—as well as large parts of the non-Western world under the umbrella of the Non-Aligned Movement (NAM)—frequently complained about bias, prejudice, and ethnocentrism, not least with regard to the media coverage of the Iranian revolution, the armed struggle for Palestine, and the growing presence of Muslim minorities in the West (Said 1981). In 1981, the OIC launched its first resolution to call for a new "international information order characterized by justice, impartiality and morality, so that our nation may be able to show to the world its true qualities, and refute the systematic media campaigns aimed at isolating, misleading, slandering and defaming our nation."[20] The idea of establishing a new "international information order" emanated directly from a UNESCO initiative—supported by NAM—that addressed the lack of media representation on behalf of the Global South. But when the OIC adopted the concept in its own official discourse, the campaign was couched in religious language. Just as the adoption of the Cairo Declaration can be seen as a response to the general spread of liberal human rights, the OIC's growing preoccupation with defending Islam can be perceived as a response to the globalization and rising hegemony of Western media. So, in order to explain the OIC's advocacy of cultural protectionism throughout the 1980s, we need to take into account both domestic and regional reasons as well as external factors and developments on the global scene. All in all, OIC discourse on free speech and religion throughout the 1980s and 1990s was characterized by an intransigent and particularistic religious rhetoric permeated with references to Islam. However, this way of framing the issue would later change.

The Path to Showdown: Polarization in the UN System and Domestic Free Speech Norms in the OIC's Dominant Member States

As should be evident by now, the blasphemy issue held a central role in OIC internal official discourse throughout the 1980s, but what circumstances motivated the OIC member states to take the free speech issue to the UN at the turn of the millennium? A main reason can be found in the polarization and confrontation in the corridors of the UN throughout the 1990s, when powerful OIC members were increasingly under scrutiny, not least due to gross human rights violations in the area of free speech and religiously motivated censorship, resulting in explicit criticism in UN human rights forums, in country reports by UN special rapporteurs, in statements by other member states, and by human rights NGOs with consultative status in the UN system (Langer 2014:167). This criticism entailed conflict and counterattacks, which—at least partly—explain the atmosphere prior to the first UN resolution combating defamation of religions in 1999.[21]

Pakistan received more criticism than any other OIC member during the 1990s, first and foremost due to the country's draconian blasphemy laws.[22] In an extensive country report in 1996, UN rapporteur Abdelfattah Amor argued that "applying the death penalty for blasphemy appears disproportionate and even unacceptable, especially in view of the fact that blasphemy is very often the reflection of a very low standard of education and culture, for which the blasphemer is never solely to blame."[23] Similar reports on Pakistan's restrictive free speech policies were also produced by NGOs with consultative status in the UN such as Amnesty International (Amnesty International 1994) and Human Rights Watch (Human Rights Watch 1993). Speaking on behalf of the OIC in 1999, Pakistan's UN ambassador Munir Akram

> reminded the Commission that Islam was a religion of peace which had enunciated the concept of human rights more than 14 centuries earlier. The OIC member States therefore found it extremely disturbing that at recent sessions of the Commission and the Sub-

> Commission, attempts had been made to misinterpret the divine tenets of Islam and to cast Islam in the most negative light possible.[24]

Blasphemy, apostasy, and speech deemed insulting are also serious crimes in many leading member states of the OIC, and the list of citizens who are penalized for blasphemous crimes in many of these countries is long (Freedom House 2010; Alfandari, Baker, and Atteya 2011; Marshall and Shea 2011; Human Rights *First* 2012). Within the OIC group at UN headquarters in Geneva, Pakistan has enjoyed the role as the OIC's coordinator on human rights issues, primarily because Pakistan has been able to mediate between two old foes, Iran and Saudi Arabia. Pakistan's key role within the UN machinery in Geneva is interesting because Pakistan enforces some of the world's most restrictive blasphemy laws, which have been subject to vehement international criticism. Legal offences relating to religion were first codified by India's British rulers in 1860 and were inherited by Pakistan after its independence in 1947, but the 1980s paved the way for Pakistan's current blasphemy laws (Siddique and Hayat 2008:310), which were part of a larger Islamization of Pakistani politics and legal structures under General Zia ul-Haq's regime from 1977 to 1988 (Halliday and Alavi 1988; Forte 1994; Mayer 2006:2; Jahangir 2011). These laws are first and foremost used to target religious minorities and nonconforming members of the Muslim majority and have fostered a climate of intolerance, intimidation, extrajudicial mob violence, and severe persecution (Amnesty International 2001; Freedom House 2010; U.S. Commission on International Religious Freedom 2015b).

The main financial contributor to the OIC's budget and the country that hosts the OIC's Jeddah headquarters, Saudi Arabia, strictly enforces an extreme interpretation of Sunni Islam commonly known as Wahhabism, which criminalizes all dissent from official and state-sanctioned religious interpretation. The law combines royal decrees and Sharia, and in a string of royal decrees addressing terrorism in the second decade of this century, the kingdom classified atheism as a new form of terrorism and virtually defined all dissident thought or expression as terrorism (Human Rights Watch 2014; Withnall 2014). Furthermore, Saudi officials continued to call for an international instrument criminalizing blasphemy (*Saudi Gazette* 2015).

A third key player in the OIC human rights machinery in Geneva is Egypt. Despite profound differences regarding the role of religion in state law, Egypt is likewise upholding laws that serve as de facto blasphemy laws, for instance

Article 98(f) in the country's penal code, which prohibits "ridiculing or insulting heavenly religions" (Marshall and Shea 2011:62). Despite the fact that the main body of Egypt's legislation remains civil, the religious establishment at the prestigious Al-Azhar University, an authoritative institution within Sunni Islam, exercises its power over religious matters by banning books, issuing fatwas, and filing lawsuits on blasphemy, apostasy, and related matters (Marshall and Shea 2011:61–82). Egypt was also the number one OIC member state mobilizing the Islamic world against Denmark in the wake of the Danish cartoons of the prophet Muhammad (Klausen 2009) and has—along with Saudi Arabia—staunchly opposed new compromises with the West on the issue of free speech vis-à-vis religion.[25]

Defamation of Religions Enters the UN: A Norm Struggle from 1999 to 2010

After the aforementioned confrontations in the UN system throughout the 1990s, Pakistan launched the first resolution combating "defamation of religions" in the UN Commission on Human Rights in 1999.[26] The decision triggered a new front in the long and passionate struggle to define the scope of legitimate speech vis-à-vis religion, but it also signaled a discursive change in the OIC's rhetoric. After 1999, OIC's spokespersons in the UN system gradually distanced themselves from religious particularism and formulated their arguments in secular and liberal language while embracing the idea of universal normative standards for all. Instead of subordinating the secular international human rights regime to religious doctrines, the OIC gradually sought to reinterpret the meaning of specific human rights, such as freedom of expression, and in doing so to enunciate the reality that the content of each and every norm is contested, negotiated, and renegotiated by competing political actors. The content of the "universal" depends on the outcome of international political power struggles.

In the OIC's first UN resolution in 1999, Islam was still the only religion exclusively mentioned, which gave the impression of a partisan and biased approach. However, the resolution was written in secular language and without the usual references to religion so visible in OIC internal documents—thus indicating how self-proclaimed religiously motivated actors are forced to adapt to, or translate, a secular language when introducing domestic norms within the secular structures of the UN (Bettiza and Dionigi 2014; Kayaoglu 2014). In other words, when the OIC promotes domestic censorship norms entrenched in duty-based, communitarian legal and political systems at the international level, it strategically employs a rights-based, secular human rights language.

The concept of "defamation" is present in almost all Western legal systems and is closely related to libel and slander, but in a modern context, the concept is usually applied in order to protect individual reputation against false speech and baseless accusations (Langer 2014:200–1). But historically, defamation law was also used to protect public peace and order, and the English Licensing Order of 1643 issued by the English parliament aimed to suppress "the many false, forged, scandalous, seditious, libelous and unlicensed papers, pamphlets, and books to the great *defamation of religion* and government" (Blitt 2011a:130). In other words, blasphemy prohibitions and laws against defamation of religions have historically been an integrated part of Western legal systems despite a massive decline in the last century (Hare and Weinstein 2009), just as blasphemy laws in the Muslim world were originally installed by Western colonial powers. According to one influential OIC diplomat, the word "defamation" was chosen in order to pursue a language which already had a basis in Western law.[27] Nevertheless, the coupling of "defamation" with "religion" was a new, innovative, and controversial move, which according to skeptics threatened free speech ideals and was inconsistent with the international human rights framework (Blitt 2010; Temperman 2012). This is first and foremost because religions and other collective idea systems per definition cannot be defamed; second because the only rights-holders in human rights thinking are individuals and not their political, religious, or other ideas; and third because there is no objective way to verify or falsify religious truth claims, which makes it difficult to establish concrete criteria in order to determine what precisely constitutes the defamation of a religion.

While pledging to respect universal human rights and legal obligations, the OIC's first resolution "expresses its concern at the use of the print, audiovisual or electronic media or any other means to spread intolerance against Islam."[28] The sponsors of the resolution were also "alarmed at the negative stereotyping of Islam," and the resolution urged all member states to "counter intolerance" based on religion or belief. At the commission's meeting on the resolution, Pakistani delegate Ambassador Akram explained the background for the decision to launch the new resolution:

> In the past few years, there had been new manifestations of intolerance and misunderstanding, not to say hatred, of Islam and Muslims in various parts of the world. It was to be feared that those manifestations might become as widespread and endemic as anti-semitism had been in the past. There was a tendency in some countries and in the international media to portray Islam as a religion hostile to human rights, threatening to the Western world and associated with terrorism and violence, whereas, with the Quran, Islam had given the world its first human rights charter. No other religion received such constant negative media coverage. That defamation campaign was reflected in growing intolerance towards Muslims. The Commission on Human Rights had to stand up against that campaign.[29]

Evidently the Pakistani ambassador sought to establish a causal link between defamation of Islam and "growing intolerance towards Muslims" while drawing a parallel to anti-Semitism. In other words, the argument was not to protect Islam for its own sake but to defend individual believers from the harm caused by defamation. Hence, this argument brings the individual into focus in line with the prevailing human rights discourse in the UN. The OIC's first draft was titled "defamation of Islam" and only addressed the Islamic religion, but after European pressure and a passionate internal theological debate between hardliners and pragmatists within the OIC, the OIC ambassadors settled for the title "defamation of religions," which became the recurrent title for years to come.[30] This seemingly minor change was especially problematic for Saudi Arabia and other religiously conservative members of the OIC, because in their eyes the very purpose of the resolution was to shield Islam specifically from insult in an age where the global flow of information cannot be controlled and contained to the same extent as before. Furthermore, the word "religions" in plural was problematic, with the "s" in the end implicitly recognizing religious pluralism and thereby undermining Islam as the only true theological revelation. But a compromise was a precondition for consensus, and the resolution was adopted without a vote in 1999 and again in 2000. The discursive shift from "Islam" to "religions"—away from particularistic language toward a more inclusive and neutral language—illustrates how OIC's normative agency was constrained by other normative actors from the very beginning. Such constraints were simultaneously shaping OIC's discursive transformation.

Despite consensus, the EU group in Geneva had expressed reservations from the beginning,[31] and when members of the commission convened in 2001, it marked the end of consensus and the beginning of polarization. Proponents in favor of the resolution increasingly framed the issue in the context of well-known secular categories such as racism, discrimination, hate speech, Islamophobia, and freedom of religion. Opponents pointed out that preventing discrimination of individuals on the grounds of religion or belief was completely in line with existing international law, but to demand respect for religion *as such* and thereby shield religion from legitimate debate was a completely different—and highly problematic—endeavor. Western countries argued that the only rights-holders in human rights thinking were individuals, not religions or other collective belief systems, and the resolution was undermining the right to speak freely about religion as exemplified in the Muslim world, where dissidents and minorities were being prosecuted in court and persecuted in civil society.

Throughout the next decade, the OIC never made an actual attempt to legally define defamation of religions, and the Western bloc in the Human Rights Council gradually came to perceive the OIC's campaign as an attempt to legitimize domestic free speech norms and redefine international free speech ideals. In an attempt to establish a causal link between defamation of religions and the rights of individual believers, the OIC's 2001 draft claimed that "defamation of religions . . . leads to violations of the human rights of their adherents."[32] In a revised draft later adopted as Resolution 2001/4, the text "encourages states, within their respective constitutional systems, to provide adequate protection against all human rights violations resulting from defamation of religions" (L.7/Rev.1, para. 3). The Pakistani representative also argued that "when traditional forms of racism tend to disappear, the world sees a rise in new forms of racism just as dangerous" (SR.61, para. 2). In other words, the OIC's diplomats argued that defaming a religion was a manifestation of racism, substantially broadening the common meaning of "racism." According to one British diplomat frequently negotiating this resolution with the OIC, "to frame the issue as a matter of racism was a wise move by the OIC. The fight against racism unifies all states and the global human rights movement, and to conceptualize 'defamation of religions' as an emerging form of racism was a way of legitimizing the campaign as a new human rights challenge that the international community had to deal with."[33]

Because the previous two resolutions had been adopted without a vote, the vote in 2001 unveiled the actual fault lines in the commission. No Western country voted in favor, and the twenty-eight countries voting in support of the resolution were from Africa, Asia, the Middle East, and South America.[34] Roughly speaking, the commission split into Western countries opposing and non-Western and developing countries supporting the resolution, including many Christian-majority states from Africa and Latin America, refuting the idea that the issue was a clash between the Muslim world and the Christian world. The opposing countries were from Eastern and Western Europe and North America plus Japan. The fact that Russia and even China—a self-declared nonreligious communist state—voted in favor of the resolution also illustrated the traditional strategic solidarity in NAM in the UN system. Even though the OIC was the only group actively lobbying for the resolution, the Global South—represented by NAM—supported the resolution and thereby transcended religious boundaries.

Within the EU presidency, there was a growing sense of an orchestrated campaign by the non-Western world on many different fronts to redefine the very meaning of human rights and renegotiate the content of international law. The "Dialogue Among Civilizations" was an Iranian initiative endorsed by the UN in 1999, which included the rejection of the "desecration of moral, religious and cultural values,"[35] and within the EU, the OIC's resolution triggered the sense that "this circus moves around from institution to institution."[36] One diplomat in the EU's chairmanship and a leading negotiator on the defamation resolution explained it as follows: "In 1999, we managed to change the resolution from 'defamation of Islam' to 'defamation of religions,' and we considered this a victory. At that time, we did not see any danger and were too slow to react. We were naïve, passive and had a legalistic approach. But in 2001, we realized that we had to take a firm stance, which triggered an internal debate in the EU. Eventually, the EU members agreed to reject the resolution because it fundamentally threatened our free speech ideals."[37]

When the UN Commission on Human Rights convened in March 2002, the defamation issue had become a routine source of conflict with a certain ritualistic predictability regarding the arguments and the voting pattern. After the breakdown of negotiations in 2001 and no consensus to consider, the OIC was less constrained and therefore adopted stronger language in the years to come. The events of 9/11 triggered new concerns for the spread of Islamophobia in the West, and the UN's special rapporteur on racism, the Senegalese Dodou Diène, submitted several reports that recognized and strengthened the OIC's argument. He approached defamation of religions as a new form of human rights violation and was preoccupied with the "amalgamation of race, religion and culture."[38]

Before the Danish cartoon affair in 2005, no leading newspaper in Europe had reported on the defamation resolutions (Langer 2014:179), and the resolutions were adopted every year in the UN Commission on Human Rights (in 2006 replaced by the Human Rights Council due to institutional reforms). In 2005, the resolution also reached the General Assembly in New York, and in 2006, new patterns became visible in the OIC's discourse. From the first resolution in 1999, all resolutions contained the word "defamation" in the title, but in 2006, eleven OIC member states put forward a resolution entitled "Incitement to Racial and Religious Hatred and the Promotion of Tolerance" on behalf of the OIC.[39] The resolution's short text contained references to Article 20(2) in the International Covenant on Civil and Political Rights (ICCPR), which stated that "any advocacy of national, racial or religious hatred that constitutes incitement to discrimination, hostility or violence shall be prohibited by law" (ICCPR 1966). In other words, the OIC was now explicitly framing defamation of religions as a manifestation of hate speech in violation of international law. Since the early 1990s, OIC had called for a new and binding legal instrument to outlaw defamation of religions, but without explicitly abandoning this ambition, the OIC was increasingly utilizing existing legal provisions in international law while justifying its campaign on the basis of existing free speech prohibitions in UN conventions. Again, we see how the meaning of seemingly "fixed" norms was constantly being redefined and reinterpreted by normative agents in the UN system. While broadening the scope of existing hate speech provisions in international law, the OIC was also addressing the need for a new legal blasphemy prohibition, which could be realized by adopting an additional protocol to the ICCPR or the International Convention on the Elimination of All Forms of Racial Discrimination (ICERD). This ambition to outlaw religious defamation has remained persistent.

However, and in a somewhat contradictory fashion, OIC representatives also claim that existing legal provisions are sufficient, as defamation of religions constitutes a violation of Article 20(2) in the ICCPR. In other words, material insulting the Prophet Muhammed violates international law. By broadening the interpretation of this inherently ambiguous free speech article in the ICCPR, the OIC seeks to redefine the content of "universal" free speech norms. When the United States ratified the ICCPR, it expressed reservations with regard to Article 20(2) due to its incompatibility with American free speech ideals enshrined in the First Amendment to the U.S. Constitution. Therefore, and with renewed assertiveness, the OIC has claimed to defend and uphold international human rights law, while the United States and Europe have failed. This argument challenges head-on the Western monopoly of defining the meaning and the implications of international law. However, the OIC's argument was undermined when, in 2011, the UN Human Rights Committee, a body of independent experts who interpret UN treaties, made clear that there was no legal basis for OIC's interpretation of the aforementioned article in the ICCPR: "Prohibitions of displays of lack of respect for a religion or other belief system, including blasphemy laws, are incompatible with the Covenant. . . . Nor would it be permissible for such prohibitions to be used to prevent or punish criticism of religious leaders or commentary on religious doctrine and tenets of faith."[40] Hence, according to the Human Rights Committee, criminalizing defamation of religions is incompatible with international law.

The United States Enters the Picture: The Beginning of the End for the OIC's Defamation Agenda

As part of institutional reforms in 2006, the UN dismantled the Commission on Human Rights and established the Human Rights Council, as the commission was regarded as an ineffective and politicized body due to regionalism and group tactics shielding the world's worst human rights violators (Freedman 2013:197). However, when the so-called reform did not meet U.S. expectations, especially because membership criteria were not enforced in practice and allowed systematic violators of human rights to achieve membership, the Bush administration chose to stay out of the council and later boycotted the council all together. In the laconic words of U.S. Ambassador John Bolton: "We want a butterfly. We're not going to put lipstick on a caterpillar and declare it a success" (*Economist* 2006).

After Obama's presidential victory in 2008 and his famous Cairo speech in Egypt, the United States joined the Human Rights Council again as part of a renewed multilateral engagement with the Muslim world.[41] According to U.S. diplomats, the newly appointed Secretary of State Hillary Clinton was immediately preoccupied with the defamation debate in the Human Rights Council (Nossel 2012), and the U.S. mission in Geneva perceived the OIC's campaign as dangerous for two main reasons: firstly, the defamation agenda legitimized gross human rights violations in the Muslim world, especially against minorities and dissenting individuals. Secondly, the defamation agenda could potentially redefine—and undermine—freedom of expression as an international human right. Despite UN resolutions being non-binding, they have, in the words of former U.S. ambassador Jeane Kirkpatrick a tendency, like "ground water," to seep into international court opinions and gradually change existing interpretations of international law (Marshall and Shea 2011:320).

Seeking to dismantle the entrenched divide between the OIC and the Western bloc, the U.S. mission in Geneva approached its Egyptian counterpart and proposed a partnership on a new resolution on freedom of expression (Nossel 2012:5). After months of negotiations with huge compromises on both sides, the alliance was announced, sending shockwaves through the UN system. The resolution was adopted by consensus[42] and triggered criticism in the United States, both because the language of the resolution was perceived as vague and imprecise and because the U.S.-Egypt partnership was seen as a generous U.S. recognition of an autocratic Middle Eastern regime grossly violating the right to free expression (Peretz 2009).

However, the U.S.-Egypt alliance soon dissolved as the United States set out to dismantle the comfortable majority supporting the OIC's resolution. The United States approached members from Latin America, Africa, the Middle East, and Asia, and with a combination of stick and carrot, persuasion and pressure, the superpower's influence on the voting pattern in the council soon materialized.[43] As a result of this diplomatic offensive, more and more countries switched sides, and the gap between the no votes and the yes votes decreased rapidly. Prior to the vote in the spring of 2011, the OIC had two options. It could either compromise on a new resolution with the United States and the European Union, or it could stick to its own resolution and risk defeat. The multilateral activism of the U.S. mission, both in Geneva and in different capitals in OIC member states, split the influential OIC members into two main groups. With memories still fresh of the assassination of Pakistani minority minister Shahbaz Bhatti and the reformist Punjab Governor Salman Taseer (assassinated because of their vocal opposition to Pakistan's blasphemy laws), Pakistan was inclined to compromise, as was Turkey. OIC secretary-general at the time, the Turkish Ekmeleddin İhsanoğlu, supported a compromise and was heavily involved in the negotiations, and Pakistan and Turkey held extensive talks with the United States and the UK, which led the negotiations on behalf of the EU. The strongest opposition came from Egypt and Saudi Arabia, who vehemently opposed any compromise. After unfruitful meetings within the OIC group, Pakistan took an unusual decision and called for a vote.[44] The majority voted in favor of abandoning the old resolution and accepted a new text more in line with Western hate-speech laws. The EU and the United States argued that the new resolution, eventually adopted as a consensus resolution,[45] was an unequivocal victory for free speech, as it underpinned the belief that religious people have rights, but not religions per se. The resolution's only passage on legal measures is defined narrowly and completely in line with U.S. free speech law, encouraging states to adopt "measures to criminalize incitement to imminent violence based on religion or belief."[46] In other words, incitement to "imminent violence" is the only legitimate free speech infringement. The narrowness in the words "imminent violence" demonstrates the fingerprints of the United States. According to one dissatisfied Egyptian diplomat in Geneva opposing the compromise, "the very purpose of OIC's long struggle was to protect our religion and our Prophet from insult and defamation. Therefore, resolution 16/18 was a huge defeat. Due to American pressure, the support for our resolution was gradually diminishing, but we should have continued our efforts instead of giving in to Western pressure, even if our resolution had been defeated."[47]

Hillary Clinton called the new compromise a "landmark achievement" (U.S. State Department 2011), and Secretary-General Ekmeleddin İhsanoğlu, who was very influential during the negotiations, called the resolution "a poster child of OIC-US-EU cooperation" (Petersen and Kayaoglu 2013). The paramount question was, of course, whether the new resolution marked any substantial change. Were the profound conflicts resolved? Did the international community reach a new consensus on the scope and the implications of international free speech norms?

Unsurprisingly, the answer is no. Unaffected by the new and widely praised consensus, a press release from the OIC in early 2011 made it clear that the organization "did not back down from its position" (Mchangama 2011a). Pakistan's UN ambassador at the time, Masood Khan, reiterated that the ultimate objective was still "a new instrument or convention" addressing defamation (Blitt 2010:21). During the March session of the Human Rights Council in 2011, Secretary-General İhsanoğlu reiterated his call for a UN observatory "to monitor acts of defamation of all religions" (İhsanoğlu 2011) and asserted that the "perception that supporting [defamation of religion] would throttle one's right to freedom of expression is only a myth" (Blitt

2011b:362). Pakistan's ambassador, Zamir Akram, also stated that "this resolution does not replace the OIC's earlier resolutions on combating defamation of religions which were adopted by the Human Rights Council and continue to remain valid" (Blitt 2011b:368). Likewise, the Saudi Arabian ambassador emphasized that "this text . . . is not replacing the other existing text which also criminalizes attack on religion" (Blitt 2011b:363).

Five years after the so-called diplomatic breakthrough, old fault lines are still intact, and the OIC's goal remains the same: to establish a binding international legal instrument that prohibits defamation of religions. While pursuing this goal, the OIC's discourse remains contradictory. Sometimes, the organization pursues its agenda within the framework of existing measures, and at other times, new legal measures are called for (Mayer 2015). This latter ambition is exactly what the OIC has sought to do in another UN institution, the so-called Ad Hoc Committee on the Elaboration of Complementary Standards. This committee was mandated to "elaborate . . . complementary standards in the form of either a convention or additional protocol(s) to the International Convention on the Elimination of All Forms of Racial Discrimination, filling the existing gaps in the Convention, and also providing new normative standards aimed at combating all forms of contemporary racism, including incitement to racial and religious hatred."[48] The Ad Hoc Committee has been chaired by the former Algerian ambassador to the UN, Idriss Jazairy, who has endorsed and promoted the OIC's position on freedom of expression. During an interview in 2015, the Pakistani Mission in Geneva made it clear that Pakistan still wanted new international legal standards to protect religion, and this ambition was being pursued within the Ad Hoc Committee: "We still agree that there is a need for such an instrument to combat defamation of religions. In this regard, we are also engaged in the Committee on the Elaboration of Complementary Standards where the issue of religious intolerance is being discussed as a contemporary form of racism. It is a step by step approach where we may start with some kind of soft law leading towards [a] binding instrument in the long term. Such universally agreed international standards will also assist in strengthening domestic laws/regulations on this crucial subject."[49]

Such statements strengthen the argument of those who claim that for the OIC, Resolution 16/18 was merely a tactical shift, where the same goal was pursued by other means. When the defamation agenda was defeated, the OIC embarked on a new strategy that aimed to broaden existing hate-speech provisions by redefining the scope and the meaning of concepts such as racism and hate speech. This discursive strategy may be more likely to succeed in secular human rights forums. Most Western states have abolished blasphemy laws or ceased to enforce them but, excepting the United States, nearly all have hate-speech laws in place which are actively enforced.

Resolution 16/18 also sparked the so-called Istanbul Process, a series of meetings monitoring the implementation of the resolution. Five meetings have been held as of this writing; the third meeting in Geneva in 2013 (Petersen and Kayaoglu 2013) and the fifth meeting in Saudi Arabia in June 2015—attended by this author—revealed old fault lines. The central bone of contention was still how to interpret existing free speech provisions in international law and how to interpret the phrase "incitement to imminent violence" in Resolution 16/18. During the meeting in Jeddah in June 2015, OIC members claimed that offensive cartoons violated international human rights law and should be criminalized, while countries including Chile, the UK, and the United States argued that such far-reaching interpretations leave UN conventions null and void and undermine the very right to speak freely about religion. According to this argument, it has never been—and should never become—a human right to live your life without the risk of someone offending your religious beliefs.

Conclusion: Employing Human Rights Language to Undermine Human Rights

From the late 1970s the call to combat certain speech forms targeting religion have been integrated into the OIC's internal discourse, and from the early 1990s, the OIC has called for a new international legal instrument curtailing blasphemy or defamation of religions. In 1999, the OIC group in Geneva launched a UN resolution combating "defamation of religions," which was adopted every year and triggered massive UN reporting until 2011, when the new consensus Resolution 16/18 was unanimously adopted. The United States was the primary actor undermining the OIC's political support for the defamation agenda, and in that sense, the OIC's long-term project was defeated. However, Resolution 16/18 and the subsequent Istanbul Process have shown that the normative struggle to define the content of universal free speech norms remains open.

Over time, the OIC's discourse on free speech norms has evolved. During the 1980s, after the Rushdie Affair and during several confrontations in

UN human rights forums in the 1990s, OIC rhetoric was permeated with references to religious principles, but the 1999 UN resolution marked a new phase in OIC human rights discourse, where references to God, religious symbols, or holy scriptures were significantly toned down. On the contrary, the OIC deliberately sought to promote its agenda by utilizing secular human rights language. By framing religious defamation as acts of, for example, racism, hate speech, intolerance, or discrimination, OIC representatives argued that to combat such defamation was a way of protecting the human rights of individual believers. Despite such translation of arguments, the West still found the OIC's agenda problematic and opposed the resolution from 2001 onward. This development prompted a second discursive change, when the OIC started to utilize more systematically concrete free speech prohibitions in international law, particularly Article 20(2) in the ICCPR, which was a controversial article from the very beginning of its drafting history. Despite the adoption of consensus Resolution 16/18 in 2011, the struggle to interpret free speech norms globally remains wide open, and the OIC is still the key actor challenging free speech norms as interpreted and applied by the West.

This clash between the OIC and the West is frequently portrayed as a clash between universalism and cultural relativism, but this conceptualization misses the point. The OIC's human rights discourse is permeated with the recognition of the universality of human rights and the pledge to promote universalism. Therefore, the correct question to ask is not how the OIC challenges universal human rights, but how it seeks to *redefine* the content of universal norms, *reinterpret* international law, and *renegotiate* the substantial meaning of "universality." Despite OIC attempts to frame censorship as a way of protecting the human rights of individuals, I would still argue that the OIC represents a nonliberal version of universalism that challenges the liberal human rights tradition, first and foremost because the consequences of OIC's policies are rigorous censorship that empowers and arms political and religious elites against vulnerable deviating minorities and dissenting individuals. The enforcement of blasphemy laws in the Muslim world illustrates the implications of banning defamation of religions. Furthermore, the OIC frequently justifies censorship in the context of Islamophobia in the West while arguing for the need to protect Muslim minorities. However, if the OIC's leadership were truly committed to minority protection as a general principle, the human rights record in many powerful OIC member states would most likely be less alarming (U.S. Commission on International Religious Freedom 2015a). Hence, the OIC is strategically utilizing prevalent human rights language in order to undermine human rights as it is commonly understood. In the words of Fred Halliday, "If there is a conflict between Western and internationally established codes of conduct and those of the Islamic states it is not one between universalism and particularism, but between two, apparently divergent and contradictory, forms of universalisms" (Halliday 1995:159). According to this argument, the "universal" is a tabula rasa, a signifier devoid of substance, and "universal norms" are therefore a result of normative struggles between rival actors in the UN who all seek hegemony. Therefore, international norms are also dynamic in terms of content and meaning. The OIC's persistent attempt to either install "defamation of religions" as a new human rights violation or to reinterpret existing norms illustrates the ongoing political struggle to define the content of "universality."

By approaching the OIC as a vehicle for international norm diffusion, this chapter analyzes OIC attempts to rearticulate the right to freedom of expression by introducing a new norm, namely the call to criminalize defamation of religions internationally. As argued, this agenda represents an attempt to limit free speech vis-à-vis religion and internationalize repressive blasphemy laws as enforced domestically in OIC's leading member states. The devastating free speech record in states such as Egypt, Iran, Pakistan, Turkey, and Saudi Arabia speaks its own unequivocal language. Implementing the OIC's human rights agenda internationally would therefore represent a detrimental attack on the right to speak freely about religion as codified in international law.

Notes

Parts of this chapter have also been published in: Skorini, Heini, and Marie Juul Petersen. 2017. "Hate Speech and Holy Prophets: Tracing the OIC's Strategies to Protect Religion." In *Religion, the State and Human Rights*, ed. Anne Stensvold. London: Routledge.

The interviews conducted in this research are anonymized according to the wishes of all interviewees. For the reader's information, the majority of the interviewees are former or current diplomats, civil servants, and UN ambassadors. Furthermore, I have also interviewed one NGO representative present in the UN Human Rights Council Geneva and one academic. The interviewees come from the United States, Europe, the Middle East, and Southeast Asia.

1. UN General Assembly, E/CN.4/1999/L.40, 1999.

2. OIC Resolution 31/10-P, 1979.

3. Many OIC members have never ratified the ICCPR, and other OIC members have only ratified the convention with far-reaching reservations motivated by religious concerns (see https://treaties.un.org/; Langer 2014:361).

4. OIC Resolution 31/10-P, 1979.

5. OIC Final Communiqué, "Third Islamic Summit Conference, The Mecca Declaration of the Third Islamic Summit Conference," 1981, para. 6 (see http://ww1.oic-oci.org/english/conf/is/3/3rd-is-sum.htm).

6. OIC Resolution 4/3-P (IS), 1981.

7. Anonymous interviews, former Pakistani diplomat, telephone interview with author, Denmark-New York, July 4, 2015; researcher on the OIC, Skype interview with author, Denmark-Malaysia, May 13, 2015; OIC diplomat, interview with author, Jeddah, June 3, 2015; Pakistani diplomat, Skype interview with author, Denmark-Islamabad, May 3, 2015.

8. Anonymous interviews, former Pakistani diplomat, telephone interview with author, Denmark-New York, July 4, 2015; Egyptian diplomat, interview with author, Geneva, June 17, 2015; British diplomat, Skype interview with author, Tel Aviv-London, January 26, 2015.

9. Anonymous interview, Pakistani diplomat, Skype interview with author, Denmark-Islamabad, May 3, 2015.

10. UN Human Rights Treaty, E/CN.4/1989/SR.41, para. 19–21, 1989.

11. OIC Final Communiqué, 1989, "18th Islamic Conference of Foreign Ministers," para. 46 (see http://www.oic-oci.org/english/conf/fm/18/18%20icfm-final-en.htm).

12. Ibid.

13. OIC, Dakar Declaration, 1991, "Sixth Islamic Summit Conference," ch. 3 (see: http://www.oicoci.org/english/conf/is/6/6th-is-sum(declaration).htm).

14. OIC Resolution 3/6-C (IS), 1991.

15. Ibid.

16. OIC Resolution 17/21-C, 1993.

17. OIC, Cairo Declaration on Human Rights in Islam, p. 10 (see https://www.oic-iphrc.org/en/data/docs/legal_instruments/OIC_HRRIT/571230.pdf).

18. UN General Assembly, A/CONF.157/PC/62/Add.18, 1993.

19. See: http://www.oic-iphrc.org/en/legal/.

20. OIC Final Communiqué 1981, "Third Islamic Summit Conference, The Mecca Declaration of the Third Islamic Summit Conference," para. 6 (see: http://ww1.oic-oci.org/english/conf/is/3/3rd-is-sum.htm).

21. See, for instance, the 1996 report by the UN Special Rapporteur on religious intolerance, Abdelfattah Amor, E/CN.4/1997/91, as well as the 1994 report by the UN Special Rapporteur on the human rights situation in Sudan, Gaspar Biro, E/CN.4/1994/48, paras. 66–85. In both cases, Muslim-majority member states reacted with fury (*Washington Post* 1994; E/CN.4/1996/57, paras. 37–8).

22. UN E/CN.4/1995/91, p. 71 (see: https://documents-dds-ny.un.org/doc/UNDOC/GEN/G94/751/53/pdf/G9475153.pdf?OpenElement).

23. UN E/CN.4/1996/95/Add.1, para. 82.

24. UN E/CN.4/1999/SR.2, para. 63.

25. Anonymous interview, Egyptian diplomat, interview with author, Geneva, June 17, 2015.

26. UN E/CN.4/1999/L.40.

27. Anonymous interview, former Pakistani diplomat, telephone interview with author, Denmark-New York, July 4, 2015.

28. UN E/CN.4/1999/L.40.

29. UN E/CN.4/1999/SR.61, paras. 1–2.

30. Anonymous interview, UN diplomat, interview with author, Geneva, June 17, 2015.

31. UN E/CN.4/1999/SR.62, para. 9.

32. UN E/CN.4/2001/L.7.

33. Anonymous interview, British diplomat, Skype interview with author, Tel Aviv-London, January 26, 2015.

34. Countries voting in favor: Algeria, Argentina, Brazil, Cameroon, China, Colombia, Costa Rica, Cuba, Ecuador, Indonesia, Libya, Kenya, Madagascar, Malaysia, Mauritius, Mexico, Niger, Pakistan, Peru, Qatar, Russia, Saudi Arabia, Syria, Senegal, Thailand, Uruguay, Venezuela, and Vietnam. Countries voting against: Belgium, Canada, Czech Republic, France, Germany, Italy, Japan, Latvia, Norway, Poland, Portugal, Romania, Spain, UK, and the United States. Abstentions: Burundi, Guatemala, India, Liberia, Nigeria, South Africa, South Korea, Swaziland, and Zambia.

35. UN A/54/116, 1999.

36. Anonymous interview, Swedish diplomat, interview with author, Copenhagen, May 5, 2015.

37. Anonymous interview, Swedish diplomat, interview with author, Copenhagen, May 5, 2015.

38. Anonymous interview, former UN special rapporteur, interview with author, Jeddah, June 4, 2015.

39. UN A/HRC/1/L.16. The countries were Algeria, Iran, Jordan, Lebanon, Malaysia, Morocco, Oman, Pakistan, Qatar, Sudan and Tunisia.

40. UN CCPR/C/GC/34, para. 48. The irony is that during the negotiations on the ICCPR in the early 1950s, U.S. representative Eleanor Roosevelt fought staunchly against this particular article (E/CN.4/SR.174, para. 27), but the voting bloc backed by the Soviet Union succeeded in adopting it anyway.

41. Anonymous interview, U.S. diplomat, interview with author, Jeddah, June 4, 2015.

42. UN A/HRC/RES/12/16.

43. The WikiLeaks database contains more than two hundred documents with the sentence "defamation of religions." These documents reveal just how comprehensively U.S. diplomacy was operating in all corners of the world. (See WikiLeaks 2009, Cable 09STATE122639_a.)

44. Anonymous interview, former OIC diplomat, interview with author, Geneva, June 17, 2015.

45. UN A/HRC/RES/16/18.

46. UN A/HRC/RES/16/18, para. 5.

47. Anonymous interview, Geneva, June 17, 2015.

48. A/HRC/RES/6/21, preamble (http://ap.ohchr.org/documents/E/HRC/resolutions/A_HRC_RES_6_21.pdf).

49. Anonymous interview, Pakistani diplomat, email interview with author, Denmark-Geneva, May 28, 2015.

Works Cited

Alfandari, Julia Yael, Jo Baker, and Regula Amnah Atteya. 2011. "Defamation of Religions: International Developments and Challenges on the Ground: SOAS International Human

Rights Clinic Project." SOAS School of Law Research Paper No. 09/2011. London: School of Oriental and African Studies and Cairo Institute for Human Rights Studies.

Amnesty International. 1994. *Pakistan: Use and Abuse of the Blasphemy Laws*, July 26. https://www.amnesty.org/en/documents/asa33/008/1994/en/.

———. 2001. *Pakistan: Insufficient Protection of Religious Minorities*, May 14. https://www.amnesty.org/en/documents/asa33/008/2001/en/.

Aswad, Evelyn. M. 2013. "To Ban or Not to Ban Blasphemous Videos." *Georgetown Journal of International Law* 44: 1313–28.

Bettiza, Gregorio, and Dionigi, Filippo. 2014. "Beyond Constructivism's Liberal Bias: Islamic Norm Entrepreneurs in a Post-Secular World Society." EUI Working Paper MWP 10. Badia Fiesolana: European University Institute.

Blitt, Robert C. 2010. "Should New Bills of Rights Address Emerging International Human Rights Norms? The Challenge of 'Defamation of Religion.'" *Northwestern Journal of International Human Rights* 9 (1): 1–26.

———. 2011a. "The Bottom up Journey of "Defamation of Religion" from Muslim States to the United Nations: A Case Study of the Migration of Anti-Constitutional Ideas." *Studies in Law, Politics, and Society,* (Special Issue Human Rights: New Possibilities/New Problems) 56: 121–211.

———. 2011b. "Defamation of Religion: Rumors of Its Death Are Greatly Exaggerated." *Case Western Reserve Law Review* 62 (2). http://dx.doi.org/10.2139/ssrn.2040812.

Chase, Anthony. 1996. "Legal Guardians: Islamic Law, International Law, Human Rights Law, and the Salman Rushdie Affair." *American University International Law Review* 11 (3): 375–435.

Dobras, Rebecca J. 2009. "Is the United Nations Endorsing Human Rights Violations? An Analysis of the United Nations' Combating Defamation of Religions Resolutions and Pakistan's Blasphemy Laws." *Georgia Journal of International and Comparative Law* 37: 339.

Economist. 2006. "The UN's Human Rights Council: A Caterpillar in Lipstick?" March 2. http://www.economist.com/node/5577499.

———. 2014. "Bad-Mouthing: Pakistan's Blasphemy Laws Legitimise Intolerance." November 27. http://www.economist.com/news/asia/21635070-pakistans-blasphemy-laws-legitimise-intolerance-bad-mouthing.

Farrior, Stephanie. 1996. "Molding the Matrix: The Historical and Theoretical Foundations of International Law Concerning Hate Speech." *Berkeley Journal of International Law* 14 (1). https://scholarship.law.berkeley.edu/bjil/vol14/iss1/1/.

Freedman, Rosa. 2013. *The United Nations Human Rights Council: A Critique and Early Assessment*. Abingdon: Routledge.

Freedom House. 2010. *Policing Belief: The Impact of Blasphemy Laws on Human Rights*. https://freedomhouse.org/sites/default/files/Policing_Belief_Full.pdf.

Forte, David F. 1994. "Apostasy and Blasphemy in Pakistan." *Connecticut Journal of International Law* 10: 27.

Graham, L. Bennett. 2009. "Defamation of Religions: The End of Pluralism?" *Emory International Law Review* 23: 69.

Grinberg, Maxim. 2006. "Defamation of Religions v. Freedom of Expression: Finding the Balance in a Democratic Society." *Sri Lanka Journal of International Law* 18: 197.

Halliday, Fred. 1995. "Relativism and Universalism in Human Rights: The Case of the Islamic Middle East." *Political Studies* 43: 152–67.

Halliday, Fred, and Hamza Alavi. 1988. *State and Ideology in the Middle East and Pakistan*. London: Palgrave.

Hare, Ivan, and James Weinstein, eds. 2009. *Extreme Speech and Democracy*. Oxford: Oxford University Press.

Human Rights *First*. 2012. *Blasphemy Laws Exposed: The Consequences of Criminalizing "Defamation of Religions."* http://www.humanrightsfirst.org/wp-content/uploads/Blasphemy_Cases.pdf.

Human Rights Watch. 1993. *Persecuted Minorities and Writers in Pakistan*, September 19. https://www.hrw.org/legacy/reports/1993/pakistan/.

———. 2014. *Saudi Arabia: New Terrorism Legislations Assault Rights: Campaign to Silence Peaceful Activists*, March 20. https://www.hrw.org/news/2014/03/20/saudi-arabia-new-terrorism-regulations-assault-rights.

İhsanoğlu, Ekmeleddin. 2010. *The Islamic World in the New Century: The Organization of the Islamic Conference, 1969–2009*. London: Hurst.

———. 2011. "Statement by the H. E. Prof. Ekmeleddin İhsanoğlu, Secretary-General of the Organization of the Islamic Conference, at the High Level Segment of the 16th Session of the Human Rights Council." March 1. http://www.humanrightsvoices.org/assets/attachments/documents/9429hrc16sessionoic.pdf.

Jahangir, Asma. 2011. "Pakistan's Tenets of the Faith." *New Statesman*, April 14. http://www.newstatesman.com/asia/2011/04/pakistan-laws-women-religious.

James, Vaughn E. 2009. "Defamation of Religion versus Freedom of Expression: Finding the Balance." *Fides et Libertas* 43: 44–45.

Kayaoglu, Turan. 2014. "Giving an Inch Only to Lose a Mile: Muslim States, Liberalism and Human Rights in the United Nations." *Human Rights Quarterly* 36 (1): 61–89.

Khan, Ali. 2007. "Combating Defamation of Religions." *American Muslim*, January 1. https://ssrn.com/abstract=954403.

Klausen, Jytte. 2009. *The Cartoons That Shook the World*. New Haven, CT: Yale University Press.

Krook, Mona Lena, and Jacqui True. 2012. "Rethinking the Life Cycles of International Norms: The United Nations and the Global Promotion of Gender Equality." *European Journal of International Relations* 18 (1): 103–27.

Langer, Lorenz. 2014. *Religious Offence and Human Rights: The Implications of Defamation of Religions*. Cambridge: Cambridge University Press.

Marshall, Paul, and Nina Shea. 2011. *Silenced: How Apostasy and Blasphemy Codes Are Choking Freedom Worldwide*. Oxford: Oxford University Press.

Mayer, Ann Elizabeth. 2006. *Islam and Human Rights: Tradition and Politics*. 4th ed. Boulder, CO: Westview.

———. 2015. "The OIC's Human Rights Policies in the UN: A Problem of Coherence." *Matters of Concern* series working paper no. 2015/4. Copenhagen: Danish Institute for Human Rights. https://www.humanrights.dk/publications/oics-human-rights-policies-un-problem-coherence.

Mchangama, Jacob. 2011a. "The OIC vs. Freedom of Expression." *National Review*, April 7. http://www.nationalreview.com/article/264113/oic-vs-freedom-expression-jacob-mchangama.

———. 2011b. "The Sordid Origin of Hate-Speech Laws." *Policy Review* 170: 45–58.

Nossel, Suzanne. 2012. *Advancing Human Rights in the UN System*. New York: Council on Foreign Relations.

Peretz, Marin. 2009. "U.S., Egypt Co-Sponsor a Resolution on Freedom of Opinion and Expression. What the Hell Is Going On? Only the A.P. Reported This: I Wonder Why." *New Republic*, October 5. https://newrepublic.com/article/69993/us-egypt-co-sponsor-resolution-freedom-opinion-and-expression-what-the-hell-going-here.

Petersen, Marie Juul, and Turan Kayaoglu. 2013. "Will Istanbul Process Relieve the Tension Between the Muslim World and the West?" *Washington Review of Turkish and Euroasian Affairs*, September 30.

Pew Research. 2014. "Which countries still outlaw apostasy and blasphemy?" http://www.pewresearch.org/fact-tank/2014/05/28/whichcountries-still-outlaw-apostasy-and-blasphemy.

Said, Edward W. 1981 *Covering Islam: How the Media and the Experts Determine How We See the Rest of the World*. New York: Pantheon.

Saudi Gazette. 2015. "Saudi Official: Criminalize Vilification of Religious Symbols." July 26. http://english.alarabiya.net/en/News/middle-east/2015/07/26/Saudi-official-Criminalize-vilification-of-religious-symbols.html.

Siddique, Osama, and Zarah Hayat. 2008. "Unholy Laws and Holy Speech: Blasphemy Laws in Pakistan—Controversial Origins, Design Defects, and Free Speech Implications." *Minnesota Journal of International Law* 17 (2): 303.

Temperman, Jeroen. 2012. "Blasphemy, Defamation of Religions & Human Rights Law." *Netherlands Quarterly of Human Rights* 26 (4): 517–45.

U.S. Commission on International Religious Freedom. 2015a. *Annual Report 2015*. http://www.uscirf.gov/sites/default/files/USCIRF%20Annual%20Report%202015%20%282%29.pdf.

———. 2015b. *Pakistan*. http://www.uscirf.gov/sites/default/files/Pakistan%202015.pdf.

U.S. State Department. 2011. "Secretary Clinton: Adoption of Resolution 16/18 Countering Religious Intolerance a 'Landmark Achievement.'" Press statement, March 24, 2011. https://geneva.usmission.gov/2011/03/24/adoption-of-resolution-at-human-rights-council-combating-discrimination-and-violence/.

Washington Post. 1994. "The Next Rushdie?" March 26. https://www.washingtonpost.com/archive/lifestyle/1994/03/26/the-next-rushdie/f306048f-37d4-4022-94d7-db739cf3c915/.

———. 2011. "Shahbaz Bhatti, Pakistan's Sole Christian Minister, Is Assassinated in Islamabad." March 2. http://www.washingtonpost.com/wp-dyn/content/article/2011/03/01/AR2011030101394.html.

WikiLeaks. 2009. Cable 09STATE122639_a. https://wikileaks.org/plusd/cables/09STATE122639_a.html.

Withnall, Adam. 2014. "Saudi Arabia Declares All Atheists Are Terrorists in New Law to Crack Down on Political Dissidents." *Independent*, April 1. http://www.independent.co.uk/news/world/middle-east/saudi-arabia-declares-all-atheists-are-terrorists-in-new-law-to-crack-down-on-political-dissidents-9228389.html.

CHAPTER 6

Competing Perceptions: Traditional Values and Human Rights

Moataz El Fegiery

Introduction

Over the last three decades, international human rights constituencies have expanded, and their language has become a source of inspiration for social movements, political activists, and marginalized groups all over the world (Goodhart 2008; Chase 2012; Risse, Roop, and Sikkink 2013). However, the debate on cultural relativism and the universal applicability of human rights continues to inform international politics and is occasionally revisited in the UN. Since its adoption of the Cairo Declaration on Human Rights in Islam in 1990,[1] the Organization of Islamic Cooperation (OIC) has become a key international player in this debate, and on most of its positions it has been an outspoken advocate for cultural relativism and has provided an alternative interpretation of certain human rights (Mayer 2012; Cismas 2014; Kayaoglu 2015). A clear example of this can be seen in the OIC's efforts at the UN Human Rights Council (HRC) to restrict the scope of freedom of expression under the pretext of protecting religions, especially Islam, from contempt or defamation (Leo, Gaer, and Cassidy 2011; Langer 2014).

Another legal and political battlefield has emerged at the UN HRC concerning the relationship between human rights, culture, and religion—the so-called respect for traditional values. This process began in October 2009 with a resolution entitled *Promoting Human Rights and Fundamental Freedoms,* initiated by Russia and sponsored by OIC member states.[2] This resolution and two similar resolutions adopted by the HRC on April 8, 2011[3] and October 9, 2012[4] proposed a series of activities at the HRC with the objective of exploring "how a better understanding of traditional values of humankind underpinning international human rights norms and standards can contribute to the promotion and protection of human rights and fundamental freedoms." The "traditional values" argument has been perceived suspiciously or condemned by many other states as well as key international and regional human rights nongovernmental organizations (NGOs). This chapter examines how traditional values are defined and framed by different actors involved in this debate, arguing that the introduction of this new frame of reference by Russia and the OIC aimed to undermine the universality of certain human rights and most specifically lesbian, gay, bisexual, transgender, and intersex (LGBTI) rights. The first section of this chapter introduces the traditional values resolutions, examines the political context of their emergence in the HRC, engages more specifically with the concept of traditional values and analyses its contradictory and ambiguous nature. The second section explores how the relationship between traditional values and human rights has been framed by different actors who contributed to the discussion of traditional values in the HRC. The final section discusses the extent to which international human rights law can tolerate the derogation from some aspects of its norms in the name of culture or traditions. The analysis in this paper draws on the HRC's documents related to the process of traditional values of humankind, as well as publications and commentaries by representatives of OIC member states[5] and NGOs.

Traditional Values Agenda in the Human Rights Council

Between 2009 and 2012, the UN Human Rights Council adopted three resolutions under the title *Promoting Human Rights and Fundamental Freedoms Through a Better Understanding of Traditional Values of Humankind* which were initiated by Russia with the support of OIC member states. The main focus of the resolutions was to advocate the importance of traditional values in international human rights discourse. Quoting the Vienna Declaration of the first World Conference on Human Rights,[6] the 2009 resolution stated that "the significance of national and regional particularities and various historical, cultural and religious backgrounds must be borne in mind." This resolution requested that the Office of the UN High Commissioner for Human

Rights (OHCHR) organize a workshop for an exchange of views on "how a better understanding of traditional values of humankind underpinning international human rights norms and standards can contribute to the promotion of and protection of human rights and fundamental freedoms." The workshop was convened in Geneva on October 4, 2010 with the participation of representatives of states, national human rights institutions, NGOs, and independent experts from different continents and comprised divergent perspectives on the implications of traditional values for the respect for human rights.[7] In his statement at the workshop, the representative of the Moscow Patriarch of the Russian Orthodox Church "warned against abstract determinations in the field of human rights": and stated that "international authorities while making human rights interpretations regarding specific countries should make a thorough examination of the national context."[8] China's representative delivered a similar message, stating that "the concept of human rights should not be monopolised by a few countries and that it was actually deeply rooted in the traditional value system of every country."[9]

The 2011 resolution requested that the HRC Advisory Committee[10] conduct a study on the promotion of human rights and fundamental freedoms through a better understanding of traditional values of humankind. In its seventh session, the Advisory Committee established a drafting group of ten experts, and in December 2011, the rapporteur of the drafting group, the Russian academic Vladimir Kartashkin, submitted a preliminary study to the eighth session of the Advisory Committee, held in February 2012.[11] Many of the views raised in this preliminary study triggered intense disagreement among the Advisory Committee members.[12] The most controversial point in this draft was its argument that "the different approach of states and other civilizations to the way they perceive some norms of current international law must be respected."[13] The draft also suggested that human rights should be contingent on individual "responsible behaviour" in respect of the state and society and emphasized the role of the family in preserving and transmitting traditional values.[14] However, it did not recognize the diverse forms of families under international human rights law and did not provide an equal assessment of the potential positive and negative contributions that the family institution can bring to human rights, particularly the rights of women, children, and LGBTI.

In August 2012, the drafting group submitted another preliminary study to the ninth session of the Advisory Committee, and the final study based on this new preliminary version was submitted to the twenty-second session of the HRC (February 25–March 22, 2013).[15] The final study took an opposite direction from the first preliminary version by highlighting the ambiguous and paradoxical nature of the term "traditional values" and its potentially dangerous implications for the universality of human rights.[16] It, however, argued for the critical and innovative engagement with societal traditions to further the implementation of international human rights law.[17] It also recognized that "family" can have various forms and meanings,[18] and emphasized that "human rights are inalienable and inherent in human person, and are not conditional upon responsible behavior."[19]

The 2012 resolution requested that the OHCHR collect information from UN member states and other relevant stakeholders, such as national institutions of human rights and NGOs, on best practices in the application of traditional values while promoting and protecting human rights. The OHCHR submitted the final report of this consultative process to the twenty-fourth session of the HRC (September 9–27, 2013)[20] (UN HRC 2013). In its submission, the European Union "stressed the need for caution, pointing to the possible danger of introducing the concept of traditional values in the human rights realm as there was no clear-cut universally agreed definition."[21]

Most of the submissions made by states highlighted the use of traditional values in their domestic practices to promote human rights and avoided introducing traditions to limit certain rights.[22] However, there was disagreement among NGOs. Several Christian NGOs from Latin America, Romania, and the United States adopted the conservative philosophy behind the traditional values agenda. Out of thirty-five submissions made by NGOs, sixteen argued that human rights should not in any way threaten the family, often defined as a union between a man and a woman. On the other end of the spectrum, human rights NGOs from different regions—including Russia and the Muslim world—were critical of the use of traditional values-based arguments in their societies to restrict human rights.

Voting behavior in the three resolutions reflected the presence of two major political alliances with two different views on this matter. One alliance consisted of Russia, China, and Cuba together with the member states of the OIC. Mauritius was the only OIC member state that voted against the first resolution, while Indonesia in its support for the resolution was keen to emphasize that its purpose was to contribute to strengthening human rights, not weakening them. The second alliance consisted of EU member states, Canada, Switzerland, the United States, as well as a number of Western allies, including Botswana, Costa Rica, Japan, Mexico, and the Republic of Korea. Some countries in the Global South and Eastern Europe chose to abstain from voting, including Argentina, Benin, Bosnia and Herzegovina, Brazil, Chile, Guatemala, Peru, the Republic of Moldova, Ukraine, and Uruguay.

The polarization between the two alliances has been considered a trend at the HRC since its establishment in March 2007. While the structure of the alliances has changed on some issues, the two have usually taken opposite positions with respect to issues related to the debate on human rights universality, religion and freedom of expression, and LGBTI rights. This trend has led to what the Cairo Institute for Human Rights Studies (CIHRS 2010:225) and others have termed a "West against the rest" type of international solidarity within UN mechanisms that rights-hostile states often use to push through policies designed to weaken the UN human rights system. While many states and human rights NGOs opposed the ambiguous content of the traditional values resolutions, their skepticism also had much to do with its sponsors, most of whom were known for their invocation of cultural or religious traditions to justify their own human rights abuses and limit the scope of international human rights law. This explains why much of the commentary made by key local and international human rights NGOs has focused on the negative aspects of traditional values (CIHRS 2009b; Human Rights Watch 2009; Reid 2012, 2013).

The most delicate point of contention in the OIC's position on traditional values is the assumption that their understanding of traditions is the most authentic one. For example, according to a statement made by Egypt's representative during the discussion of traditional values at the HRC, "Traditional values should not be confused with traditions or practices that were harmful, these had to be fought within the values upon which societies were built." However, it was necessary, according to the Egyptian representative, to differentiate between these harmful practices and what constituted traditional values.[23] But herein lie many unanswered questions. By which criteria are certain practices dismissed and considered harmful and others defended as authentic? The test for this selection is ambiguous and is most likely left to the discretion of the political elite dominating state and religious institutions. If conservative Islamists had been in power, one might have seen the Egyptian representative change his attitudes toward practices such as female genital mutilation or child marriage and consider them traditions and not harmful practices. When the Muslim Brotherhood (2013) was in power in Egypt, it invoked "Islamic values" to protest issues related to gender equality addressed by the fifty-seventh session of the UN Commission on the Status of Women. Egypt has also been among the leading states in driving the so-called defamation of religions agenda, arguing for special protection of religions, and has attempted to obstruct the contribution of NGOs to the debate on the protection of human rights under Islamic law at the HRC. For instance, in June 2008, representatives from Egypt and Pakistan opposed any critical discussion of the treatment of women under Islamic law by human rights NGOs at the HRC (Dacey and Koproske 2008:7). Commenting on this incident, former UN High Commissioner for Human Rights Louise Arbour said, "It is very concerning in a council which should be the guardian of freedom of expression, to see constraints or taboos, or subjects that become taboo for discussion" (CIHRS 2009a:192). In May 2016, Egypt, on behalf of the OIC, blocked the participation of eleven LGBTI NGOs from attending the UN High-Level Meeting on Ending AIDS (Nichols 2016).

The reference to traditional and religious values in opposition to human rights has been apparent in the positions taken by Russia and the OIC with respect to LGBTI rights. Russia and OIC member states, except Mauritius, rejected the two resolutions on human rights, sexual orientation, and gender identity adopted by the HRC on July 14, 2011[24] and October 2, 2014.[25] In February 2012, Zamir Akram, then ambassador of Pakistan, sent a letter on behalf of the OIC to Laura Dupuy Lasserre, the ambassador of Uruguay and the former president of the HRC, protesting the work of the HRC on what Akram and the OIC considered to be "a controversial notion like sexual orientation and gender identity" (UN Islamic Group to UN HRC 2012). In this letter, the OIC invoked traditional values to reject any interpretation of international human rights treaties that involved the protection of lesbian, gay, bisexual, and transgender individuals. During the panel discussion on discrimination and violence based on sexual orientation and gender identity convened by the HRC in March 2011, Mauritania, on behalf of the Arab group[26] explicitly dismissed the debate on sexual orientation and warned that it would further the discord within the HRC. Russia, joined by the Arab group and the majority of the member states of the African group, reaffirmed the importance of respecting different cultural and religious values and rejected what they considered "an attempt to impose concepts and notions on certain behaviors which did not fall into the internationally agreed set of human rights."[27] This position is consistent with anti-LGBTI legislation in Russia (Wilkinson 2014) and most OIC member states (Mayer 2012).

Following the traditional values initiative, Russia and OIC member states initiated another process in the HRC under the title of "The Protection of the Family." This initiative came as a reaction to the inclusion of the LGBTI rights in the work of the HRC since 2011. At the urging of member states of the OIC and Russia, the HRC adopted a resolution, supported by twenty-six member states, "reaffirming that the family is the natural and fundamental group unit of society and is entitled to protection by society and the state."[28] Under this resolution, the HRC decided to convene a panel discussion in its twenty-seventh session on the protection of the family. The HRC adopted another resolution on the protection of the family on 1 July 2015,[29] requesting that OHCHR prepare a report on the impact of the implementation of the international human rights obligation of family members to realize adequate standards of living. The two resolutions highlighted states' responsibility to protect the family institution without considering the individual rights of the members of this institution. They also ignored the diversity of families, including single-parent families or same-sex couples. Saudi Arabia proposed an amendment to the 2014 resolution to define marriage as a union between men and women. On the other hand, an amendment proposed by Uruguay and sponsored by Argentina, Chile, Colombia, Croatia, Guatemala, the United States, and the EU, to add a reference to "various forms of the family"[30] was obstructed by Russia, which invoked the rules of procedures to adjourn the consideration of this amendment. In return, Saudi Arabia withdrew its proposed amendment.[31]

The Western bloc raised the same concerns during the deliberation on the 2015 resolution on the protection of the family, and all of their attempts to amend the text were blocked or rejected. For instance, Brazil, Chile, South Africa, and Uruguay proposed an amendment, including a reference to the existence of various forms of the family, but it was blocked by Russia and OIC member states. Pakistan proposed an amendment to the same resolution to explicitly limit the definition of marriage to a union between a man and a woman. However, this was withdrawn following the obstruction of the amendment proposed by Brazil, Chile, South Africa, and Uruguay. Albania, Denmark, and Norway proposed that the resolution should emphasize the rights of individual family members, and Albania, Ireland, and Norway suggested the omission of a vague sentence stating that "the family plays a crucial role in the preservation of cultural identity, traditions, morals, heritage and value system of the society." However, the two proposals were rejected.[32]

On the other hand, human rights NGOs coming from OIC member states highlighted how the discourse on traditional values has been employed in their countries to limit the scope of international human rights and justify abuses. Well aware of the role of international human rights in the transformation of domestic practices, they adopted a critical and evolutionary perspective of traditions. In its first reaction to the 2009 HRC resolution, the Cairo Institute for Human Rights Studies, a prominent NGO active in the Arab region, rejected the introduction of "traditional values" to the international human rights framework, arguing that the concept had "no basis in international human rights instruments" (CIHRS 2009b). It then pointed out that this concept justifies repression, discrimination, and other violations of human rights, especially women's rights. Similarly, in a written submission to the UN HRC, Nazra for Feminist Studies[33] (2011) referred to "the history of the use of traditional values to undermine the rights of women human rights defenders in Egypt, as the violations were based largely on traditional, patriarchal values regarding what it meant to be a respectable woman." CIHRS and Nazra for Feminist Studies have argued that traditions are diverse and open to competing interpretations. They have pointed to the debate on women's rights in Egypt as an obvious example of this, arguing that for decades, reforms in the personal status laws have been dismissed by the state under the pretext of respecting "Islamic traditional values." But when the state comes to the conclusion that traditional values do not support certain practices and have declared them harmful, other conservative forces challenge these reforms and accuse the government of violating traditions.

In their campaigns, NGOs from the Muslim world joined cross-regional coalitions to convey their concerns globally. Human rights groups from Bangladesh, Egypt, Sudan, Turkey, and regional NGOs including CIHRS and Women Living Under Muslim Laws formulated a statement sponsored by sixty NGOs from all continents which was submitted to the HRC Advisory Committee in August 2011. This joint statement highlighted the transformative role of international human rights law, maintaining that "a human rights-based approach often requires changes to the status quo in order to ensure compliance with international standards."[34] The evolutionary nature of traditions was also highlighted in the statement, noting that "a practice or belief that has existed over a period of time or is practiced by a majority does not provide it with worth or validity." The rights of LGBTI, long seen as a taboo in most OIC member states, were addressed by this coalition of NGOs, which expressed concerns about the refusal of the sponsors of traditional values resolutions to recognize that different types of families exist and require protection, such as families with parents of the same sex or gender.[35] Another important remark made by this coalition of NGOs is that the purpose of international human rights is to "protect groups that have traditionally faced marginalization or exclusion," and according to them, an argument based on traditional values may risk exposing these groups to danger.

Human Rights and the Challenge of Culture and Traditional Practices

The problematic character of the concept of traditional values was highlighted in a workshop held by OHCHR in 2010, which concluded that "there is a danger in making something as undefined and constantly evolving as 'traditional values' the standard for human rights."[36] The idea of "traditional values" or "cultural specificities" has been repeatedly introduced to the debate as a form of resistance to the system of rights established by international human rights treaties. The proponents of this theory tend to essentialize the meaning of traditions and cultures by claiming that a certain value or practice is authentic and representative of a tradition. Such understandings of culture as static, essentialist, and homogenous have been refuted countless times by numerous scholars. Preis (1996), for example, argues that the study of culture and human rights should consider the complexities and the evolving nature of cultural interactions in different contexts.

Traditions usually encompass a wide range of competing values and practices. The identification of specific practices or value systems as mainstream by a group of people at certain periods of history does not mean that these practices or values were not challenged by other individuals, but rather that those dissidents were marginalized or excluded in different ways. The practice of power is decisive in shaping culture. In the words of Sally Merry, "culture is hybrid and porous and . . . the pervasive struggle over cultural values within local communities is competitions over power" (2005:9). The history of premodern Islam is full of examples of certain intellectual schools or practices being dismissed and excluded for the sake of other views or practices. One can argue that international human rights challenges those who aim to maintain a structure of exclusion and hierarchy instead of providing spaces for dissidents and marginalized groups to express themselves on an equal basis.

Another place from which to question the authenticity claim is that "traditions . . . are often newly created for political purposes or borrowed from others" (Merry 2005:13). Certain values or practices have been selectively taken out of their historical context, reframed, and introduced as authentic traditions in paradigmatically different sociopolitical settings. For example, the idea of the "Islamic state" or Sharia as state law is an example of what has been considered "an invention of tradition" (Tibi 2012:12). Abdullahi An-Na'im holds that "the notion of an Islamic state is a postcolonial innovation based on a European model of the state" (2008:7).

Against this background, I argue that the issue at stake in this debate is not *who* has the right to present an authentic definition of a tradition, since the interpretation of traditions will always be a source of disagreement, but *how* a society can peacefully manage competing claims about traditions. One can find differences in the understanding of traditions among states that represent the same civilizational and cultural background. For example, OIC member states' attitudes toward Islam and human rights were not monolithic during the drafting of the Universal Declaration of Human Rights (UDHR; Waltz 2004). Contesting claims about traditions also takes place within populations that adhere to the same cultural heritage. For example, Islamic feminists challenge family laws that some Muslim authorities see as an authentic expression of Islamic legal traditions (Mayer 2008). Legal claims based on traditions can also be made by religious minority groups in opposition to laws applied by the majority. For example, members of Muslim minorities in some Western states may claim certain legal rights or arrangements based on specific interpretations of their traditions that may contravene their constitutional and legal orders (An-Na'im 2014). Meanwhile, members of a certain minority group may adhere to conflicting understandings of their traditions. For instance, some Orthodox Christians in Egypt oppose the strict regulations of marriage and divorce applied by their Church, considering them a misinterpretation of the tenets of their religion (Shaham 2010).

Therefore, a key challenge in the human rights discourse is how states can strike a balance between competing claims made by certain communities to preserve their traditions and the protection of individual rights—particularly the right to equality before the law and nondiscrimination. Liberal theorists argue that a minority group cannot evoke its autonomy as a group to violate the individual rights of its members (Kymlicka 2001:342; Rawls 2005:466–74), and according to this view, "individuals should be able to leave the communal track and transfer their disputes to civil courts at their own will, especially when there is a direct and imminent threat by communal norms and institutions to the constitutionally protected rights and freedoms of individuals" (Sezgin 2013:15).

Thus the issue of traditional values and human rights is not to be simplified as a conflict between an arrogant universal human rights morality and relativist moralities. Peter Jones points out that "the world is in much larger measures one characterized by rival universalisms" (1994:219). Alternatively, the universal morality of human rights can be defended as a tool of settlement of potential conflict that can arise between rival universalisms. Human rights can fulfil this task by achieving a balance between the individual and society without sacrificing the autonomy and freedom of the individual. Human rights also provides subcultural groups within a society the right to preserve their traditions and values without imposing them on those members who may deviate from the dominant interpretation of certain traditions within the same group.

To summarize, traditions become a threat to the universality of human rights when they are invoked to provide states with unchecked discretion in the implementation of their obligations under international human rights law. One, however, needs to consider that societal traditions may not always be seen as a threat to human rights, since the engagement with traditions can be supportive of the implementation as well as the development of international human rights. Through a process of what can be called an inclusive universalism (Baderin 2003:29), different cultural traditions can contribute to a universal conception of human rights.

In many societies, human rights defenders translate international law into local justice, seeking to strengthen the cultural legitimacy and resonance of human rights, what Merry (2005) calls vernacularization—or as suggested by An-Na'im (1990) work to achieve cultural legitimacy of international human rights. On this point, Merry explains that "in order for human rights ideas to be effective . . . they need to be translated into local terms and situated within local contexts of power and meaning. They need in other words to be remade in the vernacular" (2005:1). This was arguably the dominant theory for independent experts who took part in UN activities on traditional values. For example, Tom Zwart proposes "the receptor approach" under which human rights practitioners need to promote human rights through the traditional arrangements already in place in certain countries or they may add new elements to these arrangements (2012, 2014).

During the discussion of traditional values, human rights NGOs from OIC member states mostly focused on real and potential threats posed by this framework to international human rights law. However, the possibility that "traditional values" could also, under certain circumstances, positively contribute to human rights has not been dismissed in the work of many human rights groups in the Muslim world. For example, a coalition of prominent Arab NGOs state in one of their documents on political reform in the Arab world that "cultural or religious particularities should not be invoked as a pretext to doubt and to question the universality of the principles of human rights. The 'particularities' that deserve celebration are those entrenching the citizen's sense of dignity and equality, which enrich his/her culture and life and enhance his/her participation in their own country's public affairs" (CIHRS 2004:14).

Some OIC member states have introduced a conception of traditions as supportive of the implementation of international human rights. For instance, Mauritius has pointed out that it draws on traditional values in human rights education at schools. They claim that certain values such as respect, love for truth, life, family, parents, education, wisdom, nature, compassion, honesty, peace, cooperation, and solidarity are found in the holy books, and that these values enforce the culture of human rights.[37] Jordan argued that its constitution "lays down rights, duties and state responsibilities with regard to equality, dignity and freedom as reflections of values derived from Arabic and Islamic culture based on the state religion."[38] Pakistan declared that "the teaching of Islam is the Magna Carta of human rights as the principles of human rights were enunciated by the Holy Prophet, insinuating a total harmony between the interpretations of Islam in Pakistan and international human rights."[39] Oman reiterated that several human rights could be found in Islam, such as the right to life, work, and education, declaring the launch of a number of official initiatives on Islam and human rights to correct misconceptions about Islam.[40] Traditions are not monolithic and they can, under certain circumstances, facilitate the implementation of international human rights norms in local contexts (Baderin 2003, 2007). However, the influence of religious legal traditions in the practices of major OIC member states such as Egypt, Iran, Pakistan, and Saudi Arabia restrict the scope of certain human rights norms, in particular religious freedom (El Fegiery 2013), gender equality (Cismas Chapter 7), the rights of religious minorities, freedom of expression (Hashemi 2008), the rights of the child (Hashemi 2007), and the prohibition of discrimination based on sexual orientation (Mayer 2012).

Furthermore, a distinction needs to be made between a critical engagement with traditions for the purpose of cultural or religious reform and a pragmatic engagement with traditions in an eclectic way to facilitate or improve the implementation of some human rights but without challenging the underlying assumptions that restrict other human rights.

This distinction does not seem clear in the work of the UN human rights bodies. For instance, the UN HRC Advisory Committee study states that "many States have taken positive steps to adopt laws based on traditional and religious values in order to introduce changes in conformity with international human rights standards."[41] The study points to the personal status law reforms in Egypt as an example of this trend, in that the reforms adopted by the Egyptian government have improved the status of women in the family.

However, the elimination of other forms of discrimination against women will not be possible without a drastic transformation of Muslim legal traditions. Other Muslim scholars and practitioners challenge traditional methodological construction of Islamic law and present new methods for dealing with the Qur'an and sunna. For example, Islamic feminism has been recently transformed from theory to action through the establishment of regional and global networks of human rights activists. A prominent example of this movement is Musawah, a global movement for equality and justice in Muslim family law that combines human rights defenders and scholars from OIC member states. The Musawah Framework for Action underlines that the values of justice and equality constitute the core universal values of the Qur'an (2009:12). Musawah argues that the adherence to justice and equality between men and women in Muslim family laws is possible through a new interpretation of Islamic sources (2009:15–7).[42]

Furthermore, the one-sided relation between traditions and human rights, where transformation in the former is needed to accommodate the latter, is not the only way for traditions to be positively relevant to human rights. Traditions and different cultural perspectives hold value and merit that could enrich the existing human rights system. The possible implications of cultural diversity for the articulation of international human rights prompted the United Nations Educational, Scientific and Cultural Organization (UNESCO) back in 1947 to invite prominent scholars belonging to different cultural and religious backgrounds to submit their views on the possibility of reaching an agreement among divergent cultures on a list of human rights. UNESCO received seventy responses, which reflected American, Chinese, European, Hindu, Islamic, and socialist perspectives and customary legal traditions, prompting the agency to conclude that "the sources of human rights were present in their traditions, even though the language of rights was a relatively modern European development" (Glendon 2002:73). The rights of indigenous peoples is another example where traditional values can possibly allow for the development of human rights. The struggle of indigenous peoples in many regions across the world highlights "the inherent rights of indigenous peoples which derive from their political, economic and social structures and from their cultures, spiritual traditions, histories and philosophies, especially their rights to their lands, territories and resources."[43]

Engaging Cultures Without Jeopardizing the Universal Applicability of Human Rights

A relevant issue in the traditional values debate is the extent to which international human rights law can tolerate the derogation from some aspects of its norms in the name of culture or religion. There are different answers to this question in human rights theories and practice. The preliminary study on traditional values prepared by Russian academic Vladimir Kartashkin states in one of its key conclusions that since many rights and freedoms are interpreted differently in different states, "the different approach of states and civilizations to the way they perceive some norms of current international law must be respected."[44] The meaning of "inclusive universalism" to realize human rights in non-Western societies is a source of heated debate in human rights literature. For example, Mashood Baderin argues that an inclusive universalism requires "a multi-cultural or cross cultural approach to the interpretation and application of human rights principles" (2003:28–29). According to Baderin, there is no global homogeneous legal understanding of the substance of human rights, neither between Western and non-Western states nor, for that matter, within Western states (28). This leads him to the conclusion that international human rights schemes should consider the contextual cultural values of non-Western societies such as Muslim societies, but he also invites Muslim communities to demonstrate an evolutionary interpretation of their legal traditions (6). He suggests that the doctrine of margin of appreciation, which has been recognized by the European Court of Human Rights (ECHR), can provide the international human rights system with "the flexibility needed to avoid confrontation between Islamic law and international human rights law" (235). Similarly, Jack Donnelly proposes the concept of relative universality as an appropriate way to mediate the tensions that arise from the multiple interpretations given to international human rights norms. Donnelly states that societies should be given certain flexibility to deviate from international human rights norms when "a particular conception or implementation is, for cultural or historical reasons, deeply embedded within or of unusually great significance to some significant group in society" (Donnelly 2007:231).

It is true that we have not realized yet "a uniform, coherent, uncontested human rights regime" (Alston and Goodman 2013:488) and that the reality is that states, international and regional human rights organs, and NGOs still disagree on the scope of many rights, in Western and non-Western countries. As noted by Nehal Bhuta, "The catalogue of rights found today in [international treaties] represents a word-smithed bricolage of rights claims derived from heterogeneous traditions and specific political projects" (2012:126).

In the absence of a world court of human rights, the UN treaty bodies and independent experts have been guiding the interpretation process of the international human rights treaties. The International Court of Justice has examined numerous human rights cases involving issues such as the right of self-determination, states' reservations to human rights treaties, and human rights in occupied territories. Its case law has played a crucial role in disclosing the existence of rules of customary international law (Higgins 2007:745–46). Regional human rights systems have also developed remarkable jurisprudence on human rights (Bonello 2005:117; Roht-Arriaza 2005). Introducing the ambiguous and broad concept of "traditional values" to the lexicon of international human rights without thorough clarification of its meaning and clear criteria for its use can obfuscate further the content of human rights treaties and block the consolidation of its universality.

In many clauses of international human rights treaties, the practical means of human rights protection are left to states' discretion, which can imply various domestic practices and institutions. The only condition is that the domestic discretion does not justify a departure from the core moral values of human rights. Jones submits that this will "look less like [a] different local expression of the same morality than conflicting understanding of what is morally permissible" (1994:217). Other scholars, however, have been suspicious of the idea of relative universality or weak relativism. Diane Orentlicher wonders by which criteria some cultural practices will therefore be tolerated, and other practices not (2001:143–44). She submits that engaging with the foundational sources of domestic cultures to legitimatize human rights will effectively promote and defend the moral validity of universal human rights to all human beings (154–56). Mayer believes that the method developed by Baderin provides Muslim states with an excuse to escape their international human rights obligations on the ground of cultural and religious values (2005:302–6). Moreover, Niaz Shah refers to the possible dangers of applying the margin of appreciation in the international human rights system, as suggested by Baderin (Shah 2008:471). He argues that states will apply it to misuse their discretionary powers and unjustifiably limit human rights; for instance, "the statutory laws of many Muslim states do not prevent polygamy, which can be condoned under the doctrine of marginal appreciation, making it difficult to achieve gender equality" (472).

According to Eva Brems, the margin of appreciation doctrine is applied by the ECHR in cases for which there is no agreement among states on the means for protecting or restricting a right (2004:14). In this situation, the ECHR asserts that states are best suited to decide as long as this principle is not used arbitrarily to justify violations. James Sweeney asserts that "the doctrine has been presented as a valuable tool for recognizing and accommodating limited local variations within a nevertheless universal model of human rights" (2005:474). I submit that while different cultural and religious traditions should be invited to contribute to international human rights law within the dialogue among civilizations and inclusive universalism, international human rights bodies should not tolerate practices that fall short of its well-established interpretations of international human rights treaties, such as those to protect and promote gender equality, freedom of religion, equality between Muslims and non-Muslims, and the prohibition of torture and cruel punishment.

However, the articulation of human rights discourses at the domestic level is deeply intertwined in complicated networks of social, economic, political, and cultural power that cannot be addressed only by technical and abstract legal norms. The international human rights system as suggested by Brems (2004:13–4) should be flexible enough to accommodate the cultural and socioeconomic conditions that might obstruct the application of international human rights law in some societies. As proposed by Brems, the principle of progressive realization of human rights, recognized in the International Covenant on Economic, Social, and Cultural Rights,[45] can be extended to other human rights, whereby states can delay their compliance with certain human rights due to contextual cultural or political factors. Brems explains that, in order to invoke this principle, states should clearly demonstrate their commitment to comply with these rights and adopt practical steps to do so (2004:14). Certain core rights and some aspects of human rights cannot be violated in the name of the principle of progressive realization of human rights. While the principle of progressive application of human rights is not a judicial doctrine, such as the doctrine of margin of appreciation, it can guide the human rights treaty bodies to consider contextual factors in societies without sacrificing the essence of some fundamental human rights norms. The use of this principle might be necessary in some Muslim societies where, even if a state has the political will to enforce certain rights, it still needs to lay the groundwork domestically and engage in dialogue with certain cultural, religious, and social groups. Such states need to be politically and technically supported by human rights treaty bodies.

Conclusion

Threats to international human rights law continue to emerge from within international organizations supposedly tasked with the promotion and development of this law. These organizations have long been venues for states' disputes over the interpretation of international human rights treaties. The rise of the traditional values agenda shows the ability of the alliance of China, Russia, and the OIC to regressively influence the debate on human rights in Geneva. The concept of "traditional values" is contradictory and paradoxical, and the claim of authenticity made by many OIC member states and Islamists about the relationship between international human rights and Islamic legal traditions is questionable given the diverse and conflicting interpretations of these traditions. The arguments and actions of the authors and sponsors of traditional values resolutions have demonstrated time and again that this agenda has been introduced to challenge certain human rights norms and disrupt their interpretation and development, particularly in the area of LGBTI rights. Nevertheless, and not insignificantly, Western states, UN independent experts, and human rights NGOs including human rights defenders from the OIC's member states have played a significant role in containing this agenda at the UN HRC.

The OIC's sponsorship of the "traditional values" agenda shows the continuation of the organization's conservative attitudes toward international human rights treaties and their enforcing mechanisms. To be sure, the level of commitment of the OIC's member states to international human rights in their domestic legal jurisdiction varies widely. One should recall that the contribution of Turkey and other so-called moderate Muslim states such as Indonesia, Malaysia, and Morocco was decisive in the establishment of the IPHRC, which was one result of the organizational reforms proposed by former secretary-general of the OIC, Ekmeleddin İhsanoğlu. However, this has not changed the conservative actions of the OIC toward human rights at the international level.

The endorsement of the "traditional values" and the "family" agenda seemed a strategic choice for many OIC member states, including Egypt, Iran, Pakistan, and Saudi Arabia, to cover up their repressive domestic policies and human rights failures. The OIC has also failed to provide space for independent NGOs and human rights defenders from their member states to interact with its activities and work. As concluded by Turan Kayaoglu, "The organization's state centric nature complicates the functioning of its human rights mechanisms" (2015:95). Most importantly, the domestic politics and geopolitical interests of influential and wealthy OIC member states (particularly Saudi Arabia) still represent a major factor in determining the collective policy choices of this organization in international human rights forums. This tendency was apparent in 2015 and 2016 when Saudi Arabia used its diplomatic ties with key Western states and most OIC member states and its financial leverage on the UN to prevent the UN HRC from condemning crimes committed by Saudi Arabia against civilians during its military operations in Yemen (Human Rights Watch 2016).

Finally, the negative side of the traditional values debate should not overshadow the relevance of cultural traditions in the implementation or expansion of human rights. Traditional values can be introduced to facilitate the application of or expand the scope of international human rights. The inclusivity of different cultural and civilizational traditions in international human rights is a legitimate demand and helps legitimize human rights in local contexts.

Notes

1. *Cairo Declaration on Human Rights in Islam*. August 5, 1990. A/CONF.157/PC/62/Add.18.

2. *Promoting Human Rights and Fundamental Freedoms Through a Better Understanding of Traditional Values of Humankind*. October 12, 2009. UN Doc. A/HRC/res/12/21.

3. *Discriminator Laws and Practices and Acts of Violence Against Individuals based on their sexual Orientation and Gender Identity.* November 17, 2011. A/HRC/19/41.

4. *Promoting Human Rights and Fundamental Freedoms Through a Better Understanding of Traditional Values of Humankind.* October 9, 2012. A/HRC/RES/21/3.

5. In this chapter, "Muslim states" refers to states where the majority of the population is Muslim, members of the OIC, or states that recognize Islam as their official religion or consider Islamic law an official source of domestic legislation in their constitutions.

6. *Vienna Declaration and Program of Action.* Adopted June 25, 1993. A/CONF.157/24, para. 5.

7. *Workshop on Traditional Values of Humankind.* December 13, 2010. A/HRC/16/37.

8. Ibid., para. 20.

9. Ibid., para 61.

10. The Human Rights Council Advisory Committee acts as a think tank for the HRC. It is composed of eighteen experts who serve for three years in a personal capacity. Candidates are nominated by all member states of the UN and elected by the HRC according to a balanced geographic distribution. *Resolution on the Human Rights Council,* March 15, 2006. A/Res/60/251.

11. The drafting group consisted of Chairperson Ahmer Bilal Soofi (Pakistan), Rapporteur Vladimir Kartashkin (Russia), Obiora Chinedu Okafor (Nigeria), Anantonia Reyes-Prado (Guatemala), Mona Zulficar (Egypt), Dheerujall Seetulsingh (Mauritius), Laurence Boisson de Chazournes (France), Shiqiu Chen (China), Alfred Ntunduguru Karakora (Uganda), and Chinsung Chung (Republic of Korea).

12. *Preliminary Study on Promoting Human Rights and Fundamental Freedoms Through a Better Understanding of Traditional Values of Humankind Prepared by Professor Vladimir Kartashkin.* August 24, 2011. A/HRC/AC/8/4.

13. Ibid., para. 62.

14. Ibid., paras. 40–48, 49–55.

15. *Study of the Human Rights Council Advisory Committee on Promoting Human Rights and Fundamental Human Rights and Fundamental Freedoms Through a Better Understanding of Traditional Values of Humankind.* December 6, 2012. A/HRC/22/71.

16. Ibid., paras. 7–12.

17. Ibid., paras. 52–72.

18. Ibid., para. 58.

19. Ibid., para. 30.

20. *Summary of Information from States Members of the United Nations and Other Relevant Stakeholders on Best Practices in the Application of Traditional Values while Promoting and Protecting Human Rights and Upholding Human Dignity.* June 17, 2013. A/HRC/24/22.

21. Ibid., para. 3.

22. See submissions by Belarus, Bosnia, and Herzegovina, Brunei, Guatemala, Honduras, Indonesia, Iraq, Jordan, Mauritius, Pakistan, Oman, Qatar, Serbia, Spain, Sri Lanka, and Syria.

23. *Workshop on Traditional Values.* A/HRC/16/37, para. 63.

24. *Joint Written Statement by the Association for Women's Rights in Development and other NGOs.* August 3, 2011. A/HRC/AC/NGO/1. Twenty-three states voted in favor of the resolution: Argentina, Belgium, Brazil, Chile, Cuba, Ecuador, France, Guatemala, Hungary, Japan, Mauritius, Mexico, Norway, Poland, Republic of Korea, Slovakia, Spain, Switzer-

land, Thailand, Ukraine, United Kingdom of Great Britain and Northern Ireland, United States of America, and Uruguay. Nineteen states voted against: Angola, Bahrain, Bangladesh, Cameroon, Djibouti, Gabon, Ghana, Jordan, Malaysia, Maldives, Mauritania, Nigeria, Pakistan, Qatar, Republic of Moldova, Russian Federation, Saudi Arabia, Senegal, and Uganda. Three states abstained: Burkina Faso, China, and Zambia.

25. *Human Rights, Sexual Orientation and Gender Identity.* October 2, 2014. A/HRC/RES/27/32. Twenty-five states voted in favor of the resolution: Argentina, Austria, Brazil, Chile, Costa Rica, Cuba, Czech Republic, Estonia, France, Germany, Ireland, Italy, Japan, Mexico, Montenegro, Peru, Philippines, Republic of Korea, Romania, South Africa, the former Yugoslav Republic of Macedonia, United Kingdom of Great Britain and Northern Ireland, United States of America, Venezuela (Bolivarian Republic of), and Viet Nam. Fourteen states voted against: Algeria, Botswana, Côte d'Ivoire, Ethiopia, Gabon, Indonesia, Kenya, Kuwait, Maldives, Morocco, Pakistan, Russian Federation, Saudi Arabia, and United Arab Emirates. Seven states abstained: Burkina Faso, China, Congo, India, Kazakhstan, Namibia, and Sierra Leone.

26. In this chapter, "Arab group" refers to the twenty-two member states of the League of Arab States: Algeria, Bahrain, Comoros, Djibouti, Egypt, Iraq, Jordan, Kuwait, Lebanon, Libya, Mauritania, Morocco, Oman, Palestine, Qatar, Saudi Arabia, Somalia, Sudan, Syria, Tunisia, United Arab Emirates, and Yemen. All of them are also members of the OIC.

27. "Human Rights Panel on Ending Violence and Discrimination Against Individuals Based on Their Sexual Orientation and Gender Identity." Geneva, March 7, 2012. http://www.ohchr.org/Documents/Issues/Discrimination/LGBT/SummaryHRC19Panel.pdf.

28. *Protection of the Family.* June 25, 2014. A/HRC/26/L.20/Rev.1. Twenty-six states voted in favor of the resolution: Algeria, Benin, Botswana, Burkina Faso, China, Congo, Côte d'Ivoire, Ethiopia, Gabon, India, Indonesia, Kazakhstan, Kenya, Kuwait, Maldives, Morocco, Namibia, Pakistan, Philippines, Russian Federation, Saudi Arabia, Sierra Leone, South Africa, United Arab Emirates, Venezuela, and Viet Nam. Fourteen states voted against: Austria, Chile, Czech Republic, Estonia, France, Germany, Ireland, Italy, Japan, Montenegro, Republic of Korea, Romania, United Kingdom of Great Britain and Northern Ireland, and United States of America. Six states abstained: Argentina, Brazil, Costa Rica, Mexico, Peru, and the former Yugoslav Republic of Macedonia.

29. *Protection of the Family.* July 1, 2015. A/HRC/29/L.25. Twenty-nine states voted in favor of the resolution: Algeria, Bangladesh, Bolivia, Botswana, China, Congo, Côte d'Ivoire, Cuba, El Salvador, Ethiopia, Gabon, Ghana, India, Indonesia, Kazakhstan, Kenya, Maldives, Morocco, Namibia, Nigeria, Pakistan, Paraguay, Qatar, Russian Federation, Saudi Arabia, Sierra Leone, United Arab Emirates, Venezuela, and Viet Nam. Fourteen states voted against: Albania, Estonia, France, Germany, Ireland, Japan, Latvia, Montenegro, Netherlands, Portugal, Republic of Korea, South Africa, United Kingdom of Great Britain and Northern Ireland, and United States of America. Four states abstained: Argentina, Brazil, Mexico, and the former Yugoslav Republic of Macedonia.

30. *Protection of the Family: Amendment to Draft Resolution A/HRC/26/L.20/Rev.1.* June 24, 2014. A/HRC/26/L.37.

31. *Report of the Human Rights Council on Its Twenty-Sixth Session.* December 11, 2014. A/HRC/26/2, paras. 189–99.

32. *Report of the Human Rights Council on Its Twenty-Ninth Session.* November 25, 2015. A/HRC/29/2, paras. 269–92.

33. Nazra for Feminist Studies is a feminist NGO based in Egypt. The organization works for the promotion of gender equality in the Middle East and North Africa. For more information, see http://nazra.org/en.

34. *Joint Written Statement by the Association for Women's Rights in Development and Other NGOs.* August 3, 2011. A/HRC/AC/NGO/1, 2.

35. Ibid., 6.

36. *Workshop on Traditional Values of Humankind.* December 13, 2010. A/HRC/16/37, para.70.

37. *Summary of Information from States Members of the United Nations and Other Relevant Stakeholders on Best Practices in the Application of Traditional Values While Promoting and Protecting Human Rights and Upholding Human Dignity.* June 17, 2013. A/HRC/24/22, para. 16.

38. Ibid., para. 14.

39. Ibid., para. 17.

40. Ibid., para. 19, 20, 21.

41. *Study of the Human Rights Council Advisory Committee on Promoting Human Rights and Fundamental Human Rights and Fundamental Freedoms Through a Better Understanding of Traditional Values of Humankind.* December 6, 2012. A/HRC/22/71, para. 49.

42. See also the *Paris Declaration on Means of the Renewal of Religious Discourse,* drafted and signed by a group of Muslim human rights defenders and prominent scholars (Cairo Institute for Human Rights Studies 2003).

43. *Declaration on the Rights of the Indigenous Peoples.* September 7, 2007. G.A. Res.61/295, A/RES/47/1.

44. *Preliminary Study on Promoting Human Rights and Fundamental Freedoms Through a Better Understanding of Traditional Values of Humankind Prepared by Professor Vladimir Kartashkin.* August 24, 2011. A/HRC/AC/8/4, paras. 60–62.

45. *International Covenant on Economic, Social and Cultural Rights.* Adopted on December 16, 1966; entered into force January 3, 1976. 993 UNTS 3.

Works Cited

Alston, Philip, and Ryan Goodman. 2013. *International Human Rights.* Oxford: Oxford University Press.

An-Na'im, Abdullahi A. 1990. *Toward an Islamic Reformation: Civil Liberties, Human Rights, and International Law.* Syracuse, NY: Syracuse University Press.

———. 2000. "Islam and Human Rights: Beyond the Universality Debate." *American Society of International Law Proceedings* 94: 95–103.

———. 2008. *Islam and the Secular State: Negotiating the Future of Shari'a.* Cambridge, MA: Harvard University Press.

———. 2014. *What Is an American Muslim? Embracing Faith and Citizenship.* Oxford: Oxford University Press.

Baderin, Mashood A. 2003. *International Human Rights and Islamic Law.* Oxford: Oxford University Press.

———. 2007. "Islam and the Realization of Human Rights in the Muslim World: A Reflection on Two Essential Approaches and Two Divergent Perspectives." *Muslim World Journal of Human Rights* 4 (1): DOI: 10.2202/1554-4419.1117.

Brems, Eva. 2004. "Reconciling Universality and Diversity in International Human Rights: A Theoretical and Methodological Framework and Its Application in the Context of Islam." *Human Rights Review* 5 (3): 5–21.

Bhuta, Nehal. 2012. "Rethinking the Universality of Human Rights: A Comparative Historical Proposal for the Idea of Common Ground with Other Moral Traditions." In *Islamic Law and International Human Rights Law: Searching for Common Ground*, ed. Anver M. Emon, Mark S. Ellis, and Benjamin Glahn, 123–42. Oxford: Oxford University Press.

Bonello, G. 2005. "The European Court of Human Rights." In *The Essentials of Human Rights*, ed. Rhona Smith and Christien van den Anker, 115–18. London: Routledge.

Cairo Institute for Human Rights Studies. 2003. *The Paris Declaration on Means of the Renewal of Religious Discourse*. Cairo: CIHRS.

———. 2004. *The Second Independence, Towards an Initiative for Political Reform in the Arab World*. Cairo: CIHRS.

———. 2009a. *Roots of the Unrest: Human Rights in the Arab Region 2010*. Cairo: CIHRS.

———. 2009b. "UN Takes One Step Forward and Two Big Leaps Back." Cairo: CIHRS.

———. 2010. *Bastion of Impunity, Mirage of Reform: Human Rights in the Arab Region in 2009*. Cairo: CIHRS.

Chase, Anthony. 2012. *Human Rights, Revolution, and Reform in the Muslim World*. Boulder, CO: Lynne Rienner.

Cismas, Ioana. 2014. *Religious Actors and International Law*. Oxford: Oxford University Press.

Dacey, Austin, and Colin Koproske. 2008. "Islam and Human Rights: Defending Universality at the United Nations." Amherst, NY: Centre for Inquiry International. https://www.centerforinquiry.net/uploads/attachments/ISLAM_AND_HUMAN_RIGHTS.pdf.

Donnelly, Jack. 2007. "The Relative Universality of Human Rights." *Human Rights Quarterly* 29 (2): 281–306.

El Fegiery, Moataz. 2013. "Islamic Law and Freedom of Religion: The Case of Apostasy and Its Legal Implications in Egypt." *Muslim World Journal of Human Rights* 10 (1): 1–26.

Glendon, Mary Ann. 2002. *A World Made New: Eleanor Roosevelt and the Universal Declaration of Human Rights*. New York: Random House.

Goodhart, Michael E. 2008. "Neither Relative nor Universal: A Response to Donnelly." *Human Rights Quarterly* 30 (1): 183–93.

Hashemi, Kamran. 2007. "Religious Legal Traditions, Muslim States and the Convention on the Rights of the Child: An Essay on the Relevant UN Documentation." *Human Rights Quarterly* 29 (1): 194–227.

———. 2008. *Religious Legal Traditions, International Human Rights Law and Muslim States*. Leiden: Martinus Nijhoff.

Higgins, Rosalyn. 2007. "Human Rights in the International Court of Justice." *Leiden Journal of International Law* 20 (4): 745–51.

Human Rights Watch. 2009. "UN Human Rights Council: 'Traditional Values' Vote and Gaza Overshadow Progress." http://www.hrw.org/news/2009/10/05/un-human-rights-council-traditional-values-vote-and-gaza-overshadow-progress.

———. 2016. "UN: Suspend Saudi Arabia from Human Rights Council." https://www.hrw.org/news/2016/06/29/un-suspend-saudi-arabia-human-rights-council.

Jones, Peter. 1994. *Rights.* Issues in Political Theory series. London: Palgrave.

Kayaoglu, Turan. 2015. *The Organization of Islamic Cooperation: Politics, Problems, and Potential.* London: Routledge.

Kymlicka, Will. 2001. *Contemporary Political Philosophy: An Introduction.* 2nd ed. Oxford: Oxford University Press.

Langer, Lorenz. 2014. *Religious Offence and Human Rights: The Implications of Defamation of Religions.* Cambridge: Cambridge University Press.

Leo, Leonard A., Felice D. Gaer, and Elizabeth K. Cassidy. 2011. "Protecting Religions from 'Defamation': A Threat to Universal Human Rights Standards." *Harvard Journal of Law and Public Policy* 34 (2): 769–803.

Mayer, Ann Elizabeth. 2005. "International Human Rights Law and Islamic Law by Mashood Baderin." *American Journal of International Law* 99 (1): 302–6.

———. 2008. "The Reformulation of Islamic Thought on Gender Rights and Roles." In *Islam and Human Rights in Practice: Perspectives Across the Ummah*, ed., Shahram Akbarzadeh and Benjamin MacQueen, 12–31. London: Routledge.

———. 2012. *Islam and Human Rights: Tradition and Politics.* 5th ed. Boulder, CO: Westview.

Merry, Sally Engle. 2005. *Human Rights and Gender Violence: Translating International Law into Social Justice.* Chicago: University of Chicago Press.

Musawah. 2009. "Musawah Framework of Action." In *Wanted: Equality and Justice in the Muslim Family*, ed. Zainah Anwar, 11–22. Selangor: Musawah.

Muslim Brotherhood. 2013. "Muslim Brotherhood Statement Denouncing UN Women Declaration for Violating *Shari'a* Principles." *Ikhwan Web.* http://www.ikhwanweb.com/article.php?id=30731.

Nazra for Feminist Studies. 2011. "Traditional Values and Human Rights Violations in Egypt." http://www.ohchr.org/Documents/Issues/HRValues/NazraFeministStudies.pdf.

Nichols, Michelle. 2016. "Muslim States Block Gay Groups from UN AIDS Meeting; U.S. Protests." http://www.reuters.com/article/us-un-lgbt-aids-idUSKCN0Y827F.

Orentlicher, Diane F. 2001. "Relativism and Religion." In *Human Rights as Politics and Idolatry*, by Michael Ignatieff, 141–59. Princeton, NJ: Princeton University Press.

Preis, Ann-Belinda S. 1996. "Human Rights as Cultural Practice: An Anthropological Critique." *Human Rights Quarterly* 18 (2): 286–315.

Rawls, John. 2005. *Political Liberalism.* 2nd ed. New York: Columbia University Press.

Risse, Thomas, Stephen C. Ropp, and Kathryn Sikkink, eds. 2013. *The Persistent Power of Human Rights: From Commitment to Compliance.* New York: Cambridge University Press.

Reid, Graeme. 2012. "'Traditional Values' Code for Human Rights Abuse?" Human Rights Watch. http://www.hrw.org/news/2012/10/17/traditional-values-code-human-rights-abuse.

———. 2013. "The Trouble with Tradition: When 'Values' Trample Over Rights." In *World Report 2013.* Washington: Human Rights Watch. https://www.hrw.org/world-report/2013/country-chapters/africa.

Roht-Arriaza, Naomi. 2005. *The Pinochet Effect: Transnational Justice in the Age of Human Rights.* Philadelphia: University of Pennsylvania Press.

Shah, Niaz A. 2008. "Women's Human Rights in the Koran: An Interpretive Approach." In *International Law and Islamic law*, ed. Mashood A. Baderin, 461–96. Surrey: Ashgate.

Shaham, Ron. 2010. "Communal Identity, Political Islam and Family Law: Copts and the Debate over the Grounds for Dissolution of Marriage in Twentieth-Century Egypt." *Islam and Christian-Muslim Relations* 21 (4): 409–22.

Sezgin, Yüksel. 2013. *Human Rights Under State-Enforced Religious Family Laws in Israel, Egypt and India*. Cambridge: Cambridge University Press.

Sweeney, James A. 2005. "Margins of Appreciation: Cultural Relativity and the European Court of Human Rights in the Post-Cold War Era." *International and Comparative Law Quarterly* 54 (2): 459–74.

Tibi, Bassam. 2012. *Islam and Islamism*. New Haven, CT: Yale University Press.

UN Islamic Group to UN HRC. 2012. "Letter Opposing Panel on Violence Against Gays." http://blog.unwatch.org/index.php/2012/02/17/letter-from-uns-islamic-group-to-unhrc-president-opposing-panel-on-violence-against-gays/.

Waltz, Susan Eileen. 2004. "Universal Human Rights: The Contribution of Muslim States." *Human Rights Quarterly* 26 (4): 799–844.

Wilkinson, Cai. 2014. "Putting 'Traditional Values' into Practice: The Rise and Contestation of Anti-Homopropaganda Laws in Russia." *Journal of Human Rights* 13(3): 363–79.

Zwart, Tom. 2012. "Using Local Culture to Further the Implementation of International Human Rights: The Receptor Approach." *Human Rights Quarterly* 34 (2): 546–69.

———. 2014. "Safeguarding the Universal Acceptance of Human Rights Through the Receptor Approach." *Human Rights Quarterly* 36 (4): 898–904.

CHAPTER 7

The Position of the OIC on Abortion: Not Too Bad, Ugly, or Just Confusing?

Ioana Cismas

Introduction

In the wake of the sociopolitical upheavals that have engulfed several states in the Middle East and North Africa since 2010, a number of new works have reflected on sexuality in Muslim-majority countries (El Feki 2013; El Said, Meari, and Pratt 2015; Eltahawy 2015). In one such study, Shereen El Feki echoes Michel Foucault (1978) and explains that if the Arab Spring is understood as a contestation of power relations, alongside political, economic, and social elements, sexuality as an instrumentalizable element of such relations cannot be neglected (El Feki 2013). This chapter aligns itself with these works insofar as it is premised on the understanding that sexuality is an element of power relations, "bound up in religion, tradition, culture, politics, and economics" (El Feki 2013:xiv). At the same time, it seeks to avoid essentializing any of these factors. Built on such premises, the aim of this chapter is to explore by means of legal analysis the position of the Organization of Islamic Cooperation (OIC) on one of the features of sexuality: abortion.

The position of the OIC and many of its member states on aspects related to sexuality is commonly described as strongly conservative. For instance, Javaid Rehman and Eleni Polymenopoulou note that the OIC has been "regularly launching arguments not only against sexual rights, but, even more substantially, against gender equality and the universality of women's rights" (2013:38) In particular the OIC's routine objections to—or in United Nations

(UN) parlance, the bracketing of—"sexual orientation" and "gender identity" in resolutions and declarations have hindered international progress on the protection of the rights of lesbian, gay, bisexual, transgender, and intersex (LGBTI) persons (Saiz 2007). But has the OIC spoken with a similarly strong voice on the issue of abortion, another central feature of sexuality? And if so, what has it said? Since abortion is a central tenet of sexual and reproductive rights and women's rights more broadly, intuitively one would assume that the OIC's stance on abortion must be, to paraphrase the title of this book, bad or ugly. Is it really so?

This inquiry into the OIC's stance on abortion is driven by a doctrinal legal approach and draws on socio-legal insights. This methodology permits an examination of the research question that is centered on the dialectic interplay between the OIC and its member states.[1] It also allows for an exploration of the relation between the OIC's normative position, as this emerges from the organization's legal instruments, and its institutional stance as revealed by discourses made on the global stage by OIC representatives. In terms of structure, therefore, this chapter first places abortion within the context of feminist thought and the current framework of international human rights law. Second, it examines relevant provisions of the main OIC human rights instruments, specifically the Cairo Declaration on Human Rights in Islam (CDHRI or Cairo Declaration) and the Covenant on the Rights of the Child in Islam (CRCI). The third part provides an analytical overview of member states' domestic legislation and policies on abortion and identifies possible explanatory variables, including political, religious, and sociohistorical factors, for the various legislative configurations. Fourth, the chapter contrasts the normative position of the OIC and the member states' legislation to the stance adopted by the OIC in selected UN forums. The conclusion assesses the findings and inquires into what ways the OIC's institutional voice on abortion could be shaped in the future.

Abortion: What's in a Term?

Central to the feminist movements of the early nineteenth century in England was the notion that "women in particular must be able 'to decide whether, when, and how to have children'" (Corrêa and Petchesky 1994:299). Rosalind Petchesky explains that there are two aspects underpinning this idea: first, the principle of bodily self-determination recognizing the "biological connection between women's bodies, sexuality and reproduction," and second, the socially constructed position of the woman in society as the principal child-carer and rearer (Petchesky 1990:2). Although the two dimensions—one biological, the other social—entail an intrinsic philosophical tension, they also espouse a certain universality. As such, despite the conceptual origins of reproductive rights in the West, birth control movements across the globe have embraced the idea that women have a right to control their bodies, including the right to refuse to bear children (Corrêa and Petchesky 1994:299). In fact, anthropologists studying ancient societies have concluded that "abortion is an absolutely universal phenomenon," not only geographically but also temporally (George Devereux as cited in Petchesky 1990:1).

Abortion occasioned some of the most intense diplomatic confrontations of the 1990s. Access to safe abortion, in addition and linked to contraception, sexual education, sexual orientation, and gender identity were all components of a battleground issue at the 1994 International Conference on Population and Development in Cairo and the 1995 Fourth World Conference on Women in Beijing. Sexual and reproductive rights pitted not only states against each other but also women's groups, religious groups of all orientations—in opposition or in coalition with the former—nongovernmental organizations, UN agencies, and various other experts (Haynes 2013:12–13). An achievement at such conferences was the acknowledgment by states that unsafe abortions led to high rates of maternal mortality and morbidity, and consequently, a commitment to reduce instances of these (UN Population Fund 1995:para. 8.20).

In the realm of international and regional human rights treaty law, abortion receives few express mentions—one of these being in the OIC's own CRCI.[2] The Convention on the Elimination of Discrimination Against Women (CEDAW 1981), where one would naturally expect to find a stipulation on abortion, entails provisions on family planning in Articles 10(h), 12(1), and 14(2). Importantly, Article 16(1)(e) requires states to "ensure, on a basis of equality of men and women . . . the same rights to decide freely and responsibly on the number and spacing of their children and to have access to the information, education and means to enable them to exercise these rights."

As such, abortion has found a place in international human rights law since 1979. The CEDAW Committee has read abortion into these provisions and others, and interpreted the states' obligations in relation to safe abortion at first timidly and in more recent times with increasing conviction.[3] In its general recommendations, the committee calls on states to include safe abortion services alongside contraception and ante- and postnatal care in sexual and reproductive health care (CEDAW Committee 2013:para. 52(c)); to prevent, investigate, and punish gender-based violations, inter alia, forced abortions (para. 65(a)); and to decriminalize abortion (CEDAW Committee 1999:para. 31(c)); CEDAW Committee 2015:para. 47(b) and 51(l)). It suggests that the criminalization of abortion is an intrinsically gender-discriminatory practice given that abortion, as a "form of behaviour . . . can be performed only by women" (CEDAW Committee 2015:para. 47(b)).

The right to sexual and reproductive health is deeply interlinked with a host of other human rights, in particular the right to life, the right not to be subjected to torture, inhuman, and degrading treatment, the right to health, and the right to privacy. As such, women who have been denied a safe abortion at the domestic level have, in recent years, held their governments accountable under various international and regional human rights treaties in spite of the fact that the latter instruments lack an explicit stipulation on abortion.[4]

An influential interpretative instrument that clarifies the normative framework on abortion is the 2016 General Comment of the Committee on Economic Social and Cultural Rights (CESCR). The CESCR considers access to safe abortion to be an integral part of the right to health, as this is stipulated in the International Covenant on Economic, Social and Cultural Rights. This general comment provides an extensive elaboration of states' obligations (to respect, protect, and fulfill) and the criteria of availability, accessibility, acceptability, and quality that they must ensure in relation to abortion, as well as their general obligation of nondiscrimination and gender equality (CESCR 2016).

The OIC's Normative Position on Abortion

Since the early 1990s, the OIC has claimed to offer "general guidance" to its member states in the area of human rights.[5] It has sought to do so through the development of a series of human rights instruments.[6] Of particular interest to this current chapter is the CDHRI, a nonbinding instrument that was adopted in 1990 by the OIC Council of Foreign Ministers, and the 2005 CRCI, a binding convention that, however, has not entered into force.[7]

Additionally, in June 2011, OIC ministers adopted the Statute of the Independent Permanent Human Rights Commission (OIC IPHRC), establishing a human rights body for the organization.[8]

It is a common practice of regional organizations to adopt human rights declarations and conventions, and to establish monitoring and enforcement mechanisms; many of these instruments entail some regional particularities. This latter observation is certainly not amiss in relation to the three OIC instruments, with the CDHRI standing out among these, and indeed, among all regional instruments, as extraordinarily particularistic. As discussed in greater detail elsewhere, the regime that the CDHRI seeks to establish is more akin to a "religionalism" given that it subjects universal standards to limitation clauses based on Sharia[9] and proclaims the latter as the sole principle of interpretation of the Cairo Declaration (Cismas 2014:253).[10]

Article 2 of the CDHRI entails provisions on the right to life that are relevant to this study's analytical focus on abortion. Those paragraphs read:

> (a) Life is a God-given gift and the right to life is guaranteed to every human being. It is the duty of individuals, societies and states to safeguard this right against any violation, and it is prohibited to take away life except for a Shari'ah prescribed reason. . . .
> (c) The preservation of human life throughout the term of time willed by God is a duty prescribed by Shari'ah.

How should these two religious limitation clauses be interpreted? In order for one to understand what a "Shari'ah prescribed reason" is and what "term of time God had willed," one must recall three fundamental interconnected aspects. First, Islam is not monolithic and does not have an overarching interpretative authority: the two main branches of Islam, Sunni and Shia, are each further divided into various schools of legal thought. Second, Sharia "is not really divine law in the sense that all its specific principles and detailed rules were directly revealed by God to the Prophet Muhammad . . . Sharia was constructed by the early Muslim jurists out of the fundamental sources of Islam, namely the Qur'an and Sunna" and other traditions (An-Na'im 1990:11, 33; Cismas 2014:252–53). Furthermore, *fiqh* represents the developing jurisprudence of Sharia that is the reasoned reflections of Muslim scholars and jurists "concerning what they consider the Shari'a to require of Muslims in the particular time and locality they find themselves," as well as the method of deducing such opinions (Ahdar and Aroney 2010:3–4; Cismas 2014:253).

Third, it is appropriate at this juncture to emphasize Anissa Hélie's observation: "It is a fact that Islam has merged with diverse cultural traditions across the world, ensuring local variations in terms of religious beliefs and practices, as well as in terms of interpretations of the scriptures" (Hélie 2012:15).

With the above aspects in mind, let us tackle the interpretation of the two religious clauses entailed by Article 2(a) and (c) of the Cairo Declaration. The Qur'an does not provide any specific pronouncements on abortion; however, it is "sensitive to a stage development between conception and childbirth" (Shapiro 2014:3–4). This has led religious scholars to adopt different perspectives on the permissibility of abortion depending on the gestational stage of the fetus (Hélie 2012:14; Shapiro 2014:3–4). Before the fourth stage (120 days), when "ensoulment" is said to occur and the fetus is thus recognized as possessing a spirit, most Sunni schools allow abortion; Shiite schools, on the other hand, prohibit termination of pregnancy except on the grounds of "fetal or maternal conditions that bring extreme difficulties for the mother or family" (Shapiro 2014:3–4). After ensoulment, abortion is generally prohibited; nonetheless all legal schools are said to provide for an exception: saving the life of the pregnant woman (Ibid). In recent years, religious scholars have not only debated the exact time when ensoulment occurs (Al-Hibri 2011:4–5) but also whether abortion should be permitted for victims of rape or incest, with some prominent clerics supporting this (Hélie 2012:14).

What emerges is that the religious limitation clauses in Articles 2(a) and 2(c) allow wide discretion for OIC member states to accommodate their specific interpretations of Sharia in relation to when life begins. Implicitly thus, the CDHRI sanctions both progressive and restrictive abortion policies. Therefore, in the area of abortion, not much is achieved in terms of the *general* guidance, which the CDHRI purports to provide to OIC member states. Much rather, the saying "to each their own" applies. At this stage, it should also be noted that Articles 2(a) and 2(c) seem largely irrelevant for OIC member states that do not employ Sharia as a source of law—indeed, as we shall see, a fair number of them do not. These observations tie into a previous assessment of the CDHRI which concluded that because the declaration disregards the variety of contexts of OIC member states, its ability to function as *genuine*—thereby increasing the level of protection—and *general*—thus addressed to all member states—guidance for OIC states in the area of human rights is questionable. At best, those states that feel unrepresented by the CDHRI provisions will disregard them. At worst, states that adopt interpretations of Sharia, which are discriminatory or fail to uphold human rights, will feel legitimized (Cismas 2014:275). What appears clear is that, given the discretion they enjoy under the CDHRI in relation to when life begins, states are not encouraged to engage critically with existing interpretations of Sharia that (severely) restrict access to safe abortion.

Article 7(a) of the CDHRI may, however, be used to interpret Articles 2(a) and 2(c) and potentially to narrow the wide discretion accorded to states in interpreting when life begins and thus what abortion policies are acceptable under the terms of the declaration—were it not for its equivocality. Article 7(a) reads, "As of the moment of birth, every child has rights due from the parents, society and the state to be accorded proper nursing, education and material, hygienic and moral care. Both the fetus and the mother must be protected and accorded special care."

Note that it is at "the moment of birth" when the rights of the child vis-à-vis third parties arise. Yet the second sentence of Article 7(a) confuses matters by stipulating that protection is due to the "fetus." Be that as it may, as the expression "fetus" is preferred to that of the "unborn child" or the "embryo," one could infer that the "term of time willed by God" commences when the embryo has reached the fetal stage. This would suggest that the CDHRI sanctions the termination of pregnancies up to the fetal stage. This interpretation nonetheless is in dissonance with the theory of ensoulment, which we have seen is prevalent among Sunni schools—the CDHRI would thus be more restrictive than those interpretations of Sharia.

Let us turn to the CRCI, an instrument aimed to bind OIC states that ratify it.[11] While Islam retains an important place in the CRCI, the instrument departs from the CDHRI model in so far as it does not subject human rights to a general Sharia limitation clause, nor does it put forward Sharia as the interpretative principle of the instrument. Certainly, the CRCI has its particularities: troubling is the instrument's silence on the right to freedom of religion, as well as the Islamic limitations clause on specific rights and the claw-back clauses that it entails (Cismas 2014:285–91). Be that as it may, the CRCI provides for international legal anchors in its preamble, acknowledging therefore that it be interpreted by the ratifying state in accord with universal human rights standards, and in particular the UN Convention on the Rights of the Child (CRC) to which all OIC states are party.

What relevance then, does the CRCI carry for our analytical focus in this section? Article 6 of the CRCI deals with the right to life of the child as follows: "The child shall have the right to life from when he is a fetus in his/her mother's womb or in the case of his/her mother's death; abortion should be prohibited except under necessity warranted by the interests of the mother, the fetus, or both of them."

Before analyzing the substance of Article 6, it is important to pause and emphasize that abortion is specifically mentioned in the CRCI. This is rare in the architecture of human rights instruments, international and regional alike. The CRCI provision is certainly more elaborate than the corresponding stipulation on the child's right to life entailed in Article 6(1) of the 1989 UN CRC. Philip Alston, who was UNICEF's legal adviser during its drafting, clarifies that the omission of the term "abortion" from the operative part of this instrument was intentional on the part of its drafters (Alston 1990:157). Instead, a preambular paragraph was inserted, referencing the preamble of the 1959 Declaration of the Rights of the Child, which in turn stipulates that special safeguards and care are due to the child "before as well as after birth" (Ibid; Declaration of the Rights of the Child: preamble). This was, on Alston's analysis, "a typical 'compromise' solution which had intentionally failed to resolve" the permissibility or impermissibility of abortion with the precise aim of accommodating "whatever position [individual states] prefer with respect to the rights of the unborn child, provided that they act in conformity with other applicable provisions of international human rights law" (Alston 1990:157).

Among such international provisions, Article 16(1)(e) of the CEDAW (1981) is particularly relevant. In this context, it is worth observing that of the eleven OIC states that have entered specific reservations to various parts of Article 16 of the CEDAW, only Niger has explicitly reserved Article 16(1)(e), which protects the same right of women and men to decide "freely and responsibly on the number and spacing of their children" (Niger 1999).

In contrast to the UN CRC, the specific provision in the CRCI allows less discretion for national interpretations on the issue of when life begins. The couching of the second sentence of Article 6 in a negative form is an important linguistic signifier: it suggests a negative (philosophical) stance on abortion, which is not in line with more recent interpretations by UN treaty bodies and certainly not with feminist thought.[12] Nonetheless, such phrasing cannot detract from the provision's substantive meaning: under the CRCI terms abortion should be permissible on request before the embryo reaches the fetal stage; after this period it should also be granted on reasons of "necessity warranted by the interests of the mother, the fetus, or both of them" (Article 6(1)). The "interests" clause could cover a wide array of grounds for termination of pregnancy, ranging from threat to the life of the pregnant women, threat to her physical and her mental health, fetal impairment, rape, incest, and potentially socioeconomic reasons. The latter ground is notably not entailed in the provision concerning medical abortion in the Protocol to the African Charter on Human and Peoples' Rights on the Rights of Women in Africa,[13] yet on a textual reading of the CRCI, socioeconomic grounds for termination of pregnancy cannot be excluded.

It should also be noted that Article 6 of the CRCI does not accord with the ensoulment theory present in many Sharia law interpretations; had such a correspondence been inscribed in the CRCI, the resulting provision would have been less restrictive in terms of gestational limits. This may have been a rare occasion when a religious limitation clause on human rights could potentially have expanded the scope of protection afforded. Although, given the differing interpretations as to the exact moment when ensoulment occurs, such a reference would likely have created legal uncertainty.

The UN CRC remains indeterminate on the issue of when life begins and implicitly also on abortion. The International Covenant on Civil and Political Rights (ICCPR)[14] and the European Convention on Human Rights (ECHR)[15] follow a similar indeterminate course. In contrast, Article 4(1) of the American Convention on Human Rights (ACHR) explicitly stipulates the protection of the right to life "from conception"; put differently, a textual reading of the ACHR would not sanction abortion.[16] When compared to the provisions of the CRC, ICCPR, and ECHR, Article 6 of the CRCI allows states less discretion to define when life begins. It could be argued that by narrowing the options available to states, the CRCI excludes the most conservative positions on abortion, while not promoting the most progressive course. It is also worth noting that the text of the CRCI does take a less conservative stance on abortion when compared with the ACHR.

Domestic Legislation of OIC Member States

States everywhere have regulated abortion through legislation and policies, permitting or criminalizing it, restricting the practice to specific legal grounds or allowing it on request, specifying further criteria for the procedure such as spousal consent, parental approval, or doctoral consent (which in practice further limit access to abortion), and sanctioning a certain time period correlated to the gestational stages within which termination of pregnancy can occur. This part of the chapter first offers an overview of the legal regulation of abortion in the OIC region; a second analytical segment puts forward a number of factors that may explain the different domestic positions on abortion assumed by OIC states.

The Big Picture: Regulation of Abortion in the OIC Region

The UN dataset *World Abortion Policies 2013* (UN Department of Economic and Social Affairs 2013) provides information on abortion legislation and related aspects in all UN member states; it thus includes data on fifty-six of the OIC member states.[17] The quantitative analysis in this section relies primarily on this dataset, cross-referencing the information with more recent data mapping produced by the Center for Reproductive Rights (CRR 2016).

Worldwide, including across OIC member states, abortion is commonly permitted on one or more of seven legal grounds: (1) to save the life of a woman; (2) to preserve a woman's physical health; (3) to preserve a woman's mental health; (4) in case of rape or incest; (5) because of fetal impairment; (6) for economic or social reasons; (7) on request. These legal grounds could be portrayed on a conservative–progressive continuum of abortion: one end would correspond to a total ban of abortion and the other end would indicate that the procedure is permissible on all seven grounds.

None of the OIC member states has legislated a total ban on abortion. As such no OIC state occupies the conservative extreme on the continuum. Based on UN data published in 2013, eighteen states would be placed toward the conservative end, as they permit abortion only to save the life of the woman (legal ground (1)): Afghanistan, Bangladesh, Brunei Darussalam, Côte d'Ivoire, Djibouti, Egypt, Gabon, Guinea Bissau, Iran, Iraq, Lebanon, Libya, Mauritania, Senegal, Somalia, Suriname, Syria, and Yemen. Four states criminalize abortion except for a combination of two grounds: the Maldives for (1) and (2); Mali and Indonesia for (1) and (4); and Oman for (1) and (5). Fourteen states allow abortion on a combination of three grounds: Algeria, Comoros, Gambia, Malaysia, Morocco, Mozambique, Nigeria, Pakistan, Saudi Arabia, Sierra Leone, Uganda, and the United Arab Emirates for (1), (2), and (3); Chad on grounds (1), (2), and (5), and Sudan on grounds (1), (4), and (5). Six OIC countries permit abortion in four circumstances: Cameroon for (1), (2), (3), and (4); Jordan, Kuwait, Niger, and Qatar for grounds (1), (2), (3), and (5); and Togo for (1), (2), (4), and (5). Three states position themselves toward the progressive end of the continuum by allowing abortion on grounds (1),

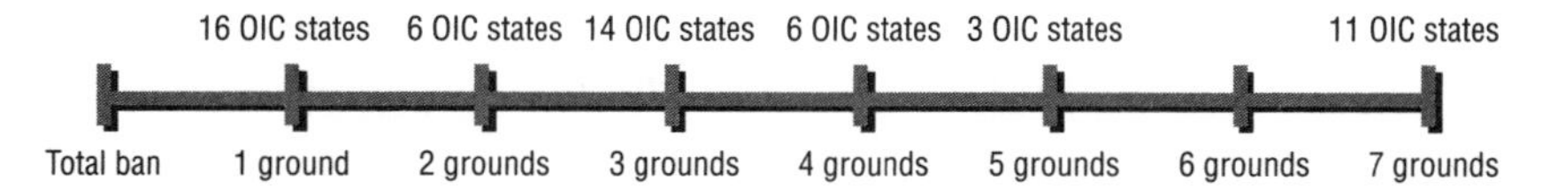

Figure 7.1. OIC states and abortion on a conservative-progressive continuum. The figure is compiled based on data from the UN Department of Economic and Social Affairs, *World Abortion Policies 2013*, and CRR, *The World's Abortion Laws* (2016).

(2), (3), (4), and (5): Benin, Burkina Faso, and Guinea. Occupying the progressive pole are eleven states that sanction termination of pregnancy on all seven grounds, including, thus, on the woman's request. These states are Albania, Bahrain, Guyana, Tunisia, Turkey, and the six Central Asian republics: Azerbaijan, Kazakhstan, Kyrgyzstan, Tajikistan, Turkmenistan, and Uzbekistan.

The general trend over time in the OIC member states is one toward liberalization on this issue: between 1996 and 2011 nineteen countries expanded the legal grounds on which they would permit abortion (UN Department of Economic and Social Affairs 2013). Data published in 2016 by the Center for Reproductive Rights lists Djibouti and Iran as decriminalizing abortion when it is performed to preserve the physical health of the woman (2), and in the case of fetal impairment (5), respectively (CRR 2016). This effectively reduces the number of OIC states to sixteen that allow therapeutical abortion only when the woman's life is at threat (see Figure 7.1). Countries that have moved in the opposite direction of the liberalization trend are Iraq and Algeria, which have criminalized abortions on grounds (3), (4), and (5) in the case of the former and (4) for the latter (UN Department of Economic and Social Affairs 2013).

Comparisons of the OIC with other regions must take into account the fact that the former is not a regional organization per se and does not, as such, cover a geographical area, but spans four continents: Africa, Asia, Europe, and Latin America. With this caveat in mind, there are some important insights to be gained from a comparative perspective. For instance, if we consider the data on states permitting therapeutic abortion in cases where a woman's life is at threat, it becomes clear that the Latin American and Caribbean region is the more conservative. Four states—Chile, the Dominican Republic, El Salvador, and Nicaragua—ban abortion without exception for preserving a woman's life. Less than 10 percent of Latin American and Caribbean countries ensure abortion on request, whereas the percentage in the

OIC is double (19.64 percent).[18] In Europe, Malta and the Holy See (which has jurisdiction over the Vatican territory) criminalize abortion in all circumstances, yet the abortion on request percentage (72.22 percent) overwhelmingly showcases the more liberal approach of European countries.[19]

Lest the comparisons with the Latin American and Caribbean region provide too optimistic a picture of the OIC states' legal acceptability of abortion, it should be recalled that maternal mortality rates remain among the highest in the world in some of the OIC countries. In 2010, in Chad and Somalia, over 1,000 women died while pregnant or within forty-two days of termination of pregnancy per 100,000 live births (UN Department of Economic and Social Affairs 2013). These countries have been ravaged by war and poverty is rampant, yet it must also be noted that the correlation between restrictive abortion policies and unsafe abortions—which often result in the death of the pregnant woman—is confirmed in these two cases (see, generally, Haddad and Nour 2009). At the same time, the OIC data provide further evidence that in order to reduce mortality rates a comprehensive policy on sexual and reproductive rights—one that prioritizes the availability and accessibility of abortion, and equally of contraception and sexual education—is essential. Alongside access to safe abortion, use of contraceptive methods has been demonstrated to be a key element in the reduction of maternal mortality (Haddad and Nour 2009). The UN dataset shows dismally low ratios of contraceptive use in OIC countries where maternal mortality ratios are 200 and over.[20]

The parallel between regions in what concerns the legal acceptability of abortion discloses an additional significant aspect: a scattered distribution. While the Latin American and Caribbean region may be more restrictive of legal abortion, there is a certain regional cohesion in this conservatism. Similarly, in Europe the majority of states embrace liberal legislation, with a small number of conservative outliers. The OIC area, however, is highly polarized: it has a strong conservative and a strong liberal pole, a strong off-center left agglomeration indicating rather conservative policies toward abortion, with the rest of the cases scattered around almost every other point on the continuum (see Figure 7.1). This reinforces the observation that, far from being a monolithic bloc, the OIC member states are diverse (Cismas 2014:243–44) and this holds equally true with regard to their abortion legislation. In the case of Latin America and the Caribbean, on the one hand, and Europe, on the other, geographic proximity, shared past experiences, and religion (in particular in relation to Latin America and the Caribbean) may explain the coagulation of policies and a gravitation of the majority of states from the respective region toward the conservative or progressive end of the continuum. Beyond the lack of a common geographic space, what factors can explain the OIC's polarization in the area of abortion policies?

The Small, Yet Important Details: Factors Influencing Abortion Legislation in OIC States

The type of political regime and the space for civil society activism, religion-state relations, and the role of Sharia as a source of law, as well as sociohistoric factors, if read in conjunction with one another and alongside other phenomena, may provide explanations for the differing configurations of domestic abortion legislation across OIC states.

Political regimes in the OIC range from democracies—albeit few and far between—to authoritarian regimes, and from war-torn societies to those that have experienced longer periods of stability. Ethnic divisions and political marginalization of minorities of all kinds, as well as sectarian fighting occur in many an OIC state. Can any correlations be made between the types of political regimes and conservative/liberal abortion policies? The highest-ranking OIC states on the Economist Intelligence Unit's (EIU) Democracy Index 2015 are the "flawed democracies" in Guyana, Indonesia, Malaysia, Senegal, Suriname, and Tunisia (EIU 2015). Among them, only Guyana and Tunisia allow abortion on request, whereas Senegal and Suriname criminalize the practice except for saving the woman's life; Indonesia has a fairly restrictive regime admitting only two grounds for abortion, whereas Malaysia, accepting three legal grounds, is slightly more progressive. Based on these, can one infer that a democratic system does not necessarily guarantee a liberal abortion regime? This would be a hazardous conclusion because it discounts an array of other factors that, in combination, may explain the abortion policies of democracies.

Of the sixteen OIC countries at the conservative end of the continuum (on the 2016 data entailed in the CRR map), fourteen appear in the EIU Democracy Index. Nine are classified as "authoritarian regimes," three are "hybrid" regimes, and Suriname and Senegal, as mentioned previously, are categorized as "flawed democracies." Overall, it could be argued that authoritarian regimes do not foster liberal reproductive polices, were it not for the five Central Asian republics that have liberal abortion policies yet are placed at the very bottom of the democratic index (EIU 2015).[21] The proposition that "almost all authoritarian regimes are repressive around matters sexual" (Altman 2004:66) holds true for Afghanistan under the Taliban, the Sudan of the past and today, as well as Yemen, although a fuller understanding of these countries' policies is gained only by examining other aspects: war, poverty, ethnic and sectarian tensions, and the influence of religion in the hands of political leaders, among others.

Attributing foremost importance to the regime type as an explanatory variable would leave us struggling to understand why Tunisia, under Habib Bourguiba and Zine El Abidine Ben Ali's repressive rule, has managed to develop one of the most liberal abortion systems in Africa, and, indeed, beyond this region. During their reign, the Tunisian state has affirmed the right of women to use contraception, encouraged and subsidized family planning, increased the number of health facilities, and subsidized abortions (UN Department of Economic and Social Affairs 2002c; Hessini 2007:79). Data from 2006 present Tunisia as having one of the highest rates of modern contraception use in the OIC area and the lowest maternal mortality rate among the African member states of the organization (UN Department of Economic and Social Affairs 2013). At the international level, on ratification of the UN CRC, Tunisia had submitted an interpretative declaration showcasing its unequivocal position on abortion: "The Government of the Republic of Tunisia declares that the Preamble to and the provisions of the Convention, in particular article 6 [on the child's right to life], shall not be interpreted in such a way as to impede the application of Tunisian legislation concerning voluntary termination of pregnancy" (Declaration of Tunisia to the CRC 1992). Before rushing to declare Ben Ali and his predecessor ultimate promoters of sexual and reproductive rights and frontrunners of the feminist movement in the OIC region, however, we should pause and recall the human rights violations to which women from "Islamist movements" were subjected during their reign (U.S. Department of State 2011; Marks 2013). Tunisia's early reforms were top-down, elite-driven policies that pursued a nationalist agenda aimed at weakening "the power of kinship groups and the religious establishment" (Chambers and Cummings 2014:30). Some of these reforms may well have also targeted certain international reputational gains.

Be that as it may, once they succeeded in gaining much-needed societal space, Tunisian women's groups played an important role in shaping the policies concerning their rights, not least in the area of abortion. For instance, Leila Hessini reports that women's groups successfully lobbied for the amendment of legislative provisions on parity requirements—these had sanctioned abortion only for those women who had five living children and provided "written agreement of both husband and wife" (Hessini 2007:79). In turn, such reforms have created additional space for women's interest groups to coagulate, and in general for civil society to emerge and grow. The wave of reforms in the 1990s is attributed largely to women's organizations and their feminist activism (European Parliament 2012:4). Against this background, it is not entirely surprising that the Arab Spring started in Tunisia and, at least at this stage, appears to have brought about a pluralist democratic regime (albeit a fragile one) in which women, including "Islamist" women, demand their rights.

Overall, the better conclusion is that, while the type of political regime, *on its own,* fails to explain the exact shape abortion policies take, it certainly correlates with the human rights situation in a country, thus including sexual and reproductive rights. Civil society movements and NGOs appear to be key elements in processes of change, yet they require a certain breathing space to emerge and develop, which in some authoritarian regimes, and in particular in those experiencing conflict, they simply will not find. Encouraging the creation and development of space for civic action could be one of the roles, which the OIC, as an institution, should prioritize.[22]

The religion-state relationship in the constitutional architecture of OIC states and the role of Sharia in their legal systems varies greatly. As such the OIC comprises self-declared secular states, such as Turkey, and theocracies, of which Iran is a paradigmatic example. It includes states in which Sharia law is not a source of legislation (e.g., Albania, Burkina Faso, Chad, Côte d'Ivoire, Turkey, and the six Central Asian republics); where it is the sole or dominant source of law in matters of both criminal proceedings and personal status (e.g., Iran, Saudi Arabia, Sudan); where it governs the personal status and the family codes (e.g., Libya, Malaysia, Morocco); and systems that use customary law alongside common or civil law, whereby customary law can be influenced by Sharia interpretations (e.g., Mali).[23] To make this already great diversity even more complex, some countries employ Sharia only in certain regions. For example, Indonesia uses civil law primarily and Sharia law for personal status matters, while in the Aceh region Sharia is used in both civil and criminal justice matters (Laiman et al. 2015). As previously discussed, Sharia interpretations themselves differ between the Sunni and Shia branches, and within these branches—given the existence of various schools of legal thought, and across countries and regions—there are yet further distinctions in interpretations.

Of the eleven OIC countries where abortion is provided on request, nine do not rely on Sharia as a source of law. Tunisia, while constitutionally recognizing Islam as the state religion, does not make recourse to Sharia as a source of law. This has been maintained, after assiduous deliberations, in the post-Arab Spring constitution of 2014 (Constitution of Tunisia 2014, Article 1; Salah-Omri 2013). In Bahrain, where abortion has been liberalized through the penal code of March 20, 1976, Sharia is the major source of legislation (UN Department of Economic and Social Affairs 2002a; Mechantaf 2010). Yemen, Oman, and the United Arab Emirates offer illustrations of abortion regulated by penal codes based on restrictive interpretations of Sharia (Hessini 2007).

Religion as a factor of singular importance presents a treacherous explanation for the restrictive abortion legislation of certain Muslim-majority countries because it fails to take into account its intersections with numerous other aspects, and with political forces in particular. In authoritarian regimes, in particular (but perhaps also in democracies), it is unclear whether religion drives repressive policies or whether authoritarians (and populists) instrumentalize religious interpretations to further their agenda.

Iran provides an interesting illustration. Before the 1979 revolution, Iran had a relatively permissive abortion policy; after the overthrow of the Shah and his replacement with the Ayatollah Khomeini, that policy was reversed: therapeutic abortion was allowed only when a woman's life was at threat (UN Department of Economic and Social Affairs 2002b). The Iranian Penal Code of 1991, which is based on Sharia, classifies abortion "as a lesser crime involving bodily injury (*oisas*), which is punishable by the payment of blood money or compensation (*diyah*)"; compensation is correlated to the gestational stages enounced in the Qur'an (63). In the early 1990s, Iran embarked on a program to control the growth of its population through improved and subsidized access to contraceptives, the promotion of family planning, including voluntary sterilization, and access to health clinics (64).[24] By 2005, a new law permitted the termination of pregnancies in the case of fetal impairment, but only "after a definite diagnosis by three experts and a confirmation by the Legal Medicine Organization" (Larijani and Zahedi 2006). Based on 2002 data, Iran had the highest ratio of contraceptive use in the OIC region and among the lowest maternal mortality rates (UN Department of Economic and Social Affairs 2013). A 2008 study concluded that the effect of modern contraceptive use on reducing the abortion rate had been 51 percent greater than that of religiosity (Erfani and McQuillan 2008). This provides an interesting reminder of the fact that the state-religion relation is not one between two elements—the state and religion—but includes a third variable: the individual and her choices. The same research suggests that abortions had been performed in unsafe circumstances because legal restrictions remained excessive. Since 2012, Iran has reversed many of its policy achievements by, for example, halting funding for family planning. In 2014, NGOs and activists flagged the new Bill to Increase Fertility Rates and Prevent Population Decline, which if adopted, would prohibit voluntary sterilization and "block access to information about contraception" (Amnesty International 2015).

On the one hand, the Iranian example shows how a theocracy can navigate the religious space to provide information and access to family planning for its population, albeit imperfectly. On the other hand, it demonstrates that as long as access to safe abortion, adequate contraception, and family planning more broadly are not considered inalienable human rights but as mere tools for population control, these will remain temporary achievements at the mercy of the ruler—be that a religious or a secular one.

Beyond the restrictive legal grounds for abortion, which in certain OIC countries may, as we have seen, be influenced by the particular relation that the state has with religion, a number of other legal hurdles exist. These include spousal approval, parental approval, and the requirement that several doctors provide their consent for the procedure. These practices are sometimes described as religiously motivated, but, if we accept that what is demanded by religion is essentially an act of interpretation, it becomes clear that they may have different motivations. Alas, in religious and secular societies alike, the practice of infantilizing women continues to inform the creation or maintenance of such practices.

Sociohistoric aspects may carry some weight in explaining a state's position on abortion. For example, the liberalized stance on abortion that the six former Soviet republics of Central Asia have adopted may be traced to the policies of the Soviet Union. While decriminalization of abortion occurred in 1955, in practice the Soviet Union's position on sexual and reproductive rights was tumultuous because it failed to adequately combine access to safe abortion with increased access to modern contraceptives and subjected women to supplementary pressures (Randall 2011).

The colonial legacy is more often invoked in connection to the homophobic approach to LGBTI rights that several Muslim-majority states have adopted (Lutchmie Persad 2010). Nonetheless, a Stockholm syndrome attachment to codes promulgated by old colonial powers is also apparent in the area of abortion legislation. For example, Indonesia modeled its fairly conservative abortion law on the Dutch criminal code; Mauritania's restrictive legislation is based on French colonial law; and Libya's highly restrictive law is derived from Italian codes (Hessini 2007).

A history of conflict in which rape was a weapon of war, or existing, ongoing large-scale sexual violence, may explain why some states, which otherwise have restrictive abortion policies, have provided an explicit exception for victims of rape. This may well be the case for Mali and Sudan.

On their own, none of these factors—the political, the religious, the sociohistorical—serve to fully explain an OIC state's position on abortion. The explanatory value of the factors lies in understanding the relations between them within a country and across time, as well as the interaction with other aspects including poverty, economic forces, a certain developmental model that embraces population control, or phenomena such as globalization.

The OIC's Position in UN Forums

Having examined the normative position of the OIC on abortion (as this results from an analysis of the CDHRI and the CRCI), and the variety of domestic legislative approaches of member states, this section has a twofold aim. First, it seeks to establish whether the OIC has acted in UN forums as a coordinated group espousing an institutional position on abortion. Second, it examines to what extent this institutional stance relates to the OIC's normative position and the member states' domestic approaches.

During the 1994 International Conference on Population and Development (ICPD) in Cairo, the OIC's institutional position on abortion was notable mainly because of its utter absence. In other words, the organization failed to articulate a common position. Interestingly, the period preceding the conference saw fervent opposition to sexual and reproductive health and rights from various quarters (Bowen 1997). Reportedly, an "unholy religious pact" was sought out by the Holy See—identified by scholars as the standard-bearer of the prohibition of abortion—with certain Muslim-majority states, in particular Iran and Libya (Abdullah 1996). As mentioned previously, the latter two states had—and have—some of the most restrictive abortion laws. During the Cairo conference itself, the "unholy alliance" between Iran and the Holy See had broken down when it became apparent that their agendas did not entirely align (Dunlop, Kyte, and MacDonald 1996). By 1994, Iran was already pursuing a program to control its population growth through contraceptives and family planning; this policy was intrinsically incompatible with the Holy See's stance, which excluded any and all means of preventing or interrupting pregnancies.[25]

Some OIC states, as well as several countries from Latin America, the Holy See, and Malta, entered reservations to and submitted interpretative statements of those provisions of the ICPD Programme of Action that concerned sexual and reproductive rights. The OIC states' reservations were generally not opposed to abortion *as such*,[26] in contrast to those entered by Latin American states, the Holy See, and Malta.[27] Rather, the former were concerned with the notion of sexual rights, which were recognized as belonging to the individual and not limited to the context of marriage, thereby extending to sexual relations outside the confines of marriage (understood as the union between a man and a woman) (Cismas 2014:59).[28] This insistence on the "traditional" family unit as the holder of sexual rights—as opposed to the individual—proved highly problematic, frustrating some of the normative advancements of the conference.

The next test for the OIC institutional position came in 1995 at the Fourth World Conference on Women in Beijing. The configurations in Beijing were very different from those in Cairo. In Beijing, women took center stage, heading the event and many of the states' delegations; the African Group assumed a leadership role, which ultimately made consensus possible on issues including sexual and reproductive health (Dunlop, Kyte, and MacDonald 1996:156–58). What remained of the "unholy alliance" were the Holy See, Malta, Sudan, and Yemen acting as a "scripted and coordinated . . . grouping that was fundamentalist in its approach" (161). Noting that the OIC had "for the first time in such a conference . . . acted as a country grouping to coordinate positions," Dunlop, Kyte, and MacDonald also observed the organization's difficulty in forming and maintaining a coherent position (161).

The statement by then OIC secretary-general, the Nigerian politician Hamid Algabid could provide some insights into the OIC's institutional position on abortion. The relevant passage reads, "If we proceed to know the truth of life, we find it a holy one, stemming from an overall principle that he who kills one person is similar to the one who kills all people; and if any one saves a life, it would be as if he saves the life of all people. Hence, the prohibition and total incrimination of the aggression committed against the fetus's right to life, through abortion" (Algabid 1995).

Two aspects make this statement baffling. The "prohibition and total incrimination of the aggression committed against the fetus's right to life" fails to accord with *any* of the OIC's member states' abortion laws. By 1995, all OIC states sanctioned abortion when the life of the pregnant woman was at threat, yet the secretary-general's statement failed to take stock of these national realities. The statement was in stark contrast with the position of those OIC states that were permitting abortion on request, or those states that did so on the grounds of health of the pregnant women, fetal impairment, rape, or incest. In addition, it appears that the OIC's normative position on abortion, as enshrined in the organization's own instruments, was also ignored. Algabid's statement was in dissonance with the OIC's Cairo Declaration, specifically the provision stipulating that the right to life of the child starts at birth (see CDHRI, Article 7(a)). To summarize, the OIC institutional position on abortion, as outlined by Secretary-General Algabid, was a rather peculiar achievement: It was more conservative than the domestic legislation in any of the OIC member states *and* the provisions of the CDHRI.[29]

In spite of this, the normative developments of Beijing were important. The Platform for Action defined sexual and reproductive rights as human rights and operationalized some of the commitments made in Cairo: among others, it encouraged states to consider "reviewing laws containing punitive measures against women who have undergone illegal abortions" (UN 1996a:40 (para. 106(k))). Only five of the OIC member states entered reservations to this latter provision: Brunei, Kuwait, Libya, Malaysia, and Mauritania. A careful reading of these reserving instruments clarifies their nuanced meaning, particularly when compared to the unequivocal language on a total ban on abortion evident in the reservations of the Holy See and of some Latin American states (UN 1996b:154–75). To illustrate, Malaysia's reservation states that "in the context of paragraph 106 (k) we wish to support the view that attention should be given to the prevention of unsafe abortions and the provision of humane management of complications from abortions as part of reproductive health care. However, abortion is not legal or permissible in Malaysia and can only be performed on medical grounds" (167).

At the UN Commission on the Status of Women—an intergovernmental body of the UN Economic and Social Council—the OIC has been noteworthy, not because of its voiced institutional opinion on abortion, but because of its silence. In 2012, the forum was embroiled in effervescent debates, which ultimately led to the failure to adopt "agreed conclusions" (Vik and Moe 2015:18). While OIC member states presented statements on behalf of the G77 and the African group, they did not do so on behalf of the OIC (Ibid).

The negotiations of the Sustainable Development Goals (SDGs) provided another occasion for the OIC to express its institutional position on reproductive and sexual rights more generally, and on abortion more specifically. In 2014, the Open Working Group (OWG) tabled the proposal on SDGs and subsequently submitted it for consideration to the UN General Assembly. At that time, state representatives spoke on behalf of several groupings; among them Benin, an OIC member state, intervened on behalf of the least developed countries, yet not on behalf of the OIC (UN General Assembly 2014a:6). Explanations of positions and reservations on the draft declaration on the SDGs were also made by OIC member states Kuwait, Lebanon, Libya, and Egypt on behalf of the Group of Arab States—not, however, on behalf of the OIC (UN General Assembly 2014b).[30] To summarize, on the occasion of the SDGs negotiations, the OIC failed anew to articulate an institutional position. A pattern had clearly emerged.

Yet again some members states—Afghanistan, Cameroon, Chad, Iran, Libya, Mauritania, Senegal, and Yemen—voiced objections to the OWG's proposed targets 3.7[31] and 5.6[32] (UN General Assembly 2014b). Of these, only Cameron, Libya, Mauritania, and Yemen raised specific objections related to the termination of pregnancies. The nearly identical reservations of the latter three states were particularly vehement in their opposition to abortion and relied on a highly misleading interpretation of the right to life as a *jus cogens* norm "applicable without distinction of birth" (UN General Assembly 2014b:4–5, 16, 21–2). *Jus cogens* norms are those select few rules of customary international law that are accepted by the international community as nonderogable and which "can be modified only by a subsequent norm of general international law having the same character" (Vienna Convention on the Law of Treaties 1980, Article 53). While the right to life has crystallized into a norm of customary international law (Petersen 2012:para. 1), and it may well have achieved the status of *jus cogens*, the scope of this right does not include the protection of life from the moment of conception. Evidence for this includes both the inconsistent state practice relating to when life begins and the equally divergent *opinio juris* on the topic. When employing the expression "applicable without distinction of birth," Libya, Cameron, Mauritania, and Yemen appeared to draw on the nondiscrimination clause in the UN CRC, read in conjunction with the preamble, which in turn references the Declaration of the

Rights of the Child (principles 4–5). As has already been discussed, this preambular clause was inserted by the drafters of the convention to allow for varied national interpretations of when life begins. In and of itself, the drafting history serves to demonstrate the lack of consensus over the issue and hence evidences the noncustomary nature, and implicitly nonperemptory nature, of the protection of life from the moment of conception.

It is correct that the nondiscrimination clause in the UN CRC imposes a duty on states to "respect and ensure the rights set forth in the Convention to each child . . . without discrimination of any kind, irrespective of the child's . . . birth" (CRC 1990: Article 2(1)). However, by providing birth as a nondiscriminatory ground, the drafters' intention was not to extend protection to the embryo or fetus (see, for a discussion, Abramson 2008:105–6). Furthermore, the subsequent practice of UN treaty bodies suggests that birth as a prohibited ground of discrimination refers to children born out of wedlock (Detrick 1999:75–78.). Such misuse of the nondiscrimination clause reveals a certain cynicism on the part of Libya, Mauritania, and Yemen, given that the CRC Committee had flagged its concern in relation to the existing discrimination of children born out of wedlock in each of the three countries (CRC Committee 1998, para. 11; CRC Committee 2001, para. 25; CRC Committee 2014, paras. 29, 35(b), and 76(d)).

Overall, we see an inability of the OIC to produce a coherent institutional stance on abortion at international conferences on population, development, and women, and in other UN forums. This silence could be explained by the OIC's internal polarization on abortion. Additional institutional and political causes may exist. What has been striking, is that on the rare occasion when the institutional voice of the OIC has spoken (through the secretary-general's statement), its tone has been retrogressive, measured against the domestic legislative approaches in OIC states and the normative position as this was embodied, at that time, by the Cairo Declaration. It was as if the OIC insisted on confirming its stereotypical portrayal as a conservative organization, even when there were possibilities for very different courses of action.

Conclusion

Control of a woman's sexuality by her father, her husband, her brother, by religion, or by the state is nothing new. A measure of control of a woman's sexuality by the woman herself, however, is new; it is an achievement of recent date. The option to have recourse to safe abortion is an integral part of a woman's control over her sexuality, understood as both reproductive and pleasurable. The framework of human rights within which access to safe abortion now finds its place represents a claim that such control can no longer be alienated to third parties. Yet, as with all human rights, the struggle is never over.

Where does the OIC fit into this struggle? Or, to paraphrase this volume's title, what is the OIC's position on abortion: good, bad, or ugly? The answer must be: not too bad, possibly ugly, and certainly confusing. To elaborate on this seemingly contradictory answer, an overview of the chapter's findings is in order.

First, the OIC's normative position as it emerged from an analysis of the Cairo Declaration, and especially the CRCI, is not too bad, although important caveats exist. The CDHRI recognizes birth, not conception, as the start of an individual's life, and thereby provides space for interpretations that sanction abortion. Yet, its equivocality (birth versus fetus in Article 7) and the (in)famous religious limitation clauses (in Articles 2(a) and 2(b), 24, and 25) provide too much space for domestic interpretations—whether conservative, progressive, or somewhere in between, any abortion policy can be accommodated. It is unlikely, however, that a total ban that fails to ensure an exception for saving a woman's life would be sanctioned. The CRCI should be acknowledged for what it is: one of the rare international instruments that explicitly mentions abortion. Potentially, its Article 6 stipulations can form the basis of a fairly progressive regime in the area of abortion. Its potential nonetheless remains uncertain: the manner in which the provision "necessity warranted by the interests of the mother, the fetus, or both of them" is interpreted—that is, to include or exclude legal grounds for abortion—will ultimately be decisive.

Second, overall and by comparison to other regions, the domestic laws on abortion in OIC member states are not the most restrictive. Were we to place the OIC's membership on a conservative-progressive continuum we would find a significant polarization: a strong conservative pole (sixteen member states permit abortion only to save a woman's life), a strong progressive pole (eleven states allow abortion on request), a strong agglomeration of countries that accept three legal grounds for abortion, with the rest of the cases scattered on the continuum. The analysis has shown that the type of political regime (whether democratic or authoritarian), the state-religion relation and the role of Sharia in the legal system, sociohistoric factors, including the legacy of colonialism and of conflict, may carry explanatory value if their intersections within a country and across time are considered. Civil society, and in particular women's groups, have emerged as an important factor in the changing legislative landscape on abortion.

Third, the OIC's position (as an institution) on abortion in international forums is difficult to identify because no (coherent) position has coagulated. When OIC Secretary-General Hamid Algabid intervened on the topic at the Beijing Conference, he did so in a manner that was more conservative than both the OIC's normative position and those of the individual countries. Cynics may therefore argue that it is preferable for the OIC not to speak with one voice on abortion, if such is the result. To unravel the OIC's mystifying silence on abortion and the unfortunate exception to such silence, we must look at causes beyond the membership's polarization on the topic. To these points, I would argue that two interrelated elements, one institutional and one political, explain the nonexisting OIC position on abortion as well as the obstacles that any initiative aiming to build such a position will have to confront.

At the institutional level, the OIC is an eminently intergovernmental organization: the power rests with states (see Kayaoglu 2015:23–37). The organs of the organization are either gatherings of state representatives of varying seniority (such as the Islamic Summit, the Council of Foreign Ministers, standing committees), or organs that should have an independent functioning yet are not entrusted with the powers to function independently. The example of the OIC IPHRC is paradigmatic for the latter case. Considering its statute, the commission lacks the most basic of powers for it to be able to function as a human rights monitoring body: that of monitoring the human rights situation in the organization's member states (Cismas 2014:297–98). This, of course, does not mean that OIC IPHRC members may not find resourceful methods to fulfill the mandate that they *should* have been entrusted with (Cismas 2011:1148–49; Kayaoglu 2015:104–5). Institutionally, the secretary-general is in a similar position to that of the OIC IPHRC, albeit with more administrative clout.[33] In practice, whether she (sic!) will take a proactive and progressive stance on any issue, including abortion, will depend on her agenda, personality, and prestige, and the space of maneuver she is granted by the OIC's powerful members. One of the most problematic aspects in the institutional architecture of the OIC is the limited space for participation provided to nongovernmental organizations (Kayaoglu 2015:105–6). The reticence of many member states to engage with civil society organizations critical of their opinions and the statist mindset of the OIC translates into a number of cumbersome administrative procedures, which effectively bar political and physical access (Cismas 2014:302–3). Women's groups and other civil society organizations from across the OIC area wishing to lobby the IPHRC or the Secretariat on abortion policies will find it difficult to do so, given that both are based in Jeddah.[34]

This brings us to the political factor. An interesting parallel can be made between the OIC and the UN Security Council. While keeping due proportion and acknowledging their many differences, the OIC and the UN Security Council have one aspect in common: a select group of states can hold other member states hostage to their politics. This fact translates, in the case of both bodies, into institutional ineffectiveness. Foremost among the "powerful" OIC states is the financial backer of the organization, Saudi Arabia, and its rival Iran. As Turan Kayaoglu explains, Malaysia, Pakistan, and Turkey have become contenders with their own interests and agendas (Kayaoglu 2015:ch. 4). For those OIC states with a progressive stance on abortion to spearhead their position within the OIC and in international forums, they would inevitably have to engage with the de facto veto-yielding states and carefully navigate the difficult institutional setting. The current times, marked by the post-MDGs activity, may offer a rare opportunity for progressive OIC states to chip away at the conservative image of this organization; they may consider couching the sexuality agenda in development terms, which ultimately could sway conservative states, or at least ensure that no blocking objections be registered. In the alternative, what we are left with is the OIC's current position: potentially not too bad, at times ugly, and in general very confusing.

Notes

1. For the relevance of the dialectic between the OIC and its member states' position on human rights, see Chapter 1 in this volume. See also Chapter 5.

2. The other express stipulation can be found in the Protocol to the African Charter on Human and Peoples' Rights on the Rights of Women in Africa, discussed later in this chapter.

3. Contrast the recommendation to decriminalize abortion in the 1999 General Recommendation A/54/38/Rev.1, para. 31(c) to the 2015 Recommendation CEDAW/C/GC/33, paras. 47(b) and 51(l).

4. For example, although abortion as such does not appear in the International Covenant on Civil and Political Rights, the Human Rights Committee found in the case *KL v Peru* that denying access to legal abortion amounted to violations of the covenant's Articles 7 (the right to be free from cruel, inhumane, and degrading treatment), 17 (the right to privacy),

and 24 (special protection of the rights of a minor). See https://www.escr-net.org/caselaw/2016/kl-v-peru-ccprc85d11532003-communication-no-11532003.

5. OIC Resolution No. 49/19-P 1990, Article. 1.

6. For a detailed analysis of these instruments, see Cismas 2014, chapter 5. See also Chapter 8, this volume.

7. According to Article 23, the CRCI enters into force after thirty days pursuant to the ratification of the twentieth member state of the OIC. Covenant on the Rights of the Child in Islam (2005), IC/9-IGGE/HRI/2004/Rep.Final, annexed to the Resolution on Legal Affairs No. 1/32-LEG, June 2005.

8. OIC/CFM Resolution on Legal Affairs No. 2/38-LEG 2011. http://ww1.oic-oci.org/38cfm/en/documents/res/LEG-RES-38-CFM-FINAL-2.pdf.

9. Limitation clauses in international human rights treaties are not unusual; however they generally follow an established form which represents a procedural guarantee that the rights thereby limited are not in fact emptied of their substantive meaning. Such clauses usually provide that restrictions on rights must be prescribed by law, must pursue a legitimate aim, and must be necessary in a democratic society. See discussion in Cismas 2014:258–65.

10. See also Chapter 4, this volume.

11. The OIC's website lacks information on the ratification status of the CRCI. While the instrument appears on the website of the OIC, the states that have become party to it are nowhere listed. https://www.oic-iphrc.org/en/data/docs/legal_instruments/OIC_HRRIT/327425.pdf. See Chapter 2 (this volume) for more details on the CRCI ratification status. See also Viljoen 2012:16 and http://www.refworld.org/docid/44eaf0e4a.html.

12. Topics that are societally sensitive are often phrased in domestic legislation in such ways as to discourage the practice, yet still permitting it. For instance, Article 115 of the Swiss criminal code (1937, with amendments, status as of March 1, 2018) provides for assisted suicide in the following terms: "Inciting and assisting suicide: Any person who for *selfish motives* incites or assists another to commit or attempt to commit suicide shall, if that other person thereafter commits or attempts to commit suicide, be liable to a custodial sentence not exceeding five years or to a monetary penalty" (emphasis added). https://www.admin.ch/opc/en/classified-compilation/19370083/201501010000/311.0.pdf.

13. Article 14(2)(c) of the Protocol to the African Charter on Human and Peoples' Rights on the Rights of Women in Africa stipulates that states take all appropriate measures "to protect the reproductive rights of women by authorising medical abortion in cases of sexual assault, rape, incest, and where the continued pregnancy endangers the mental and physical health of the mother or the life of the mother or the foetus." This is a relevant instrument not least because several OIC member states are party to it. See http://www.achpr.org/instruments/women-protocol/ratification/.

14. ICCPR, Article 6(1). For developments in the Human Rights Committee's interpretation of the covenant to ensure the protection of women seeking access to safe abortion see Zampas and Gher 2008.

15. ECHR, Article 2. The European Court of Human Rights has refrained from establishing when life begins for purposes of Article 2 of the ECHR. Instead, it accorded a wide margin of appreciation to states and reviewed the procedural obligations in respect to abortion arising under Article 8 (private life) or Article 3 (inhuman and degrading treatment). See also Wicks 2011 and Erdman 2014.

16. For an analysis of how the Inter-American Commission and Court of Human Rights have navigated therapeutic abortion cases given the stipulation of Article 4(1) of the ACHR, see Zampas and Gher 2008, and Malca 2013.

17. Information on Palestine is not available in the *World Abortion Policies 2013* website.

18. Note that Guyana is counted in both the OIC and the Latin America and Caribbean sample.

19. Note that Albania is counted in both the OIC and the European sample.

20. In Chad, for example, contraception use was 3 percent, whereas the maternal mortality ratio was 1,100 per 100,000 live births in 2010. In Uganda the contraception use was 30 percent and the maternal mortality ratio 310 (UN Department of Economic and Social Affairs 2013).

21. Kazakhstan, the sixth OIC country from Central Asia, is classified as a hybrid regime.

22. For a related discussion see Chapter 12, this volume.

23. Some extensive studies on the topic of religion as a source of law more broadly, and Sharia and the law specifically, are Stahnke and Blitt 2005, Abiad 2008, and Temperman 2010.

24. Interestingly, Iran appears to have been sensitive to developments in international conferences, including the 1994 International Conference on Population and Development in Cairo (UN Department of Economic and Social Affairs. 2002b:64).

25. The Holy See's position can be found in Pope Paul VI's encyclical letter *Humanae Vitae* of July 25, 1968. http://w2.vatican.va/content/paul-vi/en/encyclicals/documents/hf_p-vi_enc_25071968_humanae-vitae.html. The relevant passage reads: "The direct interruption of the generative process already begun and, above all, all direct abortion, even for therapeutic reasons, are to be absolutely excluded as lawful means of regulating the number of children. Equally to be condemned . . . is direct sterilization, whether of the man or of the woman, whether permanent or temporary. Similarly excluded is any action which either before, at the moment of, or after sexual intercourse, is specifically intended to prevent procreation—whether as an end or as a means."

26. The *Report of the International Conference on Population and Development* (ICPD) lists eleven OIC states that have entered reservations and interpretative statements to the ICPD Programme of Action. Of these, Libya and Yemen explicitly reserved the right to interpret the provisions related to abortion in the instrument in accordance with their national law or their religious beliefs (UN Population Fund 1995:ch. 5, paras. 13 and 19), while the United Arab Emirates interpreted "family planning" to exclude abortion (ch. 5, para. 18). It may well be that general Islamic reservations that were entered by some of the other eight OIC states sought to ensure a similar effect in relation to abortion. While acknowledging that the Programme of Action is not a binding instrument, note that the permissibility of general reservations is highly contentious in treaty law. See Cismas 2014:267–270.

27. Each of the nine Latin American states that entered reservations to the ICPD Progamme of Action specifically mentioned their opposition to the right to access safe abortion (UN Population Fund 1995:ch. 5, paras. 9, 10, 14, 15, 21, 23, 24, 26, 30). For the Holy See's lengthy and detailed statement and reservations, including the fundamental objection to a right to access safe abortion, see ch. 5, para. 27, and for Malta's statement see ch. 5, para. 29.

28. As an illustration, the Libyan delegate stated: "I wish to express a reservation, despite the discussion that took place in the Main Committee regarding the basic rights of couples and individuals. We express a reservation regarding the word 'individuals.'" (UN Population Fund 1995:ch. 5, para. 13).

29. For a more general discussion of the tensions evident between the OIC and some of its member states' human rights policies in UN forums, see Chapter 4 (this volume).

30. These statements all concerned goal 16 ("Promote peaceful and inclusive societies for sustainable development, provide access to justice for all and build effective, accountable and inclusive institutions at all levels") and referred to, inter alia, the noninclusion in the OWG proposal of language on the right to self-determination of colonial and occupied people.

31. "By 2030, ensure universal access to sexual and reproductive health-care services, including for family planning, information and education, and the integration of reproductive health into national strategies and programmes" (UN General Assembly 2014ba:12).

32. "Ensure universal access to sexual and reproductive health and reproductive rights as agreed in accordance with the Programme of Action of the International Conference on Population and Development and the Beijing Platform for Action and the outcome documents of their review conferences" (UN General Assembly 2014ba:14).

33. Charter of the Organization of Islamic Cooperation. Dakar, March 14, 2008. http://ww1.oic-oci.org/english/charter/OIC%20Charter-new-en.pdf.

34. See also Chapter 4 on the OIC's relationship with civil society.

Works Cited

Abdullah, Yasmin. 1996. "The Holy See at United Nations Conferences: State or Church?" *Columbia Law Review* 96 (7): 1835–75.

Abiad, Nisrine. 2008. *Sharia, Muslim States and International Human Rights Treaty Obligations: A Comparative Study.* London: British Institute of International and Comparative Law.

Abramson, Bruce. 2008. *A Commentary on the United Nations Convention on the Rights of the Child, Article 2: The Right of Non-Discrimination.* Leiden: Martinus Nijhoff.

Ahdar, Rex, and Nicholas Aroney. 2010. "The Topography of Shari'a in the Western Political Landscape." In *Shari'a in the West*, ed. Rex Ahdar and Nicholas Aroney, 1–31. Oxford: Oxford University Press.

Algabid, Hamid. 1995. "Statement of His Excellency Dr. Hamid Algabid OIC Secretary General, World Conference on Women, Beijing 4–15 September 1995." http://www.un.org/esa/gopher-data/conf/fwcw/conf/una/950911155632.txt.

Al-Hibri, Azizah. Y. 2011. *Family Planning and Islamic Jurisprudence.* Karamah Muslim Women Lawyers for Human Rights. http://karamah.org/wp-content/uploads/2011/10/AlhibriFamilyPlanning.pdf.

Alston, Philip. 1990. "The Unborn Child and Abortion Under the Draft Convention on the Rights of the Child." *Human Rights Quarterly* 12 (1): 156–78.

Altman, Dennis. 2004. "Sexuality and Globalization." *Sexuality Research & Social Policy* 1 (1): 63–68.

American Convention on Human Rights. OAS Treaty Series No. 36, 1144 UNTS 123. Adopted November 22, 1969; entered into force July 18, 1978.

Amnesty International. 2015. "Iran: Proposed Laws Reduce Women to 'Baby Making Machines' in Misguided Attempts to Boost Population." March 11. https://www.amnesty.org/en/latest/news/2015/03/iran-proposed-laws-reduce-women-to-baby-making-machines/.

An-Na'im, Abdullahi Ahmed. 1990. *Toward an Islamic Reformation: Civil Liberties, Human Rights and International Law*. Syracuse, NY: Syracuse University Press.

Bowen, Donna Lee. 1997. "Abortion, Islam, and the 1994 Cairo Population Conference." *International Journal of Middle East Studies* 29 (2): 161–84.

CDHRI. 1990. "Cairo Declaration on Human Rights in Islam." Resolution No. 49/19-P, Nineteenth Islamic Conference of Foreign Ministers, Cairo. August 5. https://www.oic-iphrc.org/en/data/docs/legal_instruments/OIC_HRRIT/571230.pdf.

CEDAW. 1981. Convention on the Elimination of All Forms of Discrimination Against Women. 1249 UNTS 18, adopted December 18, 1979, entered into force September 3, 1981.

CEDAW Committee. 1999. A/54/38/Rev.1, General recommendation No. 24: Article 12 of the Convention (women and health).

———. 2013. CEDAW/C/GC/30, General recommendation No. 30 on women in conflict prevention, conflict and post-conflict situations.

———. 2015. CEDAW/C/GC/33, General recommendation No. 33 on women's access to justice.

CESCR. 2016. E/C.12/GC/22. General comment No. 22 on the right to sexual and reproductive health (Article 12 of the International Covenant on Economic, Social and Cultural Rights). http://undocs.org/E/C.12/GC/22.

Chambers, Victoria, and Clare Cummings. 2014. "Building Momentum: Women's Empowerment in Tunisia." Case study report. London: Overseas Development Institute. http://www.developmentprogress.org/sites/developmentprogress.org/files/case-study-report/tunisia_case_study_-_full_report_final_feb_16.pdf.

Cismas, Ioana. 2011. "Introductory Note to the Statute of the OIC Independent Permanent Human Rights Commission." *International Legal Materials* 5 (6): 1148–60.

———. 2014. *Religious Actors and International Law*. Oxford: Oxford University Press.

Constitution of Tunisia. 2014. Translated by UNDP and reviewed by International IDEA. https://www.constituteproject.org/constitution/Tunisia_2014.pdf.

Corrêa, Sonya, and Rosalind Petchesky. 1994. "Reproductive and Sexual Rights: A Feminist Perspective." In *Population Policies Reconsidered: Health, Empowerment, and Rights*, ed. Gita Sen, Adrienne Germain, and Lincoln C. Chen, 107–23. Cambridge, MA: Harvard University Press.

CRC. 1990. Convention on the Rights of the Child. 1577 UNTS 3, adopted November 20, 1989, entered into force September 2, 1990.

CRC Committee. 1998. *Concluding Observations of the Committee on the Rights of the Child: Libyan Arab Jamahiriya*. CRC/C/15/Add.84.

———. 2001. *Concluding Observations of the Committee on the Rights of the Child: Mauritania*. CRC/C/15/Add.159.

———. 2014. *Concluding Observations on the Fourth Periodic Report of Yemen*. CRC/C/YEM/CO/4.

CRCI. 2005. Covenant on the Rights of the Child in Islam, Resolution on Legal Affairs No. 1/32-LEG. Adopted by the 32nd session of the Islamic Conference of Foreign Ministers, Sana'a, June 21–23, 2005.

CRR. 2016. *The World's Abortion Laws*. New York: Center for Reproductive Rights. http://worldabortionlaws.com.

Declaration of the Rights of the Child. 1959. *General Assembly Resolution 1386 (XIV)*. November 20.

Declaration of Tunisia to the CRC. 1992. UNTC, Online Database, Chapter IV: Human Rights, Convention on the Rights of the Child. https://treaties.un.org/PAGES/ViewDetails.aspx?src=TREATY&mtdsg_no=IV-11&chapter=4&clang=_en.

Detrick, Sharon. 1999. *A Commentary on the United Nations Convention on the Rights of the Child.* Leiden: Martinus Nijhof.

Dunlop, Joan, Rachel Kyte, and Mia MacDonald. 1996. "Women Redrawing the Map: The World After the Beijing and Cairo Conferences." *SAIS Review* 16 (1): 153–65.

EIU. 2015. Democracy Index 2015. https://www.eiu.com/public/topical_report.aspx?campaignid=DemocracyIndex2015.

El Feki, Shereen. 2013. *Sex and the Citadel: Intimate Life in a Changing Arab World.* London: Chatto and Windus.

El Said, Maha, Lena Meari, and Nicola Pratt, eds. 2015. *Rethinking Gender in Revolutions and Resistance.* London: Zed Books.

Eltahawy, Mona. 2015. *Headscarves and Hymens: Why the Middle East Needs a Sexual Revolution.* London: Weidenfeld and Nicolson.

Erdman, Joanna N. 2014. "Procedural Abortion Rights: Ireland and the European Court of Human Rights." *Reproductive Health Matters* 22 (44): 22–30.

Erfani, Amir, and Kevin McQuillan. 2008. "Rates of Induced Abortion in Iran: The Roles of Contraceptive Use and Religiosity." *Studies in Family Planning* 39 (2): 111–22.

European Convention on Human Rights. 1953. Council of Europe Treaty Series No. 5, adopted November 4, 1950, entered into force on September 3, 1953, as amended by Protocols No. 11 and No. 14.

European Parliament. 2012. "Gender Equality Policy in Tunisia, Briefing Note, Directorate General for Internal Policies, Policy Department C: Citizens' Rights and Constitutional Affairs, Women's Rights and Gender Equality." http://www.europarl.europa.eu/RegData/etudes/note/join/2012/462502/IPOL-FEMM_NT(2012)462502_EN.pdf.

Foucault, Michel. 1978. *The History of Sexuality.* Vol. 1, *An Introduction*, trans., Robert Hurley. New York: Pantheon Books.

Haddad, Lisa B., and Nawal M. Nour. 2009. "Unsafe Abortion: Unnecessary Maternal Mortality." *Reviews in Obstetrics and Gynecology* 2 (2): 122–26.

Haynes, Jeffrey. 2013. *Faith-based Organisations at the United Nations.* Badia Fiesolana: European University Institute Working Papers, RSCAS 2013/70.

Hélie, Anissa. 2012. "The Politics of Abortion Policy in the Heterogeneous 'Muslim World.'" In *Self-Determination and Women's Rights in Muslim Societies*, ed. Chitra Raghavan and James P. Levine, 3–36. Waltham, MA: Brandeis University Press.

Hessini, Leila. 2007. "Abortion and Islam: Policies and Practice in the Middle East and North Africa." *Reproductive Health Matters* 15 (29): 75–84.

Holy See. 1968. Encyclical Letter *Humanae Vitae* of the Supreme Pontiff Paul VI to his venerable brothers the patriarchs, archbishops, bishops and other local ordinaries in peace and communion with the Apostolic See. 25 July 1968.

ICCPR. 1976. International Covenant on Civil and Political Rights. 999 UNTS 171, adopted December 16, 1966, entered into force March 23, 1976.

ICESCR. 1976. International Covenant on Economic, Social and Cultural Rights. 993 UNTS 3, adopted December 16, 1966, entered into force January 3, 1976.

Kayaoglu, Turan. 2015. *The Organization of Islamic Cooperation: Politics, Problems, and Potential.* London: Routledge.

Laiman, Alamo D., Dewi Savitri Reni, Ronald Lengkong, and Sigit Ardiyanto. 2015. The *Indonesian Legal System and Legal Research*). New York: Hauser Global Law School Program. http://www.nyulawglobal.org/globalex/Indonesia1.html.
Larijani, Bagher, and Farzaneh Zahedi. 2006. "Changing Parameters for Abortion in Iran." *Indian Journal of Medical Ethics* 3 (4): 130–31. http://www.issuesinmedicalethics.org/index.php/ijme/article/view/687/1689.
Lutchmie Persad, Xavier B. 2010. "Homosexuality and Death: A Legal Analysis of Uganda's Proposed Anti-Homosexuality Bill." *Florida A & M University Law Review* 6 (1): 135–62.
Malca, Camila Gianella. 2013. "Upcoming Decision of the Inter American Court of Human Rights on Access to Therapeutic Abortion?" *PluriCourts* (blog), University of Oslo. http://www.jus.uio.no/pluricourts/english/blog/leiry-cornejo-chavez/upcoming-decision-of-the-inter-american-court-of-human-rights-on-access-to-therapeutic-abort.html.
Marks, Monica. 2013. "Women's Rights Before and After the Revolution." In *The Making of the Tunisian Revolution: Contexts, Architects, Prospects*, ed. Nouri Gana, 224–51. Edinburgh: Edinburgh University Press.
Mechantaf, Khalil. 2010. "The Constitutional Law and the Legal system of the Kingdom of Bahrain." New York: Hauser Global Law School Program. http://www.nyulawglobal.org/globalex/Bahrain.html.
Omri, Mohamed-Salah. 2013. *Tunisian Constitutionalism and the Draft Constitution of December 2012*. Open Democracy. https://www.opendemocracy.net/mohamed-salah-omri/tunisian-constitutionalism-and-draft-constitution-of-december-2012.
Petchesky, Rosalind. 1990. *Abortion and Woman's Choice: The State, Sexuality & Reproductive Freedom*. rev. ed. Boston: Northeastern University Press.
Petersen, Niels. 2012. "Life, Right to, International Protection." *Max Planck Encyclopedia of Public International Law*. Oxford: Oxford University Press. http://opil.ouplaw.com/view/10.1093/law:epil/9780199231690/law-9780199231690-e841?prd=EPIL.
Protocol to the African Charter on Human and Peoples' Rights on the Rights of Women in Africa. 2005. Adopted July 1, 2003, entered into force November 25, 2005. http://www.achpr.org/instruments/women-protocol/.
Randall, Amy E. 2011. "'Abortion Will Deprive You of Happiness!': Soviet Reproductive Politics in the Post-Stalin Era." *Journal of Women's History* 23 (3): 13–38.
Rehman, Javaid, and Eleni Polymenopoulou. 2013. "Is Green a Part of the Rainbow? Sharia, Homosexuality and LGBT Rights in the Muslim World." *Fordham International Law Journal* 37 (1): 1–52.
Niger. 1999. Reservations to the CEDAW. https://treaties.un.org/Pages/ViewDetails.aspx?src=IND&mtdsg_no=IV-8&chapter=4&lang=en#EndDec.
Saiz, Ignacio. 2007. "Bracketing Sexuality: Human Rights and Sexual Orientation—A Decade of Development and Denial at the United Nations." In *Culture, Society and Sexuality: A Reader*. 2nd ed., ed. Richard Parker and Peter Aggleton, 459–80. Abingdon: Routledge.
Shapiro, Gilla K. 2014. "Abortion Law in Muslim-majority Countries: An Overview of the Islamic Discourse with Policy Implications." *Health Policy and Planning* 29 (4): 483–94.
Stahnke, Tad, and Robert C. Blitt. 2005. "The Religion-State Relationship and the Right to Freedom of Religion or Belief: A Comparative Textual Analysis of the Constitutions of Predominantly Muslim Countries." *Georgetown Journal of International Law* 36: 947–1078.

Statute of the OIC Independent Permanent Human Rights Commission. 2011. Resolution on Legal Affairs No. 2/38-LEG, adopted by the 38th session of the Council of Foreign Ministers, Astana, June 28–30.

Temperman, Jeroen. 2010. *State-Religion Relationships and Human Rights Law: Towards a Right to Religiously Neutral Governance*. Leiden: Martinus Nijhoff.

UN. 1996a. *Report of the Fourth World Conference on Women*. Beijing, 4–15 September 1995. A/CONF.177/20/Rev.1. http://www.un.org/womenwatch/daw/beijing/pdf/Beijing%20full%20report%20E.pdf.

———. 1996b. Addendum to *Report of the Fourth World Conference on Women*. Beijing, September 4–15, 1995. A/CONF.177/20/Add.1. http://www.un.org/documents/ga/conf177/aconf177-20add1en.htm.

UN Department of Economic and Social Affairs. 2002a. *Abortion Policies: A Global Review. Country Profiles: Bahrain*. http://www.un.org/esa/population/publications/abortion/.

———. 2002b. *Abortion Policies: A Global Review. Country Profiles: Iran (Islamic Republic of)*. http://www.un.org/esa/population/publications/abortion/.

———. 2002c. *Abortion Policies: A Global Review. Country Profiles: Tunisia*. http://www.un.org/esa/population/publications/abortion/.

———. 2013. *World Abortion Policies 2013*. http://www.un.org/en/development/desa/population/publications/policy/world-abortion-policies-2013.shtml

UN General Assembly. 2014a. *Report of the Open Working Group of the General Assembly on Sustainable Development Goals*. August 12. A/68/970. https://undocs.org/A/68/970.

———. 2014b. Addendum to the *Report of the Open Working Group of the General Assembly on Sustainable Development Goals*. October 27. A/68/970/Add.1. https://digitallibrary.un.org/record/784147/files/A_68_970_Add.1-EN.pdf

UN Population Fund. 1995. *Report of the International Conference on Population and Development*. Cairo, September 5–13, 1994. A/CONF.171/13/Rev.1. http://www.refworld.org/docid/4a54bc080.html.

U.S. Department of State, Bureau of Democracy, Human Rights, and Labor. 2011. *2010 Country Reports on Human Rights Practices: Tunisia*. http://www.state.gov/j/drl/rls/hrrpt/2010/nea/154474.htm.

Vienna Convention on the Law of Treaties. 1980. 1155 UNTS 331, adopted on May 23, 1969, entered into force on January 27, 1980.

Vik, Ingrid, and Christian Moe. 2015. *Islamic Cooperation and Reproductive Rights: The Role of the OIC at the UN and in Africa*. Oslo: Scanteam.

Viljoen, Frans. 2012. *International Human Rights Law in Africa*. Oxford: Oxford University Press.

Wicks, Elizabeth. 2011. "A, B, C v Ireland: Abortion Law Under the European Convention on Human Rights." *Human Rights Law Review* 11 (3): 556–66.

Zampas, Christina, and Jaime M. Gher. 2008. "Abortion as a Human Right—International and Regional Standards." *Human Rights Law Review* 8 (2): 249–94.

CHAPTER 8

The OIC and Children's Rights

Mahmood Monshipouri and Turan Kayaoglu

Introduction

The Covenant on the Rights of the Child in Islam (CRCI)[1] was adopted at the thirty-second Islamic Conference of Foreign Ministers in Yemen, on June 28–30, 2005. Numerous countries participated in drafting it. As of this writing, however, it is still awaiting ratification by the required twenty OIC member states. One reason for the OIC's attention to children's rights is that from child labor to child soldiers, and from child brides to female genital cutting, children's rights have been central to many debates around human rights, Islam, and Muslim societies. Some point to examples in early Muslim history, such as the Qur'anic injunction regarding female infanticide and Qur'anic support for the protection of orphans' rights as examples of Muslim duties to protect and promote children's rights. Others point to contemporary examples of girls who are married before adulthood, discrimination against girls in access to health care and education, and the widespread use of child labor and child soldiers as examples of Muslim societies' inability or unwillingness to protect the rights of children.

A second reason is the increasing role of children's rights in international human rights discourse. Although children's rights have been a topic in international human rights discussions, the 1989 United Nations Convention on the Rights of the Child (UN CRC) achieved a near-universal consensus with all but two states (South Sudan and the United States) ratifying it.[2] The position of the OIC on children's rights has been influenced both by the organization's desire to be part of this global consensus and by its desire to be an authentic Islamic voice, drawing distinctions based on Muslim religious and cultural values and the OIC's support for state sovereignty and domestic jurisdiction (Kayaoglu 2015). The OIC's 2005 Covenant on the Rights of the Child in Islam attempts to bridge these differences, but is an eclectic and ambiguous document: it "Islamicizes" children's rights while also interjecting a human rights perspective advocating the well-being, health, and protection of children in OIC member states.

A third reason for the OIC's attention to children's rights is arguably part of an effort to restrict other types of human rights (Kayaoglu 2013). An emphasis on children's rights provides a means to counter liberal arguments about women's rights, gender equality, and sexual orientation. The CRCI as such emphasizes the role of the traditional family and Islamic values in protecting children's rights, distinguishing it from liberal approaches that tend to stress individual rights and freedoms rather than collective responsibilities. Moreover, questions remain about the compatibility of the CRCI with international children's rights standards but also about the extent to which OIC member states will adhere to the CRCI. Compliance is of particular concern given the CRCI's emphasis on the primacy of domestic jurisdiction and the OIC's weak monitoring and enforcement capacity.

A final reason for the OIC's attention to children's rights is the centrality of children and families to building a strong *umma*—the community of Muslims bound together by ties of religion. Islam emphasizes teaching children about Islamic beliefs and practices from an early age, and families are where children first learn about their religion and are socialized into a Muslim identity. The OIC leaders believe that without this transmission of Islamic values, practices, and perspectives to children and by extension the next generation, the umma—the Muslim umma—will get weaker with each generation. Thus, for the OIC, attention to the rights of children is attention to the future of umma.

This chapter presents the OIC's position and efforts made on behalf of children's rights in Islam within the larger context of the development of children's rights in international human rights jurisprudence. To this end, the chapter first describes the development of children's rights in international human rights. Second, it examines how Muslim states and the OIC have reacted to the UN's CRC. Third, it discusses the development and content of the CRCI. The final three sections of the chapter explore three issues related to children's rights—the definition of a child, children in armed conflicts, and child labor—to examine the overlaps, differences, and tensions between the UN's CRC and the OIC's CRCI. A study of these topics suggests that even when the OIC and the international community agree on a particular issue pertaining to the rights of children, the OIC has been ineffective in implementing these standards. Yet the OIC will continue to be the institutional voice representing Muslim states in discussions on children's rights; the OIC thus has the potential to influence the future of children's rights in the OIC region as well as globally.

Children's Rights as Human Rights

International human rights law treats children's rights as a distinct category of rights because of children's evolving capacity toward autonomy and in the context of children's reliance on the decisions of their parents, caregivers, and state authorities. Moreover, children are entitled to distinct rights due to their unique needs and vulnerabilities.

Children's rights entered into international human rights discourse as early as the 1920s. In 1924, the League of Nations adopted the Declaration of the Rights of the Child, also known as the Geneva Declaration (of the Rights of the Child). This declaration listed children's rights as those necessary for their spiritual and material development, including the right to food, health care, and shelter (Moody 2015). The 1948 Universal Declaration of Human Rights (UDHR) also acknowledged that motherhood and childhood need "social protection and assistance" and that children are entitled to "social protection." The United Nations 1959 Declaration of the Rights of the Child built on the Geneva Declaration and established the universality of children's rights, the right to protection from discrimination, and the right to special protection (Moody 2015).

Continuing the work of previous declarations, the UN member states unanimously adopted the CRC in 1989. This was the first comprehensive international treaty making children subjects of international law. It also gave children an active role in determining their own well-being by recognizing the child "as a person, with evolving capacities" (Woodhouse and Johnson 2009:7). As subjects of law, children have the right to express their opinion on all decisions affecting them and to participate in choices that affect their welfare. In other words, the best interest of the child is no longer interpreted only from an adult point of view, but rather it is also seen directly from the standpoint of the child. The CRC highlights the fact that the best course of action in securing a child's welfare cannot be determined without the involvement of the child in question.

The treaty advances children's rights in four areas (with children being defined in Article 1 as those under the age of 18). First, states should ensure that all children under their jurisdiction enjoy the rights "irrespective of the child's or his or her parent's or legal guardian's race, color, sex, language, religion, political or other opinion, national, ethnic or social origin, property, disability, birth or other status" (Article 2). Second, governmental actions affecting children should be guided by concern for the best interest of the child, such as the safety, security, well-being, and healthy development of the child (Article 3). Third, children have the right to life; freedom of expression, thought, and religion; and due process of law and other civil and political rights (for example, Articles 12–18). Fourth, children have the right to education, housing, and health care in addition to other economic, social, and cultural rights (for example, Articles 24–32).

The treaty also emphasizes the importance of parent-child relations and the right of parents to raise their children, and it asks the government to respect the rights and responsibilities of parents, which are balanced with the child's evolving capacity: "State Parties shall assure to the child who is capable of forming his or her own views the right to express those views freely in all matters affecting the child, the views of the child being given due weight in accordance with the age and maturity of the child" (Article 12).

One of the treaty's key strengths is that it recognizes that children's rights must be actively promoted if they are to be implemented—merely relying on awareness alone will not suffice. Human rights activists thus have a powerful tool in their efforts to protect children's human rights given its almost worldwide acceptance. Increasingly, it has become the dominant framework for taking up the challenge of recognizing and protecting children's rights.

The UN CRC has two optional protocols. The Optional Protocol on the Involvement of Children in Armed Conflict (OPAC) requires states take "all feasible measures" to ensure that individuals under the age of 18 do not take a "direct part" in armed conflicts (Article 1). Pursuant to this protocol, state parties must also take legal measures to prohibit independent armed groups from recruiting and using children under the age of 18 in any combat operations. The Optional Protocol on the Sale of Children, Child Prostitution, and Child Pornography (OPSC) requires states to protect children against these types of abuses, treat these exploitations as serious crimes, provide legal counsel and other support services to child victims, and cooperate with other states to halt and punish child abusers. The CRC and its protocols represent an enormous advancement in protecting children's rights.

Additionally, the CRC has a monitoring apparatus, known as the Committee on the Rights of the Child (also abbreviated CRC), which is a body of independent experts that monitors implementation of the convention. All states are required to submit regular reports to the committee on how provisions are being implemented. States must make their initial report two years after acceding to the convention and every five years thereafter. The committee assesses the national reports in tandem with the reports transmitted by national NGOs. After examining these reports, the committee then addresses its concerns and recommendations to the state in the form of "concluding observations." Thus states are subject to constant monitoring concerning children's rights in their countries.

Muslim States, the OIC, and the Covenant on the Rights of the Child

All OIC members ratified the UN CRC. Some of them, such as Albania, Azerbaijan, Bahrain, Benin, Burkina Faso, Cameroon, Chad, Gabon, Kazakhstan, Lebanon, Libya, Nigeria, and Senegal, signed it without entering any reservations (Sardar Ali 2007a:175). Others, such as Bangladesh, Indonesia, Malaysia, Mali, Tunisia, and Turkey, did not mention Islamic principles, but rather cited constitutional and national laws as the basis for their reservations (Tunisia has since withdrawn its reservations) (Sardar Ali 2007a:175; Hamid and Sein 2013:291–92). Although these reservations may not refer to Islam specifically, domestic laws in OIC member states are often shaped by Islamic law and values. Thus Islam may still influence children's rights on issues that may be at odds with international human rights, such as inheritance law and marriage age.

Some OIC members listed reservations invoking Islam. These states were Brunei Darussalam, Djibouti, Egypt, Iran, Iraq, Jordan, Kuwait, Mauritania, Morocco, Oman, Pakistan, Qatar, Saudi Arabia, Syria, and the United Arab Emirates (Sardar Ali 2007b:99). The Islamic Republic of Iran, for example, ratified it on July 13, 1994 but made the following reservation: "The Government of the Islamic Republic of Iran reserves the right not to apply any provisions or articles of the Convention that are incompatible with Islamic Laws."[3]

Some OIC members, including Afghanistan, Algeria, Bangladesh, Indonesia, Iran, Iraq, Jordan, Pakistan, Saudi Arabia, and the United Arab Emirates, argued that the personal freedoms granted to children were incompatible with the precepts of Islamic law (Sardar Ali 2007a:175–76). Most of their reservations were in response to freedom of religion, guaranteed in Article 14: "States parties shall respect the right of the child to freedom of thought, conscience and religion." The addition of a paragraph to Article 14 respecting the rights and duties of parents and, when applicable, legal guardians, "to provide direction to the child in the exercise of his or her right in a manner consistent with the evolving capacities of the child," was necessary to secure a compromise for the treaty to move forward (Hamid and Sein 2013 296–97). Other reservations concerned adoption (Article 21), special protection of and alternative care for a child deprived of family environment (Article 20), and nondiscrimination (Article 2) (Hamid and Sein 2013:292).

The OIC has, however, generally been supportive of the UN CRC. The 1994 OIC resolution *On Child Care and Protection in the Islamic World* calls on member states to "sign and ratify" the CRC, to "take necessary steps to bring their constitutions, laws and practices into the confirmation of the [CRC]," and to develop "national programs for the realization of the [CRC] objectives."[4]

The Covenant on the Rights of the Child in Islam

The OIC has long focused on issues related to children, women, and the family. While its standard-setting on women's rights has failed to live up to modern Western norms and ideals, the OIC has established standards on the rights of children and has produced several declarations and resolutions emphasizing the well-being, health, and protection of children. The Declaration on the Rights and Care of the Child in Islam (1994) places the rights of the child within the framework of strong families and a strong umma. The declaration lists eight categories of rights of children: (1) rights related to the family (the centrality of the family to the child; the importance of selecting a good wife/husband); (2) rights of the fetus (a prohibition on abortion; the fetus has an "absolute right to life"); (3) rights of infants; (4) the right of lineage (a prohibition on adoption, but reference to the *Kafalah* system); (5) the right of guardianship; (6) the right to social, health, psychological, and cultural care; (7) the right to ownership; and (8) the right to education, which includes the right to learn about Islam and the protection of children "against attempts to force them to relinquish" Islam.

The most authoritative OIC statement on children's rights is found in the 2005 Covenant on the Rights of the Child in Islam. It stands as the only (potentially) binding OIC human rights document (Kayaoglu 2013). However, after more than a decade, the covenant has yet to get the required twenty states' ratifications for it to enter into force. While it may not be brought into force, it nonetheless provides an excellent perspective on the OIC's prevailing views of children's rights.

The CRCI has two main objectives: (1) to care for and strengthen families, such that the husband and wife can raise physically and spiritually healthy children; and (2) to establish the conditions in which Muslim children can be proud of their nation, country, and religion. The document's twenty-six articles emphasize children's rights to education, health care, and a safe environment.

The CRCI explicitly stipulates the state's responsibilities to ensure that these rights are protected. In accordance with their domestic regulations, states are asked to take the necessary steps to fulfill the following obligations: the equality of children (Article 5); the protection of children from all forms of abuse, including not involving them in armed conflicts and wars (Article 17); and the protection of refugee children (Article 21). However, these responsibilities are—repeatedly and explicitly—conditioned with language deferring to the primacy of state sovereignty, domestic jurisdiction, and the principle of noninterference into domestic affairs.

In 2005, during the First Conference of Ministers in Charge of Childhood, the OIC secretary-general urged member states to ratify the CRCI and summarized the OIC's position on children's rights:

> Our responsibility toward our children stems from the values of Islam which accord priority to the child's best interests within the family, which constitutes the first nucleus of the society. Shariah guarantees full rights of the child and secures a decent living for him in terms of maternal health, pregnancy, childbirth, naming, lactation, custody, alimony, health, physical and psychological upbringing, education, and behavior that observes the noble values. Islam protects the rights of the child since he is a fetus in his mother's womb and abolishes any distinction between male and female. (İhsanoğlu 2013:126)

A comparison between the CRCI and the OIC's 1990 Cairo Declaration on Human Rights reveals some notable differences (Kayaoglu 2013). While both texts include several references to Sharia, the CRCI does not establish it as a guiding force in interpreting the document. In an apparent contradiction of the declaration, the CRCI does not restrict children's rights to those specified in the body of Islamic law. Moreover, there is language in the CRCI that could be construed as a challenge to practices that are sometimes justified through Sharia. Article 4, for instance, urges member states to make efforts to "end action based on customs, traditions, or practices that are in conflict with the rights and duties stipulated in this Covenant." Female genital mutilation could be one example of a cultural practice—linked erroneously to Sharia—that supporters of the CRCI would push states to curtail (Mosaffa 2011).

While de-emphasizing Sharia somewhat, the CRCI does not do the same for state sovereignty (Kayaoglu 2013). Thus while the CRCI downplays Sharia as a universal religious law, it strengthens and supports Sharia as domestic law. As with the Cairo Declaration, references to Sharia elevate member states' sovereign prerogatives rather than promoting a uniform religious code. Unlike the Cairo Declaration, which underscored the importance of Sharia as the only authority, the CRCI avoids direct references to Sharia and instead emphasizes Islamic values.

The CRCI emphasizes the role of the traditional family and Islamic values in protecting the rights of the child, privileging the role of collective bodies, such as the traditional family and the nation, and stressing responsibilities in securing the rights of children. These references firmly ground the document in a conservative Islamic framework and distinguish its approach from a liberal view, as that expressed in the UN CRC, emphasizing individuals rather than collectives and stressing rights rather than responsibilities.

Accordingly, there are several differences between the UN CRC and the CRCI. First, and fundamentally, the two conventions differ in their understanding and definition of what a child is. Unlike the UN CRC, which specifies that "a child means every human being below the age of 18 years unless under the law applicable to the child, maturity is attained earlier" (Article 1), the CRCI provides that "a child means every human being who, according to the law applicable to him/her, has not attained maturity" (Article 1). The vagueness of this definition of a child makes the OIC's concept at once acceptable to all its member states' local—legal and de facto—jurisdictions and potentially unsettling given the challenge it poses to the established standard set forth in the UN CRC. As discussed in the next section, this vagueness and deference to domestic jurisdiction allow, for example, discriminatory treatment against girl children.

Another controversial difference between the UN CRC and the CRCI is the child's freedom of religion. The CRCI is silent on the right of the child to freedom of thought, conscience, and religion; the emphasis is on the parents' right to raise their child as a Muslim. Article 9 of the CRCI specifies that "every child is entitled to the respect of his/her personal life. Nevertheless, the parents or legal representatives are entitled to exercise Islamic and humane supervision over the conduct of the child." This article gives parents the right to raise their children as Muslims. However, this provision is potentially in conflict with Article 14 of the UN CRC, which protects the child's freedom of religion. While the UN CRC also grants parents the right to educate their child (which may include religious education), it empowers states to act on the basis of the best interest of the child even if the state's understanding of best interest conflicts with that of the parents: "A child temporarily or permanently deprived of his or her family environment, or in whose own best interests cannot be allowed to remain in that environment, shall be entitled to special protection and assistance provided by the State" (Article 20). This skepticism of freedom of religion is consonant with the 1994 Declaration on the Rights and Care of the Child in Islam (Sardar Ali and Shail Khan 2017) that bans apostasy, as well as with the Cairo Declaration and other OIC documents (Cismas 2014:285).

Third, the two conventions differ in their conception of the family. Although the UN CRC also refers to the important role of the family in the development of the child, the CRCI emphasizes this anew by defining the family as "the cornerstone" of social order, asking states to prevent the weakening of the family. In fact, the CRCI lists this as its first objective: "To care for the family, strengthen its capabilities, and extend to it the necessary support to prevent the deterioration of its economic, social, or health conditions, and to habilitate the husband and wife to ensure their fulfillment of their role of raising children physically, psychologically, and behaviorally" (Article 2(1)). The role of the state is specifically cited in reference to the family. In particular, member states are asked to "respect the responsibilities and duties of parents" (Article 4(1)). Article 8, which is specifically about the family, indicates that "State parties shall protect the family from causes of weakness and disintegration and shall work . . . to care for the family members and cause cohesion and balance among them" (Article 8(1)). Muslim critics of the UN

CRC welcome this emphasis on the family as they have argued that its exclusive focus on the child undermines family cohesion and contradicts parents' rights and duties related to raising their children (Badamasiuy 2009).

A fourth, more practical difference between the UN CRC and the CRCI is in the area of enforcement: the CRCI calls for the establishment of an "Islamic Committee on the Rights of Child" to meet every other year to "examine the progress made in the implementation of [the] Covenant" (Article 24). Since the CRCI has not yet been ratified by the number of states required for it to enter into force, it is not yet in operation and there is no such committee.

One area in which the CRCI is more progressive than the UN CRC, however, is regarding abortion. As discussed by Ioana Cismas in Chapter 7, the CRCI is the only major international treaty that mentions abortion: "The child shall have the right to life from when he is a fetus in his/her mother's womb or in the case of his/her mother's death; abortion should be prohibited except under necessity warranted by interests of the mother, the fetus, or both of them" (Article 6). The mere fact that the document mentions abortion and specifies conditions for it distinguishes the CRCI from other international treaties, arguably providing some (albeit severely restricted) degree of legitimacy to abortion. This language is also more progressive than the OIC's earlier Declaration on the Rights and Care of the Child in Islam (1994), which banned abortion and stated that the "fetus has an absolute right to life."

Defending the Child Without Defining the Child?

While UN CRC defines a child as a human being below the age of 18, an exception is provided that "unless under the law applicable to the child, majority is attained earlier" (Article 1). The second part accommodates domestic differences—the identification of age 18 makes this a soft benchmark for international consensus on issues such as the minimum age for criminal responsibility and establishes this as a universal goal. Unlike the UN CRC, the CRCI does not stipulate an age and defers to domestic jurisdiction: "A child means every human being who, according to the law applicable to him/her, has not attained maturity" (Article 1). There is, in effect, no consensus among OIC member states on what a child is.

Most OIC members' domestic jurisdictions either directly incorporate Islamic law in their legal system or indirectly draw on Islam-infused cultural and societal norms. As such, they follow a traditional Islamic approach to defining what a child is. This approach characterizes the end of childhood in reference to a child's maturity in fulfilling certain responsibilities, such as leading prayer, fasting, or getting married. Often labeled as *aqil* and *baliq* (mature enough to understand the consequence of one's actions, adult), this approach places the age of legal maturity as the onset of puberty.

This definition introduces some variability in attaining maturity because reaching puberty differs within and between the sexes. Islamic jurists have worked to establish lower (below which a child cannot be claimed mature) and upper limits (above which a person is mature) to the age of maturity to manage this variability in the domestic legal systems. For example, four Sunni schools of law have established the lower limits for boys as 12 (Hanifi), 10 (Hanbali), and 9 (Shafi and Maliki) and the upper limits as 15 (Hanifi, Hanbali, Shafi) and 18 or 19 (Maliki). While lower limits on the age of maturity are not well-established for girls, Sunni schools have established upper limits for girls as 15 (Hanifi and Shafi) and 18 (Maliki). In general, Shias have not established lower limits on the age of maturity but establish upper limits as 15 for boys and 9 for girls. In other words, for Shias any male 15 and above and any girl 9 and above cannot claim to be a child and thus should be treated as an adult (Abiad and Mansoor 2010:57–58).

Defining Puberty

Islamic approaches that define a child in reference to the onset of puberty and thus a variable age of maturity create three problems for protecting children's rights. First, the Islamic approach sets onset of adulthood much earlier than most modern legal systems do. The Islamic approach allows for the overall physical maturity and mental capacity of a child in determining the actual legal liability of individuals, and some Muslim jurists hold that children who do not have an understanding of the gravity of their actions should not be held criminally liable. However, since the default position is defined by the age relative to the onset of puberty, this approach does not provide adequate protection for children, as reaching puberty is not the same as reaching maturity.

Second, the binary of legally liable adult versus not-liable child has not historically allowed Islamic law to develop a specialized comprehensive legal system for juveniles (Abiad and Mansoor 2010:46). The CRCI, however, has established rules to protect the legal rights of the child, including due process of law, fair trial, and consideration of the child's age (Article 19). The CRCI also asks for children to be tried in juvenile courts with rehabilitation of the child as the primary concern of such legal proceedings (Article 19). There are some signs of the development and reform of juvenile court systems to offer better protection to children (Abiad and Masoor 2010). Yet the situation in most OIC member states remains inadequate. The formal and informal attitudes that establish puberty as the benchmark for maturity have delayed the creation and the broader acceptance of juvenile legal systems. The CRCI is progressive compared to most of its member states in establishing a reformist framework for juvenile justice (ibid.:55).

Third, identifying legal adulthood with puberty discriminates against girls. For example, according to Iranian law, which is based on Shia Islam, men reach puberty at age 15 and women at age 9. There are cases where children at these ages have been found criminally liable. In a recent report, Amnesty International documented the execution of at least 73 juveniles in Iran between 2005 and 2015; 160 additional juvenile offenders have received death penalty sentences that have yet to be administered (Gladstone 2016:A8). This puberty-based definition of legal maturity entails different criminal responsibilities for the same criminal act. Legally speaking, if a 14-year-old boy commits a crime, he would be exonerated from any criminal responsibility; but if that same crime were committed by a 10-year-old girl, she would be held accountable (Monshipouri 2009:79). Despite some juvenile justice reforms identified in the report, Iran continues to trail behind the rest of the world in maintaining laws that allow girls as young as 9 and boys as young as 15 to be sentenced to death.

The significant difference in the attainment of the age of maturity for girls versus boys also allows Iranian law to establish different ages for the legal eligibility for marriage. In addition to contradicting the Universal Declaration of Human Rights, which asks for equality in all matters relating to marriage and family relations, this allows child marriages by offering legal permission for the marriage of girls as young as 9. Moreover, Iranian law even allows for marriage before reaching the age of puberty. The father (or his side of the family) has the right to enter into a marriage contract regarding a baby daughter or a baby son. Iranian civil code states: "Signing the marriage contract of a child, who has not yet reached puberty, by permission of his/her father or father's father is correct provided that the interests of the child are taken into consideration" (Monshipouri 2009:79). If such a marriage is decided, the girl or boy has no voice in later confirming or denying the father's choice of their spouse. The CRCI provisions that allow deference to domestic jurisdiction, the incorporation of Islamic values, and the privileging of parental rights over those of the child are compatible with these practices.

In short, the CRCI's deference to traditional Islamic values and to member states' domestic jurisdictions in determining the attainment of maturity undermines the effective protection of children rights. What follows is a continuation of this discussion on the deference to domestic jurisdiction, whether the CRCI provides necessary protection for children affected by armed conflicts, and the extent to which the enforcement of CRCI provisions remains crucial to the OIC's broader mission.

Child Soldiers and the OIC

In OIC member states, a large number of children fall victim to terror attacks, landmines, and foreign military intervention, resulting in injury and death. As photos of children sleeping on the streets and their bodies washing to shore show, armed conflicts cause many Muslim children to become refugees or to become internally displaced. During armed conflict, children's rights as human rights merit special attention to their protection. One element of that consensus among OIC members is the desire to prevent children from being recruited to participate in armed conflicts. In particular, the UN CRC refers to the rights of children in armed conflict:

> 1. States Parties undertake to respect and to ensure respect for rules of international humanitarian law applicable to them in armed conflicts which are relevant to the child. 2. States Parties shall take all feasible measures to ensure that persons who have not attained the age of 15 years do not take a direct part in hostilities. 3. States Parties shall refrain from recruiting any person who has not attained the age of 15 years into their armed forces. In recruiting among those persons who have attained the age of 15 years but who have not attained the age of 18 years, States Parties shall endeavor to give priority to those who are oldest. 4. In accordance with their obligations under international humanitarian law to protect the civilian population in armed conflicts, States Parties shall take all feasible measures to ensure protection and care of children who are affected by an armed conflict. (Article 38)

In 2000, the Optional Protocol to the Convention on the Rights of the Child on the Involvement of Children in Armed Conflict[5] changed the age for enlisting children in armed conflict from 15 to 18 (Article 1). Ratification of this protocol required each state to posit a binding declaration to set "the minimum age at which it will permit voluntary recruitment into its national armed forces and a description of the safeguards that it has adopted to ensure that such recruitment is not forced or coerced" (Article 3(2)).

Twenty-three OIC members have ratified the protocol and issued declarations regarding the minimum age of military service in their countries. Azerbaijan set the lowest age for voluntary military enlistment at age 17, and Afghanistan set the highest age for voluntary military enlistment at age 22; other OIC states fell within this range, with most of them setting the age for voluntary military enlistment at age 18. Although the implementation of the protocol remains weak and children younger than 18 are found in the military forces of state parties—including OIC members who signed the optional protocol—the acceptance of this optional protocol is encouraging (Mosaffa 2011).

On paper, the OIC is also supportive of the protection of the rights of children in armed conflicts. The CRCI asks states to "take necessary measures . . . to protect children by not involving them in armed conflicts or wars" (Article 17(5)). In addition, there are other, albeit somewhat specious, provisions throughout the document that may be interpreted as protective of children in armed conflicts: "The child shall be provided with legal and humanitarian assistance where needed, including access to a lawyer and interpreter if necessary" (Article 19(3)(c)) and "States Parties to this Covenant shall ensure, as much as possible, that refugee children, or those legally assimilated to this status, enjoy the rights provided for in this Covenant within their national legislation" (Article 21). These provisions indicate a clear stand of the OIC and its member states regarding the protection of the rights of children during armed conflict.

Yet the OIC and its member states have been ineffective in protecting children in armed conflicts. The reality is that children have been recruited to the militaries of OIC member states. UN reports point to the recruitment of children by the Afghan National Police[6] and the Taliban use of children as soldiers, including suicide attacks (Bleasdale 2013). There is also substantial evidence that children serve in Somalia's Transitional Federal Government forces, and Al-Shabaab forcibly recruits children as young as 10, often abducting them from their homes or schools; some of these children are later made to become suicide bombers. In Darfur, the Sudanese Armed Forces and armed groups, including the progovernment militias and factions of the rebel Sudan Liberation Army, all use child soldiers (Shorten 2015). OIC member Yemen signed an action plan with the United Nations in May 2014 to end the child recruitment by the Yemeni armed forces; however, there is still nothing in Yemeni law that criminalizes the recruitment of child soldiers (*OIC Journal* 2014:22–3). The Islamic State in Iraq and Syria (ISIS) has been using child soldiers in what may amount to war crimes (Jansen 2016:40–41). In Nigeria, Boko Haram regularly abducts children and uses them as slaves or soldiers.

The OIC would do well to use the extent of their authority to denounce the recruitment of child soldiers in OIC member states. It is understood that those who claim to act in the name of Islam often act in a rogue fashion and do not adhere to human rights appeals or codes. However, these activities that children are forced to engage in across OIC member states fall under their geographical jurisdiction.

There are issues with states' capacity and will to enforce laws regarding child soldiers. Very few states have set up specific, national mechanisms to enforce the declarations enumerated in the CRCI. A firm stance needs to be taken against those states and societies that use children in war: The OIC can ask its members to criminalize those who recruit or use child soldiers. Concrete steps toward monitoring and implementation are needed to transform the OIC's CRCI from a document of principles to one that meaningfully protects the rights of children in armed conflicts.

Child Labor and the OIC

Attempts to prevent child labor have been plagued by complex relationships among variables such as economic deprivation, cultural traditions, the local economy and power structure, and the global economy. The long-term solution lies in alleviating poverty, improving the quality of education, and expanding access to schooling for disadvantaged social groups. Protecting children in their workplaces and creating more alternatives for economic and social advancement are key components. An antipoverty development strategy will be effective only if it targets equality and educational opportunities for poor families, especially those with school-age children (Monshipouri 2003).

Although there is a growing consensus regarding the need to eliminate child labor worldwide, some legal experts take the pragmatic view that instead of seeking the total abolition of child labor, a goal which appears unrealistic except under certain circumstances, official policies should be directed at preventing child labor from being exploitative or dangerous to physical or psychological health (An-Na'im 2011:178).

Both the UN CRC and the CRCI aim to eliminate the worst forms of child labor. The UN CRC clearly states this: "States Parties recognize the right of the child to be protected from economic exploitation and from performing any work that is likely to be hazardous or to interfere with the child's education, or to be harmful to the child's health or physical, mental, spiritual, moral or social development" (Article 32). Building on the consensus the convention has established and its earlier Convention No. 138 on minimum employment age, the International Labor Organization (ILO) developed Convention No. 182 in 1999, addressing the worst forms of child labor.

Ratified by 173 of 183 states of the ILO at the end of 2010, Convention No. 182 asked states to take immediate and effective actions to prevent those under 18 from working in the worst forms of child labor:

> (a) all forms of slavery or practices similar to slavery, such as the sale and trafficking of children, debt bondage and serfdom and forced or compulsory labor, including forced or compulsory recruitment of children for use in armed conflict; (b) the use, procuring or offering of a child for prostitution, for the production of pornography or for pornographic performances; (c) the use, procuring or offering of a child for illicit activities, in particular for the production and trafficking of drugs as defined in the relevant international treaties; (d) work which, by its nature or the circumstances in which it is carried out, is likely to harm the health, safety or morals of children.

While it is true that child labor continues due to the poor enforcement of labor restrictions and related international legislation and conventions, it is difficult to end all forms of child labor in the face of extreme poverty and inadequate resources at the national level. These factors, however, cannot justify the failure of the states to pay attention to the most deprived groups.

In addition to the ILO's monitoring of child labor, the UN CRC's own Committee on the Rights of the Child (CRC) monitors child labor. Specifically, during the periodic review of examining how member states are working to realize their obligations, the committee always pays special attention to the economic situation of member states to assess if states are doing all they can to eliminate worst forms of child labor with "special attention to the most disadvantageous groups" (Besson and Bourke-Martignoni 2009:302–3).

The CRCI also addresses the issue of child labor:

1. No child shall exercise any risky work, or work which obstructs his/her education or which is at the expense of his/her health as well as physical or spiritual growth.
2. Domestic regulations of every State shall fix a minimum working age, as well as working conditions and hours. Sanctions shall be imposed against those who contravene these regulations. (Article 18)

Similar to the case of child soldiers, the OIC has not seriously addressed combating this threat to children's rights. Notably, the worst forms of child labor remain prevalent in the Muslim-majority countries of southwest Asia, such as Bangladesh and Pakistan. While there is near-universal agreement on the elimination of child labor as a compelling international norm and a goal for domestic laws, there is far less agreement regarding the actual content, nature, and practice of child labor among OIC member states, let alone how to enforce these rights.

Conclusion

The evolving trend within the OIC toward reconciling the CRCI with internationally recognized human rights principles is a promising prospect for change. However, the OIC's limited abilities to monitor or enforce compliance with human rights principles regarding children, especially on matters relating to child labor, the legal equality of boys and girls, the prohibition on child soldiers, and the protection of children in the labor market is a hindrance to effective action. The OIC has neither the resources to help its member states implement policies to protect and promote children's rights nor does it have monitoring or enforcement mechanisms to compel implementation and compliance with its rules. This is a matter that would do well to earn the OIC's undivided attention.

Notes

1. Covenant on the Rights of the Child in Islam. OIC/9-IGGE/HRI/2004/Rep. Final. http://www.refworld.org/docid/44eaf0e4a.html.

2. *Convention on the Rights of the Child.* Resolution 44.25. Adopted November 20, 1989; entered into force September 2, 1990. http://www.ohchr.org/en/professionalinterest/pages/crc.aspx.

3. *Declarations and Reservations—The Covenant on the Rights of Child.* https://treaties.un.org/pages/ViewDetails.aspx?src=TREATY&mtdsg_no=IV-11&chapter=4&clang=_en#EndDec.

4. *On Child Care and Protection in the Islamic World.* Resolution No. 16/22-C. http://ww1.oic-oci.org/english/conf/fm/22/resolution22-c.htm#16.

5. *Optional Protocol to the Convention on the Rights of the Child on the Involvement of Children in Armed Conflict.* Resolution A/RES/54/263. Adopted May 25, 2000; entered into force February 12, 2002. http://www.ohchr.org/EN/ProfessionalInterest/Pages/OPACCRC.aspx.

6. *Report of the Secretary-General to the Security Council.* A/69/926–S/2015/409. https://childrenandarmedconflict.un.org/countries/afghanistan/.

Works Cited

Abiad, Nisrine, and Farkhanda Zia Mansoor. 2010. *Criminal Law and the Rights of the Child in Muslim States: A Comparative and Analytical Perspective.* London: British Institute of International and Comparative Law.

An-Na'im, Abdullahi Ahmed. 2011. *Muslims and Global Justice.* Philadelphia: University of Pennsylvania Press.

Badamasiuy, Juwayriya Bint. 2009. *Obligations and Rights of the Parents Under the Child's Rights Act: A Shariah Perspective.* Kaduna, Nigeria: Zakara Communications.

Besson, Samantha, and Joanna Bourke-Martignoni. 2009. "Children's Convention: Convention on the Rights of the Child." In *Encyclopedia of Human Rights,* vol. 1, ed. David P. Forsythe, 302–3. New York: Oxford University Press.

Bleasdale, Marcus. 2013. "Child Soldiers." Human Rights Watch. https://www.hrw.org/topic/childrens-rights/child-soldiers.

British Institute of International and Comparative Law. 2010. "Criminal Law and the Rights of the Child: Training Workshop Summary." June 28–29, 2010. https://www.biicl.org/files/5054_rights_of_the_child_workshop.pdf.

Cismas, Ioana. 2014. *Religious Actors and International Law.* New York: Oxford University Press.

Gladstone, Rick. 2016. "Iran Faces Criticism for Execution of Minors." *New York Times,* January 25, A8.

Hamid, Abdul Ghafur, and Khin Maung Sein. 2013. "Muslim States and the Implementation of the Convention on the Rights of the Child: With Special Reference to Malaysia." In *Islam and International Law: Engaging Self-Centrism from a Plurality of Perspectives*, ed. Marie-Luisa Frick and Andrea Th. Müller, 290–308. Leiden: Martinus Nijhoff.

İhsanoğlu, Ekmeleddin. 2013. *Moderation and Modernization Vision for the Muslim World: Selected Speeches*. Jeddah: OIC.

Jansen, Michael. 2016. "A Sad Reality." *Gulf Today: Panorama*, January 15–21, 40–41.

Kayaoglu, Turan. 2013. "A Rights Agenda for the Muslim World? The Organization of Islamic Cooperation's Evolving Human Rights Framework." Brookings Doha Center Analysis Paper. Doha: The Brookings Institution.

———. 2015. *The Organization of Islamic Cooperation: Politics, Problems, and Potential*. London: Routledge.

Monshipouri, Mahmood. 2003. "Human Rights and Child Labor in South Asia." In *Human Rights and Diversity: Area Studies Revisited*, ed. David P. Forsythe and Patrice C. McMahon, 182–204. Lincoln: University of Nebraska Press.

———. 2009. "Shirin Ebadi." In *Encyclopedia of Human Rights*, vol. 2, ed. David P. Forsythe, 78–81. New York: Oxford University Press.

Moody, Zoe. 2015. "The United Nations Declaration of the Rights of the Child (1959): Genesis, Transformation and Dissemination of a Treaty (Re)constituting a Transnational Cause." *Prospects* 45 (1): 15–29.

Mosaffa, Nasrin. 2011. "Does the Covenant on the Rights of the Child in Islam Provide Adequate Protection for Children Affected by Armed Conflicts?" *Muslim World Journal of Human Rights* 8 (1): https://doi.org/10.2202/1554-4419.1220.

OIC. 2008. Charter of the Organization of Islamic Cooperation. Dakar, March 14, 2008. http://ww1.oic-oci.org/english/charter/OIC%20Charter-new-en.pdf.

OIC Journal. 2014. "Yemen Children Give Up the Childhood to Join the Fight." *OIC Journal* 28 (September/December): 22–23.

Sardar Ali, Shaheen. 2007a. "A Comparative Perspective of the Convention on the Rights of the Child and the Principles of Islamic Law: Law Reform and Children's Rights in Muslim Jurisdictions." In *Protecting the World's Children: Impact of the Convention on the Rights of the Child in Diverse Legal Systems*, 142–208. Cambridge: Cambridge University Press.

———. 2007b. "The Twain Doth Meet! A Preliminary Exploration of the Theory and Practice of as-Siyar and International Law in the Contemporary World." In *Religion, Human Rights, and International Law*, ed. Javaid Rehman and Susan C. Breau, 99. Leiden: Martinus Nijhoff.

Sardar Ali, Shaheen, and Sajiila Sohail Khan. 2017. "Evolving Conceptions of Children's Rights: Some Reflections on Muslim States' Engagement with the UN Convention on the Rights of Children." In *Parental Care and the Best Interests of the Child in Muslim Countries*, ed. Nadjma Yassari, Lena-Maria Moller, and Imen Gallah-Arndt, 285–322. The Hague: Asser.

Shorten, Kristen. 2015. "At Least 250,000 Children Being Used in Wars Around the World." *News.com.au*, January 24. http://www.news.com.au/world/at-least-250000-children-being-used-in-wars-around-the-world/story-fndir2ev-1227194842435.

Woodhouse, Barbara B., and Kathryn A. Johnson. 2009. "The United Nations Convention on the Rights of Child: Empowering Parents to Protect Their Children's Rights." In *What Is Right for Children?* ed. Martha Albertson Fineman and Karen Worthington, 7–18. Abingdon: Ashgate.

PART III

INTERSECTIONS: CONFLICTS AND COOPERATION

CHAPTER 9

The OIC and Conflict Resolution: Norms and Practical Challenges

Hirah Azhar

Introduction

Human rights and conflict resolution are intrinsically linked to one another.[1] While violent conflicts result in severe violations of human rights (including torture, death, imprisonment, destruction of livelihoods and general well-being), these violations often provide the impetus for armed, violent resistance to the state (Manikkalingam 2006). The UN charter makes explicit mention of this relationship,[2] while the Geneva Conventions, and international humanitarian law in general, can be considered the "near relations" of international human rights law (Kolb 1998). The study of conflict and conflict resolution activities therefore allow for a deeper understanding of how regional and international actors treat human rights issues.

Conflict resolution has been at the forefront of the Organization of Islamic Cooperation's (OIC) agenda since the organization's establishment in 1969, following an arson attack on the Al-Aqsa mosque in Jerusalem. In fact, Article 28 of the revised 2008 charter states the objective of "preserving international peace and security, and settling disputes through peaceful means."[3] The OIC has been present—and often actively involved—as a mediator in various conflicts affecting OIC member states since 1969. The changing nature of conflicts after the Cold War revealed the limitations of multilateral institutions such as the United Nations in comprehensively resolving conflicts (Kaldor 2012). This has been especially true for extremely violent civil wars within the Global South (e.g., Somalia) as well as the rise in violent Islamist terrorism. As a result, conflict management, conflict prevention, and humanitarian assistance have increasingly dominated the agendas of transregional intergovernmental organizations such as the OIC.

Historically, the OIC's conflict resolution efforts have focused mostly on mediation and the provision of humanitarian aid, often contributed as part of a multilateral arrangement with other actors. The organization has rarely led resolution efforts, and past efforts to do so have often lacked conviction because of the absence of a cohesive policy. Moreover, for an organization with member states that continue to witness violent internal and external conflicts, the OIC does not have a peacekeeping force, and its current mechanism for conflict resolution (the Peace, Security and Mediation Unit) remains firmly dialogue-oriented. This is particularly noteworthy because personnel from OIC member states make up a significant portion of the United Nations' various peacekeeping missions (Hashmat 2011:107).

The literature on the OIC's conflict resolution activities has focused on these issues in greater detail and can be roughly divided into two camps: assessments of the OIC's conflict resolution successes and failures; and analyses about what keeps the organization from emerging as a strong conflict resolution actor (al-Ahsan 2004; Hashmat 2011; Salah 2011; Ahmad 2012; Hossain 2012; Sharqieh 2012; Castillo 2014). Alternatively, the OIC's presence as a normative actor has seen far more diverse analysis, although with the exception of al-Ahsan (2004), Mirbagheri (2006), and Cismas (2014), none make explicit reference to the OIC's conflict resolution activities.

A study of the OIC's conflict resolution discourse and efforts can allow us to assess how the OIC treats human rights issues in practice. Indeed, as a sui generis intergovernmental organization that specifies conflict resolution as one of its primary objectives, protection of human rights should form the very cornerstone of its conflict resolution discourse. However, the OIC has historically favored a Sharia-based approach to human rights that remains inconsistent with the UN Declaration of Human Rights (see, e.g., Chapter 4, this volume). As Azin Tadjdini notes, regionalization "takes the shape of Islamization" in the OIC's case, since it consists of a group of states that "share an ideology" and consequently "enter into legal and political cooperation" (Tadjdini 2012:40). Ioana Cismas contends that this duality of politics and religious identity—"where the role of religion is intertwined with political goals"—is central to all OIC decision-making and seems to be particularly relevant to its conflict resolution approach (Cismas 2014:241). Similarly,

Salim Farrar observes that the OIC has "gradually absorbed international norms into Islamic forms" and a "religious vernacular," resulting in an "evolving and strategic" human rights agenda (Farrar 2014), while Abdullah al-Ahsan argues that the OIC has increasingly provided a "context-sensitive application of universal human rights" (al-Ahsan 2008:304).

This has created an inherently problematic equation between conflict resolution and human rights within the OIC that this chapter seeks to explore in greater detail. In particular, the analysis here focuses on two fundamental questions. First, how closely interlinked is the OIC's conflict resolution approach with its treatment of human rights? Has any shift in its conflict resolution agenda or strategy trickled down to its treatment of human rights within conflicts? Second, what tangible impact do resolution efforts on the ground have on the OIC's treatment of human rights? This chapter argues that, although the OIC's treatment of human rights has been informed by its evolving conflict resolution approach, this has had little real impact in practical terms because of the OIC's consistently lax and selective approach to human rights and its inherent shortcomings as a conflict resolution actor. The chapter first examines how closely shifts in the conflict resolution and human rights narratives of the OIC mirror one another. Is the organization's evolving conflict resolution approach a product of its rather reluctant but increasing engagement with human rights issues or vice versa? Alternatively, is there even a causal relationship between the two or are they merely symbiotic? Second, the chapter focuses on whether or not—and to what extent—changes in the organization's conflict resolution approach have influenced its treatment of human rights in practice.

In the exposition that follows, two points emerge and become self-evident. First, the OIC's conflict resolution narrative, at least, is largely in conformity with universally accepted international norms regarding human rights within a conflict resolution context. That is not to say that fundamentally Islamic norms do not inform the OIC's conflict resolution activities in any way. Indeed, there has always been both a strong religious rationale for the OIC's involvement in any particular conflict, as well as repeated references to the Qur'an and Islamic traditions in its discourse. But there is little evidence of the OIC prioritizing Islamic norms above the international community's normative approach to conflict resolution, even if the organization is predominantly concerned with Muslim-majority states and Muslim communities in non-Muslim states. Despite this, the OIC has consistently cherry-picked which human rights issues to focus on within conflict situations, mostly in conformity with the agendas of certain member states. Furthermore, as Anthony Chase (Chapter 1) observes, this acceptance of international norms does not translate into substantive changes within member states' domestic policies. Second, and perhaps paradoxically, the organization's claimed relevance as a conflict resolution actor is based *entirely* on its Islamic identity and role as a representative of Muslim-majority states, significantly limiting both its relevance and the scope of its efforts.

Background: Conflict Resolution at the OIC

The OIC's conflict resolution agenda has historically remained firmly attached to three core principles: seeking a peaceful resolution to conflicts; cooperating with regional and international organizations for this purpose (Salah 2011:19); and protecting Muslim civilians within armed conflicts (Ahmad 2012). These principles are not particularly surprising considering that the OIC's primary objective is to "promote Islamic solidarity among Member States," and maintaining peace and security among member states is an essential component of that.[4] In addition, one of the OIC charter's permanent pillars is support for Palestinian sovereignty—an issue rooted in one of the Middle East's most protracted and complex conflicts—although it has certainly moved down the organization's list of priorities in recent decades.

The belief that regional and intergovernmental organizations are better suited to resolving conflicts is an intrinsic part of the OIC's conflict resolution narrative. During a discussion at George Mason University in 2011, Secretary-General Ekmeleddin İhsanoğlu observed that regional organizations "had greater vested interests in resolving conflicts in their own backyards and a better ability to mobilize home-grown mechanisms to address the root causes of conflict" (Lyons 2011). Ambassador Tariq Salah, director of the OIC's Department of Political Affairs and Muslim Minorities, wrote that the rationale for this approach is a reaction to the world's increasingly securitized approach to conflict resolution over the years. "Short term solutions," he writes, "must give way to a proper understanding of the root causes of conflicts, which often lie in political grievances, injustice, alienation, backwardness . . . underdevelopment as well as the need for good governance" (Salah 2011:19).

The OIC's conflict resolution efforts have also been focused exclusively on Muslim-majority states or the advancement of "Muslim-minority communities in sub-state, inter-state, and international violence" (Prodromou 2014:3). A key component of its narrative is therefore support for the self-determination struggles of Muslims around the world—a notion that also informed the basis of the organization's creation. The 1990 Cairo Declaration on Human Rights in Islam (CDHRI) accordingly declared "colonialism of all types" as "one of the most evil forms of enslavement" (Article 11(b)). This clause, Farrar writes, refers both to past colonial struggles by Muslims living under European empires as well as pan-Islamic opposition to the Israeli occupation of Palestinian territories (Farrar 2014:54).

It was the Israeli-Palestinian conflict, in fact, which provided the OIC with the first opportunity to explicitly reference human rights. Garnering opposition to Israel was the organization's foremost concern immediately after its establishment, as it sought to "demonstrate to the international community Israeli actions were . . . violations of 'internationally accepted' norms" (Farrar 2014:53). The issue of human rights was therefore presented through the prism of self-determination. "In cases where . . . minorities and communities have been confronted with discrimination on the basis of their religion and have suffered from infringement of their human rights," writes former Secretary-General İhsanoğlu, "the OIC has voiced its concern and worked to secure the rights of these minorities" (İhsanoğlu 2010:98).

In terms of structure, the OIC's Council of Foreign Ministers has historically implemented the majority of its conflict resolution efforts, although certain OIC organs—such as the Humanitarian Affairs Department and the Islamic Development Bank—have assisted the council in certain areas. These include joint and independent mediation efforts; financial assistance for humanitarian relief; voting at the UN and certain regional organizations; and contributing to the UN's peacekeeping missions (Prodromou 2014).

Moving Toward a Reformed Approach

In a 2015 interview, the director of the OIC's Peace, Security and Mediation Unit, Amanul Haq, remarked, "From 1969 to 2005 . . . OIC presence on the ground was very limited and to some extent, almost nonexistent in some places."[5] In fact, pressure for a revision to the OIC's approach to peace and conflict resolution had been building since 1969. Foremost had been a growing need to return to the OIC's founding objectives and commit to a larger and more effective role in resolving conflicts within the Muslim world. This was not surprising considering the rapid rise in Islamist terrorism and the sheer number of violent conflicts affecting OIC member states. This, combined with the absence of a clear and cohesive policy on conflict resolution at the OIC, precipitated the organization's strategic shift in approach.

Following Ekmeleddin İhsanoğlu's appointment to the position of secretary-general in 2004 and the launch of the "Ten Year Program of Action"[6] (TYPOA) in June 2006, the OIC's new conflict resolution approach appeared more lucid and explicit, although indicating a shift in its ambitions for conflict resolution as more informed by humanitarian intervention and multilateral mediation. At the same time, the organization's consideration of human rights within the context of conflict resolution has shifted from the struggles of self-determination to humanitarianism. This reformation of the OIC's conflict resolution approach resulted in the 2013 launch of the OIC's Peace, Security and Mediation Unit (PSMU) and the Network for Religious and Traditional Peacemakers, of which the OIC is a founding and core group member.

At a speech at the Fourth International Turkish Asian Congress in 2009, Secretary-General İhsanoğlu remarked that the TYPOA identified conflict resolution as a prominent challenge facing OIC member states and pledged to strengthen the role of the OIC in "conflict prevention, confidence building, peace keeping, conflict resolution and post conflict rehabilitation in OIC member states as well as in conflict situations involving Muslim communities." He added that since "global stability is derived from regional stability," there was a need to strengthen regional cooperation and organization, although "cooperation among regional organizations should be based on complementarity of actions" and the "goal should be to establish efficient partnerships and cooperation among international organizations which would provide an effective international response to conflicts, wherever it occurs" (Turkish Asian Center for Strategic Studies 2009). To this end, Ambassador Salah writes that the OIC is invested in its cooperation with the UN Peacebuilding Commission and work related to postconflict rehabilitation in OIC member states, such as operating trust funds in Afghanistan, Bosnia, and Sierra Leone (Salah 2011:19).

İhsanoğlu's successors, Iyad Madani (2014–2016) and Dr. Yousef Al-Othaimeen, have largely continued with this approach (Négron-Gonzales 2015:123). At a foreign ministers' meeting specifically geared toward the OIC's mechanism of conflict resolution in 2014, it was determined that the OIC could use its *comparative advantage* and capacity for *traditional peacemaking* to great effect. Quite specifically, Amanul Haq explained that since the notion of elders (respected traditional and religious figures) is prevalent in the Muslim world, there is immense scope for continuing to utilize them in mediation situations: "The traditional mechanism of presenting issues to the elders for problem-solving and decision-making has been present in the Arab world, Afghanistan, the Subcontinent and elsewhere for a very long time," he remarked. These include tribal leaders in Afghanistan (within the jirga system) and Somalia; in some instances, he added, they "even negate the authority of the state." The UN, he added, has a very institutionalized structure for conflict resolution and is often considered western-centric. In contrast, the OIC enjoys greater diversity of influence, as its mediation work with Al-Shabaab in Somalia indicates, and can therefore successfully employ a more traditional and "culturally and religiously sensitive" form of mediation.[7]

As a result, in 2013 the OIC established the PSMU based on the mechanisms of complementarity and comparative advantage vis-à-vis other international and regional organizations, using the traditional peacemaking structure as a blueprint. The OIC's conflict resolution arm firmly pursues a preventative diplomacy agenda, using mediation, negotiations, and multiparty dialogue to enable peace.[8] The unit's structure consists of three layers: a Wise Persons' Council (WPC) at the top, consisting of "well-known Muslim personalities from around the world, including current and former state leaders" (according to Haq); followed by special envoys who implement policy on the ground based on the recommendations of the WPC; and then the secretariat, which provides administrative support to the top layers. The unique WPC organ is not a decision-making body but an advisory one where each individual puts forth his/her recommendations independently, which the OIC's council of foreign ministers then has the option of approving or disapproving.[9] The first consultative session of the WPC[10] and the special envoys of the secretary-general was held at OIC headquarters in May 2016, marking the operationalization of the OIC's conflict resolution mechanism.

In addition, the OIC established a "contact group" of OIC states on Peace and Conflict Resolution (PCR) in October 2016. First proposed by Indonesia in 2015, the contact group is designed to function as a "consultative platform" that can produce solutions for the many security challenges faced by Muslim-majority states and communities around the world, including intra- and interstate conflict resolution (Yosephine 2016). The group is not independently operational, however, and requires guidance and instructions from the OIC's institutional bodies.

At the core of the OIC's revised conflict resolution approach is its focus on the role of traditional peacemaking in mediation efforts. Accordingly, the Network for Religious and Traditional Peacemakers was jointly launched in 2013 by Finn Church Aid (FCA), the UN Mediation Support Unit, UN Alliance of Civilizations (UNAOC), Religions for Peace (RfP), and the OIC. The initiative is a "global network that consists of religious and traditional leaders and organizations supporting their mediation and peace-building efforts."[11] Its work includes, but is not limited to, providing training to mediators from states and organizations, facilitating contacts with local leaders and representatives, and conducting fact-finding missions in any particular area.

Conflict Resolution and Human Rights: An Uneasy Symbiosis

The OIC's conflict resolution mechanism is broadly guided both by Sharia and the UN's conflict resolution principles of mediation and arbitration (al-Ahsan 2004:138). This marriage of two largely heterogeneous sets of norms has presented a normative dilemma for the OIC. Which set of norms weighs more heavily on decision-making? And how can the OIC reconcile the two to pursue policies that are in conformity with both Islamic and international norms? In addition, how has the shift in the OIC's conflict resolution approach since 2005 affected this dilemma?

Between 1996 and 2005, the OIC's conflict resolution narrative struggled with reconciling Islamic and universal norms, particularly with respect to human rights. In 1999, for example, the OIC adopted the controversial Convention on Combating Terrorism, which exempted acts committed in "people's struggles including armed struggle against foreign occupation, aggression, colonialism, and hegemony, aimed at liberation and self-determination" from terrorism.[12] Since then, the OIC has tried to amend the universally accepted definition of terrorism to include this exemption, often to exclude Palestinian suicide bombing attempts from the terrorism label because they are in response to "Israeli occupation." This has had profound implications for the OIC's involvement in the Israeli-Palestinian conflict as part of a multilateral framework, since the organization is not regarded as an objective and credible actor.

Complete adherence to international law is also not a realistic option because several powerful OIC member states adhere to Sharia law or at least prioritize Sharia rulings in some matters (such as freedom of speech versus defamation of religion). As a result, member states at the OIC approved the draft statute of the International Islamic Court of Justice (IICJ) in 1987, effectively establishing the first Sharia court that could potentially solve international disputes with recourse to international law as a second option (Castillo 2014:7). However, there is little evidence to suggest that the OIC ever intends to use the Sharia court for conflict resolution purposes. Moreover, the OIC has historically shied away from taking a legally binding, judicatory position on any particular conflict; indeed, its charter calls for *noninterference* in the internal affairs of OIC member states as well as their sovereignty, independence, and territorial integrity (Castillo 2014:5).

A Shift in Discourse

In 2005, some of the TYPOA's objectives were to uphold the principles of transparency and accountability; tackle ideologies that base religious extremism on particular interpretations in Islam; and protect the rights of women, children, and minorities. From the very beginning, therefore, there was a clear focus on human rights within the OIC's post-2005 discourse. Farrar writes that the plan demonstrated the OIC's commitment to institutional reform and a shift toward the UN framework as well as a definitive departure from the Cairo Declaration (Farrar 2014:19; but see Chapter 5, this volume, for a diverging view). The TYPOA's internationalization of OIC activities also addressed state abuse of human rights (with reference to autocratic governments) as well as cooperation with international organizations/agencies for the protection of the interests and human rights of Muslim minorities living outside OIC member states.

This emphasis on the human angle of conflicts indicates recognition of the changing nature of conflicts affecting Muslims as well as the impact of a reformed human rights approach toward conflict resolution efforts. The shift toward humanitarianism is notable for emerging at the same time as the unanimous adoption of the Responsibility to Protect (R2P) principle at the UN General Assembly in 2005. The OIC accordingly adopted many of the R2P measures and has been committed to institution-building within member states to comply with the R2P's first two pillars: responsibility of the state to protect its citizens and responsibility of the international community to support the state's efforts. These include an early warning system to tackle conflicts in member states before they flare up out of control (Ahmad 2012:2) as well as the creation of an election-monitoring mechanism to ensure free and fair elections within member states (Négron-Gonzales 2015:94). However, as Melinda Négron-Gonzales notes, the OIC has never officially endorsed the UN's R2P, largely because of its third pillar: responsibility of the international community to protect civilians if the state is unable or unwilling. Perhaps most controversially, the R2P allows for the use of force if peaceful means are insufficient to protect civilians (Négron-Gonzales 2015:127). The OIC, however, is adamantly committed to the principles of state sovereignty and noninterference, at least on paper. Its 2008 charter states that the promotion of human rights is "implemented in accordance with [members'] constitutional and legal system."[13] A comprehensive adoption of the R2P by the OIC therefore remains improbable.

One major aspect of the OIC's revised conflict resolution approach has been renewed interest in preventative diplomacy, largely because of the organization's experience with the Arab uprisings from 2011 onward and the individual cases of Iraq, Libya, and Syria.[14] Accordingly, the OIC's international assistance, as part of TYPOA, is split into two areas: operational prevention (i.e., mediation and peaceful dialogue) and structural prevention (i.e., addressing the—largely socioeconomic—roots of a conflict) (Négron-Gonzales 2015:127). In particular, OIC Secretary-General İhsanoğlu focused on humanitarian intervention, with particular attention given to the crises in Libya and Syria.

In Libya, the OIC used the UN's R2P principle to employ the principle of impartiality and support international intervention as a means to protect civilians and provide humanitarian assistance. Secretary-General İhsanoğlu was particularly blunt about the "excessive use of force against civilians," and in a speech at the OIC's Council of Permanent Representatives in March 2011, he declared that international intervention was necessary for the protection of civilians, citing the human rights provision in international law along with the OIC charter and the TYPOA's provision for good governance and respect for human values and human rights. In addition, Ahmad credits the OIC's decisive approach toward the Libyan crisis as instrumental in the adoption of UN Security Council resolutions 1970 and 1973 (Ahmad 2012:3). Indeed, the OIC remained the only international organization that maintained open channels of communication with both the Gaddafi regime and Libyan rebels (Sharqieh 2012:172).

This commitment to protecting Libyan civilians from the conflict and urging international—primarily UN-led—intervention also informed the OIC's position in Syria, though to a far lesser extent. Ishtiaq Ahmad regards this humanitarian stance, supported by invoking Islamic norms forbidding the killing of civilians, to be in conformity with international humanitarian law[15] (Ahmad 2012:3–4). Moreover, though Qatar, Saudi Arabia, Turkey, and the UAE remain actively invested in both Libya and Syria, the OIC has distanced itself from Qatar and Saudi Arabia's "interventionist stance" on Syria. Indeed, the OIC has shied away from contributing to the armed conflict in any manner and has opposed the funding and arming of the Free Syrian Army—supported by a number of key OIC member states—because of its fundamental opposition, from an Islamic perspective, to the loss of civilian life (Ahmad 2012:1).

This shift in the OIC's conflict resolution approach can also be attributed to its increased focus on understanding and tackling what Amanul Haq describes as the "political and socio-economic contexts that bring forth conditions conducive to the spread of security risks and instability in the Muslim World."[16] He defines these as including "continued economic deprivation, exclusion, separation and marginalization of people, poverty, lack of opportunities, misguided development, educational structures and influences and interferences of foreign interest." The OIC's approach, he explained, is therefore focused on promoting good governance, respect for human rights, and support for progress in all. In addition, the OIC's conflict resolution approach now encompasses the areas of terrorism and violent extremism as well as cyber security, since social media has been seen to facilitate terrorist activities and recruitment. The rationale for this, Haq explains, is that the OIC is in a position to speak on behalf of all Muslims and invalidate the extremist rationale for such behavior.

The OIC's shifting focus to humanitarian intervention and preventative diplomacy is indicative of two underlying issues. First, conflict resolution and human rights appear to share a uniquely symbiotic relationship at the OIC, with the OIC increasingly using universal human rights language to articulate its reformed conflict resolution approach. On the other hand, the changing nature of conflicts affecting Muslims—such as uprisings against autocratic regimes—has brought human rights to the forefront. Second, the use of universal human rights language reflects the OIC's growing dependence on multilateral conflict resolution efforts, for which the adoption of such language is essential.

Multilateral Cooperation

A key component of the OIC's conflict resolution efforts is cooperation with other international and regional organizations, due in large part to limitations in its own capacity and resources. In this respect, there is little to suggest that there might be a conflict between the OIC's approach and international norms. Indeed, in the words of İhsanoğlu, "The OIC seeks to work firmly within the international system, and within the confines of international law and norms . . . for the purpose of conflict resolution through peaceful means" (İhsanoğlu 2010:97).

The OIC's two new conflict resolution initiatives are cases in point. Capacity-building initiatives at the PSMU, for instance, are extensively supported by the UN, especially its Mediation Support Unit.[17] Similarly, the Network for Religious and Traditional Peacemakers has so far focused on capacity-building and the collection and dissemination of ideas and solutions from traditional and religious leaders across the world. In an interview with the author, Dr. Mohamed Elsanousi, director of the secretariat of the network (Washington office), explained that the premise of the initiative is "to implement Track 1.5 where religious leaders are used to support and implement peace solutions." In fact, the initiative is "not trying to create a new institution but build a network of support and dialogue." As a result, he said, the network's primary objective is to "support other governments and organizations in conflict resolution, mediation and peace building" by providing a presence at the grassroots level. Accordingly, the network brought together religious representatives from Nigeria, Myanmar, Pakistan, and Somalia in 2014 to discuss ways to tackle violent extremism that could then inform policy decisions on the ground.[18]

This approach also extends to regional organizations. The OIC signed a Partnership Agreement with the African Union (AU) on the fight against terrorism and violent extremism in Africa in April 2015 and sought to do the same with the Association of Southeast Asian Nations (ASEAN), according to Haq.[19] In the turbulent Middle East and North Africa (MENA) region, while the organization enjoys partnering with the twenty-two–member Arab League regularly, it is also part of the tripartite OIC-Arab League-Gulf

Cooperation Council mechanism that meets frequently to discuss common issues affecting member states.[20]

However, nowhere is the OIC's increasing reliance on multilateral cooperation more evident than with the UN. OIC-UN cooperation began in October 1975 when the OIC was accepted as an observer member (Resolution 3369). Subsequent resolutions—61/49 of February 12, 2007, 63/114 of February 26, 2009, and 65/140 of April 5, 2011—have signaled mutual cooperation in the areas of international peace and security, self-determination, and the promotion and upholding of human rights (Castillo 2014:16). Indeed, this relationship has been steadily moving toward a more formalized partnership rather than the ad hoc cooperation the two organizations have enjoyed in the past.

In December 2006, the UN General Assembly passed a resolution to welcome and encourage greater cooperation between the OIC and the UN, particularly with regard to "conflict prevention, confidence-building, peacekeeping, conflict resolution, and post-conflict rehabilitation in member states as well as in conflict situations involving Muslim communities."[21] In December 2011, the OIC and UN Office for the Coordination of Humanitarian Affairs signed a memorandum of understanding, agreeing to further cooperation in the area of humanitarian crises, including the protection of civilians during armed conflicts (Ahmad 2012:2). The key rationale informing this partnership was that of comparative advantage in the area of mediation. The OIC is considered a very useful partner for the UN within the Muslim world, particularly in those areas or with those local actors where the UN does not enjoy easy access (Salah 2011:20). This has been the case in Somalia and in Libya with Gaddafi's regime. In the latter case, a series of policy decisions[22] meant that only the OIC remained in a position to speak with both sides.

During a meeting with the UN Security Council in 2013, İhsanoğlu remarked that strengthening cooperation between the United Nations and the OIC, particularly in forming early responses to disputes, would "promote multilateralism and boost the international collective security mechanism."[23] According to Ambassador Salah, this partnership can benefit from the "coordinated division of labor" and "institutional cooperation," particularly in the areas of "training, institution-building, information and experience sharing, and logistical support" (Salah 2011:21).

This relationship is not surprising considering the sheer preponderance of faith-based organizations at the UN. However, what makes the OIC-UN relationship unique is how much the UN's human rights language has made its way into the OIC's conflict resolution discourse, particularly since 2005. On the surface, therefore, it would appear that the OIC has resolved its normative dilemma with multilateral cooperation, allowing the OIC and its various conflict resolution partners to tackle specialist areas of the same conflict. In this way, the OIC retains its Sharia-based norms for the areas where it functions—such as traditional peacemaking and mediation—while adopting the UN's conflict resolution and human rights language to address the larger picture.

It is therefore useful to observe the OIC's relationship with organizations that adhere to fundamentally different norms, both in rhetoric and practice. The European Union's (EU) liberal peace-building agenda, for instance, is firmly rooted in a number of deeply entrenched norms, including universal human rights. Examining the OIC's relationship with the EU can allow for an assessment of its normative actorness (Manners 2002). On paper, it would appear that the EU and OIC have great scope for cooperation in the field of conflict resolution, particularly since they have been independently involved in many of the same crisis zones. In fact, two OIC member states, Turkey and Morocco, share a relationship with the EU that is inconceivable anywhere else (Pinfari 2017). Turkey is a candidate for EU accession and a key diplomatic influence in the Syrian civil war, while Morocco benefits from an advanced status arrangement with the EU and has been vying for full EU membership.

However, cooperation on conflict management has historically remained largely absent from the EU-OIC agenda. Recent years have seen attempts to remedy this with both sides exhibiting interest in fostering further cooperation. During Secretary-General İhsanoğlu's tenure the OIC visibly sought closer links with the EU and established multiple opportunities to cooperate on crucial issues. As a result, the first-ever high-level consultation meeting between the EU and the OIC took place in Brussels in September 2014, marking a renewal of both organizations' commitment to consolidate a multifaceted partnership. Among other things, the two sides crucially agreed on the need for a partnership to manage "crisis and post-crisis dilemmas."[24]

Both organizations are institutional donors to the UN Peace-Building Commission and liaise regularly over crisis issues,[25] but there is a fundamental disparity in their respective positions whenever the interests of member states (on both sides) are involved. Richard Gowan and Franziska Brantner note that the OIC holds a strategic advantage over the EU in large, majority-based UN forums and uses its leverage over the AU and Arab League, among others, to lobby support for its agenda (Gowan and Brantner 2008:55). There have also been tensions related to key human rights issues, indicating that the EU's strong emphasis on key universal norms—and the OIC's reluctance to adhere to them—has affected EU-OIC relations negatively. Cyprus, for instance, remains the most extensive source of contention between the EU and OIC. In 1983, the Turkish-held area of northern Cyprus declared itself the "Turkish Republic of Northern Cyprus," an entity that was only recognized by Turkey and rejected by the UN Security Council in 1984 (Resolution 550). The OIC's decision to grant observer status to the Turkish Cypriot State in 2004 was therefore seen by the EU as directly contravening international law. Indeed, the second joint EU-OIC forum was cancelled in 2004 precisely because EU member states withdrew over the Cyprus issue.

Is the OIC a Viable Conflict Resolution Actor?

In his analysis of the OIC's abysmal management of the Iran-Iraq war,[26] al-Ahsan outlines some of the key problems with the OIC's conflict resolution approach. The OIC's proactive involvement in the conflict started at the very onset of the crisis in September 1980, with the organization initially sending a goodwill mission to Tehran and Baghdad and then creating an Islamic Peace Committee during the Third Islamic Summit in Mecca and Ta'if in 1981. Since the committee identified the Shafal-'Arab waterway as the main issue of contention, it was decided that subsequent mediation efforts would focus on the root of the problem (al-Ahsan 2004:143–44). Unfortunately, the OIC was unsuccessful in bringing Iran to the negotiating table and restricting Iraq from manipulating the OIC. Consequently, it failed to broker either a cease-fire or a peace agreement. The OIC's constant appeasement of Iraq not only eroded its credibility as a fair mediator but also demonstrated that the organization was unwilling to go against the grain when the interests of key member states were at stake (al-Ahsan 2004:152).

The OIC's many shortcomings—some inherent within the organization—are key to understanding why the its evolving conflict resolution and human rights relationship has had little impact. If anything, the OIC has increasingly scaled back its conflict resolution activities to remain firmly within the relatively safer ambit of multilateral cooperation. As a result, it is difficult to assess how the OIC treats human rights within the sphere of conflict resolution. It is more useful, instead, to explore the reasons why the OIC is not equipped to resolve most conflicts and the impact those shortcomings have had on its treatment of human rights.

Successes and Failures

The OIC's early mediation successes—between the Palestine Liberation Organization and Jordan in 1970 as well as Pakistan and Bangladesh in 1971—took place right after the establishment of the organization in 1969. In both cases, however, the OIC mediated between the two sides only *after* the end of armed confrontation (al-Ahsan 2004:140–41). Since then, the OIC has been selective about the crises it tackles.[27] Moreover, while the OIC has enjoyed varying shades of success with its multifaceted involvement in Guinea, the Philippines, and Somalia to name just a few, the organization has generally floundered in the MENA region. Though there have been notable successes, such as the Sunni-Shia reconciliation in Iraq (2006), the OIC's failure to significantly influence any resolution in the Israeli-Palestinian conflict or any of the crises resulting from the Arab uprisings or the Islamist terrorist threat that the so-called Islamic State poses in Iraq and Syria, indicate deeper structural weaknesses within the organization in the face of a self-described mandate.

In Africa, the OIC's mediation efforts in Somalia and Mali have been considered a success. The violent civil war in Somalia began in 1991 after the state collapsed under immense political instability; the UN intervened in the conflict in 1993 and the OIC helped mediate the Djibouti Peace Agreement in 2008, which was signed by all countries involved as well as a number of international organizations as observers. The OIC's role in the mediation process was "instrumental," writes Salah, because it managed to persuade President Sheikh Sharif (leader of the opposition Alliance for the Re-liberation of Somalia) to join the peace process (Salah 2011:20). In addition, the OIC led humanitarian relief efforts within the region during the drought and ensuing severe food shortage in 2011, establishing the OIC Humanitarian Assistance Coordination Office in Mogadishu in an attempt to gather and distribute food supplies to areas in need (Castillo 2014:17). Because it was able to broker a deal with the Al Shabaab militant group so that humanitarian assistance could be delivered at a time when other international actors had been forced to leave or were simply not allowed access, the OIC could act as an intermediary of sorts.

In Asia, the OIC has also been involved in two mediation successes: Southern Philippines and Southern Thailand. In the former, the OIC helped broker peace agreements (1976 and 1996) between the Filipino government and the Moro people (Muslim indigenous population) living predominantly in the south of the country. The second agreement, between the government and the Moro National Liberation Front (MNLF) sought to establish peace in the independent Mindanao region in the south. In Thailand, the OIC's efforts have been less institutionalized, resulting in a joint communiqué as well as the provision of advice and support from the OIC for the purpose of assisting the Thai government in catering to its Muslim citizens (Salah 2011:20).

The African and Asian mediation success stories had two things in common: first, they were all essentially internal conflicts, and second, the OIC was part of a solid multilateral peace arrangement. In the MENA region, however, the OIC does not enjoy the benefits of an existing regional security mechanism. Barry Buzan and Ole Wæver's analysis on regional security in the MENA region indicates a "pattern of security interdependence" spanning the entire MENA region, but not cooperation (Buzan and Wæver 2003:187). The OIC's involvement in Iraq during the 1990 Gulf War demonstrates some of the key difficulties it has faced in the region. The organization adopted a resolution in its 1997 Summit Conference in Tehran condemning Iraq's attack on Kuwait and calling for compliance with all UN resolutions on the matter (based on the principle of solidarity between member states). In direct contrast, in 2003, the U.S.-led military campaign in Iraq saw the OIC stressing the principles of nonintervention in Iraqi affairs, self-determination, sovereignty, and national integrity in a declaration at the Islamic Summit Conference in Putrajaya (Castillo 2014:18). However, the OIC decided to intervene directly by facilitating a reconciliation agreement between the warring Sunnis and Shias in 2006, largely in response to the deadly violence on both sides (Sharqieh 2012:168–69). Inviting Sunni and Shia leaders to a meeting in Mecca during Ramadan, Secretary-General İhsanoğlu intervened directly to bring about a nationwide reconciliation and the signing of the Mecca Declaration. Ibrahim Sharqieh explains that the invitation to Islam's most revered location during the holiest part of the Islamic year exerted "moral pressure" on representatives of both sides to sign the document (Sharqieh 2012:168–69). The document "rejected the notion of killing among Muslims and agreed on the principle of inviolability of the human soul" (İhsanoğlu 2010:123). It was circulated widely in mosques across Iraq, writes Salah, who suggests that this particular strategy might well be useful in tackling extremism in Somalia (Salah 2011:20). However, as Négron-Gonzales notes, the initiative produced a very limited moratorium on sectarian violence in Iraq and cannot be perceived as an enduring success (Négron-Gonzales 2015:130).

Syria's protracted and violent conflict, in direct contrast to Libya, has not enjoyed decisive and assertive policy-making at the organization (Négron-Gonzales 2015:132). The OIC has never invoked R2P's third pillar and lobbied the UN to intervene through whatever means possible, despite the escalating violence in the country. Instead, the OIC has continued to uphold R2P's first pillar, which recognizes that the state is responsible for protecting its civilians. Unlike the Gaddafi regime, Bashar al-Assad's regime continues to enjoy the support of Iran, a key OIC member state. It has therefore been much more difficult to establish a definitive OIC position on the conflict. In lieu of that, the OIC has focused on asking the UN to facilitate a peaceful, negotiated resolution to the conflict and providing humanitarian assistance. Nevertheless, in August 2012, the OIC suspended Syria's membership in the organization at the Islamic Summit in Mecca in a move designed to alienate al-Assad's regime, despite strong and vocal opposition by Iran. In addition, it continues to work as co-facilitator of the Syria Humanitarian Forum, a campaign to coordinate fund-raising for humanitarian assistance. Much like the Somalian case, the OIC managed to reach a crucial agreement with Syria in 2013 to send humanitarian aid and a joint OIC-UN mission to Syria. In an unexpected move, the so-called Mecca Letter—condemning human rights violations in Syria—was also formally acknowledged by member states at the 2012 Islamic Summit in Mecca (Castillo 2014:20). Since then, the OIC has consistently claimed to offer support for all initiatives "aiming at reaching a political solution" to the crisis (OIC 2015).

Perhaps the OIC's most challenging test to date has been the Israeli-Palestinian conflict, where the OIC does not recognize one of the key actors—Israel—despite its preoccupation with the issue of Palestinian sovereignty. As a direct consequence of the Six Day War, the OIC was established in 1969 and its charter lists the Palestinian issue as one of its key concerns, pledging member states' commitment to supporting the struggle of the Palestinian people. In practical terms, the OIC has provided official Muslim representation on the issue at the UN and its various bodies. It was instrumental in Palestine's approval as an observer member by the UN General Assembly and has inexhaustibly campaigned on related subjects at the UN and

Human Rights Council (HRC). These have included calling for action against alleged Israeli human rights abuses and building settlements as well as advocating a two-state solution and consequently, Palestinian statehood.

Despite this, interviews with OIC representatives reveal that the Palestinians appear unwilling to actively seek any tangible political support from the OIC for conflict resolution efforts. Instead, "they use the organization's status and resources for soft support" such as voting at the UN, claims Dr. Shaher Awawdeh, political officer for Palestine and Al Quds Affairs at the OIC. He adds that the Palestinians fluctuate between selecting the Arab League and the OIC as their representative at the UN and during peace negotiations based on what sort of support they require. For all Jerusalem-related negotiations, for instance, the OIC is both consulted and asked to provide its considerable fifty-seven-member support. The Palestinians initially accepted the OIC's offer to serve as a mediator between Fatah and Hamas. "We were the first organization to arrive on the occasion of the Fatah-Hamas split in 2007 and were . . . essentially the first mediator," recalls Awawdeh, who came with Secretary-General İhsanoğlu. That effort did not succeed, however, and subsequent offers by the OIC to mediate between the two sides have not been accepted, in part due to the schism within Hamas itself. Since then, the OIC has downgraded its resolution efforts in the conflict by excluding it from the new PSMU entirely. According to Haq, this is because the conflict has been "prioritized as an Arab issue and is therefore dealt with primarily through the Arab League."[28]

Problems at the OIC

These case studies do allow for a few conclusions about how the OIC's conflict resolution efforts have affected human rights in practical terms. First, until 2005, the charter's core principles of "non-interference in domestic affairs" and respect for the "sovereignty, independence and territorial integrity of each Member State" significantly hampered the OIC's capacity for supporting humanitarian intervention (Ahmad 2012:2), such as in Iraq during the Gulf War. In addition, the principle of sovereignty deprives stateless conflict actors—such as the Sahrawis in the Western Sahara—from bringing their case to the OIC.

Second, the organization is fundamentally heterogeneous; member states are not only spread over three continents but also share neither the same language nor the same ethnic or cultural identity. Since member states do not speak with one voice, individual members have often pursued their own interests, sometimes in direct opposition to the OIC's professed stance. Egypt's peace treaty with Israel in 1978 (after the end of the Arab-Israeli war in 1973), for example, led the OIC to suspend the state in 1979 (but re-admitting it in 1984). Similarly, after the Oslo I Accord was signed in 1993, some OIC states established trade links with Israel—in opposition to the economic boycott of Israel—while others[29] continued to provide funds to the Palestinian Authority. Conversely, Yasser Arafat's support for Saddam Hussein during the Gulf War in 1990 led to the widespread expulsion of the many Palestinians working in Gulf countries without OIC interjection (Hossain 2012:302). In general, it has been fairly easy for certain member states to pursue their own agenda. Egypt's continued closure of the Rafah border crossing, for instance, has not even earned a slap on the hand from the OIC.[30]

The prodemocracy Arab uprisings that spread through the MENA region from 2010 onward are also indicative of the OIC's inconsistent conflict resolution approach. With key OIC member states dealing with growing hostilities at home, a summit meeting was held in March 2011, which ended up focusing only on the humanitarian crisis in Libya. Thus began a process of the OIC cherry-picking which uprisings would receive a tongue-lashing and which would be largely ignored. As Ishtiaq Hossain notes, though the Gaddafi regime's human rights violations against its own people were openly condemned by Secretary-General İhsanoğlu, no mention has ever been made of Bahrain's many human rights violations in the same context (Hossain 2012:306). Indeed, Bahraini forces were joined by troops from Saudi Arabia and the UAE for the express purpose of physically (and sometimes fatally) subduing the mainly Shia-Bahraini protestors. Key Arab and Gulf states, in fact, have sporadically witnessed prodemocracy protests, including perhaps the OIC's most influential member state, Saudi Arabia. This is exacerbated by the fact that the OIC functions almost exclusively without any legal consequences for member states. Unlike other international and regional actors, the OIC's mediation efforts are largely seen as nonbinding and nonpunitive, making use of the carrot and not *both* the carrot and the stick with member states involved in conflict situations (Sharqieh 2012:171).[31] The exception, of course, is when the OIC does enforce embargos and adopts other soft power measures, but it depends entirely on the relative strength and influence of the member states concerned.

Third, the absence of sufficient political will to firmly handle mediation and conflict management processes greatly hinders the OIC's commitment to upholding peace within and between member states for Muslim minorities in non-Muslim states. Continued involvement in Thailand's ongoing separatist conflict in its deep south, for instance, is offered only if the Thai government is happy to receive the OIC's help. On a trip to Bangkok, Secretary-General Madani stated that the OIC was in Thailand not to "impose or put itself into the situation," but to facilitate ongoing developments.[32]

This weakness is exacerbated by the OIC's chronic financial shortcomings and the resultant funding of its activities by member states, which then assume a disproportionate amount of political leverage. The OIC's activities are largely funded by Saudi Arabia,[33] followed by the other large OIC economies, such as Iran, Kuwait, Malaysia, Turkey, and the UAE.[34] Historically, Saudi Arabia and Iran have been dominant voices that have steered the OIC toward predominantly political issues (Hakala and Kettis 2013:6). Conversely, larger Muslim-majority states such as Malaysia, Morocco, and Turkey have become increasingly involved and largely prefer to focus on moderation, cultural exchange, dialogue, and good governance. Since the OIC operates on the basis of consensus, this absence of any real cohesion within the organization and the excessive influence of member states such as Iran, Saudi Arabia, and the other Gulf states have historically hampered the OIC's role in mediation and conflict management.

Nowhere is this more apparent than in the Middle East, where Sunni-Shia rivalry pits two vocal members—Iran and Saudi Arabia—against one another as soon as there are any religious undertones in any political crisis. Iraq, Lebanon, and Syria are prime examples of this as well as the OIC's inconsistent handling of the Arab uprisings. The area's regional hegemony is so pervasive, in fact, that it has systematically influenced the majority of conflicts within its boundaries. While Saudi Arabia accuses Iran of instigating protests in Bahrain and within its own oil-rich and Shia-dominated northeastern province, Iran accuses Qatar, Saudi Arabia, and Turkey of arming Syrian rebels.

The combined effect of these factors is key to understanding why the OIC's dynamic conflict resolution and human rights relationship has not produced many visible results. The OIC, writes Salah, is "better placed to deal with conflicts in the Muslim World" particularly in cases where only the OIC's Islamic identity and representation of all Muslim states can help broker ceasefire and peace agreements (Salah 2011:21). However, the organization's many obstacles to effective conflict resolution, and the very particular, specialist advantages it can offer, do not allow for the practical adoption of international human rights norms.

Conclusion

It is important to understand just how inherently problematic the conflict resolution-human rights relationship is at the OIC. The appearance of a gradual incorporation of international norms, for instance, comes with a reformed conflict resolution approach that seeks to work in tandem with other actors. As this chapter argues, a supposed disparity between the OIC's conflict resolution approach and its actions on the ground stems largely from the paradoxical nature of its normative treatment of conflict resolution. The OIC's shift toward humanitarianism and even stronger multilateral cooperation necessitated the adoption of universally acceptable international norms regarding conflict resolution. However, this shift has occurred in spite of the fact that the organization's comparative advantage and raison d'être are rooted in its Islamic identity and representation of the Muslim world.

The OIC's new focus on complementarity and traditional peacemaking is a reflection of its resource and capacity constraints and its conscious decision to work within the existing international conflict resolution framework. These constraints have necessitated collaboration with richer, better-organized, and politically strong organizations and actors for multiparty mediation where the OIC can best use its specific skill set (Castillo 2014:6). They have also required the OIC to adopt universal human rights language, at least in all conflict resolution discourse. In practice, however, the OIC's lack of cohesion and control over member states has not allowed for adherence to those international norms. So while the answer to whether conflict resolution and human rights share a symbiotic relationship at the OIC is yes, it is significantly limited by the OIC's compromised role as a conflict resolution actor.

One important issue has been left out of this analysis because it goes beyond the scope of this chapter: whether conflict resolution efforts at the OIC can facilitate the unanimous adoption of universal human rights or impair the process. After all, greater OIC involvement in conflict situations "may limit the possibilities for durable peace arrangements that conform to international human rights law and for sovereignty principles crucial to global order and security," writes Elizabeth Prodromou (2014:4). While this is a relevant concern, the OIC's consistent downsizing of its conflict resolution efforts and use of universal human rights language indicate a reluctance to deviate from international human rights law in this regard. And so the questions that must now be asked are: how ambitious is the OIC's conflict resolution approach and is it enough to significantly alter the application of international human rights law to conflict situations?

Nevertheless, analyses of the OIC's conflict resolution efforts can continue to contribute positively to the literature on the OIC and human rights. The dynamic relationship between both entities provides an interesting window through which to observe how the organization handles competing norms in practice. The Arab uprisings are a prime example of how the OIC has had to reformulate its stance on human rights abuses—almost overnight—within OIC member states. As Secretary-General İhsanoğlu remarked at an OIC conference at Sabancı University in Istanbul, "The OIC has a strong desire to build national dialogue between governments and the opposition forces. . . . The OIC also aims to promote human rights, which does not have a good record in Muslim countries, as well as build bigger capacities in preventive diplomacy" (*Hürriyet Daily News* 2011). The OIC's stance on the Rohingya, for instance, is constantly evolving. So while Secretary-General Madani declared that depriving the Rohingya of their citizenship "was a human rights issue" during a recent trip to Thailand, he also added that Thailand, Bangladesh, and ASEAN could help resolve this matter.[35]

Mere acknowledgment that OIC member states have a human rights problem is a—very small—step in the right direction. At the very least, it has opened up the OIC's conflict resolution approach for a wider discussion within the human rights discourse.

Notes

1. Henceforth, "conflict resolution" is used as an umbrella term for all activities that seek a resolution to violent conflicts, including preventative diplomacy, mediation, arbitration, multilateral efforts, and humanitarian relief.

2. See preamble of UN charter.

3. Charter of the Organization of Islamic Cooperation. Dakar, March 13–14, 2008. http://www.oic- oci.org/docdown/?docID=33&refID=9.

4. Ibid., Article 2(a)(1).

5. Amanul Haq, interview with author, OIC headquarters, Jeddah, 2015. All Haq quotes are from this interview. All interviews were conducted and recorded openly, and quotes are used with the express permission of the interviewees.

6. For more information, see http://www.oic-iphrc.org/en/data/docs/legal_instruments/OIC%20Instruments/TYPOA-%20AEFV/TYPOA-EV.pdf.

7. Haq, interview with author.

8. "OIC Operationalizes Its Conflicts Resolution Mechanism." 2016. Organization of Islamic Cooperation. May 18. http://www.oic-oci.org//topic/ampg.asp?t_id=11205&t_ref=4407&lan=en.

9. Haq, interview with author.

10. The WPC consists of Abdullah Gül, former president of Turkey, Dr. Susilo Bambang Yudhoyono, former president of Indonesia, and General Abdulsalami Abubakar, former head of state of Nigeria, among others.

11. As stated on the network's website: https://www.kirkonulkomaanapu.fi/en/donors/international-networks/network-religious-traditional-peacemakers/.

12. Convention on Combating International Terrorism, Article 2.

13. Charter of the Organization of Islamic Cooperation, 1.

14. Shaher Awawdeh, interview with author, OIC headquarters, Jeddah. 2013. All Awawdeh quotes are from this interview.

15. The 1949 Geneva Convention and Additional Protocols, 1977.

16. Speech at the Turkish Asian Center for Strategic Studies in 2015.

17. Haq, interview with author.

18. Mohamed Elsanousi, in video call with author, 2015. All Elsanousi quotes are from this interview.

19. Haq, interview with author.

20. Haq, interview with author.

21. *Resolution Adopted by the General Assembly.* Sixty-First Session. Agenda item 108 (q).

22. As Sharqieh explains, the UN's relationship with the Gaddafi regime "deteriorated" after UNSC Resolution 1973 approved NATO intervention while the regime cut ties with the Arab League after the organization called for a no-fly zone in Libya. Alternatively, the AU was considered "too close" to the regime and was therefore rejected as a neutral party by the rebels (Sharqieh 2012:171).

23. *Cooperation Between the UN and Regional and Subregional Organizations in Maintaining International Peace and Security.* 2013. UNSC/11161, October 28. https://www.un.org/press/en/2013/sc11161.doc.htm.

24. "Saudi Arabia: OIC and EU Agree to Settle a Common Ground for Partnership in Different Areas." 2014. *Mena Report,* March 2. https://www.highbeam.com/doc/1G1-382680467.html.

25. Most notably in the Philippines and Guinea.

26. See al-Ahsan 2004 for a more detailed account of the OIC's mediation efforts in the Iran-Iraq war.

27. With the exception of the Iran-Iraq war, the OIC decided not to intervene in any other conflicts during the 1970s, such as in Libya, Sudan, or the Western Sahara.

28. Haq, interview with author.

29. Most notably Saudi Arabia, Kuwait, and the UAE.

30. Though certain member states, such as Malaysia in 2010, have called on Egypt to open the border on a permanent basis.

31. The OIC's "stick," explains Sharqieh, is the use of "moral power," which was seen to be effective in Iraq's Sunni-Shia reconciliation in 2006 and the OIC's mediation and humanitarian efforts in Somalia but has not been applicable in every case.

32. "OIC Ready to Assist on Unrest in Deep South." *Bangkok Post*, January 14, 2016. http://www.bangkokpost.com/news/politics/825428/oic-ready-to-assist-on-unrest-in-deep-south.

33. Saudi Arabia pledged $1 billion to the Poverty Alleviation Fund within the Islamic Development Fund at the OIC at the 2006 summit, while Iran pledged $1 million and the UAE $2 million to the Islamic Solidarity Fund (Hossain 2012:299).

34. *New Scale of Member States Mandatory Contributions to Annual Budgets of the General Secretariat and its Subsidiary Organs, 2006–2007.* Resolution No. 3/33-AF.

35. "OIC Ready to Assist on Unrest in Deep South." 2016. *Bangkok Post*, January 14. http://www.bangkokpost.com/news/politics/825428/oic-ready-to-assist-on-unrest-in-deep-south.

Works Cited

Ahmad, Ishtiaq. 2012. "The Organisation of Islamic Co-operation's Position on the Protection of Civilians in Armed Conflicts." Norwegian Centre for Conflict Resolution (NOREF) policy brief. https://www.files.ethz.ch/isn/157048/0042c466c06c8c9e2b8f790e5ddbbd88.pdf.

al-Ahsan, Abdullah. 2004. "Conflict Among Muslim Nations: Role of the OIC in Conflict Resolution." *Intellectual Discourse* 12 (2): 137–57.

———. 2008. "Law, Religion and Human Dignity in the Muslim World Today: An Examination of OIC's Cairo Declaration of Human Rights." *Journal of Law and Religion* 24 (2): 569–97.

Buzan, Barry, and Ole Wæver. 2003. *Regions and Powers*. Cambridge: Cambridge University Press.

Castillo, Victor. 2014. "The Organization of Islamic Cooperation in Contemporary International Society." *Revista Electrónica de Estudios Internacionales* 27: 171–91.

Cismas, Ioana. 2014. *Religious Actors and International Law*. Oxford: Oxford University Press.

Farrar, Salim. 2014. "The Organisation of Islamic Cooperation: Forever on the Periphery of Public International Law?" *Chinese Journal of International Law* 13 (4): 787–817.

Gowan, Richard, and Franziska Brantner. 2008. "A Global Force for Human Rights? An Audit of European Power at the UN." *European Council on Foreign Relations*. Policy paper, September. https://www.files.ethz.ch/isn/91657/Global_Force_Human_Rights_EU_0908.pdf

Hakala, Pekka, and Andreas Kettis. 2013. *The Organization of Islamic Cooperation: Defined—for Better and Worse—by Its Religious Dimension*. Brussels: Directorate-General for External Policies of the European Union.

Hashmat, Ahmad S. 2011. "The OIC's Potential, Capabilities and Constraints for International Conflict Resolution." *Strategic Studies* 31 (1): 107–35.

Hossain, Ishtiaq. 2012. "The Organization of Islamic Conference (OIC): Nature, Role, and the Issues." *Journal of Third World Studies* 29 (1): 287–314.

Hürriyet Daily News. 2011. "OIC Supports National Dialogue in Arab Spring." December 7. Istanbul. http://www.hurriyetdailynews.com/default.aspx?pageid=438&n=oic-supports-national-dialogue-in-arab-spring-2011-07-12.

İhsanoğlu, Ekmeleddin. 2010. *The Islamic World in the New Century: The Organization of the Islamic Conference, 1969–2009*. London: Hurst.

Kaldor, Mary. 2012. *New and Old Wars: Organized Violence in a Global Era*. Cambridge: Polity Press.

Kolb, Robert. 1998. "The Relationship Between International Humanitarian Law and Human Rights Law: A Brief History of the 1948 Universal Declaration of Human Rights and the 1949 Geneva Conventions." *International Review of the Red Cross* no. 324. https://www.icrc.org/eng/resources/documents/article/other/57jpg2.htm.

Lyons, Terrence. 2011. "S-CAR Hosts the OIC: Conflict Resolution in the Islamic World." *S-CAR News*. http://activity.scar.gmu.edu/newsletter-article/s-car-hosts-oic-conflict-resolution-islamic-world.

Manikkalingam, Ram. 2006. "Is There a Tension Between Human Rights and Conflict Resolution? A Conflict Resolution Perspective." Armed Groups Project working paper 7 (June).

Manners, Ian. 2002. "Normative Power Europe: A Contradiction in Terms?" *Journal of Common Market Studies* 40 (2): 235–58.

Mirbagheri, Farid. 2006. "Islam and Liberal Peace." Unpublished conference paper presented at the March 22 Annual Meeting of the International Studies Association, San Diego, CA.

Négron-Gonzales, Melinda. 2015. "Organization of Islamic Cooperation." In *International Organizations and the Implementation of the Responsibility to Protect: The Humanitarian Crisis in Syria*, ed. Daniel Silander and Don Wallace, 90–109. Abingdon: Routledge.

Organization of Islamic Cooperation. 2005. "Ten-Year Programme of Action to Meet the Challenges Facing the Muslim Ummah in the 21st Century." Third Extraordinary Session of the Islamic Summit Conference, December 7–8. https://www.humanrights.ch/upload/pdf/170320_10_year_programm_of_action.pdf.

Pinfari, Marco. 2017. "Introduction: Middle East and North Africa." In *The EU, Regional Integration and Conflict Resolution*, ed. Thomas Diez and Nathalie Tocci, 51–55. New York: Palgrave Macmillan.

Prodromou, Elizabeth. 2014. "OIC Memorandum 5: The OIC and Conflict Resolution." Global Governance Watch. http://www.globalgovernancewatch.org/library/doclib/20140815_OICMemo5.pdf.

Salah, Tariq Ali Bakheet. 2011. "The Role of the OIC in Mediation and Facilitation: Challenges and Successes." *OIC Journal* 16: 19.

Saudi Press Agency. 2015. "OIC Welcomes the Results of Talks on the Syrian Crisis." https://www.spa.gov.sa/1414282.

Sharqieh, Ibrahim. 2012. "Can the Organization of Islamic Cooperation (OIC) Resolve Conflicts?" *Peace and Conflict Studies* 19 (2): 162–79.

Tadjdini, Azin. 2012. "The Organisation of Islamic Cooperation and Regional Challenges to International Law and Security." *Amsterdam Law Forum* 4 (2): 36–48.

Turkish Asian Center for Strategic Studies. 2009. "SCO Secretary-General participates in 4th International Turkish-Asian Congress in Istanbul." Press release, June 16. http://www.tasam.org/en/Icerik/3296/sco_secretary-general_participates_in_4th_international_turkish-asian_congress_in_istanbul.

Yosephine, Liza. 2016. "OIC Adopts Resolution on Peace, Conflict Resolution Contact Group." *Jakarta Post*, October 19. http://www.thejakartapost.com/news/2016/10/19/oic-adopts-resolution-on-peace-conflict-resolution-contact-group.html.

CHAPTER 10

Fragmented Aid: The Institutionalization of the OIC's Foreign Aid Framework

Martin Lestra and M. Evren Tok

Introduction

Although the Organization for Islamic Cooperation (OIC) was not established with the explicit purpose of providing aid to the world's underprivileged, its founders were motivated, at least in part, by a wish to impersonate and enhance "Islamic solidarity" in the face of widespread poverty in Muslim-majority countries (İhsanoğlu 2010:3). Diverse OIC institutions emerged, including the Islamic Development Bank (1975), the Islamic Solidarity Fund (1974), and the Islamic Centre for Development of Trade (1981), dealing with both humanitarian and developmental concerns (Kayaoglu 2015:17). These entities signaled an initiative to address the wide range of needs and, progressively, to align aid with the third generation of human rights—rights to economic and social development (Iqbal 2007). Thus, only recently did the OIC stress again the need to ensure the "right to development" for members of the *umma*.[1]

By claiming to institutionalize "Islamic solidarity," the OIC raised high expectations from the outset, particularly in the realm of foreign aid. There were several reasons for justifying the OIC's role in this capacity. First, charity was part and parcel of many member states' core religious texts and practices. Second, the OIC emerged in the context of decolonization as the collective voice of the putative global Muslim community (*umma*). In the field of aid, it offered an alternative framework for cooperation among developing countries (Choudhury 1998; İhsanoğlu 2010), which could run counter to that of dominant Western bilateral and multilateral donors such as UN agencies and OECD members (Barakat and Zyck 2010:4; Hynes and Carroll 2013:4). Third, the OIC member states included some of the world's largest aid donors and some of the poorest countries. This meant that the OIC had both an inherent motive to act in relief and development as well as some means to do so. Fourth, at face value, aid was a suitable issue area for OIC cooperation, and it was supported in that respect by politics-averse members such as Saudi Arabia (Kayaoglu 2015:45; Svoboda et al. 2015:7).

For these reasons, foreign aid was a most likely case in which the OIC could act as a credible, effective, and cohesive alternative to established frameworks. However, what started as a promising political enterprise led to a puzzling outcome. Today, the OIC projects the image of a fragmented system of aid provision. Some OIC aid agencies, such as the Islamic Development Bank (IDB), are well-recognized and visible in the field of aid provision; others, including the Islamic Solidarity Fund (ISF), are marginal. Moreover, confusion remains as to what extent the OIC secretariat, rather than its member states, is leading the OIC's aid efforts. Finally, the OIC's aid provision remains scattered and uncoordinated, lacking direction and impact. Why is it that an organization bound by a common religious identity and charitable principles—encouraged by the need to define alternatives to mainstream Western foreign aid and looking for politically neutral activities on which all member states could agree—has not been able to build up a consolidated and coherent aid provision system?

In this chapter, we argue that the fragmentation of the OIC aid system results from the asymmetrical intergovernmental relationship between a small number of aid donors (notably the hydrocarbon-rich Gulf states) and a large and increasing pool of aid recipients (notably African states). We argue that, empowered by the asymmetrical setting of the OIC (there are very few donors with whom to compete), each donor has pushed forward its national aid champion, deteriorating the multilateral endeavor of OIC aid in the process. Simultaneously, because most members of the OIC are developing countries, their increasing demands have led to the design of additional aid institutions within this framework, and this has been to the detriment of a cohesive OIC aid system. The combination of these two trends explains why the OIC system is fragmented, structurally underfunded, and difficult to reform.

We discuss the OIC's aid fragmentation in three sections.[2] The first section provides an overview of the OIC's history of aid assistance. This includes a discussion of the OIC's shift to Africa. The second section discusses the OIC's aid culture, focusing in particular on the organization's emphasis on sovereignty and solidarity and its ambiguous relations with Western aid practices and agencies. The third section discusses the organizational issues that have led to this aid fragmentation.

The OIC Humanitarian Assistance System: A Brief History

While the original 1972 OIC charter did not mention humanitarian or development aid, the organization did from the outset recognize the needs of the poorest populations of the world, many of whom lived in Muslim-majority countries (Bakhit 2008). From early on, for instance, the OIC disbursed aid to Palestine,[3] and member states coordinated relief efforts in the midst of massive refugee flows after the 1979 Soviet Union invasion of Afghanistan (İhsanoğlu 2010:175). Despite these various efforts, the OIC's "longing" for a consolidated mechanism of aid assistance only materialized in the past decade, reflected in the revised 2008 charter's explicit recognition of the need to "cooperate and coordinate in humanitarian emergencies"[4] (İhsanoğlu 2010:175; Fan, cited in Sezgin and Dijkzeul 2015:313). What follows is a drawing of important events and shifts in the history of OIC aid provision, followed by an overview of the various actors involved in this policy.

Before the 2004 tsunami in Southeast Asia, the OIC's collective humanitarian efforts were ad hoc and short-lived. Structures emerged during specific humanitarian crises but rarely outlived them. For instance, during the Balkan conflicts in the 1990s, member states engaged in coordinated action to provide aid to the region, but their interest in pooling humanitarian efforts waned after the Dayton Accords.[5] Throughout the late 1990s and early 2000s, coordination of OIC humanitarian action was limited, consisting mainly of small OIC funds to Afghanistan (2002) and Sierra Leone (2003). A study by the Overseas Development Institute suggests that it was not until 2004 and the tsunami in Southeast Asia that the OIC once again emerged as a significant humanitarian player (Svoboda et al. 2015:8). The OIC contributed over $500 million altogether; however, aid was not coordinated and the OIC only managed to develop a fund for child victims of the tsunami (OIC 2005; Svoboda et al. 2015:8). This prompted a realization within the OIC secretariat that the organization's humanitarian structures were ill-fitted to support the OIC's impersonation of "Islamic solidarity" at the global level

(İhsanoğlu 2010:178). Hence, the 2005 OIC Extraordinary Islamic Summit Conference in Mecca marked a shift for OIC aid provision (Bakhit 2008; Cavalli 2009:34; İhsanoğlu 2010:176). There, foreign ministers of OIC member states presented the "Ten Year Program of Action" (TYPOA) under the title "Solidarity in Action." The aim of this reform package was to define "a clear strategy on Islamic relief action" to guarantee respect for the basic rights of Muslims throughout the globe (İhsanoğlu 2010:5–8; Svoboda et al. 2015:1).[6] Pursuant negotiations led to the establishment of the Islamic Conference Humanitarian Affairs Department (ICHAD) in 2007, which was placed under the OIC general secretariat and was responsible for the realization of the new strategy and the coordination of member states' humanitarian efforts (Fan, cited in Sezgin and Dijzkeul 2015:309).[7]

Humanitarian aid consolidation progressed in 2012 when OIC member states formally granted consultative status to nongovernmental organizations,[8] following the first OIC conference for OIC member-state NGOs working on humanitarian relief (Bakhit 2008:6). Twenty such organizations were granted consultative status in 2013 and were expected to provide guidance as well as technical and material support to OIC humanitarian aid and development initiatives (for further analysis of the OIC's cooperation with NGOs in general, see Chapter 12, this volume).[9] Additionally, in 2014, the OIC called for the establishment of an operational arm of OIC relief action: the Humanitarian Emergency Response Fund (Negrón-Gonzales 2015:97).[10] Beginning in 2011, the OIC expanded its humanitarian involvement in Somalia (2011), followed by the Philippines, India, Thailand, Italy, Trinidad, and Tobago, and, latterly, in the humanitarian crises of Syria and Yemen.[11]

The Islamic Development Bank and the Islamic Solidarity Fund

The first generation of OIC humanitarian actors comprised the IDB and ISF. The IDB (established in 1975) is the strongest multilateral organ of the OIC aid framework, with financial might that is disproportionate to other OIC institutions. For instance, the IDB's single "emergency package" for the 2004 tsunami ($443 million) outspanned the combined resources of other OIC aid institutions over decades.[12] Second, the IDB has been the most dynamic OIC institution. On closer examination, the IDB's traction is unsurprising. It is an "affiliated" institution, which allows it relative autonomy from OIC General Secretariat budget regulations.[13] It enjoys a closer working relationship with OIC donors, notably Saudi Arabia, which holds about a quarter of its shares (Islamic Development Bank 2012a:2).

The Islamic Solidarity Fund (ISF, established in 1974), though largely unknown,[14] was another forerunner of the OIC's aid system. Its main financing instrument is its *waqf*, which is based on voluntary contributions of OIC member states (İhsanoğlu 2010:40), notably those of Saudi Arabia.[15] The ISF funds diverse initiatives related to *dawa* (or proselytization), health, refugees, and so on. It is considered as "scattered all over."[16] It was placed under an emergency committee[17] with a clear focus on relief, though with limited success in its capacity to deal with natural catastrophes. It has remained largely unchanged since the 1970s.

The Islamic Solidarity Fund for Development (ISFD) reinforced the development activities of the IDB. It targets developing countries (Islamic Solidary Fund for Development undated; İhsanoğlu 2010:209; Islamic Solidarity Fund for Development 2011) and focuses on developmental goals, namely the reduction of poverty and illiteracy, the building of productive capacities, and the eradication of epidemics (Islamic Development Bank 2012a). Although similar to the ISF in its use of *waqf* to finance its projects, the ISFD has modeled its working methods on those of Western private financial companies.[18]

Since 2008, ICHAD has been the official humanitarian centerpiece of the OIC. Nested within the OIC secretariat, it is recognized as the member states' interlocutor on the topic of humanitarian affairs.[19] Its mission is to coordinate member states' actions during the policy-making phase by establishing pooled aid funds and by helping define humanitarian priorities.[20] It also plays a role in the implementation phase by creating OIC field offices, organizing donor conferences, and supervising OIC aid funds (Barakat and Zyck 2010:26).[21]

The Shift to Africa and OIC Aid Practice in Somalia

Africa's membership is central to informing OIC aid efforts. Of all OIC members, African states represent the largest group (twenty-seven states) and the latest accessions to the organization.[22] Due to the low cost of OIC membership, poorer Muslim-majority countries joined the OIC partly to benefit from wealth redistribution and economic benefit schemes (İhsanoğlu 2010:6; Bacik 2011:602; Kayaoglu 2015:17). Accordingly, the scope of OIC aid has notably increased on the African continent, although the lion's share of OIC-IDB development aid still goes to the Middle East and Asia (Islamic Development Bank 2015:1). As Barakat and Zyck (2010:45–46) point out, the recent surge in the use of "Arab agencies" (including the IDB) is driven not by crises in the Middle East—such as the 2003 U.S. invasion of Iraq—but by increased aid to African states. OIC reports corroborate this finding. Most beneficiaries of the Special Assistance Program of the IDB in 2014, for instance, were African states. Similarly, three out of the four beneficiaries of the IDB Trust Funds in 2015 were African states (Islamic Development Bank 2015:8).[23] Furthermore, the IDB-funded Special Program for the Development of Africa, implemented in twenty-two African states, has mobilized increased amounts of aid that surpassed its "initial commitment" (Islamic Development Bank 2012b). Finally, the ISFD has also granted priority to "the least developed member countries [LDMCs], especially those in sub-Saharan Africa" (Islamic Development Bank 2012a).

The OIC campaign to provide relief aid during the 2011 famine in Somalia may be considered one of the OIC's largest humanitarian successes (Fan, cited in Sezgin and Dijzkeul 2015:313). The organization played three simultaneous roles in technical, diplomatic, and donor contexts.

In its operational and technical role, the OIC set up its ICHAD office in Mogadishu at the peak of the crisis and acted as a coordinator for forty local charities, international aid agencies, and civil society organizations under the umbrella of the "OIC Coalition" (Sharqieh 2012:168; OIC 2013). From the onset, this organizational setting helped overcome many bureaucratic hurdles in the crisis-stricken country.

Building on its thorough understanding of local Somali culture and the Islamic identity of the organizations under its banner, the OIC was able to facilitate negotiations to get humanitarian access to areas under the authority of the Al-Shabaab Islamist militant group (Sharqieh 2012:170; Svoboda et al. 2015:13–14). As former assistant secretary-general Bakhit pointed out (2014:7), bringing the OIC's coalition of local NGOs into an alliance with other international actors "represents a new form of local access to affected populations, a system that needs further integration into international and regional humanitarian coordination framework to access crisis affected populations." In that regard, the OIC's efforts were conceived as complementary to those of the UN, in particular "with regard to inaccessibility of aid to certain areas of Somalia that are off-limits to international UN staff" (IRIN 2011).

Finally, aid agencies working with the OIC recognized its positive attributes as a donor. They highlighted the less cumbersome paperwork processes of the OIC—particularly in applying to join the OIC Coalition—as opposed to the UN. Local partners, for their part, expressed an appreciation of ICHAD, particularly for the ease with which they could apply for funds. In brief, despite some shortcomings—accountability and coordination issues with mainstream aid systems (IRIN 2011)—the OIC's performance in Somalia became a milestone in the history of OIC aid provision.

OIC Aid Culture

OIC aid discourses and practices reveal an acute concern for the preservation of sovereignty while attempting to embody traits of an "Islamic aid culture" (Petersen 2011:38). They also reveal ambiguous relations with other international and Western donors and agencies. As with other regional organizations, the OIC is "mindful of member states' sovereignty concerns" (Svoboda et al. 2015:7; see also Chapter 3, this volume), and these concerns are reflected in its aid provision.[24] The OIC favors the provision of aid bilaterally and directly to recipient governments, rather than through intermediary international NGOs (Barakat and Zyck 2010:32).

Furthermore, OIC aid seeks to strengthen the state. It promotes a kind of "carrot only" diplomacy, by which it offers aid as pecuniary compensation in instances of conflict (Al Maznaee 2009; Hossain 2012; Sharqieh 2012:170; see also Chapter 9, this volume, on OIC conflict resolution involvement).[25] In the Philippines and Myanmar, for instance, the OIC has always advocated in favor of the reintegration of the respective Moro and Rohingya minorities into the national community (Sharqieh 2012:165–67; OIC 2015b). Respect for sovereignty has been the baseline of the OIC's humanitarian assistance, although it received some criticism for its often noninterventionist stance, as expressed by the Bosnian leadership in the 1990s in the context of the Balkan conflicts (Barakat 2010:19).

The OIC evidently stands out in the humanitarian landscape as a religiously motivated intergovernmental organization. As such, it has the potential to promote an alternative approach to the dominant, secular "culture of development aid,"[26] that would benefit from greater cultural and religious resonance and legitimacy among certain recipient communities. Two features, in particular, seem to distinguish the organization from others.

One especially salient feature of the OIC's "Islamic" approach is its high degree of flexibility. OIC donors—and Gulf states in particular—are able to mobilize and disburse aid resources rapidly. Tightly knit personalized networks across donor and recipient countries (Kamrava and Babar 2012; Fargues and Venturini 2015), and high levels of popular support for donorship (especially in the month of Ramadan)[27] are some of many factors that make resource mobilization particularly effective in Gulf states. In 2011, $6.8 million was raised in three hours through a telethon for Somalia in Qatar (IRIN 2011). OIC donors are also swift providers of aid because they work bilaterally (Barakat and Zyck 2010:32) rather than through multilateral settings. Their aid is also made readily available, often in monetary form, directly for recipients' use. Thus, at the receiving end of the aid chain, aid professionals point to the easy access to OIC funds (Barakat and Zyck 2010). This aspect of bilateralism can often work to great effect when need is desperate and time is of the essence.

However, the direct availability of funds with a minimum of paperwork decreases accountability. Unlike Western donors of the OECD, the OIC does not align with formalized development standards of development or humanitarian aid. Moreover, the OIC asks for very little reporting from its partners and rarely evaluates the effectiveness of their aid provision (Barakat and Zyck 2010; IRIN 2011). Yet these characteristics are recognized by the OIC and OIC-related aid organizations as features indigenous to Islamic aid culture. In the words of Naeema Hassan Al-Gasseer, the former World Health Organization director for the Eastern Mediterranean, "We do things without saying that we're doing it. It is part of Islamic culture" (IRIN 2011).

In addition to the strain between sovereignty and solidarity, another element of tension in the OIC's aid culture is its ambiguous position with regard to Western, international, and other aid agencies. While the "Islamic" approach of the OIC could in theory give the OIC added value compared to other donors, in practice OIC aid is similar to that of other donors, whether in terms of focus areas, methods, or principles. OIC aid agencies are generally modeled after mainstream, international aid institutions. ICHAD, for instance, modeled itself after United Nations Office for the Coordination of Humanitarian Affairs (OCHA) (Svoboda et al. 2015:14), and the IDB after the World Bank (Touati 2011). The paradox is that while OIC aid institutions have largely imitated Western donors, their cooperation with those donors remains limited.

Western donors did not look favorably on OIC aid efforts at the outset. The OIC's privileging of Muslims in Bosnia-Herzegovina added to fears that it would fuel religious-based grievances in conflict zones (Svoboda et al. 2015:8), and this decreased Western confidence in the OIC's capacity to integrate existing aid frameworks. While faith-based aid has enjoyed renewed legitimacy in the aftermath of the Cold War,[28] Western donors remain concerned that OIC members overlook crucial steps in the aid chain, notably procurement and program supervision (Barakat and Zyck 2010:45). The OIC is also seen as having little commitment within multilateral aid agencies, insofar as it is poorly represented and underutilizes existing multilateral financing tools (Kroessin 2007:36; İhsanoğlu 2010).

Conversely, OIC officials and partners are critical of UN and Western donors. In fact, promoters of the OIC originally conceived it as a "South-South" alternative to Western multilateralism (İhsanoğlu 2010:9; Islamic Development Bank 2015:1). Western multilateralism—epitomized by the UN—was perceived to be unreliable "owing to the delicate international political power balances in which [it] operate[d]" (İhsanoğlu 2010:6). Individual OIC members also hold grievances against UN aid agencies. Gulf donors, for instance, resent being considered second-rate players, if not "banks," by their Western counterparts (IRIN 2011; UN Development Program 2012), and they criticize the UN's high administrative costs.[29] Finally, OIC partners (NGOs, charities, etc.) resent the asymmetrical nature of their relationship with the UN and fear being "swallowed up" by it (IRIN 2011).

Despite these issues, the OIC has progressively become a part of the existing humanitarian landscape. The OIC joined the UN as an observer in 1975 (Kayaoglu 2015:85). The two organizations have explored possible complementarities in the field of relief, as enacted, for instance, in the joint OIC-OCHA Plan of Action for 2015–2016 (OCHA 2011).[30] More generally, Secretary-General İhsanoğlu declared "cooperation with all organizations in the humanitarian domain" to be a "major objective" for the OIC (İhsanoğlu 2010:181), which translated into numerous rapprochements with multilateral and bilateral partners.

There has also been a proliferation of common initiatives at the operational level. Joint official visits, fact-finding missions, funds, working groups, NGO capacity-building trainings, conferences, and strategies have been developed between the OIC and a variety of humanitarian and political actors, including international nongovernmental organizations (OIC 2014a:3; OIC 2015b:4–6).

Interestingly, in their quest to become well-respected donors some OIC aid institutions—the IDB and ICHAD—have come closer to resembling Western institutions than their OIC counterparts. The IDB is involved in most global policy-making circles—from the World Bank to the OECD and the Bill and Melinda Gates Foundation (Kayaoglu 2015:111). The ISF, on the other hand, remains largely unknown. This newfound proximity between influential OIC institutions and Western donors may indicate a shift in the position of OIC member states towards increasing participation in Western multilateral schemes. In the last decade, for instance, Saudi Arabia, Turkey, and the UAE have significantly increased their funding to Western multilateral organizations (OECD 2015), which has been to the detriment of aid provided through the OIC or other alternative frameworks (the Arab League or the Gulf Cooperation Council). As one ICHAD official remarked, "[member states] just give tips to the OIC, compared to the UN."[31]

In short, despite initial distance and ongoing distrust, the OIC has "faced the imperative of dealing with global issues *as defined* by global actors" (Kayaoglu 2015:20; author emphasis). Today, the OIC and its larger member states condone the UN agenda for development (Hossein 2012). OIC officials express their wish "to be part of global initiatives to fight poverty, to achieve MDGs, to save human lives, regardless of religion" (Al Maznaee and Kebe 2009).

Fragmentation of OIC Aid Structure and Practices

International aid organizations are meant to increase donor coordination and aid effectiveness (Abbott and Snidal 1998; Martens 2002; Milner and Tingley 2013). Over the years, the OIC has consolidated its status as a humanitarian actor, while also becoming increasingly complex and fragmented.[32] This section discusses two main sources of fragmentation: the preferences of a few donors, and the power of recipient countries. These dynamics undermine the OIC's cohesion and effectiveness in delivering aid and perpetuate organizational inefficiencies.

Organizational Inefficiencies

OIC aid efficiency is hindered in a number of key ways. First of all, the aid institutions of the OIC have overlapping and often unclear operational mandates, a characteristic that the TYPOA reforms have not been able to rectify. The IDB and the ISFD, which were created with the purpose of focusing on developmental goals (İhsanoğlu 2010:46), often engage in humanitarian relief (İhsanoğlu 2010:46, 209), as was the case with the 2004 tsunami, the Sahel droughts (OIC 2005; OIC 2013), and more recently the outbreaks of meningitis and Ebola in Africa (Islamic Development Bank 2015:5).[33] Conversely, institutions set up for humanitarian purposes have also explored developmental activities. The humanitarian body of the OIC, ICHAD, has "focused more on recovery and development-oriented activities related to basic services and livelihoods" than on core humanitarian work (Svoboda et al. 2015:9). While such overlaps may stem from unclear mandates, they may also result from expansionist institutional strategies, where each institution promotes itself within the OIC aid system. An ISFD official thus recognizes that, despite the clear mandate granted to his institution, on occasions "inventing a role for the bank" is part of the job.[34]

Second, the OIC's agenda offers little predictability. Aid organs of the OIC depend on the voluntary contributions of member states. The ISF's financing instrument—the *waqf*—for example, makes it "an endowment with no mandatory contributions by Member States" (İhsanoğlu 2010:40). As a result, though the OIC has repeatedly expressed its gratitude for member states' generosity,[35] it is powerless when donor rhetoric does not translate into practice. For instance, the OIC Secretariat is still waiting on the would-be Humanitarian Emergency Relief Fund.

Third, the increasing number of aid-related institutions within the OIC has not been matched with adequate funding on the part of member states. This has led to multiple administrations being created by ICHAD without the necessary budget resulting in underfunded aid administrations (Kayaoglu 2015:111).[36] This issue is likely to become an increasingly sensitive topic in light of the expansion of the OIC's humanitarian agenda (Bakhit 2008:6; İhsanoğlu 2010:181; Shaikh 2014). With more work and more institutions, but with stagnating levels of funding, the OIC aid system presents the image of an overstretched framework in which many poorly funded institutions cannot live up to the rhetoric and expectations set by their member states. In short, organizational inefficiencies hinder donor coordination within the OIC. This internal challenge is as important, if not more so, than the external one facing the OIC: integrating into the global humanitarian landscape.

Reliance on a Few Donors and the Power of Bilateralism

If OIC humanitarian aid experienced tremendous growth—from $599 million to $2.2 billion[37]—between 2011 and 2013 (COMCEC 2015:2), this is attributable to *very few OIC member states*, notably the hydrocarbon-rich monarchies of the Gulf (Kayaoglu 2015:13). Dependence on these few donors—who often disagree on the focus of funding—has been detrimental to "a clear strategy on Islamic relief action."[38]

Though OIC bilateral donorship is not limited to Gulf states, the disproportionate size of Saudi Arabia's aid, and the increasing humanitarian activism of the UAE and Qatar, coupled with the regional demise of other sizeable players of the OIC (Egypt, Iraq, and Libya for instance), has led to further donor concentration in the OIC aid system (Almezaini 2011). Except for Turkey, whose aid disbursements continued to increase over the past decade, no other OIC member has provided a substantial alternative to Gulf donorship. By their single aid contributions, these few states may affect the outcome of relief operations. In Bosnia, by 1997, three countries—Kuwait, Qatar, and Saudi Arabia—pledged half of the resources donated by OIC members to Bosnia's reconstruction (Barakat and Zyck 2010:19).[39]

The Power of Bilateralism

The OIC's largest donor, Saudi Arabia, has been crucial in defining the orientation of aid institutions. A major funding authority of the ISF[40] and the IDB, it has contributed to establishing the latter's success story as an "island of efficiency" (Hertog 2010:101) within the OIC's aid landscape. Similarly to Saudi Arabia, Qatar is scaling up its efforts by creating the Darfur Development Bank (*Gulf Times* 2015).[41] By committing to multilateralism, the OIC framework is thus being used to extend national influence.

Rather than pooling resources, OIC donors create new aid institutions that are not supported by other OIC donors. Consequently, aid administrations proliferate without sufficient funding. For instance, the Saudi-backed ISFD has only collected a quarter of its $10 billion target funds (Islamic Solidarity Fund for Development 2011). Indeed, while Saudi Arabia provides more than half of the $2.6 billion to the institution, other wealthy donors have shown little commitment. Qatar contributes no more than Algeria, and the UAE has offered no contribution to the fund (Islamic Solidarity Fund for Development 2012). Thus donor-driven fragmentation among the small number of OIC donors is particularly acute—and surprising—given their claims for consensus and religious solidarity.[42]

At the operational level, weak coordination between OIC aid institutions is also the result of donors bringing bilateralism into the OIC's multilateral forum. In Bosnia, the OIC's contributions were relatively small compared to what individual OIC member states were providing bilaterally. In Somalia, the OIC logo never appeared on the aid that was delivered through the OIC coalition from its member states (Svoboda et al. 2015:8, 14). These anecdotes underline the fact that OIC foreign aid really boils down to the foreign aid of individual OIC member states. Like most other aid-providing institutions in the world—such as the United Nations and the European Union—the OIC aid provision system has to deal with its donor member states, particularly the Gulf donors. But "going bilateral" is especially salient among OIC donors.[43]

These (re)emerging donors are developing and consolidating their strategic foreign aid priorities. This is the case for Qatar, Turkey, and the UAE, as it is true for China and India in other regions (Neumayer 2003; Villanger 2007; Stuenkel 2011; Ozerdem, cited in Sezgin and Dijkzeul 2015).[44] Bilateralism in the OIC trumps multilateralism because the latter is perceived to water down the visibility of individual states (Svoboda et al. 2015:9). At the operational level, aid providers are more likely to receive aid bilaterally from OIC donors than from the OIC itself. In Somalia for instance, a "few received occasional small financial contributions from ICHAD for particular projects," while "some of the OIC's partners [were] able to access resources from OIC members [Saudi Arabia and Turkey]" (Svoboda et al. 2015:14).

Disagreements Among Major Member States

The roots of fragmentation are quite clear. In an aid framework dominated by very few donors, bilateral undertakings result in consequences for the whole. However, there are several reasons why OIC donors might want to "go bilateral." Most notable are the political differences between OIC donors. Also, disputes over how aid is disbursed among donor states affect the OIC as a whole, which evidently undermines the capacity of foreign aid in improving domestic vertical and horizontal accountability systems to better serve citizens.

OIC aid is best understood as a minimal common denominator. Indeed, "apart from placing the Palestinian cause at the top, there has been no clear prioritization of aims guiding institutional development" in the OIC (Kayaoglu 2015:18). This general observation holds for the OIC aid policy: throughout the organization's history, Palestine has mobilized the OIC's aid assistance (Islamic Development Bank 2015:7).[45] Increasingly, aid to Palestine has been presented by the OIC as the necessary condition to protect the "economic, social and cultural rights of the Palestinian people."[46] But politics or other interests repeatedly play out against the cohesion of OIC aid action (Hernandez and Vadlamannati 2013). The Syrian conflict continues to highlight major donor disagreements about the priorities and recipients of aid (Solmaz 2016); and following the U.S. invasion of Iraq, OIC states sided with their respective sectarian Sunni and Shia allies and did not disburse aid to support dialogue between the two communities (Sharqieh 2012:169). Disagreements within the OIC are not just the monopoly of Iran and Saudi Arabia. Barakat and Zyck point out that Iran and Qatar engaged in similar sectarian-based provisions of aid in post-2006 Lebanon (Barakat and Zyck 2010:26). Nor are these disagreements solely political. Commercial ventures, for example, have also spurred competition between Saudi Arabia and Turkey in Somalia (Khashoggi 2013).

Finally, disagreements on how aid should be disbursed exist. In developing countries, OIC donors and national agencies each "c[o]me with their own style" (IRIN 2011). This implies that disagreements on aid provision are not only an intergovernmental challenge; similar competing visions of aid take place *within* each donor country, among government agencies, para-public organizations, and wealthy charities.

Within the OIC system, different conceptions—more or less favorable to "developmentalize Islamic aid"—may coexist (Petersen 2011:15). Some organizations favor an approach that privileges strict humanitarian aid, providing food and medication, while others adopt a more developmental approach that involves building schools and mosques (IRIN 2011). The Turkish humanitarian campaign for Somalia bears witness to the heterogeneous and uncoordinated approach to humanitarian aid through the government's Directorate of Religious Affairs, the Turkish Red Crescent, and the Humanitarian Relief Foundation (ABNA 2011). Diverging views may also be present at the end of the aid chain, as donors and implementing partners might not share the same conception of how, where, or to whom aid should be disbursed.[47]

Aid is an important portfolio item for OIC donors (Almezaini 2011). Controlling the aid purse is a motive for domestic competition. For instance, reforms to foreign aid in Qatar and the UAE have led to "turf wars" between bureaucrats of the ministries of finance and of foreign affairs, as each has attempted to maintain (or gain) control over aid provision.[48] This makes internal coordination of the aid agenda more difficult and affects the OIC, as some domestic organizations decide to work with the OIC, particularly more "traditional" charities, while others prefer to collaborate with the UN.[49] Thus, in addition to other asymmetries of power in the OIC, domestic feuds within donor countries contribute to the overall fragmentation of the system.

That OIC donor states prefer bilateral initiatives over multilateral ones may explain the marginalization of the OIC as an aid forum, but—at least not completely—its fragmentation. If aid institutions continue to be created under the OIC—some thriving, others failing—that is because donors, empowered by the asymmetries of the OIC (there are very few donors with whom to compete), have "bilateralized" the multilateral by supporting their own aid champion.

Recipient-Driven Fragmentation: the Power of the Needy

We have examined how the role of the larger donors has often been detrimental to the OIC's multilateral aid cohesion. However, this displays only one side of the coin. Indeed, how does the presence within the OIC of a majority of aid-recipient countries affect the system? At the 2016 World Humanitarian Summit in Istanbul, OIC Secretary-General Madani characterized the OIC as "a unique organization in as far as humanitarian issues are concerned as it includes amongst its members some of the most generous global humanitarian donors and at the same time a number of countries that constitute the biggest humanitarian challenge for the international community" (OIC 2016). Because of this "unique" configuration, donor-recipient relationships in the OIC are a two-way street: recipients also drive reforms. Indeed, to echo former assistant secretary-general Bakhit, "the OIC . . . could not sit idle and let things happen without intervening given the important number of its Member States which were in need of humanitarian assistance" (Bakhit 2008).

It is often assumed that in donor-recipient relationships, donors exercise a high degree of leverage over recipients. However, recipients can also put pressure on donors (Nielson and Tierney 2003). This is particularly true when the number of recipients exceeds the number of donors, and when recipients

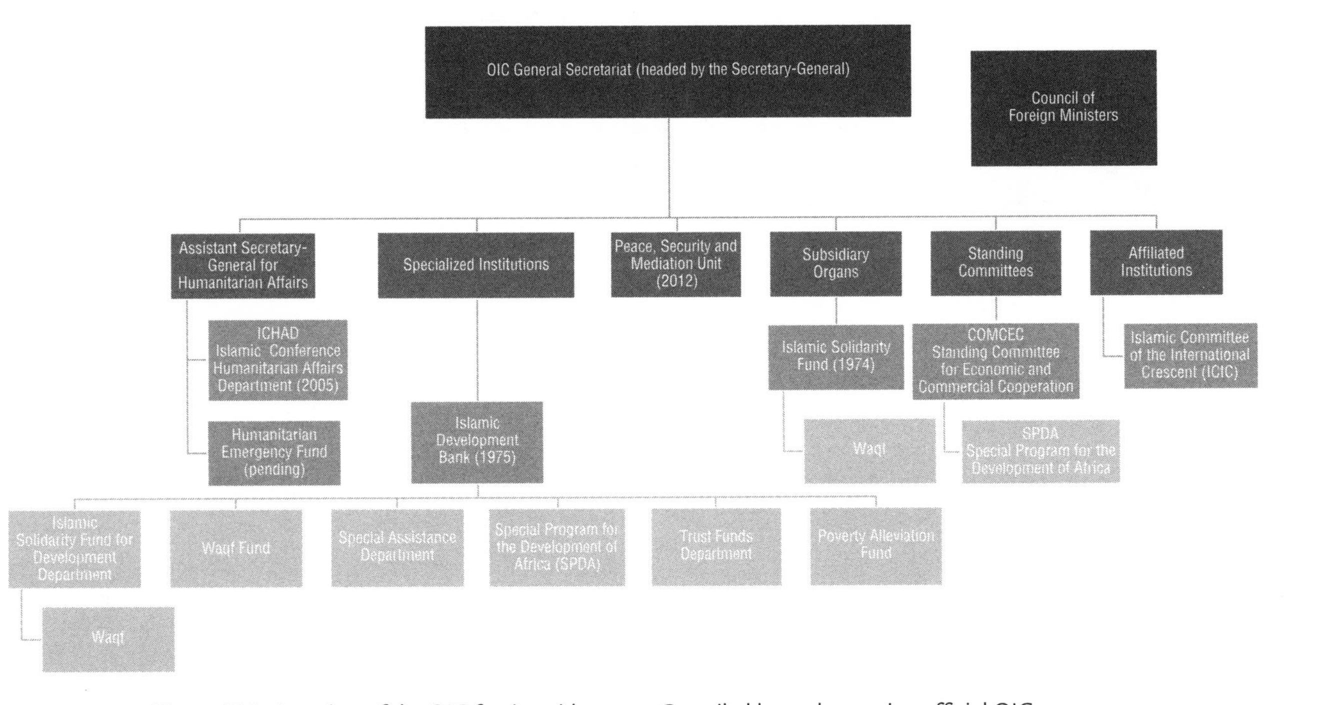

Figure 10.1. Overview of the OIC foreign aid system. Compiled by authors using official OIC sources.

have close allies among the community of donors. Created to promote Islamic solidarity, the OIC has been undeniably sensitive to the demands placed on it by its needy member states (Fan, cited in Sezgin and Dijkzeul 2015:312). As an aid consultant in Abu Dhabi told one of the authors, "It is harder in this [regional] arena to refuse than in others."[50] Similarly, an official from the IDB Special Assistance Fund thus recalls that when "the President of Senegal wanted the fund, Saudi Arabia paid."

Thus, in the mid-1970s, with twenty-four member states, aid institutions were created "in response to the demands of poor states facing growing hardship with rising oil prices caused by other, oil-rich, OIC members" (Kayaoglu 2015:17). Gulf donors, in particular, were under great pressure to redistribute their hydrocarbon rent after the oil boom of the 1970s.[51] This trend perpetuated over time as wealth inequality among OIC member states continued to grow. While the UAE and Qatar today rank at the top of wealthy nations (Espinoza, Fayad, and Prasad 2013:20), most states in need of humanitarian assistance are also OIC members. This has increased the pressure on the OIC's foreign resources as existing member states continue to request assistance. Thus, in 2004, after the tsunami in Southeast Asia, demands for assistance from the president of Indonesia at the Tenth Islamic Summit were answered by Saudi Arabia: "With the support and assistance of the Saudi Government, the OIC diligently embarked on a comprehensive plan to take full care of all the child victims of the tsunami in the region of Banda Aceh" (İhsanoğlu 2010:177).

This fact was aggravated by the enrolment of new OIC members—notably African—states also hoping to receive OIC aid (Kayaoglu 2015:17). Hence, in 2009, with fifty-seven member states, an OIC official similarly remarked that "here [in the Muslim world], there are more disasters, more poverty, there's a demand for humanitarian support—a need which has become even more pressing with the climate changes in recent years."[52] Recipient countries' administrations were even progressively shaped into "charity economies," designed to capture external aid locking in their pressure on OIC donors to continue providing aid (Nonneman 1988:28). In short, the recipients have added to the fragmentation of the OIC aid framework as increasing numbers of recipients have piled demands on the few OIC donors. Increasing—albeit legitimate and indeed desperate—demands for assistance have taxed a donor network that lacks a robust administration system. The small number of donors have not been able to cope adequately with fast-increasing demands and the resulting response to those in need has been compromised and fragmented.

Conclusion

A decade of reforms within the OIC was meant to open new horizons for the demonstration of "Islamic solidarity in action" (İhsanoğlu 2010; Rezaei 2012:196). With regard to foreign aid, although some consolidation has occurred, the OIC's aid system has become increasingly fragmented. Several aid "worlds" coexist within the OIC. Some perform well while others have no strategy, and almost all fail to achieve improvements in realizing human rights. Some are integrated in the humanitarian landscape while others are disappearing into oblivion. The main reason for this fragmentation, we argue, is to be found in the particular distribution of donors and recipients within the OIC, rather than in other factors, such as the sometimes tense relationship with Western donors or the cultural roots of Islamic aid. Fragmentation within the OIC aid system results from the role played by a few donors, on the one hand, and by an increasing pool of aid recipients, on the other. It has, by and large, undermined most of the OIC aid institutions to the benefit of member state agencies. It has also progressively overstretched an organization that cannot cope with increasing demands while facing systematic underfunding.

Notes

1. *Abu Dhabi Declaration on the Right to Development.* OIC Independent Permanent Human Rights Commission. http://www.oic-iphrc.org/en/data/docs/articles_studies/iphrc_abu_dhabi_outcome_2016.pdf.

2. We rely on several first-hand resources, including speeches, conventions, press statements, and official data. These data have been supplemented by interviews conducted over the last seven years with officials from the OIC system, representative officials on the board of these organizations, and charities from some major OIC aid donors (Qatar and the UAE).

3. Until 2000, the Islamic Development Bank's only trust funds were two funds dedicated to the Palestinian people: Al-Aqsa Fund and Al-Quds Fund (IDB 2015:7–8).

4. Charter of the Organization of Islamic Cooperation. Dakar, March 14, 2008, Article 1(19). http://ww1.oic-oci.org/english/charter/OIC%20Charter-new-en.pdf.

5. The Dayton Accords were reached on November 21, 1995 by the presidents of Bosnia, Croatia, and Serbia. They ended the war in Bosnia. They also preserved Bosnia as a single state

made up of two parts: the Bosnian-Croat federation and the Bosnian Serb Republic (see Clinton, Bill. 2017. "Dayton Accords." *Encyclopedia Britannica*. https://www.britannica.com/event/Dayton-Accords).

6. "Rights" were mentioned twenty times in the declaration. See *Makkah Al-Mukarramah Declaration*. Third Session of the Extraordinary Islamic Summit Conference, Makkah. December 7–8, 2005. https://reliefweb.int/report/iraq/makkah-al-mukarramah-declaration-iraqi-situation-mecca-document.

7. *On the Establishment of a Department of Humanitarian Affairs,* Resolution No. 11/35-C, Thirty-Fifth Session of the Council of Foreign Ministers, Kampala, Uganda, June 18–20, 2008.

8. *On the Humanitarian Activities of the OIC*. Resolution No. 1/42-ICHAD Forty-Second Session of the OIC Council of Foreign Ministers, Kuwait, May 27–28, 2015.

9. "The NGOs [benefiting from consultative status] come from all member states. However, their importance to aid work was reinforced to OIC member states as soon as 2004 after the tsunami in Southeast Asia, and operational cooperation deepened in particular as of 2006 in Lebanon" (İhsanoğlu 2010:177–78). *On the Humanitarian Activities of the OIC*. Resolution No. 1/39-ICHAD. Thirty-Ninth Session of the Council of Foreign Ministers, Djibouti, Republic of Djibouti, November 15–17, 2012. http://ww1.oic-oci.org/english/conf/fm/39/ICHAD-FINAL.pdf.

10. With the aim of raising initial capital of $100 million, it is still in the making as of this writing.

11. *On the Humanitarian Activities of the OIC*. Resolution No. 1/40-ICHAD. Fortieth Session of the Council of Foreign Ministers, Conakry, Republic of Guinea, December 9–11, 2013.

12. The ISF, for instance, has committed $207 million since 1973 (Habib Shaikh 2014), and the Islamic Solidarity Fund for Development (ISFD, launched in 2005) $433 million in the last decade (Islamic Development Bank 2012a).

13. According to OIC rules, "membership to these [specialized] organs is optional and open to OIC Member States. *Their budgets are independent* of the budget of the General Secretariat" (OIC 2016).

14. The authors have found only one instance that mentioned a specific interaction between ISF and the UN South-South Cooperation Unit (International Quran News Agency 2007).

15. Ibrahim Abdullah al-Khuzayem (director, Islamic Solidarity Fund, OIC), in interview with Marie Juul Petersen, Jeddah, 4 October 2011.

16. Atta Al-Manane Bakhit (Assistant Secretary-General for Humanitarian Affairs, Organisation of the Islamic Conference), in interview with Marie Juul Petersen, Jeddah, October 27, 2009.

17. *The Expansion of Activities of the Islamic Conference*. Resolution No. 7/8-AF. Eighth Islamic Conference of Foreign Ministers, Benghazi, Libya. May 16–22, 1977. http://ww1.oic-oci.org/english/conf/fm/All%20Download/Frm.08.htm#RESOLUTION No. 7/8-AF.

18. Ahmed Maaty (Islamic Solidarity Fund for Development, Islamic Development Bank), interview conducted by Marie Juul Petersen, Jeddah, October 5, 2011.

19. Since 2009 the OIC Council of Foreign Ministers has produced specific resolutions on the state of humanitarian affairs. See, for example, *On the Humanitarian Affairs of the OIC*. Resolution No. 1/36-ICHAD. Thirty-Sixth Session of the Council of Foreign Ministers, Damascus, Arab Republic of Syria, May 23–25, 2009. http://ww1.oic-oci.org/36cfm/w/en/res/36CFM-ICHAD-RES-FINAL.pdf.

20. Fouad Ali Al-Maznaee (director of Humanitarian Affairs Department, OIC), in interview with Marie Juul Petersen, Jeddah, 26 October 2009. See OIC charter, Article 29. ICHAD "may, *with the approval of the Islamic Summit or the Council of Foreign Ministers,* establish special funds and endowments (*waqf*) on a voluntary basis as contributed by Member States, individuals and Organizations" (OIC 2008: Article 29, italics added). See also Resolution No. 1/41-ICHAD, *On the Humanitarian Activities of the OIC.* Forty-First Session of the Council of Foreign Ministers, Jeddah, Kingdom of Saudi Arabia, June 18–19, 2014.

21. Resolution No. 1/36-ICHAD and Resolution No. 1/41-ICHAD.

22. These are Togo (1997), Guyana (1998), and Côte d'Ivoire (2001).

23. The four new beneficiaries are Comoros, Niger, Somalia, and the minority Rohingya community in Myanmar (IDB 2015:7).

24. *On the Establishment of an OIC Humanitarian Emergency Response Fund.* Resolution No. 2/40-ICHAD. Fortieth Session of the Council of Foreign Ministers, Conakry, Republic of Guinea, December 9–11, 2013.

25. Fouad Ali Al-Maznaee, Director, Abdoulaye Kebe, Professional Officer, ICHAD, in interview with Marie Juul Petersen, Jeddah, October 1, 2011.

26. This culture of development aid after World War II "was increasingly institutionalized with the establishment of intergovernmental organizations such as the United Nations and the World Bank as well as governmental aid agencies such as DfID, Danida, and USAID" (Petersen 2011:72).

27. Communication officer, Noor Dubai, in interview with Martin Lestra, Dubai, November, 23, 2011. Ali Al Suwaidi (general manager, Sheikh Eid Charitable Association), in interview with Martin Lestra, Doha, February 21, 2016.

28. Notwithstanding the climate of distrust toward Muslim faith-based organizations after 9/11 (Petersen, 2011; Benthall and Lacey 2014).

29. Aid consultant, Ministry of International Cooperation and Development, in interview with Martin Lestra, Abu Dhabi, October 24, 2015.

30. See also *On the Humanitarian Activities of the OIC.* Resolution No. 1/41-ICHAD. Forty-First Session of the Council of Foreign Ministers, Jeddah, Kingdom of Saudi Arabia, June 18–19.

31. Atta el-Mannan Bakhit (assistant secretary-general, ICHAD), in interview with Marie Juul Petersen, Jeddah, October 2, 2011.

32. See Figure 10.1 for an overview of the OIC foreign aid system.

33. Resolution No. 1/36-ICHAD.

34. Ahmad Maaty (ISFD), in interview with Marie-Juul Petersen, Jeddah, October 5, 2011.

35. OIC resolutions abound with references to OIC member states' intermittent bilateral contributions.

36. See *On the Humanitarian Activities of the OIC.* Resolution No. 1/41-ICHAD.

37. This is the equivalent of a 4 percent to 14 percent share of the total of international humanitarian aid.

38. See *Makkah Al-Mukarramah Declaration.* https://reliefweb.int/report/iraq/makkah-al-mukarramah-declaration-iraqi-situation-mecca-document.

39. In addition to money and funds, OIC Gulf member states also host the headquarters of OIC aid institutions and provide and advocate for OIC access to specific sensitive zones: in Gaza, ICHAD convoys were dependent on Saudi (and Hashemite) Red Crescent charities (Bakhit 2008; OIC 2015b).

40. Ibrahim Abdullah al-Khuzayem (director, Islamic Solidarity Fund, OIC), in interview with Marie Juul Petersen, Jeddah, October 4, 2011.

41. See also Fuad Ali Al-Maznaee (director, Abdoulaye Kebe, Professional Officer, ICHAD), in interview with Marie Juul Petersen, Jeddah, October 1, 2011.

42. Atta Al-Manane Bakhit (assistant secretary-general for Humanitarian Affairs, OIC), in interview with Marie Juul Petersen, Jeddah, October 27, 2009.

43. OIC donors in the majority still provide soft loans to support specific projects and programs, rather than committing to the core budget of the OIC institutions they have themselves created.

44. In the OIC, the UAE and Qatar are scaling up their national programs with the Qatar Development Fund and the Ministry of International Cooperation and Development, respectively, just as Saudi Arabia and Kuwait had done before them. Aid consultant (Ministry of International Cooperation and Development), in interview with Martin Lestra, Abu Dhabi, October 24, 2015.

45. Still today, Palestine is the OIC's common aid denominator. In 2013 and 2016, OIC foreign ministers called for the establishment of an "Islamic Financial Safety Net" for Palestinians and for further commitments to the existing Al-Quds and Al-Aqsa Funds (Kayaoglu 2015:64; OIC 2016).

46. *Report of the Secretary-General on the OIC Independent Permanent Human Rights Commission*. Fortieth Session of the Council of Foreign Ministers, Conakry, Republic of Guinea, December 9–11, 2013.

47. Again, this is particularly true for Gulf donors, who rely extensively on implementing agencies to carry out their work. Moza Mohamed Al Murar (general manager office), Abdul Hamid Najib Abdul Hay (advisor, Zayed Bin Sultan Al Nahyan Charitable and Humanitarian Foundation), in interview with Martin Lestra, Abu Dhabi, November 18, 2015.

48. GCC official, in interview with Martin Lestra, Doha, February 11, 2016.

49. Aid consultant (Ministry of International Cooperation and Development), in interview with Martin Lestra, Abu Dhabi, October 24, 2015.

50. Ibid.

51. Records from the UAE, Kuwait, and Qatar show that as early as the 1960s, Gulf leaders were under pressure to provide assistance to their neighbors, particularly Jordan and Sudan (Burdett, 2002).

52. Atta Al-Manane Bakhit (Assistant Secretary-General for Humanitarian Affairs, Organisation of the Islamic Conference), in interview with Marie Juul Petersen, Jeddah, October 27, 2009.

Works Cited

Abbott, Kenneth W., and Duncan Snidal. 1998. "Why States Act Through Formal International Organizations." *Journal of Conflict Resolution* 42 (1): 3–32.

ABNA. 2011. "Turkey Urges 57-Country Organization of Islamic Cooperation to Aid Somalia." *Ahluul Bayt News Agency*, August 7. http://en.abna24.com/service/europe/archive/2011/08/07/258087/story.html.

Almezaini, Khalid S. 2011. *The UAE and Foreign Policy: Foreign Aid, Identities and Interests.* Abingdon: Routledge.

Bacik, Gokhan. 2011. "The Genesis, History, and Functioning of the Organization of Islamic Cooperation (OIC): A Formal-Institutional Analysis." *Journal of Muslim Minority Affairs* 31 (4): 594–614.

Bakhit, Atta Al-Mannan. 2008. "The OIC Humanitarian Activities." Speech presented at OIC Inter-institutional Forum on the Occasion of the Celebration of the 60th Anniversary of the Universal Declaration on Human Rights, Geneva.

———. 2014. "Humanitarian Challenges: Perspectives from the South and Islamic Countries." Presented at the Annual WFP Partnership Consultation, October 29–30, Rome. http://documents.wfp.org/stellent/groups/public/documents/newsroom/wfp269388.pdf. Accessed January 17, 2016.

Barakat, Sultan, and Steven A. Zyck. 2010. "Gulf State Assistance to Conflict-Affected Environments." Research paper, Kuwait Programme on Development, Governance and Globalisation in the Gulf States. London: London School of Economics.

Benthall, Jonathan, and Robert Lacey. 2014. *Gulf Charities and Islamic Philanthropy in the "Age of Terror" and Beyond.* Berlin: Gerlach.

Burdett, Anita L. P. 2002. *Records of the Emirates,* vol. 6, *1966–1971.* Slough: Archive Editions.

Cavalli, Giacomo. 2009. "The New Organization of the Islamic Conference Charter." *Perspectives on Federalism* 1 (Single issue): 29–35.

Choudhury, Masudul Alam. 1998. "Some Long-Term Goals for the Organization of Islamic Conference." *Pakistan Economic and Social Review* 36 (2): 111–46.

COMCEC. 2015. *Improving Basic Services Delivery for the Poor in the OIC Member Countries.* Ankara: COMCEC Coordination Office.

Espinoza, Raphael A., Ghada Fayad, Ananthakrishnan Prasad. 2013. *The Macroeconomics of the Arab States of the Gulf.* Oxford: Oxford University Press.

Fargues, Philippe, and Alessandra Venturini. 2015. *Migration from North Africa and the Middle East: Skilled Migrants, Development and Globalisation.* London: I.B. Tauris.

Gulf Times. 2015. "Deputy PM discusses Setting Up of Darfur Development Bank." http://www.gulf-times.com/story/467339/Deputy-PM-discusses-setting-up-of-Darfur-Development.

Hernandez, Diego, and Krishna C. Vadlamannati. 2013. "Politics of Religiously Motivated Lending: The Case of the Islamic Development Bank." Unpublished presentation. International Political Economy Society. https://ncgg.princeton.edu/IPES/2013/papers/F310_rm1.pdf.

Hertog, Steffen. 2010. *Princes, Brokers, and Bureaucrats Oil and the State in Saudi Arabia.* Ithaca, NY: Cornell University Press.

Hossain, Ishtiaq. 2012. "The Organization of Islamic Conference (OIC): Nature, Role, and the issues." *Journal of Third World Studies* 29 (1): 287.

Hynes, William, and Peter Carroll. 2013. *Engaging with Arab Aid Donors: The DAC Experience.* IIIS Discussion Paper No. 424. https://papers.ssrn.com/sol3/papers.cfm?abstract_id=2267136.

İhsanoğlu, Ekmeleddin. 2010. *The Islamic World in the New Century: The Organization of the Islamic Conference 1969–2009.* London: Hurst.

International Quran News Agency. 2007. "OIC Body Receives UNDP South-South Cooperation Award." http://www.iqna.ir/en/news/1614984/-oic-body-receives-undp-south-south-cooperation-award.

Iqbal, Khurshid. 2007. "The Declaration on the Right to Development and Implementation." *Political Perspectives* 1 (10): 1–39.

IRIN. 2011. "Arab and Muslim Aid and the West—'Two China Elephants.'" IRIN News and Analysis, October 19. http://www.irinnews.org/analysis/2011/10/19.

Islamic Development Bank. 2010. "Who We Work With." http://thatswhy.isdb.org/irj/go/km/docs/documents/IDBDevelopments/Internet/thatswhy/en/who-we-work-with.html.

———. 2012a. "The Islamic Solidarity Fund for Development." Jeddah: IDB. http://www.isdb.org/irj/go/km/docs/documents/IDBDevelopments/Internet/English/IDB/CM/ISFD/ISFD_brief.html.

———. 2012b. "Special Program for the Development of Africa." *Progress Report.* Islamic Development Bank Group, April. http://www.isdb.org/irj/go/km/docs/documents/IDBDevelopments/Internet/English/IDB/CM/Publications/SPDA/2012-4_SPDA_Outreach_en.pdf.

———. 2015. *41 Years in the Service of Development.* Jeddah: IDB. http://www.isdb.org/irj/go/km/docs/documents/IDBDevelopments/Internet/English/IDB/CM/Publications/41%20Years%20in%20the%20Service%20of%20Development.pdf.

———. 2016. "Kuala Lumpur Office—Malaysia." Jeddah: IDB. http://www.IDB.org/irj/go/km/docs/documents/IDBDevelopments/Internet/English/IDB/CM/About%20IDB/Organization/ROK.html.

———. 2017. "ISDB Chart." http://www.isdb.org/irj/go/km/docs/documents/IDBDevelopments/Internet/English/IDB/CM/About%20IDB/Senior%20Officials/IDB_Chart.pdf.

Islamic Solidarity Fund for Development. 2011. *Fourth Annual Report.* Jeddah: IDB. http://www.isdb.org/irj/go/km/docs/documents/IDBDevelopments/Internet/English/IDB/CM/ISFD/ISFD%20Annaul%20Report%201432H.pdf.

———. 2012. "Presentation." Jeddah: IDB. http://www.isdb.org/irj/go/km/docs/documents/IDBDevelopments/Internet/English/IDB/CM/ISFD/ISFD_brief.html.

———. 2013. "Strategic Partners." Jeddah: IDB. https://isfd.isdb.org/EN/who_we_are/Pages/Strategic-Partners.aspx.

———. (undated). *ISFD Brochure.* Jeddah: IDB. http://www.isdb.org/irj/go/km/docs/documents/IDBDevelopments/Internet/English/IDB/CM/ISFD/Brochure/ISFD.pdf.

Kamrava, Mehran, and Zahra Babar. 2012. *Migrant Labor in the Persian Gulf.* London: Hurst.

Kayaoglu, Turan. 2015. *The Organization of Islamic Cooperation: Politics, Problems, and Potential.* London: Routledge.

Khashoggi, Jamal. 2013. "Are Turks in Somalia for the Hajj or to Sell Beads?" *Arab Saga* (blog). http://arabsaga.blogspot.com/2013/01/are-turks-in-somalia-for-hajj-or-to.html. Accessed June 5, 2018.

Kroessin, Mohammed R. 2007. "Worlds Apart? Muslim Donors and International Humanitarianism." *Forced Migration Review.* http://www.fmreview.org/FMRpdfs/FMR29/36.pdf.

Martens, Bertin. 2002. *The Institutional Economics of Foreign Aid.* Cambridge: Cambridge University Press.

Milner, Helen and Dustin Tingley. 2013. "The Choice for Multilateralism: Foreign Aid and American Foreign Policy." *Review of International Organizations* 8 (3): 313–41.

Negrón-Gonzales, M. 2015. "Organization of Islamic Cooperation." In *International Organizations and the Implementation of the Responsibility to Protect: The Humanitarian Crisis in Syria,* ed. Daniel Silander and Don Wallace, 90–109. Abingdon: Routledge.

Neumayer, Eric. 2003. "What Factors Determine the Allocation of Aid by Arab Countries and Multilateral Agencies?" *Journal of Development Studies* 39 (4): 134–47.

Nielson, Daniel L., and Michael J. Tierney. 2003. "Delegation to International Organizations: Agency Theory and World Bank Environmental Reform." *International Organization* 57 (2): 241–76.

Nonneman, Gerd. 1988. *Development, Administration and Aid in the Middle East.* London: Routledge.

OCHA. 2011. UN and Organization of Islamic Cooperation Strengthen Ties on Humanitarian Affairs. http://www.unocha.org/story/un-and-organization-islamic-cooperation-strengthen-ties-humanitarian-affairs.

OECD. 2015. "Multilateral Aid 2015: Better Partnerships for a Post-2015 World." Paris: OECD. http://www.oecd.org/dac/financing-sustainable-development/multilateral_aid_2015_in_figures.pdf.

OIC. 2005. "The OIC Commends Its Member States for Their Support and Solidarity in Alleviating the Tsunami Victims' Plight in Asia." *Reliefweb*, January 13. http://reliefweb.int/report/indonesia/oic-commends-its-member-states-their-support-and-solidarity-alleviating-tsunami.

———. 2013. *Resolution No. 1/40-ICHAD on the Humanitarian Activities of the OIC*, 40th Session of the Council of Foreign Ministers, Conakry, Republic of Guinea, December 9–11. https://www.oic-oci.org/subweb/cfm/40/fm/en/docs/ICHAD-40-CFM%20-RES-FINAL-ENG.pdf.

———. 2014. "Report of the OIC-OCHA Joint Mission to Iraq." https://www.oic-oci.org/upload/pages/departments/ichad/oic_ocha_iraq_2014_en.pdf.

———. 2015a. "Islamic Declaration on Global Climate Change | International Islamic Climate Change Symposium." http://islamicclimatedeclaration.org/islamic-declaration-on-global-climate-change.

———. 2015b. "OIC Continues to Mobilize Efforts for Political and Humanitarian Assistance to Rohingya Refugees." *Reliefweb,* May 24. http://reliefweb.int/report/myanmar/oic-continues-mobilize-efforts-political-and-humanitarian-assistance-rohingya.

———. 2016. *Final Communique of the 13th Islamic Summit of the Heads of State/Government of the OIC Member States.* http://www.oic-oci.org/oicv2/m/en/topic/?t_id=11093&t_ref=4364&lan.

Petersen, Marie Juul. 2011. "For Humanity or for the Umma? Ideologies of Aid in Four Transnational Muslim NGOs." PhD diss., University of Copenhagen.

———. 2012. *Islamic or Universal Human Rights? The OIC's Independent Permanent Human Rights Commission.* DIIS report. Copenhagen: Danish Institute for International Studies. http://pure.diis.dk/ws/files/66504/RP2012_03_Islamic_human_rights_web.pdf.

Rezaei, Alireza. 2012. Review of *The Islamic World in the New Century: The Organization of the Islamic Conference, 1969–2009*, by Ekmeleddin İhsanoğlu. *Middle East Journal* 66 (1): 196–97.

Sezgin, Zeynep, and Dennis Dijkzeul. 2015. *The New Humanitarians in International Practice: Emerging Actors and Contested Principles.* Abingdon: Routledge.

Shaikh, Habib. 2014. "OIC Seeks Support for Islamic Solidarity Fund." *Arab News,* April 22. http://www.arabnews.com/news/559306.

Sharqieh, Ibrahim. 2012. "Can the Organization of Islamic Cooperation (OIC) Resolve Conflicts?" *Peace and Conflict Studies* 19 (2): 162–79.

Stuenkel, Oliver. 2011. "India's and Brazil's Foreign Aid and Their Roles in the Future Development Architecture." Presentation at the workshop A Future for Aid Data, University of

Birmingham, Birmingham, UK, November 1, 2011. http://www.birmingham.ac.uk/Documents/college-social-sciences/government-society/idd/research/aid-data/workshop-31-10-11/oliver-stuenkel.pdf.

Svoboda, E., Steven A. Zyck, Daud Osman, and Abdirashid Hashi. 2015. "Islamic Humanitarianism? The Evolving Role of the Organization for Islamic Cooperation in Somalia and Beyond." London: Overseas Development Institute. https://www.odi.org/publications/9218-islamic-humanitarianism-evolving-role-organisation-islamic-cooperation-somalia-and-beyond.

Touati, Sylvain. 2011. "L'Islam et Les ONG Islamiques Au Niger." Institut Français des Relations Internationales, January. https://www.ifri.org/fr/publications/enotes/lislam-ong-islamiques-niger.

UN High Commissioner for Refugees. 2015. "Gulf Donors and NGOs Assistance to Syrian Refugees in Jordan." *Reliefweb*, May 12. http://reliefweb.int/report/jordan/gulf-donors-and-ngos-assistance-syrian-refugees-jordan.

———. 2016. "Gulf Donors and NGOs Assistance to Syrian Refugees in Jordan." *Reliefweb*, May 12. http://reliefweb.int/report/jordan/gulf-donors-and-ngos-assistance-syrian-refugees-jordan.

CHAPTER 11

Governance of Refugees in the OIC

Zeynep Şahin Mencütek

Introduction

In the words of Sadako Ogata, former United Nations High Commissioner for Refugees, "the refugee issue must be put to all governments and peoples as a test of their commitment to human rights" (UNHCR 1991). Indeed, the link between human rights and the plight of refugees is inextricable. Violations of human rights, persecution, and violence ultimately cause mass refugee exoduses and internal displacements. During the process of seeking asylum, many displaced people encounter destination countries' restrictive measures such as border closures, rejections, and detentions, as well as cruel, inhuman, or degrading treatment. The respect for human rights is the most important aspect of the protection of refugees throughout their journey in seeking asylum, during their stay in host countries, and (ideally) during their voluntary and safe repatriation to their origin countries. But while everyone has the right to seek asylum from persecution,[1] states also have the right to accept or deny asylum applications.

Approximately 70 percent of the world's refugees reside in OIC member states. Although the OIC region is a major host (as well as a main source) of refugees, the issue has not in reality been at the forefront of the OIC's agenda. Ongoing conflicts, human rights abuses, as well as lack of resources make protection of these refugees and internally displaced persons (forced migrants) difficult. Their presence also creates a serious economic and social burden on localities where they seek asylum. With the OIC region being in the unique position of both host and source of the greatest number of forced migrants, this has created a need for a legal framework and policies for the protection of these vulnerable populations in OIC member states.

This chapter aims to trace the genealogy of the OIC's refugee initiatives by examining the existing structures, policies, and practices of the OIC regarding the protection of forced migrants and discussing to what extent member states share the refugee burden. The study also explains the major shifts in OIC policies, analyzing the factors that have influenced the changes in its initiatives.

Based on an analysis of the Islamic Summit resolutions and declarations from 1969 to 2016, the OIC's main outputs regarding the protection of forced migrants have been limited to rather weak policy programs, information exchange activities, and a few concrete initiatives, such as a trust fund for returned refugees. One notable exception is the Palestinian refugee issue, which has been a permanent item on the OIC's agenda; numerous resolutions have addressed the organization's concerns over the conditions of Palestinian refugees, urging member states to provide support. Only in 2012 did the OIC draft a basic legal instrument about refugee protection, the Ashgabat Declaration. Many of the OIC's initiatives have remained suggestive, as the OIC has avoided developing a binding treaty, which would set mechanisms of monitoring, adjudication, and sanctions—requiring the compliance of member states. This chapter argues that, despite frequent references to Islamic law about forced migration, the OIC's declarations and resolutions are primarily indebted to international law and closely resemble United Nations High Commissioner for Refugees (UNHCR) statements. It also proposes that the evolution in OIC policies have been driven mainly by two factors: the protracted forced migration situations that have caused a disproportional spread of refugee burdens among member states, and calls by the UNHCR for the OIC to take concrete action. The OIC's limited action in relation to the ongoing Syrian refugee crisis and Rohingya refugees have made it clear that the organization lacks effective mechanisms for collective action and burden sharing.

This chapter has five sections. The first section gives an overview of international refugee law and the role of international organizations in refugee protection to provide comparative insights. The second section traces the roots and evolution of refugee governance in the OIC, laying the groundwork for a discussion of the main characteristics of the OIC's policies in the third section. Testing the practical refugee protection commitment of the OIC, the fourth section explores the position of the OIC in relation to the Syrian refugee crisis and the Rohingya refugees. The last section makes tentative conclusions, seeking to place the OIC in broader debates on the role of intergovernmental organizations to develop, spread, and implement norms and policies for refugee protection.

Overview of International Refugee Law and Organizations

Refugees are people who cross international borders to seek safety due to human rights abuses, persecution, and conflicts in their country of origin. The protection of refugees is guaranteed under International Humanitarian Law (IHL), the Refugee Convention of 1951, and the 1967 Convention and Protocol Relating to the Status of Refugees (hereafter collectively called the Convention). While the Convention was originally drafted to address the refugee situation in Europe before 1951, the 1967 Protocol broadened its applicability by removing geographical and time limits.[2] These key documents introduced the non-refoulement right of refugees, outlining that a refugee should not be returned to a country where he or she faces serious threats to his or her life or freedom (Article 33). The Convention also lists a set of positive rights, ensuring refugees' access to work (Articles 17–19), housing (Article 21), education (Article 22), public relief and assistance (Article 23); and access to courts (Article 16). It also protects refugees' freedom of religion (Article 4), freedom of movement within the territory (Article 26), and right to obtain identity and travel documents (Articles 27 and 28).

Globally, the UNHCR is the fundamental organization dealing with refugees and internally displaced persons (IDPs). Since 1995, UNHCR has committed to six main goals for the protection of refugees by focusing on burden sharing, including (1) strengthening implementation of the Convention; (2) protecting refugees within broader migration movements; (3) sharing burdens and responsibilities more equitably and building capacities to receive and protect refugees; (4) addressing security related concerns more effectively; (5) redoubling the search for durable solutions; and (6) meeting the protection needs of refugee women and refugee children (UNHCR 2006:17).

Until recently the OIC's involvement with refugees had largely included the gathering of data and publishing relevant statements about the refugee burden in the Muslim world with the intent of raising awareness and attracting funds to ameliorate similar crises. The organization has gradually introduced resolutions and declarations, which are nonbinding guidelines that provide a general framework for action. These guidelines set collective norms and rules and delineate some distributive goals such as calling on member states to extend their financial aid to refugee-hosting countries. In recent years however, the OIC has moved beyond simply publishing data to a more proactive stance, largely due to the refugee burden in member states and increased collaboration with UNHCR.

The Genealogy of OIC Initiatives

The massive migration of people from and to OIC countries started long before the organization was even established. In 1947, for instance, nearly 7 million Muslims were moved from India to Pakistan; in 1949, the forced flight of Palestinians began; in 1956, more than 200,000 Algerians fled to Morocco and Tunisia—to mention just a few examples. The increasing number of civil wars and international conflicts since the end of the Cold War as well as human rights violations and state failures have made forced migration a common phenomenon for many in the OIC region. Some of the most protracted and complex forced migration situations in the last decades are found in Afghanistan, Iraq, Palestine, Syria, and Sudan.

As of 2017, the vast majority of the world's forcibly displaced people come from OIC member states: Around half of all refugees originate from four OIC countries: Syria (5.5 million), Afghanistan (2.5 million), Sudan (1.4 million), and Somalia (1.0 million).[3] At the same time, OIC member states including Lebanon, Turkey and Jordan are among the leading refugee host countries. Five of six top refugee host countries are OIC members: Turkey, Pakistan, Lebanon, Iran, Ethiopia, and Jordan. Additionally, there are some 5.3 million Palestinian refugees living in Lebanon, Syria, Jordan, the West Bank, and Gaza. Turkey was the largest refugee-hosting country from 2014 to 2017, replacing Pakistan, which had occupied this rank for over a decade. The ratio of refugees to population is the highest in Lebanon, where one in six people is a refugee, and Jordan, where it is one in eleven.[4]

Many host states have had a consistent history of resisting the international refugee rights regime. Twenty-two OIC member states[5] have not signed the Convention, believing that international refugee law would erode their sovereignty and preferring instead to protect the status quo based on temporary protection. Signing the Convention would place a legal constraint on states to decide who may enter and remain on their territory and would introduce a set of rights standards that would have to be reflected in domestic law (Gammeltoft-Hansen 2014:574). In countries that have not signed the Convention, refugees are denied access to legal and political means to protect their basic rights.

In this context, UNHCR has viewed the OIC as a partner since the early 1980s, although many OIC members are not party to the Convention. UNHCR nonetheless has signed memorandum of understanding agreements with governments of nonsignatory countries to outline formal relationships with member states. This allows UNHCR some legitimacy to involve itself in the forced migrant-related issues in those territories. Due to its mission to protect and assist refugees around the world, UNHCR has supported outcomes that would result in the OIC developing policies to address the causes and impacts of forced migration in member countries as well as to develop durable solutions for them.

Refugee Issues in the OIC's Policy Programs from 1981 to 2000

The first time the OIC explicitly addressed refugee issues was at the 1981 Mecca Summit, where UNHCR was invited to participate.[6] The outcome document from the summit, the Mecca Declaration, "expressed its extreme concern over the conditions of Afghan refugees, and urged the provision of assistance to them and the creation of favorable conditions for their return to their homes."[7] Referring to Islamic solidarity, the OIC called on its members to provide financial and material aid not only to Afghan, but also Eritrean refugees. A few years later, at the 1984 Islamic Summit, the issue of Palestinian refugees was discussed. The summit produced the resolution entitled *The Palestine Question and the Situation in the Middle East*, condemning Israel for dismantling Palestinian refugee camps in the West Bank, Gaza Strip, Jordan, and Lebanon.[8]

While the OIC's refugee policies were initially focused on member-state action, in 1987 the organization for the first time explicitly encouraged integration into the international refugee regime. At the Islamic Summit in Kuwait, the organization urged its member states to cooperate with UNHCR, calling on them to "contribute towards meeting the humanitarian requirements of the refugees in cooperation with the efforts exerted by the UNHCR and other international organizations," thus "strengthening cooperation with UNHCR."[9] At the same summit, the OIC also adopted a separate resolution specifically on refugees, including the issue in its policy programs.[10]

In the 1990s, the issue of refugees became a more frequent item on the agenda of the Islamic Summits, reflecting the growing refugee/IDP crisis and the increasing number of armed conflicts in Muslim countries. Rights of refugees were included in almost all policy programs, and in a more elaborated style than the resolutions published in the 1980s. The OIC regularly expressed its appreciation to countries hosting refugees, donor member states, and UNHCR for extending humanitarian assistance to refugees in Muslim countries. For example, at the 1994 Casablanca Summit, the OIC called on member states and Islamic financial institutions to provide aid to refugees in the name of Islamic solidarity. More specifically, the same summit addressed the need to facilitate the return of Azeri, Bosnian, and Malian refugees to their homelands, to provide assistance for the Afghan refugees in Iran and Pakistan, and to work closely with UNHCR.[11] At the 1997 Tehran Summit, the OIC expressed its concerns for host countries' security, stability, and infrastructure, often under risk of collapse due to the presence of refugees. Echoing UNHCR, the OIC underlined the need for refugees' voluntary repatriation and the resettlement of returning refugees, as in the cases of Bosnia Herzegovina, Mali, and Sudan.[12]

Refugee rights were also a central part of the 1990 Cairo Declaration on Human Rights in Islam, stating that "Every man shall have the right, within the framework of Sharia's, to free movement and to select his place of residence whether inside or outside his country and if persecuted, is entitled to seek asylum in another country. The country of refuge shall ensure his protection until he reaches safety, unless asylum is motivated by an act which Sharia's regards as a crime."[13] Although the article ensured the right of free movement and asylum seeking, it also introduced an escape clause: If the host country considered that a person is fleeing due to a crime that is defined in Sharia, the person is not entitled to protection.

The main pillars of the OIC's refugee policy can be summarized as (1) to encourage member states to increase their humanitarian assistance, specifically financial assistance to refugees and refugee hosting member states; (2) to collaborate with UNHCR regarding voluntary repatriation and resettlement;

(3) to develop Islamic discourse on refugee rights in line with the international refugee regime.

Limited Implementation in the 2000s

At the 2000 Doha Summit, the OIC took its first steps in developing an instrument for the implementation of its refugee policy. The summit endorsed a resolution to set up the Trust Fund for Urgent Return of the Refugees and Displaced Persons, focusing in particular on Eastern Bosnia and Herzegovina, and asked member states to contribute to the fund.[14] After the Doha Summit, OIC resolutions made extensive references to refugee situations and called on member states to shoulder heavy refugee flows from member states (such as Afghanistan, the Gambia, and Yemen). Resolutions also discussed the return and reintegration of refugees to Mali and the Palestinian territories. In 2003, sixteen years after its first independent resolution on refugees in 1987, the OIC issued another independent resolution titled *The Problem of Refugees in the Muslim World*.[15] It was the first time the OIC had identified the 1951 Convention as the main instrument of refugee protection and called on member states to sign and ratify the Convention.

Despite the increasing number of refugee-related resolutions and other initiatives, the refugee issue was not reflected in the OIC's "Ten Year Program of Action" (TYPOA), launched in 2005, which reorganized the institution, introduced reforms, and identified institutional priorities.[16] While the program emphasized the importance of human rights, good governance, and anti-Islamophobia (Kayaoglu 2015:20), there was little mention of forced migration or other refugee-related issues, apart from a short sentence in the section called "Supporting Development and Poverty Alleviation in Africa" (Article 2[4]).

Although the OIC did not prioritize the issue of forced migration in its TYPOA, it continued to address the issue in several other documents. For example, the 2005 Covenant on the Rights of the Child in Islam touched on the rights of refugee children, noting that "states parties to this Covenant shall ensure, as much as possible, that refugee children, or those legally assimilated to this status, enjoy the rights provided for in this Covenant within their national legislation" (Article 21, 11).[17] Similarly, the 2006 Ministerial Conference observed that "there is a growing perception among OIC member states that refugee burdens are disproportionately spread. They believe that the international community is not supportive enough in helping them cope with the burden resulting from the presence of refugees and not active in seeking political settlements to resolve the refugee producing crises that have affected the Muslim world for so many years."[18]

In 2012, UNHCR and the OIC co-organized an International Conference on Refugees in the Muslim World in Turkmenistan (UNHCR 2012b). The conference's main message was to acknowledge the fact that OIC member states host a great number of refugees. The conference also referred to Islamic perspectives by stating, "We recognize that over fourteen centuries ago, Islam laid down the bases for granting refuge, which is now deeply ingrained in Islamic faith, heritage and tradition" (Ashgabat Declaration 2012: Article 2; UNHCR 2012a).

The UNHCR used this opportunity to clarify its expectations to the OIC member states. António Guterres, head of UNHCR, urged member states to accede to the Convention and to include principles of asylum into national legislation (Guterres 2009; Ashgabat Declaration 2012). The UNHCR also sought to create a joint committee for the implementation of the Ashgabat Declaration, which had been drafted by the OIC as a basic legal instrument about refugee protection. Within two months, the joint committee, made up by the OIC on Humanitarian Affairs and the Middle East and North Africa Bureau of the UNHCR, held its first series of meetings in Geneva to discuss implementation of the Ashgabat Declaration. The joint committee reiterated cooperation on protracted refugee issues in the Muslim world and discussed the formulation of a common two-year action plan (Corcoran 2014).

While the Ashgabat Declaration served as a platform for information exchange, it failed to introduce concrete policies or monitoring mechanisms. The proposed 2015 plan for developing the OIC's 2025 Program of Action only included a limited reference on the issue, subsumed under the heading "Joint Islamic Humanitarian Action" proposed by Turkey, with the OIC pledging to "maintain support for UNRWA [United Nations Relief and Works Agency for Palestine Refugees in the Near East] to enable it to carry out its mandate, and mobilize international pressure on Israel to comply with UN resolution No. 194 as to enable the Palestinian refugees to exercise their rights including the Right to Return to their homes and Repatriation."[19]

To summarize, the OIC has developed limited initiatives regarding the implementation of refugee policies over the last decades. They have included forced migration in the OIC's agenda, particularly by addressing the protracted refugee situations in Muslim countries to mobilize member states' and international support. They have prioritized the collaboration with the UNHCR by urging member states to sign the Convention and organize future joint conferences. However, the only tangible instrument launched by the OIC has been the creation of the aforementioned trust fund as an instrument for easing the share of financial burden.

Major Characteristics of the OIC's Refugee Policy

There are four principal characteristics which define the OIC's approach to refugees. Perhaps most obviously the OIC has indicated a preference for working with UNHCR rather than developing its own set of policies. While UNHCR collects data on forced migrant situations all over the world, the OIC works as an information-sharing platform for its member states. Additionally the OIC works with UNHCR to obtain financial, legal, and logistical help on refugee issues. It has appropriated the rights language of UNHCR, focusing on voluntary return, resettlement, and burden sharing as exemplified in the resolutions discussed in the previous section. This cooperation has been beneficial for the OIC considering the long-term expertise of UNHCR in standardizing the refugee rights language and in developing protection mechanisms adoptable to various host countries. This cooperation is indeed promising in that it signals a willingness on the part of the OIC to offer future support to UNHCR, particularly with burden sharing and resettlement, which both necessitate a large number of states' willingness to act.

The UNHCR for its part has referred to the important place of refugee protection in Islamic law and tradition, arguably adopting the language of OIC member states in order to find common ground for refugee protection. Instead of imposing its own discourse of "rights" and "responsibility," the UNHCR invokes themes and principles that might resemble Islamic discourse—a discursive strategy that can be observed in the UNHCR's many initiatives with the OIC (Abou-El-Wafa 2009).

A second defining characteristic of OIC policy is the attempt to integrate an Islamic perspective on the protection of forced migrants, explicating the compatibility between Islamic values and law and the international refugee regime in the 1990s and 2000s. Similarly, the secretary-general has emphasized this connection on various occasions. In 2009, for instance, Ekmeleddin İhsanoğlu stated that "Islamic Sharia applies the equitable and tolerant rules to refugees and how it is keenly concerned with their welfare and interests, while confirming human integrity and man's right to free decent life" (İhsanoğlu 2009:11). The OIC's references to Sharia and the need for Islamic action in addressing refugee protection were intensified in parallel with the worsening of refugee situations in member states. This emphasis on Sharia in refugee rights is closely related to El Fegiery's argument (Chapter 6) that since the adoption of the Cairo Declaration on Human Rights in Islam in 1990, the OIC has become an advocate of an alternative interpretation of certain human rights. However, a lack of theoretical coherence in the OIC's statements regarding human rights can be detected in its statements about Islamic refugee rights (see Chapter 4).

Among scholars of Islam, however, there is little clarity as to what constitutes Islamic refugee rights. Muslim scholars of human rights such as Musab Hayatli (2012) state that Sharia does not propose a comprehensive legal system for the protection of forced migrants. For example, while there may very well be a right to seek asylum, states do not have any obligation to provide asylum (Hayatli 2012:2–3). Also, even if Islamic law does provide rights to refugees, as some would claim, in practice Muslim countries rarely invoke these rights (Zaat 2007; Elmadmad 2008). Instead, the notion of "guest" has been widely used in Muslim countries' political discourses on forced migration, with most states giving preference and favorable treatment to fellow Muslims or Arabs.

Third, OIC refugee policies carry the imprint of a strong intergovernmental structure that allows for very little supranational authority. As is well-known, the strength of an intergovernmental system depends on the level of authority the organization has over its member states. In the case of the OIC, member states are reluctant to hand over power to the organization and turn it into an autonomous supranational organization, preferring instead to safeguard their sovereignty (see Chapters 1 and 3).[20] The mandate of the OIC does not allow the organization to intervene in the internal affairs of member countries, and, as such, the OIC is not able to address the root causes of forced migration or propose solutions for the treatment and protection of refugees in host countries. Furthermore, the OIC's ability to maneuver on the issue has been constrained by the fact that many of its members have different political views on migration-related issues, with some of the leading members such as Kuwait, Saudi Arabia, and the United Arab Emirates implementing rather restrictive migration policies and rejecting asylum to refugees. Finally, there are few opportunities for nongovernmental organizations (NGOs) and transnational civil society movements to interact with the OIC, although they play a vital role in refugee protection by urging states and governmental organizations to advance refugee rights and take action on protection issues (see Chapter 12 for a more general discussion on the OIC and civil society).

A fourth and final characteristic of OIC refugee policies is the lack of resources for implementation. Most OIC resolutions have been characterized by ambiguous terminology, avoiding concrete, practical solutions, standard-setting for protection and rights, effective burden-sharing among states, monitoring, and enforcement of compliance. This means that the OIC does not have the tools to assure the compliance of member states. The OIC has also continually avoided the identification and establishment of mechanisms to adjudicate possible disputes among member states and provide authoritative interpretations of the policy program. In the case of member noncompliance, the OIC rarely exerts authority to impose sanctions such as moral pressure, exclusion from membership, suspension of certain rights, or the imposition of fines. Moreover, it lacks the financial resources for assisting refugees and host member states. As Hirah Azhar discusses in Chapter 9, the OIC's chronic financial shortcomings, accompanied by diverging priorities of donor member states, have presented a serious challenge to building sustainable refugee protection problems.

The OIC's Refugee Policies in Practice: A Look at the Syrian and Rohingya Refugee Crises

Having sketched the genealogy of the OIC's refugee policies and identified some of its main characteristics, let us now take a look at how this policy unfolds in practice, zooming in on two recent refugee crises.

The Syrian Refugees

The tragedy of the Syrian refugees has received surprisingly little attention from the OIC. Although the organization noted that it had been following developments with deep concern from the beginning, it was only in September 2015 that the OIC raised its voice on the issue; around the same time Syrian refugees began to arrive in large numbers at European borders (European Commission 2015; OIC 2015f). In fact, an overview of 220 OIC news stories from 2015 shows no discussion of the Syrian refugee crisis before September of that year. Around that time, OIC Secretary-General Iyad Amin Madani expressed his shock and dismay at the harsh treatment by the Hungarian police of Syrian refugees who sought to enter Serbia, as displayed in international media. He called on the Hungarian government to respect international humanitarian law and the human rights of the refugees (*Alummah World* 2015). He then issued a call to the international community to deal with the crisis in September, stating that "this is neither a Syrian, nor Middle Eastern, nor European nor Muslim crisis. This is an international humanitarian crisis, in which precious lives are perishing" (OIC 2015a).

Reflecting growing international concern, the OIC held an emergency meeting of its executive committee on the humanitarian crisis in Syria on September 13, 2015. The committee's final declaration echoed previous OIC declarations, adopting the common discourse on refugee governance by addressing root causes, prioritizing burden sharing, and urging member states to join the 1951 Convention. Furthermore, the committee called on member states to consider adopting the OIC's Ashgabat Declaration. Unlike previous declarations, the emergency meeting declaration explicitly addressed the main causes of the Syrian refugee crisis, condemning the Assad regime and extremist groups, especially Daesh (ISIS) for their atrocities against civilians. This is an important shift from earlier declarations, insofar as the OIC normally takes a more apolitical stance, avoiding placing blame for humanitarian crises.

As it had done on other occasions, the OIC called on the international community and the UN Security Council to find a political solution, such as the creation of a multidimensional UN peacekeeping operation in Syria as a prelude to restoring security and stability in the country. Unlike previous occasions, however, this time the OIC publicly called on OIC member states to open their doors to the Syrian refugees, invoking principles of Islamic compassion and solidarity. The meeting encouraged member states to share the burden of refugees fairly, helping neighboring countries that had borne a disproportionate share of this burden. In particular countries such as Turkey, Jordan, Lebanon, Iraq, and Egypt were commended for their generosity in welcoming Syrian refugees (OIC 2015b). Three concrete policy suggestions were made: (1) to provide financial resources to the Emergency Fund; (2) to inform the OIC General Secretariat of refugee-related assistance and activities; and (3) to convene a ministerial meeting to adopt a plan of action or a strategy on refugee issues in the OIC region (OIC 2015b).

The OIC's inattention to the Syrian refugee crisis until 2015 can be attributed to three characteristics of OIC policies. First of all, the OIC did not want to intervene in the internal affairs of Syria (a member state) until its suspension in 2012. Second, many of its member states have varying political stances regarding the Syrian civil war and the relevant forced migration issues. The OIC does not have supranational authority that may require member states to take action, such as accepting refugees within their territories. But even if the OIC had such power, as the EU does, member states still have sovereignty to decide on their own refugee policies. As has been observed in the migration-linked crisis within the EU since 2015, member states might still resist the common policies imposed by a supranational authority.

In spite of the OIC's growing interest in the plight of refugees, what remained was the lack of resources for assisting refugees and host member states and for their implementation. As with previous crises, the OIC had to ask member states to increase humanitarian assistance to refugees, but it failed to introduce any enforcement mechanism—it just voiced its request. The OIC has never gone so far as to impose fines or sanctions in cases of noncompliance. Further, due to the lack of its own financial resources, the OIC has had a very poor record itself of allocating funding to Syrian refugees. The OIC was not among the top twenty-five donor countries and organizations that contributed to the Syria Humanitarian Response Plan in 2016, although the European Commission ranked in fourth place and UN agencies in twenty-third place. On the same list, Kuwait and Qatar, and Saudi Arabia—as the only three OIC member states—ranked in thirteenth, sixteenth and eighteenth place, respectively (Humanitarian Response Plan 2016). What is also noteworthy is that there is no record showing that the OIC provides funds to refugee camps in main host countries, whereas UNHCR takes primary responsibility for providing services to refugees living in camps in Jordan and urban refugees in Lebanon. As Lestra and Tok discuss in Chapter 10, the OIC's financial problems in refugee issues are a reflection of the OIC's general aid system, in which the large and increasing pool of aid recipients in the OIC arena outnumber the small number of aid donors, notably the Gulf States, including Saudi Arabia.

The Rohingya Refugees

In addition to the Syrian refugee situation, the OIC also engaged in the plight of the Rohingya refugees, asylum-seekers, and economic migrants who were stranded on boats in the Andaman Sea and Straits of Malacca (OIC 2015c).

The OIC has tried to mobilize efforts to assist Rohingya refugees across Southeast Asia, mainly through the provision of humanitarian assistance. The OIC's special envoy for Myanmar raised the issue at the OIC Ministerial Contact Group Meeting on the Rohingya Minority in May 2015. Some member countries made pledges to share the financial cost of refugees, and Malaysia and Indonesia promised to accept the Rohingya boat migrants as refugees and provide them with temporary shelter.[21] The OIC took part in providing basic needs and services, including food distribution, medical services, and education to the Rohingya refugees living in the camps and to IDPs. The organization was involved in service provision and worked with its network of humanitarian NGOs in hosting countries particularly during Ramadan (*Arab News* 2016). Differing from its limited involvement in previous refugee crises, this time the OIC communicated with many NGOs to launch a comprehensive action plan for refugee protection and prepared to launch a media awareness campaign across its member states. The minority Rohingya community in Myanmar also became a new beneficiary of the Islamic Development Bank Trust Funds in 2015 along with Somalia, Niger, and Comoros (Islamic Development Bank 2015:7).

Furthermore, the OIC advocated for internally displaced people to be able to return to their homes and for humanitarian assistance to reach the community that was affected by the conflict as well as for the protection of the community's status and rights, full citizenship, and equal opportunity (OIC 2015e). It issued a resolution on Myanmar's government: "Situation of human rights of Rohingya Muslims and other minorities in Myanmar . . . to ensure the return of all refugees and persons displaced from their homes, including Muslims." The resolution was adopted by consensus at the UN Human Rights Council in Geneva on July 3, 2015 (OIC 2015g).

It can be claimed that the OIC succeeded in having an impact at the international level, as it acted as a bloc at the UN to attract attention to the forced migration situation of Rohingya Muslims. In contrast to the Syrian case, OIC displayed an interest in the forced migration situation in Myanmar in the early days of the crisis. This attentiveness can be attributed to the location of the crisis and the possible stance of the member states. Myanmar is not a member state of the OIC and many member states do not have any interest or stake in this country. Attention to Rohingya Muslims may have been perceived as a politically neutral activity on which all member states could agree. Member states likely tended to approach the forced migration of a Muslim minority from a non-Muslim country from a humanitarian perspective (rather than a political one). The OIC may well have felt more comfortable in voicing its concerns about the suffering of Rohingya Muslims, working with many NGOs and trying to launch a comprehensive plan.

On the other hand, as was the case with Syria, the OIC's lack of financial resources was evident. While the organization provided substantial humanitarian assistance to forced migrants, the initiatives remained limited. As Lestra and Tok argue (Chapter 10), the case of the Rohingya Muslims displays again two reoccurring characteristics of the OIC's aid provision. First, it remains confusing to what extent the OIC secretariat, rather than its member states, is leading aid efforts; second, their aid provision, even in a limited sector such refugee assistance, is scattered and not fully coordinated, resulting (in this case) in a less-than-coherent refugee protection plan.

Conclusion

Although the international refugee regime has its own international convention and a specialized UN agency, UNHCR, efforts cannot be implemented without sustainable regional and intergovernmental cooperation. Given that most of the world's refugees and IDPs are in OIC member states, its support is urgently needed, and both refugee hosting member states and UNHCR value the collaborative possibilities the OIC presents to effect concrete actions to tackle the growing refugee burden.

This chapter focuses on the OIC's involvement in the refugee issue, examining its legal framework, policies, and practices. It traces the historical evolution of OIC refugee governance, describing how the organization's policies have gradually improved over time. The growing refugee/IDP crisis, along with the increasing armed conflicts in member states, have prompted the OIC to recognize the impact and importance of the refugee issue and to consider possible solutions that are compatible with the international refugee regime.

The chapter highlights four relevant characteristics of the OIC's approach to refugee needs. First, the OIC seems to prefer working with the UNHCR rather than developing its own set of policies. In collaboration with UNHCR, the OIC has proposed the 1951 Convention as the main instrument for refugee protection, arguing for the creation of favorable conditions for refugee return as the most preferred solution. Rather than trying to resist or bloc the language of refugee rights, it uses common terminology thanks to UNHCR's longstanding efforts to collaborate. Second, the OIC tries to show that there is a compatibility between Islamic law and the international refugee regime, the former having the capacity to enhance the latter. Thus, the OIC has made a rhetorical adoption in their ideology where refugee rights are sourced from both international law and Islam. Third, the OIC's refugee policies reflect the organization's strong intergovernmental structure. The OIC avoids intervening in the internal affairs of member countries, and, as such, the OIC is able to address neither root causes of forced migration nor violations of refugee rights in the member states. The fourth characteristic of OIC refugee policies is the lack of resources for implementation. It has done little in terms of establishing concrete enforcement or monitoring mechanisms.

The OIC's response to recent forced migration cases of Syrians and Rohingya Muslims exemplifies its limited capabilities. With the Syrian refugee issue, it became involved very late due to differing stances among member states regarding the Syrian civil war. Similarly to previous cases, the OIC prepared a declaration, called for burden sharing among member states in reference to the principles of Islamic compassion and solidarity, and urged member states to sign the 1951 Convention. Unlike previous cases, the OIC asked member states to accept Syrian refugees. But, as of the end of 2017, member states and the OIC have had a poor record of allocating funding to Syrian refugees. In the case of Rohingya Muslims forcibly displaced from Myanmar, the OIC displayed a much faster response in the delivery of assistance compared with that of the Syrian crisis. It also worked to raise the visibility of the issue at the UN level.

As demonstrated in these two recent cases, the OIC has been far from advancing current refugee rights or developing a substantive policy and instruments in refugee governance. It is equipped with few and relatively weak mechanisms for refugee protection despite its potential and the urgency of the issue. As it is not in a position to be active in developing burden share policies in refugee hosting countries and ensuring the protection of refugees, the OIC has attempted to emphasize the issue by reasoning and dialogue with governments. It has functioned as an information exchange forum, rather than an operative, protective, and coordinating body.

Nevertheless, despite its shortcomings and problems, the OIC has significant potential to develop an agenda on refugee protection mechanisms, create policies, and collaborate with not only its member states but also international organizations such as UNHCR and many other NGOs. Using its moral authority and Islamic legitimacy, the OIC could promote the international refugee regime in its member states. It could pressure member states that force their citizens to migrate and/or violate basic rights of refugees to comply with international refugee rights. Moreover, the OIC could easily manage the issue of resettlement strategically as both a responsibility and a burden-sharing tool, promoting and coordinating this through mutually agreeable arrangements. It could work on furthering local integration of refugees. It is undeniably clear that there is a need for a comprehensive refugee protection framework for internally or externally forced migrants initiated by the states and intergovernmental organizations such as the OIC. The OIC would do well to answer the call for much-needed action in a more coherent manner.

Notes

1. Universal Declaration of Human Rights, Article 14(1). http://www.ohchr.org/EN/UDHR/Documents/UDHR_Translations/eng.pdf.

2. "The 1951 Convention Relating the Status of Refugees and Its 1967 Protocol," 4. http://www.unhcr.org/4ec262df9.html.

3. See UNHCR, *Global Trends: Forced Displacement in 2016*. June 21, 2017, p. 3. http://www.refworld.org/docid/594aa38e0.html.

4. Ibid.

5. Nonsignatory countries include Bahrain, Bangladesh, Brunei Darussalam, Comoros, the Gambia, Guyana, Indonesia, Iraq, Jordan, Kuwait, Lebanon, Libya, Malaysia, Maldives, Oman, Pakistan, Palestine, Qatar, Saudi Arabia, Syrian Arab Republic, United Arab Emirates, and Uzbekistan.

6. The OIC's first two summits, in 1969 and 1974, did not include any discussions about refugees, asylum seekers, or migrants. See OIC's official web page on Islamic Summits http://ww1.oic-oci.org/english/conf/is/3/3rd-is-sum.htm.

7. Mecca Declaration of the Third Islamic Summit Conference. http://ww1.oic-oci.org/english/conf/is/3/3rd-is-sum.htm.

8. *On the Palestine Question and the Situation in the Middle East.* Resolution No. I / 4-P (IS). http://ww1.oic-oci.org/english/conf/is/4/4th-is-sum(political).htm#01.

9. Cairo Declaration. http://www.refworld.org/docid/3ae6b3822c.html.

10. *On Refugees.* Resolution 23/5-P (IS). http://ww1.oic-oci.org/english/conf/is/5/5th-is-sum(political).htm#23.

11. Casablanca Declaration. http://ww1.oic-oci.org/english/conf/is/7/7th-is-summit.htm#CASABLANCA%20DECLARATION.

12. Final Communique of the Eighth Session of the Islamic Summit Conference. http://ww1.oic-oci.org/english/conf/is/8/8th-is-summits.htm#FINAL%20%20COMMUNIQUE.

13. Cairo Declaration, Article 12. http://www.refworld.org/docid/3ae6b3822c.html.

14. *On Action Programme on Bosnia and Herzegovina and the Assistance Mobilization Group—B&H.* Resolution No. 10/9-P (IS). http://ww1.oic-oci.org/english/conf/is/9/9th-is-sum-political_1.htm#10.

15. *On the Problem of Refugees in the Muslim World.* Resolution No. 15/10-P (IS). http://ww1.oic-oci.org/english/conf/is/10/10%20is-pol-e1.htm#RESOLUTION NO. 15/10-P(IS).

16. "Ten-Year Programme of Action to Meet the Challenges Facing the Muslim Ummah in the 21st Century." http://ww1.oic-oci.org/ex-summit/english/10-years-plan.htm.

17. Covenant on the Rights of the Child in Islam. http://www.refworld.org/docid/44eaf0e4a.html.

18. OIC Ministerial Conference on the Problems of Refugees in the Muslim World, November 27–29, 2006. 13. http://www.unhcr.org/45ab8dd72.html; UNHCR (2006).

19. "The OIC-2025 Programme of Action," 18. https://www.oic-oci.org/docdown/?docID=16&refID=5.

20. From a comparative perspective, the OIC is not an exception among intergovernmental organizations engaged in refugee governance, insofar as many of these organizations also serve primarily as a platform for member-state coordination rather than work autonomously to enforce and monitor member-state actions.

21. Qatar donated $50 million, while Pakistan made a special grant of $5 million in food aid. Turkey promised to donate $1 million and to send a Turkish naval ship with aid workers to assist the migrants. In June 2015, the OIC arranged for aid packages to be distributed to over 1,500 Rohingya refugees in Kajang, Malaysia (OIC 2015d).

Works Cited

Abou-El-Wafa, Ahmed. 2009. *The Right to Asylum Between Islamic Shari'ah and International Refugee Law: A Comparative Study.* Cairo: UNHCR.

Alummah World. 2015. "OIC Express Dismay at Harsh Treatment of Syrian Refugees by Hungary." September 20. http://alummahworld.com/article/452/refugees.

Arab News. 2016. "Rohingya Refugees in Myanmar Receive OIC Ramadan Aid." June 26. http://www.arabnews.com/node/945261/saudi-arabia.

"Ashgabat Declaration of the International Ministerial Conference of the Organization of Islamic Cooperation on Refugees in the Muslim World." 2012. *Forced Migration Review* (special issue on Islam, Human Rights and Displacement). http://www.fmreview.org/FMRpdfs/Human-Rights/ashgabat.pdf.

Corcoran, Ann. 2014. "How Tight Is the UNHCR with the Organization of Islamic Cooperation?" *Refugee Resettlement Watch* (blog), November 22. https://refugeeresettlementwatch.wordpress.com/2014/11/22/how-tight-is-the-unhcr-with-the-organization-of-islamic-cooperation/.

Elmadmad, Khadija. 2008. "Asylum in Islam and in Modern Refugee Law." *Refugee Survey Quarterly* 27 (2): 51–63.

European Commission. 2015. "European Commission Statement Following the Vote of the European Parliament in Favour of an Emergency Relocation Mechanism for a Further 120,000 Refugees." Press release, September 17. Brussels. http://europa.eu/rapid/press-release_STATEMENT-15-5664_en.htm.

Gammeltoft-Hansen, Thomas. 2014. "International Refugee Law and Refugee Policy: The Case of Deterrence Policies." *Journal of Refugee Studies* 27 (4): 574–95.

Guterres, António. 2009. "Foreword." In *The Right to Asylum Between Islamic Shari'ah and International Refugee Law: A Comparative Study*, by Ahmed Abou-El-Wafa, 3–7. Cairo: UNHCR.

Hayatli, Musab. 2012. "Islam, International Law and the Protection of Refugees and IDPs." *Forced Migration Review* (June): 2–3.

Humanitarian Response Plan. 2016. "Syria Humanitarian Response Plan 2016" (total funding per donor). https://fts.unocha.org/appeals/501/donors?order=total_funding&sort=desc.

İhsanoğlu, Ekmeleddin. 2009. "Foreword." In *The Right to Asylum Between Islamic Shari'ah and International Refugee Law A Comparative Study*, by Ahmed Abou-El-Wafa, 9–13. Cairo: UNHCR.

Islamic Development Bank. 2015. *42 Years in the Service of Development*. Jeddah: Islamic Development Bank.

Kayaoglu, Turan. 2015. *The Organization of Islamic Cooperation: Politics, Problems, and Potential*. London: Routledge.

OIC. 2015a. "Appeal to the International Community by the OIC Secretary-General to Counter the Syrian Refugee Crisis." September 5. http://www.oic-oci.org/topic/?t_id=10404&t_ref=4107&lan=en.

———. 2015b. "Final Communiqué of the Open-Ended Emergency Meeting on the Syrian Refugee Crisis." September 13. https://reliefweb.int/report/syrian-arab-republic/final-communiqu-open-ended-emergency-meeting-syrian-refugee-crisis.

———. 2015c. "OIC Calls for Humanitarian Action to Address the Plight of Rohingya and Bangladeshi Refugees." May 17. http://www.oic-oci.org//topic/ampg.asp?t_id=10089&t_ref=3995&lan=en.

———. 2015d. "OIC Continues Efforts to Provide Humanitarian Aid to Rohingya Refugees." August 3. http://www.oic-oci.org//topic/ampg.asp?t_id=10322&t_ref=4077&lan=en.

———. 2015e. "OIC Continues to Mobilize Efforts for Political and Humanitarian Assistance to Rohingya Refugees." May 24. http://www.oic-oci.org//topic/ampg.asp?t_id=10123&t_ref=4006&lan=en.

———. 2015f. "OIC Convenes an Emergency Meeting to Mobilize Efforts to Address Syrian Refugee Crisis." September 10. https://mffcoexist.wordpress.com/2015/09/10/oic-convenes-an-emergency-meeting-to-mobilize-efforts-to-address-syrian-refugee-crisis/.

———. 2015g. "OIC-Proposed Resolution on Human Rights of Rohingya Gets Adopted by UN Human Rights Council." July 3. http://www.oic-oci.org//topic/ampg.asp?t_id=10248&t_ref=4052&lan=en.

UNHCR. 1991. Press release REF/1666. February 18.

———. 2006. "OIC Ministerial Conference on the Problems of Refugees in the Muslim World." Working document. http://www.unhcr.org/45ab8dd72.html.

———. 2012a. "Ancient Principles Inform Current Laws, UNHCR Chief Tells Gathering on Muslim Refugees." *Ashgabat Conference News*, May 11.

———. 2012b. "International Conference on Refugees in Muslim World Opens in Ashgabat, Turkmenistan." Ashgabat Conference briefing notes. May 11. http://www.unhcr.org/4facf6690.html.

Zaat, Kirsten. 2007. "The Protection of Forced Migrants in Islamic Law." UNHCR Policy Development and Evaluation Service working paper no. 146. December 6. http://www.unhcr.org/cgi-bin/texis/vtx/search?page=search&docid=476652cb2&query=protection.

CHAPTER 12

The OIC and Civil Society Cooperation: Prospects for Strengthened Human Rights Involvement?

Marie Juul Petersen

Introduction

Recent years have seen an increasing involvement of the Organization of Islamic Cooperation (OIC) in the international human rights system, witnessed, for example, in the establishment of the Independent Permanent Human Rights Commission (IPHRC), efforts to ensure consensus on Resolution 16/18, and the introduction of human rights language into core organizational documents such as the revised OIC charter and its "Ten Year Program of Action."[1] Parallel to its increasing attention to human rights, the OIC has also claimed a willingness to strengthen its cooperation with civil society, including, among other things, the introduction of a system granting "consultative status" to certain NGOs. While the OIC's human rights work in the UN and the work of the IPHRC have been analyzed in a number of articles, including several contributions to this volume (e.g., Chapters 3, 4, and 5), little attention has been given to the OIC's initiatives in the area of civil society cooperation (but see Ameli 2011 for a brief analysis). How, if at all, does this strengthened cooperation with civil society influence the OIC's human rights involvement? Can organizations with consultative status and other civil society partners of the OIC contribute to improving the human rights involvement of the organization in ways that, for instance, the IPHRC has not been able to? Building on an empirical analysis of the OIC's relations with civil society, this chapter seeks to answer these questions, exploring mechanisms for cooperation and the kinds of organizations included in this cooperation.[2]

At least in theory, civil society organizations can contribute to improving the human rights involvement of international organizations in several different ways. Overall, the mere existence of mechanisms for civil society cooperation in itself strengthens the right to association and the right to public participation. More specifically, civil society organizations can contribute to building human rights capacities within the OIC, they can provide information on human rights violations occurring in member states, and they can challenge the OIC to engage more actively through advocacy and lobbying activities. As such, civil society organizations "could potentially give the OIC a more forceful push regarding human rights beyond what [member] states could or would do on their own" (Chase 2015:22). The chapter argues that this inherent potential of civil society organizations is impeded by a number of factors: one, the OIC limits its cooperation to humanitarian organizations, displaying a preference for relatively apolitical, service-oriented NGOs rather than advocacy organizations more directly engaged in human rights issues; two, cooperation is subject to the approval of individual member states, thus preserving the power of authoritarian states and blocking civil society cooperation with more democratically oriented member states; and three, the OIC limits cooperation to conservative, Islamic NGOs, thus contributing to the strengthening of antipluralist, mononormative developments in the organization and its member states.

A Brief History of OIC Cooperation with Civil Society

Historically, the OIC has not had strong or well-established relations with civil society. The original OIC 1972 charter, the 1990 Cairo Declaration on Human Rights in Islam, as well as other key OIC documents all fail to mention the role of civil society, freedom of association, or mechanisms for civil society participation and influence in the OIC.[3] In its first decades, the OIC's partnership with civil society was limited to a few religious institutions such as Al-Azhar University in Egypt and the Association of Muslim Scholars, which were sometimes invited to attend the sessions of the organization or its regular conferences on Islamic *fiqh* (jurisprudence).[4] In the 1990s, the OIC's Research Center for Islamic History, Art and Culture (IRCICA), under the leadership of Ekmeleddin İhsanoğlu (who would later become secretary-general of the OIC), introduced mechanisms for more formal cooperation, entering into partnerships with a number of cultural and educational institutions and organizations. These included formal cooperation agreements with twelve universities and NGOs, including International Islamic Relief Organization of Saudi Arabia (IIROSA) (1994), Qatar University (1991), the International Islamic Call Society (1984), and Jordan University (1984). The partnerships entailed the publication of greeting cards bearing reproductions of calligraphic works, of albums of historical photographs of Mecca and Medina, and posters of Islamic monuments, as in the case of IIROSA.[5] Likewise, the organization's Islamic Solidarity Fund, for years the organization's main vehicle for humanitarian aid, also engaged in some cooperation with civil society organizations in its countries of operation. Overall, however, cooperation was ad hoc and unsystematic, reflecting a lack of formal mechanisms and procedures.[6]

This unwillingness to engage with civil society in a more strategic, formal manner reflects a deep-seated skepticism of civil society among OIC member states, who feared that civil society organizations might challenge their (in many cases illegitimate) power and authority. Like few other intergovernmental organizations, the OIC values the principles of self-determination and noninterference above all else, and the organization is, as noted repeatedly in its charter, determined "to respect, safeguard and defend the national sovereignty, independence and territorial integrity of all Member States."[7] This fear of NGOs as a threat to national sovereignty was evident in the resolution adopted at the 2000 Islamic Summit Conference calling "for a halt of the unjustified campaigns launched by some Governmental (*sic*) and NGOs against a number of Member States, focusing on the demand to abolish the Sharia ordained punishments and other penalties under the 'protection of human rights' slogan."[8]

Apart from political fear, many member states also share a more ideological skepticism of civil society, seen by many to be a "Western" concept. As Secretary-General Iyad Madani has said, "I do not want to use the term 'civil society' because it is an ambiguous term, and sometimes takes on an ideological meaning" (Mansur 2014). Many member states, he noted, perceive civil society as "fronts used to realize foreign interests."

Finally, since the 1990s, NGO connections with militant Islamic groups and movements such as Al-Qaeda and ISIS have also become a concern for member states, increasing their skepticism of NGOs. In particular, beginning with the war in Afghanistan in the 1980s certain NGOs became involved in armed struggles. They provided weapons and equipment, supported the mujahedeen financially, and facilitated contacts with volunteers who wanted to join them. A case in point is the Saudi Office for Services to the Mujahedeen, founded by a militant member of the Muslim Brotherhood (Ghandour 2003; 2004) and allegedly particularly active in supporting the mujahedeen. According to a now-declassified 1996 CIA report, the organization's Peshawar office funded at least nine training camps (CIA 1996:6), in parallel with its provision of assistance to Afghan refugees (Hegghammer 2010:43). Relations between certain NGOs and militant Islamist groups continued throughout the 1990s, and according to the above-mentioned CIA report, as many as thirteen Muslim organizations operating in Bosnia during the war were engaged in the conflict in various ways, sponsoring volunteer fighters, shipping weapons and military equipment into Bosnia, and providing visas and fake ID cards to Arab combatants (Hegghammer 2010:49). The involvement of some transnational Muslim NGOs in the 1993 and 1998 attacks on American territories—first the World Trade Center and then U.S. embassies in Kenya and Tanzania—led to increased skepticism and control over these organizations, manifested in a decrease in public funding, arrests of individuals, and bans on certain organizations. With the attacks of September 11, 2001, things worsened. After it became clear that the attacks, which killed almost 3,000 people, had been carried out by radical Islamic groups, suspicions quickly arose as to the involvement of certain transnational Muslim NGOs in planning and financing the attacks. Within a year, a number of NGOs, including the al-Haramain Foundation, the Revival of the Islamic Heritage Society, the Global Relief Foundation, and Benevolence International Foundation, were designated terrorist organizations by the U.S. government, accused of supporting or being otherwise related to Al-Qaeda. Other governments followed suit, banning a number of transnational Muslim NGOs from working in their territories. In 2003, for instance, the Saudi Arabian government closed down Al Haramain's office in Somalia on the grounds that the organization was supporting Al-Qaeda (Harmer and Cotterrell 2005:19). In the following years, especially authoritarian governments in OIC member states would use anti-terror legislation to clamp down on both illegitimate and legitimate civil society organizations.[9]

Changing Tides: "The Trend Towards Cooperation and Coordination"

While many of these concerns are still very present among member states, recent years have nonetheless witnessed a shift in the ways in which the organization deals with civil society, at least rhetorically. As noted by Secretary-General Ekmeleddin İhsanoğlu in his book *The Islamic World in the New Century*, cooperation with civil society is a development to which the OIC has "given foremost importance" in recent years (İhsanoğlu 2010:174).[10] While this is perhaps an overstatement, the focus on civil society has been consolidated in a number of documents. Most importantly, the "Ten Year Program of Action" (TYPOA), which was adopted in 2004, calls for "support [to] the trend towards cooperation and coordination between individual relief efforts of Islamic States and Islamic civil society institutions on the one hand, and international civil society institutions and organizations on the other hand"[11] (TYPOA, Section III.1). Furthermore, the program encourages the OIC to "seriously endeavour to enlarge the scope of political participation, ensure equality, civil liberties and social justice, and . . . promote transparency and accountability, and eliminate corruption in the OIC Member states" (TYPOA, Section 8(1)). Thus, the program introduced language that had been decidedly absent in most of the organization's former documents (Ameli 2011:152). Similarly, the 2011 statute for the Independent Permanent Human Rights Commission (IPHRC) encouraged the commission to promote and support "civil society organizations active in the area of human rights" (Article 15).[12] Finally, and more broadly, member states also agreed to devise "mechanisms to involve civil society organizations in Muslim countries and in the West for creating amity between people" (İhsanoğlu 2010:100). In concrete terms, then, cooperation with civil society was to include three main categories of civil society organizations: humanitarian organizations, human rights organizations, and organizations involved in the promotion of peace and conflict resolution. The following takes a closer look at how these partnerships have played out in practice.

But let us first consider some of the reasons for this rhetorical emphasis on civil society cooperation. To begin with, there was an increasing awareness among member states of the need for the OIC to strengthen its legitimacy and support in member-state populations. In the 1980s and 1990s many people were not even aware of the organization (hence the nickname "Oh I See")—and among those that were, most considered it to be an irrelevant gathering of paralyzed states, capable of agreeing only on yet another condemnation of Israel or a fatwa on theological details while lacking any initiatives that would make a real difference for people on the street. Through activities such as cooperation with civil society organizations, an increase in humanitarian aid, and the establishment of a human rights commission, the OIC hoped to improve its image, signaling a greater willingness to reach out to the wider populations in member states.[13] The need for such a sea change, of course, only grew after the Arab revolutions, demonstrating that popular demands for welfare, democracy, and rights are difficult to ignore in the long run.

Second, the increased attention to civil society and the willingness for cooperation may reflect changes in power relations internally in the OIC taking place at that time. Historically, Saudi Arabia and Iran, both major contributors to the organizational budget, had been dominant voices within the OIC. While they have indeed maintained a strong position in the organization, the 2000s saw the emergence of new powerful voices, with Turkey and other so-called moderate Muslim states such as Indonesia, Malaysia, and Morocco gaining increasing clout. While Saudi Arabia and Iran have, to say the least, had little tradition with strong civil society movements or participation, countries such as Turkey, Malaysia, Morocco, and Indonesia brought differing histories and perspectives. Contributing further to this shift in the power balance was the fact that Secretary-General İhsanoğlu was from Turkey and had a strong interest in and rapport with civil society, in part due to his past as a director of IRCICA.

Third, and on a more concrete level, the increased attention to civil society was prompted by a number of humanitarian disasters in member states, most importantly the Indian Ocean tsunami in 2004, which made it painfully clear to all that the poor coordination and cooperation between the OIC and civil society had very real ramifications in terms of lives affected due to ineffective aid provision. As then-director of ICHAD Atta el Manane Bakhit noted, the OIC "could not sit idle and let things happen without intervening given the important number of member states which were in need of humanitarian assistance" (Svoboda et al. 2015:3). Similarly, İhsanoğlu notes that "there was such a wide vacuum between the OIC and the NGO community in the Muslim world that a partnership was obligatory if the resource disbursement should reach those affected through credible channels" (İhsanoğlu 2010:177).

What, then, does OIC civil society cooperation look like in practice? The following sections present and analyze the main venues for formal, institutionalized civil society cooperation that have been established in recent years, thereby discussing the ways in which they may block or facilitate OIC human rights involvement in the future. As noted above, civil society cooperation falls (or was envisaged to fall) within three main categories: namely, cooperation with humanitarian organizations, with human rights organizations, and with organizations involved in peace and conflict resolution. Exploring these three areas of cooperation, this chapter discusses different scenarios for the future of OIC-civil society cooperation.

Humanitarian Organizations

The OIC's strongest vehicle for civil society cooperation today is the Humanitarian Affairs Department, or ICHAD.[14] While the OIC had previously cooperated with individual humanitarian organizations on an ad hoc basis, more systematic cooperation began only after the tsunami in 2004, with the OIC Alliance for the Safeguard of the Children Victims of the Tsunami being the first larger OIC-NGO partnership. In the following years, interaction with humanitarian organizations accelerated, including initiatives in Palestine and Lebanon. In 2008, against this background, the president of Senegal convened a meeting for civil society organizations before the Eleventh Islamic Summit of OIC member states in Dakar, Senegal, gathering sixty NGOs from twenty-seven OIC member states. "This is a historic moment in the history of the OIC and the Islamic Ummah in general," stated then-director of the OIC Humanitarian Affairs Department, Atta Manane Bakhit (IRIN 2008). Since then, the OIC-supported Conference of Civil Society Organization in the Islamic World has been held annually; the 2013 conference in Istanbul reportedly gathered more than 400 participants from 230 organizations to discuss "the rising role of civil society organizations in the Islamic world."[15]

In parallel to this, OIC member states began discussing possibilities for the organization to grant consultative status to humanitarian NGOs. The topic was first brought up at the 2007 Conference of Foreign Ministers (Ameli 2011:160), and at the Thirty-Ninth Session of the Council of Foreign Ministers, held in Djibouti in November 2012, the Rules for Granting OIC Consultative Status to Humanitarian Non-Governmental Organizations were finally approved.[16] According to the rules, consultative status can be granted to humanitarian NGOs headquartered in an OIC member state, as long as they are registered officially and accredited to work in the activity specified in the application for consultative status. Organizations outside OIC member states that are "affiliated to Muslim minorities and communities [and] work in the field of humanitarian relief" can also apply if they are accredited in the states where they work (Article 3(2)). Organizations with consultative status are allowed to "hold a periodic meeting prior to the ordinary sessions of the Islamic Summit or Council." Furthermore, they may—at the invitation of the secretary-general—participate in the plenary sessions of the Council of Foreign Ministers, ministerial meetings, and meetings of the standing committees (Articles 7(2) and 8(1)). Consultative status is granted by the Council of Foreign Ministers, at the recommendation of the secretary-general. According to the rules, the organizations with consultative status are obliged to "collectively set up an appropriate mechanism to facilitate the coordination and consultation" with the OIC. Responding to this requirement, the Council of Humanitarian Organizations was established in Doha in December 2014 at a meeting hosted by the Qatar Charity Foundation and attended by seventeen NGOs with consultative status.[17]

Operational partnerships between the OIC and individual civil society organizations were also strengthened. An oft-mentioned example is the 2011 Humanitarian Alliance in Somalia, coordinated by the OIC and involving up to forty international and national Islamic NGOs. While Western NGOs and donor agencies had difficulties gaining access to Al-Shabaab-controlled areas of the country, the OIC alliance managed to negotiate access, providing emergency relief to hundreds of thousands of people.[18] Cooperation also includes other activities of a strategic character. Together with IIROSA and the International Committee of the Red Cross (ICRC), for instance, ICHAD launched an initiative to discuss relations between Islamic law and international humanitarian law, inviting NGO representatives, legal experts, and Islamic scholars from more than twenty countries to a series of workshops in 2013 and 2014. ICHAD also cooperated with the Humanitarian Forum, the Humanitarian Policy Group at the Overseas Development Institute, and the Jordan Hashemite Charity Organization in organizing a series of meetings under the heading "Humanitarian Action in the Arab World," supported by the United Nations Office for the Coordination of Humanitarian Affairs (OCHA).[19]

Human Rights Organizations

In addition to the establishment of ICHAD, OIC member states discussed the establishment of the IPHRC, and here requirements for civil society participation were also an important part of the discussion. İhsanoğlu himself noted in 2012 that the role of civil society should not be confined to humanitarian action but also include "environmental protection, human rights, dialogue among civilizations, cultures and religions, as well as woman and child affairs and the fight against organized crime" (*OIC Newsletter* 2012).[20] The statutes of the IPHRC state that "the Commission shall promote and support the role of Member State-accredited national institutions and civil society organizations active in the area of human rights" (Article 15), and the rules of procedure mention "civil society organizations active in the field of human rights" several times.[21]

Initially, the IPHRC's commissioners seemed keen to ensure cooperation with civil society. The first session, held in Jakarta under the leadership of the Indonesian commissioner Siti Ruhaini in 2012, was open to participation from civil society organizations. The Indonesian NGO Human Rights Working Group participated in much of the session and wrote an extensive report afterward, summing up the main discussions of the meeting and concluding optimistically that "the first session of IPHRC in Jakarta . . . has successfully involved the participation of civil society and observers from Member States" and that the commission was "open and accessible" with regard to participation in the session as well as access to commissioners and documents (Human Rights Working Group 2012:5).

Since then, however, civil society organizations have not participated in sessions of the IPHRC. At the IPHRC's third session in Jeddah in 2013, an ad hoc working group was established to discuss mechanisms for cooperation with national human rights institutions (NHRIs)[22] and civil society organizations. The working group formulated a set of draft *Arrangements for Consultation with Relevant Parties Including Civil Society Institutions, Non-Governmental Organisations and Individuals* (Adam 2014:13). The document has been a topic for discussion at a number of sessions since then, but the commission has not been able to reach consensus. Asked about the developments in this area, a staff member from the IPHRC secretariat said that the commission will "soon be finalizing the arrangements for interaction with the NGOs and broader civil society" (interview with the author). A representative from the Asian Forum for Human Rights and Development who has followed the process is more pessimistic: "From the last conversations I had it doesn't look like they will be adopted—apparently some commissioners are skeptical" (interview with the author). Instead, at its fifth session in Jeddah in 2014, the commission decided to invite national human rights institutes (NHRIs) from OIC member states to all future meetings. While this is of course laudable, cooperation with NHRIs cannot be equated with—or be considered a substitute for—civil society cooperation. Many NHRIs in OIC member states are quasigovernmental entities with little autonomy and few connections to civil society.

Apart from the inability to agree on formal mechanisms for civil society cooperation, a number of practical obstacles further impede cooperation. Most important in this respect is the decision to place the IPHRC secretariat and its sessions in Jeddah, making it practically impossible for non-Saudi civil society organizations to interact with the commission, due—among other things—to the country's restrictive visa procedures and strict NGO legislation. Indonesia initially expressed an interest in hosting the IPHRC's secretariat, something which would have greatly facilitated civil society cooperation, taking into account the existence of a strong civil society in Indonesia and the country's relatively relaxed NGO legislation. This, however, was blocked by Saudi Arabia and Iran, and it was decided by the Council of Foreign Ministers to place the secretariat in Jeddah. Also, original plans to rotate the location of IPHRC sessions among member states, precisely in order to facilitate civil society participation, were cancelled and presently all regular sessions are held in Jeddah.

Organizations Involved in Peace and Reconciliation

Finally, the OIC envisaged reforms in the area of civil society cooperation with organizations involved in "creating amity between people," as quoted above. An important vehicle for this kind of cooperation was to be the OIC's Peace, Security and Mediation Unit (PSMU), established in 2013 on a decision by the CFM in 2012 (see Chapter 9 for an analysis of this and other OIC conflict resolution initiatives). However, as of this writing the unit has maintained a very low profile (in fact, it is not even listed on the OIC's website)—perhaps a reflection of the difficulties surrounding its establishment. Several member states opposed the establishment of the unit, fearing that it would inevitably interfere with internal member state conflicts. In the end, the unit was established as part of the secretary-general's office.

It is difficult to find information about the unit's work, as outside of its launch no public statements have been issued and there is no attached website. On its launch, the OIC stated that the unit was "expected to function principally through monitoring current and potential crisis situations and undertake timely diplomatic response . . . coupled with identifying and analyzing major root causes of conflicts and determining ways and means to address them." The statement further noted that the PSMU would "seek to interact with the OIC Member States and other international and regional organizations to share experiences in mediation and conflict resolution" (Kuwait News Agency 2013). There was no mention of PSMU cooperation with civil society in member states.

The PSMU's first initiative, the 2014 Network for Religious and Traditional Peacemakers, reflected this preference for engagement with international NGOs over civil society organizations from member states. The network was established in cooperation with Religions for Peace and Finn Church Aid, with an aim to involve religious leaders in "culturally and religiously sensitive" conflict resolution, according to an OIC staff member as quoted by Hirah Azhar (Chapter 9). The network consists of twenty-three international NGOs, research institutes, and donor agencies, including Pax Christi, World Vision, the Tony Blair Faith Foundation, and the Swiss Peace Foundation. Interestingly, out of these, only three are based in OIC member states—the Al Amana Centre with headquarters in Oman, Kalam Research & Media in the United Arab Emirates, and the Libyan Institute for Advanced Studies. A fourth, KAICIID Dialogue Center, based in Austria, is funded by the Saudi Arabian government.

Civil Society: Humanitarian, Government-Friendly, and Islamic

Against this background, how can we characterize the OIC's underlying conceptions of civil society, and what does this mean for the organization's involvement with human rights? Three main points can be advanced. First, the OIC seems to prefer cooperation with humanitarian organizations to any other kind of civil society organization. An obvious reason for this is that such organizations are often less politically engaged than, for example, human rights organizations, and as such are less of a threat to member-state authority. Furthermore, and contrary to human rights activism which can of course be highly divisive, the provision of humanitarian aid is almost unequivocally perceived to be something positive by OIC member states as well as their populations. Humanitarian organizations thus represent a more acceptable form of civil society, or as Madani prefers to call them, "voluntary associations." While some humanitarian organizations today are of course heavily involved in "political" activities such as advocacy and lobbying, and many take an explicitly rights-based approach to humanitarian aid (for instance Christian Aid or Oxfam), the group of organizations that have been granted consultative status with the OIC are almost without exception what one may call "traditional" humanitarian organizations. Apart from Islamic Relief Worldwide and Muslim Aid, none of them include human rights in their activities, focusing instead on the provision of relief, the celebration of religious holidays, mosque construction, and financial aid as well as nonpolitical service provision. Such activities are in line with the underlying OIC conception of civil society, that is, a contributor to "security, development and social peace" as formulated by Cevdet Yilmaz, Turkish Minister of Development, in his keynote speech at the OIC's Fifth Conference of Civil Society Organizations in the Islamic World.[23]

There is of course a possibility that human rights–oriented organizations are not interested in cooperating with the OIC, and this is the reason why we see so few of these organizations. However, that does not seem to be the case. Some do express doubts about the possibilities for influence in the OIC, thus questioning whether involvement is worth the effort. As a representative from the Asian Forum for Human Rights and Development noted in an interview with the author, "Is it even worth it trying to influence the OIC? That is what we ask ourselves." Together with other organizations such as the Indonesian Human Rights Working Group and the Forum for Democratic Global Governance, they have persistently tried to establish relations with the OIC but have had little success. In June 2011, a coalition of more than 230 human rights and media organizations from OIC member countries petitioned the OIC to ensure greater involvement of civil society in the IPHRC, sending a letter to the OIC's secretary-general. According to a representative from Mazlum-der, the OIC has never given any official response to that letter.[24]

Second, albeit closely related to the above, the OIC seems to prefer cooperation with government-friendly organizations. The rules for consultative status grant individual member states absolute power in deciding which organizations can be granted consultative status, thus effectively ensuring that only government-friendly organizations are included. The secretary-general may recommend consultative status to certain organizations, but the Council of Foreign Ministers (CFM) has the final word; likewise individual member states may block the secretary-general's invitations to organizations to participate in sessions of the CFM, ministerial meetings, or standing committee meetings (Articles 5(4) and 8(2)).

A closer look at the group of humanitarian organizations with consultative status confirms this; the vast majority, if not all, of these organizations have historically had very close relations to their governments. Since the 1970s, many OIC member states have nursed informal alliances with national Islamic movements and organizations, including humanitarian NGOs, employing a strategy of co-optation of Islamic organizations and persons into governmental bureaucracy while at the same time boosting their religious legitimacy (Ghabra 1997:59f; Alterman and von Hippel 2007:71). The International Islamic Charitable Organization (IICO) of Kuwait and IIROSA of Saudi Arabia, two of the largest NGOs with OIC consultative status, serve as examples of this. In Kuwait, for instance, two IICO chairmen have served as minister of Awqaf, and the organization has received generous material support from the government, including a plot of land for the organization's headquarters. In Saudi Arabia, IIROSA's relations with the government have also been close from the beginning, and the minister of defense, together with the highest religious authority in the kingdom, were among the first donors to the organization. Several government representatives have served on the board and as members of the IIROSA general assembly. Additionally, IIROSA funds have been channeled by Saudi embassies to charitable projects abroad (Observatoire de l'Action Humanitaire 2008).

Recommendations from the OIC's Fifth Conference of Civil Society Organizations in the Islamic World testify further to the consensual, amicable relations between those civil society organizations and the OIC. Devoid of any criticism of the OIC, the NGOs' recommendations instead "commended the efforts exerted by the OIC to energize the role of civil society"; "commended the valuable role of H. E. Professor Ekmeleddin İhsanoğlu in supporting the civil society and humanitarian organizations in the Muslim world"; "expressed its thanks to the 40th CFM"; and applauded ICHAD for being "an oasis for the humanitarian organizations in the Muslim world" (OIC 2013:3). As an anonymous observer to the OIC conference noted in an interview, rather than challenge the OIC, these organizations are primarily interested in increased cooperation, encouraging the OIC to engage with, mobilize, and potentially fund civil society.[25]

The IPHRC's decision to cooperate with national human rights institutions rather than civil society also reflects this focus on government-friendly organizations. While in principle independent, many OIC member-state NHRIs (although not all) are closely related to and part of government structures, meaning that cooperation is unlikely to threaten government authority and power.

Third, and perhaps most troubling, the OIC prefers cooperation with Islamic civil society organizations. While there are no formal requirements as to religious identity in the Rules for Granting Consultative Status, much civil society rhetoric emphasizes the religious quality of civil society, and in practice all organizations that have been granted consultative status, as well as most other organizations with which the OIC cooperates, have a self-proclaimed, often rather conservative, Islamic identity. In fact, the OIC does not cooperate with any Christian, Buddhist, Hindu, or secular civil society organizations from its member states. The only examples of cooperation with non-Islamic organizations are OIC partnerships with international NGOs from nonmember states, such as the Network of Religious and Traditional Peacemakers.

This preference for conservative Islamic organizations further alienates human rights organizations. While many humanitarian organizations in OIC countries have an explicit Islamic identity, most human rights organizations are secular, Christian, or interfaith (as is the case with the human rights organizations mentioned above). There are a few Muslim human rights organizations, primarily in Indonesia, Turkey, and Malaysia, but their take on Islam does not seem to fit that of the OIC and its most powerful member states. Liberal Muslim organizations such as the transnational women's movement Musawah or the Malaysian Sisters in Islam have not succeeded in establishing relations with the OIC; on the contrary, their relationship seems to be somewhat confrontational. Musawah, for instance, has very actively engaged with members of the UN Committee on the Elimination of Discrimination against Women on issues related to Islam and women's rights. They have been particularly critical of the so-called Sharia reservations to CEDAW upheld by many OIC member states and have argued for alternative interpretations of Islamic law, compatible with women's rights. While individual staff members of the OIC headquarters have expressed an interest in cooperating with Musawah, it seems unrealistic to expect such cooperation to materialize, taking into consideration the religiously conservative leanings of powerful member states such as Egypt, Iran, Pakistan, and Saudi Arabia.

Instead, the organizations with whom the OIC cooperates almost all display a relatively conservative religious identity, often associated with the Muslim Brotherhood or Salafi ideology. Again, IICO and IIROSA may serve as illustrative examples. The IICO was established by Yusuf Qaradawi, one of the key figures in the Islamic resurgence and closely related to the Muslim Brotherhood; IIROSA is part of the Salafi-oriented Muslim World League, which also enjoys close relations with the Muslim Brotherhood. Normatively, these organizations are in line with core OIC values and principles. These are organizations for whom notions of *umma* and *ikhwan* are essential; humanitarian aid is about Islamic solidarity and brotherhood, not about an abstract, universalized humanity. More specifically, most of these organizations share the OIC's skepticism of certain human rights, such as women's rights and gender equality, arguing instead for the importance of family values, complementarity, and women's right to protection (Petersen 2015).

Conclusion

This restricted understanding of civil society as consisting primarily of humanitarian, government-friendly, and religiously conservative organizations does not hold much promise for strengthened OIC human rights involvement. Not only have human rights organizations so far been consistently excluded from cooperation, OIC mechanisms for civil society cooperation practically exclude *any* government-critical organization from participating, thereby effectively avoiding challenges to state power and authority. Furthermore, its affinity for a particular group of civil society organizations is counterproductive to the strengthening of pluralist communities, nondiscrimination, and rights of minorities.[26] As such, the OIC's cooperation with civil society counters, rather than strengthens, core principles of the human rights regime. More specifically, many of these organizations may agree with the OIC on its skepticism of specific human rights, including certain women's rights, and as such actively contribute to legitimizing OIC attempts at blocking or reinterpreting such rights at the UN level.

This does not mean, however, that OIC cooperation with civil society cannot lead to stronger human rights involvement in particular areas. As for the IPHRC, there is little doubt that the adoption of mechanisms for civil society cooperation has dire prospects (and even if they are adopted, the location of the secretariat means that few civil society organizations will be able to participate in sessions). However, even if cooperation with NHRIs does not hold the same potential for challenging member-state violations of human rights, there is still reason for quiet optimism. A few OIC member state NHRIs, including the Ugandan Human Rights Commission, are strong, independent, and well-established, with solid human rights knowledge and the capacity to criticize and challenge not only member states but also the IPHRC and the OIC as such. Similarly, the PSMU and its work on peace and conflict resolution might also present openings for a greater focus on human rights. It is difficult to engage in, for example, the conflict between Muslims and Buddhists in Burma (an explicit priority of the OIC) without applying a minority rights perspective—and even more so, if the unit continues its cooperation with international NGOs firmly grounded in a human rights approach such as Religions for Peace and Pax Christi.

Finally, it is probably within the group of humanitarian organizations with consultative status in the OIC that we find the most realistic prospects for stronger human rights involvement. While these organizations may currently have little or no human rights knowledge, lacking the capacity to push for stronger OIC involvement in human rights, this might very well change. The engagement with international humanitarian law, for instance, may lead to greater human rights capacities. As noted above, a number of OIC partner organizations are involved in discussions on international humanitarian law, an area closely linked to—and sharing some of the same basic principles as—international human rights law.

Another possibility lies with Muslim NGOs outside the OIC member states. As noted above, North American and European humanitarian organizations are increasingly engaging with human rights. This includes European Muslim NGOs such as Islamic Relief Worldwide and Muslim Aid, which both have consultative status with the OIC. Enjoying a strong reputation and clout in the OIC Council of Humanitarian Organizations, such NGOs may influence other humanitarian organizations, motivating them to engage more explicitly with human rights and, in turn, pushing a human rights agenda within the OIC. An initial step could be a focus on the right to health and other economic, social, and cultural rights, which are seen by most OIC member states to be less controversial than civil and political rights. Islamic Relief Worldwide is increasingly applying a rights-based approach to its work in the areas of health, water, and education. Similarly, Muslim Aid is adopting a rights discourse. Addressing a workshop on "The Role of NGOs in the Implementation of OIC Strategic Health Plan of Action 2014–2023" in Ankara, Muslim Aid's CEO approached the issue from a human rights perspective, stating that "the right to enjoy health security is fundamental to ensure a healthy and prosperous society."[27]

Even in the area of women's rights, to the OIC perhaps the most controversial of all human rights, these organizations may be able to push the OIC in the right direction. Islamic Relief's policy advisor on gender, Iman Sandra Pertek, was invited to speak at the seventh session of the IPHRC in May 2015, where she encouraged OIC member states to "integrate gender-based violence programming into all humanitarian and conflict responses, including prevention, recognising the root causes of violence, empowering women and girls, working with men and boys, challenging discriminatory social norms and working with local leaders, including faith leaders."[28]

Such modest statements are a far cry from Musawah's radical calls to "restore the egalitarian message of the Qur'an" and demand full rights for women, but they may nonetheless resonate with some people in the OIC, perhaps contributing to pushing the organization a small step in the right direction toward stronger human rights involvement. Thus, while the kinds of organizations preferred by the OIC for cooperation may not be capable of—or interested in—pressuring the OIC toward adoption of a more wholehearted human rights policy, they may nonetheless be able to gently push the organization slowly in the right direction.

Notes

1. Charter of the Organization of Islamic Cooperation. Dakar, March 14, 2008. http://ww1.oic-oci.org/english/charter/OIC%20Charter-new-en.pdf; Ten Year Programme of Action. http://www.oic-iphrc.org/en/data/docs/legal_instruments/OIC%20Instruments/TYPOA-%20AEFV/TYPOA-EV.pdf.

2. The analysis builds primarily on OIC documents as well as data gathered from interviews conducted with staff members at the OIC headquarters (Jeddah, October 2011) and interviews with staff from NGOs cooperating with the OIC (Kuwait City, June 2008; Jeddah,

October 2009; Birmingham, July 2014), conducted in connection to previous research projects. See for example Petersen 2012a, 2014, and 2015.

3. However, the Cairo Declaration does mention freedom of expression (Article 22) and participation in government (Article 23), two arguably essential aspects of civil society, albeit subject to specific Sharia limitation clauses.

4. Civil Freedom Monitor: Organization of Islamic Cooperation, International Center for Not-for-Profit Law. http://www.icnl.org/research/monitor/oic.html.

5. http://www.ircica.org/content/irc478.aspx.

6. A number of OIC-affiliated institutions, including the Islamic Solidarity Sports Federation, the Youth Forum for Dialogue and Cooperation, and the International Union for Muslim Scouts, however, have all had relatively strong relations with civil society since their inception. Insofar as they are not institutionally part of the OIC but merely affiliated with the organization, they have not been included in the present analysis.

7. This is repeated in different ways in Articles 1(3), 2(2), 2(4), and 2(6) of the revised charter (2008).

8. The full text of the resolution can be found here: http://www.iri.edu.ar/publicaciones_iri/anuario/CD%20Anuario%202005/Demo/08-islamic%20conf-res%205.pdf.

9. For in-depth analyses of the situation of international Muslim NGOs before and after 9/11, see Petersen (2012b; 2014; 2015). On the implications of the "War on Terror" for civil society more generally, see Howell and Lind (2009). On the implications of the "War on Terror" for civil society more generally, see Howell and Lind (2009).

10. Early signs of attention to civil society had begun in the late 1990s. In the 1999 Teheran Declaration of Dialogue Among Civilizations, for instance, member states acknowledged that "[r]epresentatives of civil society can play an instrumental role in promoting the culture of dialogue within various societies and should also participate in such dialogue" (Segesvary 2000:102).

11. The revised charter does not specifically mention civil society but notes that "the Organization will enhance its cooperation with the Islamic and other Organizations in the service of the objectives embodied in the present Charter" (Article 26).

12. Statute of the OIC Independent Permanent Human Rights Commission. OIC/IPCHR/2010/STATUTE. https://oichumanrights.files.wordpress.com/2011/08/resolution-oic-iphrc-and-statute.pdf.

13. While many civil society organizations in OIC member states have historically seemed to be either unaware of, or uninterested in, the OIC, some have directed their demands explicitly at the OIC. In 2008, for instance, one of the largest Turkish human rights organizations, Mazlum-der, sent a letter to Secretary-General İhsanoğlu calling for the establishment of an independent human rights commission. İhsanoğlu then invited Mazlum-der to a meeting, during which he informed the organization about the ongoing efforts to establish such a commission.

14. See Chapter 10 for a detailed analysis of the OIC's humanitarian engagement. See also Svoboda et al. (2015) for an analysis of the organization's involvement in Somalia.

15. https://www.ihh.org.tr/en/news/islamic-civil-society-organizations-meet-in-istanbul-1957.

16. Rules for Granting OIC Consultative Status to Humanitarian Non-Governmental Organizations. http://www.oic-oci.org/oicv3/upload/pages/conventions/en/human_non_gov_org_applying_form_en_14_jan_2014.pdf.

17. The Council of Humanitarian Organizations includes the following organizations: Qatar Charity Foundation, Foundation Sheikh Thani Ibn Abdullah for Humanitarian Services (or Raf Organization, Qatar), the Eid Foundation (Qatar), the Islamic Dawa Organization (Sudan), Islamic African Relief Agency (Sudan), Al-Zubair Charity Foundation (Sudan), IHH (Turkey), International Islamic Relief Organization (Saudi Arabia), the World Assembly of Muslim Youth (Saudi Arabia), Islamic Relief Worldwide (Britain), Zamzam Foundation (Somalia), Al-Ameen for Development (Morocco), Imam Khomeini Relief Foundation (Iran), International Islamic Charitable Organization (Kuwait), Jordan Hashemite Charity Organization (Jordan), Cooperation Organization of Palestine, and the Association of Mali for Peace and Salvation. The board of the council is made up of four organizations: the International Islamic Relief Organization, which serves as vice-president, the Qatar Charity Foundation as rapporteur, Islamic Relief Worldwide of Britain as treasurer, and IHH as member. The council's president is to be elected from outside the humanitarian organizations "among professionals with extensive experience in humanitarian work and international regulations" (Shaikh 2014). A number of working groups have been established, including one on Islamic law and international humanitarian law (led by Qatar Charity), on humanitarian diplomacy (IHH and Imam Khomeini Foundation), studies and research (IIROSA), media (Al-Ameen for Development), capacity building and skills development (Raf Organization), and orphans (IIROSA and Zubair Corporation) (information from OIC media department).

18. However, critics note that the alliance was never very effective beyond Mogadishu, in part because it was haunted by the political alignment of the OIC with the federal government and associated with the UN (Svoboda et al. 2015).

19. For further information, see https://www.odi.org/sites/odi.org.uk/files/odi-assets/events-documents/5066.pdf.

20. İhsanoğlu's successor, Secretary-General Iyad Madani, stated similar concerns, albeit with an important difference—he did not mention human rights: "We have opened the doors of dialogue with voluntary associations in terms of the humanitarian relief dimension and this is great. But voluntary organizations are not just relief organizations, and their work addresses other social aspects such as health, education, women's rights, and the environment, which are among the long list of concerns that would be of interest to the OIC. For the future, we are working towards finding a way in which member states can be more open to community volunteerism" (Mansur 2014).

21. More specifically, "Commission may periodically submit to the Council reports which may include . . . activities in support of the role of Member State-accredited national institutions and civil society organizations active in the field of human rights. . . . A mandated thematic analysis of the status of promotion and protection of human rights in Member States to be conducted, *inter alia,* on the basis of [among other things] reports of Member State-accredited national human rights institutions and civil society organizations active in the area of human rights" (Rule 39); technical cooperation may be conducted in cooperation with "civil society organization active in the area of human rights" (Rule 57); and the "Secretariat may assist Commission in keeping it informed of the principal initiatives undertaken and results achieved in the field of promotion and protection of human rights by Member State-accredited National Human Rights Institutions and civil society organizations active in the area of human rights" (Rule 59). Rules of Procedure of the OIC Independent Permanent Human Rights Commission. http://www.oic-iphrc.org/en/data/docs/about/IPHRC%20-%20RULES%20OF%20PROCEDURE%20-%20FINAL/IPHRC%20-%20

Rules%20of%20Procedure%20-%20Final%20-%20Adopted%20by%2039th%20CFM%20-%20EV.pdf.

22. NHRIs are independent institutions with a mandate to protect, promote, and monitor human rights compliance in a given country. See the website of the Global Alliance of National Human Rights Institutions (GANHRI, https://nhri.ohchr.org) for further information.

23. http://www.bscsif.ro/executive-director-of-bscsif-attended-the-fifth-conference-of-the-civil-society-organizations-in-the-islamic-world/.

24. See also Asian Forum for Human Rights and Development's working paper "Understanding the Role of the Organisation of Islamic Cooperation in Human Rights" (Adam 2014) for a critical assessment of the OIC's human rights involvement in general.

25. This emphasis on cooperation rather than criticism as the key role of civil society is spelled out in the OIC's Rules for Granting Consultative Status: NGOs with consultative status are only allowed to submit "written activity oriented statements about their activities" and may only speak and deliver statements "on the contents of these written contributions" (Rules for Granting Consultative Status, Article 8(4)); in other words, they are not supposed to challenge or question OIC or member state practices, but must stick to mere summaries of their own activities.

26. This focus on conservative, Muslim organizations points to deeper fragmentations in civil society everywhere in the so-called Muslim world. When the OIC advances an understanding of Islamic civil society as the only "true" or "authentic" civil society, it mirrors in reverse a common—and equally particularistic—conception of authentic civil society as inherently secular and progressive, which was until recently dominant in much civil society literature (see Turner 1994 for discussions of this).

27. https://www.muslimaid.org/media-centre/press-release/greater-collaboration-between-oic-and-ngos-to-eradicate-preventable-diseases/.

28. http://www.islamic-relief.org/gender-just-and-family-centred-policies-and-programmes/.

Works Cited

Adam, Ahmed. 2014. "Understanding the Role of the Organization of Islamic Cooperation in Human Rights." Working paper. Bangkok: FORUM-ASIA.

Alterman, Jon B., and Karin von Hippel, eds. 2007. *Understanding Islamic Charities*. Washington, DC: Center for Strategic and International Studies.

Ameli, Saied Reza. 2011. "The Organisation of the Islamic Conference, Accountability and Civil Society." In *Building Global Democracy? Civil Society and Accountable Global Governance*, ed. Jan Aart Scholte, 146–62. Cambridge: Cambridge University Press.

Chase, Anthony Tirado. 2015. "The Organization of Islamic Cooperation: A Case Study of International Organizations' Impact on Human Rights." Matters of Concern series working paper. Copenhagen: Danish Institute for Human Rights.

CIA. 1996. "Report on NGOs with Terror Links." *Wikisource*. http://en.wikisource.org/wiki/CIA_Report_on_NGOs_With_Terror_Links.

Ghabra, Shafeeq N. 1997. "Balancing State and Society: The Islamic Movement in Kuwait." *Middle East Policy* 5 (2): 58–72.

Ghandour, Abdel-Rahman. 2003. "Humanitarianism, Islam and the West: Contest or Cooperation?" *Humanitarian Exchange Magazine* 25: 14–17. http://odihpn.org/magazine/humanitarianism-islam-and-the-west-contest-or-cooperation/.

———. 2004. "The Modern Missionaries of Islam." In *In the Shadow of "Just Wars": Violence, Politics and Humanitarian Action*, ed. Fabrice Weissmann, 325–40. Ithaca, NY: Cornell University Press.

Harmer, Adele, and Lin Cotterrell. 2005. *Diversity in Donorship: The Changing Landscape of Official Humanitarian Assistance*. HPG Research Report. London: Overseas Development Institute. https://www.odi.org/sites/odi.org.uk/files/odi-assets/publications-opinion-files/275.pdf.

Hegghammer, Thomas. 2010. *Jihad in Saudi Arabia: Violence and Pan-Islamism Since 1979*. Cambridge: Cambridge University Press.

Howell, Jude, and Jeremy Lind. 2009. *Counter-Terrorism, Aid and Civil Society*. New York: Palgrave Macmillan.

Human Rights Working Group. 2012. *Monitoring Report*. Jakarta: Human Rights Working Group. www.hrwg.org.

İhsanoğlu, Ekmeleddin. 2010. *The Islamic World in the New Century: The Organization of Islamic Conference 1969–2009*. London: Hurst.

IRIN. 2008. "OIC and Islamic NGOs Pledge Support for Humanitarian Work." March 13. http://www.irinnews.org/news/2008/03/13/oic-and-islamic-ngos-pledge-support-humanitarian-work.

Kuwait News Agency. 2013. "OIC Launches New Peace, Security Unit." March 20 http://www.kuna.net.kw/ArticleDetails.aspx?id=2299703&Language=en.

Mansur, Wael Abu. 2014. "In Conversation with the Head of the Organization of Islamic Cooperation." *Asharq al-Awsat*, July 9. https://eng-archive.aawsat.com/w-abumansur/interviews/in-conversation-with-the-head-of-the-organization-of-islamic-cooperation.

Mayer, Ann Elizabeth. 2012. *Islam and Human Rights. Tradition and Politics*. 5th ed. Boulder, CO: Westview Press.

Observatoire de l'Action Humanitaire. 2008. *International Islamic Relief Organisation*. Link no longer available.

OIC. 2013. "Final Communique. The Fifth Conference of Civil Society Organizations in the Islamic World. Istanbul, Turkey, 11–12 Safar 1435H, 14–15 December 2013." OIC/NGOs-5/2013/ICHAD.

OIC Newsletter. 2012. "Ihsanoglu: Granting Consultative Status to NGOs Opens Avenues for Partnerships with Civil Society Organizations." *OIC Newsletter*, 2. January 11. https://www.oic-oci.org/newsletter/?lan=en.

Petersen, Marie Juul. 2012a. *Islamic or Universal Human Rights? The OIC's Independent Permanent Human Rights Commission*. DIIS Report. Copenhagen: Danish Institute for International Studies.

———. 2012b. "Trajectories of Transnational Muslim NGOs." *Development in Practice* 22 (5–6): 763–78.

———. 2014. "Sacralized or Secularized Aid? Positioning Gulf-based Muslim Charities." In *Gulf Charities and Islamic Philanthrophy in "The Age of Terror" and Beyond*, ed. Robert Lacey and Jonathan Benthall, 25–52. Berlin: Gerlach.

———. 2015. *For Humanity or for the Umma? Aid and Islam in Transnational Muslim NGOs*. London: Hurst.

Segesvary, Victor. 2000. *Dialogue of Civilizations: An Introduction to Civilizational Analysis.* Lanham, MD: University Press of America.

Shaikh, Habib. 2014. *Four NGOs Join OIC Rights Body. Arab News*, April 11. http://www.arabnews.com/news/553821.

Svoboda, Eva, Steven A. Zyck, Daud Osman, and Abdirashid Hashi. 2015. "Islamic Humanitarianism? The Evolving Role of the Organization for Islamic Cooperation in Somalia and Beyond." HPG working paper. London: Overseas Development Institute.

Turner, Bryan. 1994. *Orientalism, Postmodernism and Globalism.* Abingdon: Routledge.

CONTRIBUTORS

Hirah Azhar is head of the Middle East program at the Centre for Geopolitics and Security in Realism Studies in London and has a master's degree in theory and history of international relations from the London School of Economics. She has previously completed a research fellowship in the Department of Political Science at the American University in Cairo and worked as an editor for an English newspaper in Saudi Arabia as well as a blog editor for the LSE's foreign policy think tank IDEAS. Her recent publications include (with M. Pinfari) "Israel-Palestine: The Mediterranean Paradox," in *The EU, Promoting Regional Integration, and Conflict Resolution,* ed. T. Diez and N. Tocci (Palgrave, 2017).

Mashood A. Baderin is professor of law at the School of Oriental and African Studies (SOAS), University of London. He teaches and researches in the areas of Islamic law, international law, and human rights law, with particular interest in the interaction between human rights law and Islamic law in Muslim-majority states. He has published widely in this area, including *International Human Rights and Islamic Law* (Oxford University Press, 2005). Baderin was appointed by the UN Human Rights Council as the UN Independent Expert on the Situation of Human Rights in the Sudan from May 2012 to November 2014. He is a barrister and solicitor of the Supreme Court of Nigeria.

Anthony Tirado Chase is a professor in international relations at Occidental College. Chase is a theoretician of human rights, most often in the context of the Middle East. His current research focuses on interdisciplinary approaches to human rights theorizing, transitional justice, and controversies around sexual orientation and gender identity-related rights—topics that inform his most recent article, "Human Rights Contestations: Sexual Orientation and Gender Identity" (*International Journal of Human Rights,* 2016). Other publications include *Handbook on Human Rights and the Middle East* *and North Africa* (Routledge, 2017) and *Human Rights, Revolution, and Reform in the Muslim World* (Lynne Rienner, 2012).

Ioana Cismas is senior lecturer at the York Law School and the Centre for Applied Human Rights. She has previously taught at Stirling Law School, has been a scholar-in-residence at the Center for Human Rights and Global Justice at NYU Law, and a research fellow at the Geneva Academy of International Humanitarian Law and Human Rights. She has provided legal and policy advice to United Nations mechanisms, governments, and non-governmental organizations. Ioana's research examines the roles of state and non-state actors in international law and explores the intersections between legal accountability and legitimacy. Her recent publications include *Religious Actors and International Law* (Oxford University Press, 2014).

Moataz El Fegiery is the Middle East and North Africa coordinator at the International Foundation for the Protection of Human Rights Defenders. He was the director of Cairo Institute for Human Rights Studies, an associate researcher at the Foundation of International Relations and Dialogue (FRIDE), and MENA deputy director of the International Centre for Transitional Justice. El Fegiery holds master's and doctoral degrees in law from the School of Oriental and African Studies (SOAS), University of London. His publications include "Islamic Law and Freedom of Religion: The Case of Apostasy and Its Legal Implications in Egypt" (*The Muslim World Journal for Human Rights*, 2013) and *Islamic Law and Human Rights: The Muslim Brotherhood in Egypt* (Cambridge Scholars Publishing, 2016).

Turan Kayaoglu is professor of international relations in the Politics, Philosophy, and Economics Program in the Interdisciplinary Arts and Sciences Department and Associate Vice chancellor for Research at the University of Washington, Tacoma. His publications include *Legal Imperialism: Sovereignty and Extraterritoriality in Japan, the Ottoman Empire and China* (Cambridge University Press, 2010) and *The Organization of Islamic Cooperation: Politics, Problems, and Potential* (Routledge, 2015). He is editor-in-chief of *Muslim World Journal of Human Rights.*

Martin Lestra is a postdoctoral researcher at the University of Toulouse Jean Jaurès. He earned a PhD in political science at the European University Institute and the Ecole des Hautes Etudes en Sciences Sociales. His dissertation explored the coherence and transparency of the foreign aid of Qatar and the United Arab Emirates. Lestra was a visiting researcher at New York University in Abu Dhabi and Qatar University during his fieldwork research in 2015–2016. He has published on Gulf affairs, including foreign aid, migration, and higher education, in the *Oxford Middle East Review,* the *Middle East Law and Governance Journal,* and the *Journal of Arabian Studies,* and was co-editor of *The Gulf Monarchies Beyond the Arab Spring: Changes and Challenges* (European University Institute, 2015).

Ann Elizabeth Mayer is an emeritus associate professor of legal studies and business ethics at the Wharton School of the University of Pennsylvania. She has taught as a visiting professor at Georgetown, Princeton, and Yale. She earned a PhD in modern middle eastern history from the University of Michigan, a JD from the University of Pennsylvania, and a Certificate in Islamic and Comparative Law from the School of Oriental and African Studies, London. Her research areas include Islamic law in contemporary Middle East and North Africa and international human rights law, with an emphasis on women's international human rights. She has published extensively, and the fifth edition of her book *Islam and Human Rights: Tradition and Politics* was published in 2012 (Westview Press).

Mahmood Monshipouri is a professor and chair of the Department of International Relations at San Francisco State University. He is also a lecturer at the University of California, Berkeley. He is the editor, most recently, of *Information Politics, Protests, and Human Rights in the Digital Age* (Cambridge University Press, 2016) and *Inside the Islamic Republic: Social Change in Post-Khomieni Iran* (Oxford University Press, 2016). Currently, he is working on a project on the Middle East and its changing security architecture.

Marie Juul Petersen is a senior researcher at the Danish Institute for Human Rights. She holds a PhD from the Institute for Regional and Cross-Cultural Studies at University of Copenhagen. Her research interests include Islam, human rights, and development, and she has written extensively on these topics, including *For Humanity or for the Umma? Aid and Islam in International Muslim NGOs* (Hurst, 2016) and "Islamic Charity, Social Order, and the Construction of Modern Muslim Selfhoods in Jordan" (*International Journal of Middle East Studies,* 2014, with Dietrich Jung). She has also written a number of reports, including *Islamic or Universal Human Rights? The*

OIC's Independent Permanent Human Rights Commission (Danish Institute for International Studies, 2012).

Zeynep Şahin Mencütek holds a PhD in politics and international relations from the University of Southern California. She taught international relations at Gediz University, Turkey, until July 2016. Currently, she holds an associate fellow position at the Kate Hamburger Kolleg/Center for Global Cooperation Research (University of Duisburg–Essen) and a senior fellow position at the Swedish Research Institute Istanbul. She has written extensively on migration, refugee policies, and gender in the Middle East, including "State Diaspora Policy as a Supplement of Foreign Policy: Insights from Turkey" (*Balkan and Near Eastern Studies*, 2017 with Bahar Başer) and "International Migration and Foreign Policy Nexus: The Case of Syrian Refugees in Turkey" (*Migration Letters*, 2015 with Ela Gökalp Aras). She has written *Refugee Governance, State and Politics in the Middle East* (Routledge, 2018).

Heini í Skorini is an assistant professor at the University of the Faroe Islands (Denmark) and has a PhD in international relations from King's College London, Department of War Studies. His current research addresses the study of human rights norms in international relations, the nexus between religion and politics, and free speech vis-à-vis religion. Skorini's publications include "Hate Speech and Holy Prophets: Tracing the OIC's Strategies to Protect Religion" (with Marie Juul Petersen) in Anne Stensvold's *Religion, the State and the United Nations* (Routledge, 2017). He has also coproduced the world's first podcast on the history of free speech, together with human rights lawyer Jacob Mchangama (published in 2018 by Columbia University in New York).

M. Evren Tok is an assistant dean for Innovation and Community Advancement and assistant professor at Hamad Bin Khalifa University, Doha/Qatar. He has a long background in research, project management, and grant management in Qatar and beyond. His most recent research grant, for a four-year project funded by Qatar National Research Fund, is entitled "Localizing Entrepreneurship Education in Qatar: QNV 2030 and Beyond." Tok also acted as project investigator, senior researcher, and project consultant in various UN agencies and other international organizations. Tok's most recent publication, in collaboration with Leslie Pal and Lolwah Al Khater, is an edited volume entitled *Policy Making in a Transformative State: The Case of Qatar* (Palgrave MacMillan, 2016).

INDEX

ACKNOWLEDGMENTS

This study is the culmination of five years of work. In 2013, a group of scholars came together in a workshop organized by the Danish Institute for Human Rights (DIHR). The workshop provided a forum for preliminary discussions on the OIC and human rights, identifying main questions and issues that we would explore in an edited volume on the topic.

Based on these discussions, the group organized two panels at the International Studies Association's Human Rights Joint Conference in Istanbul in 2014. A subset of these papers was later published in the DIHR working paper series *Matters of Concern*.

The members of the group met again at the DIHR in March 2015 for an in-depth discussion of their papers and the development of a common framework for this volume. Several participants later gathered in Seattle, Washington, to present on a panel titled "The Organization of Islamic Cooperation's Engagements with Human Rights" at the annual meeting of the Law and Society Association in May 2015.

The editors would like to thank all the contributors to the book for their inspiring conversations over the last couple of years, their excellent chapters, and their generous cooperation with the extensive revision process.

We want to thank the OIC bureaucrats that have been supportive of this project. We are especially appreciative of their willingness to share vital insights into the OIC's intricate politics and complex diplomacy even though they knew the project's critical tone toward the organization's human rights record and agenda.

We also extend our immense gratitude to the Danish Institute for Human Rights for their support of the two Copenhagen workshops as well as their financial support for the copyediting of the chapters.

Heidi Betts has been an invaluable help in editing the manuscript, displaying a unique sense of style, language, and content. We are grateful to her for saving us from many embarrassing mistakes, improving the clarity of our text, elevating our arguments, and ensuring the cohesiveness of the edited volume.

We would like to thank Peter Agree of the University of Pennsylvania Press for his support and patience for this project.

We dedicate this book to our children. Mona and Nana (Marie's children) and Mai and Rumi (Turan's children), we hope that your generation will continue to advance human rights.